Political Violence in Ireland

POLITICAL VIOLENCE IN IRELAND

Government and Resistance since 1848

CHARLES TOWNSHEND

CLARENDON PRESS · OXFORD

1983

Oxford University Press, Walton Street, Oxford OX2 6DP
London Glasgow New York Toronto
Delhi Bombay Calcutta Madras Karachi
Kuala Lumpur Singapore Hong Kong Tokyo
Nairobi Dar es Salaam Cape Town
Melbourne Auckland
and associated companies in
Beirut Berlin Ibadan Mexico City Nicosia

Oxford is a trade mark of Oxford University Press

Published in the United States by
Oxford University Press, New York

British Library Cataloguing in Publication Data
Townshend, Charles
   Political violence in Ireland
   1. Ireland—History—1692-
   2. Ireland—Politics and government—
   1837-1901   3. Ireland—Politics and
   government—20th century
   I. Title
   941.508   DA951
   ISBN 0-19-821753-6

Library of Congress Cataloging in Publication Data
Townshend, Charles.
   Political violence in Ireland.
   Bibliography: p.
   Includes index.
   1. Violence—Ireland—History. 2. Ireland—
Politics and government—19th century. 3. Ireland
—Politics and government—20th century. 4. Insur-
gency—Ireland—History.   I. Title.
HN400.3.Z9V57 1983   303.6'2'09415   83-15122
ISBN 0-19-821753-6

Typeset by Joshua Associates, Oxford
Printed in Great Britain
at the University Press, Oxford

For Kate

Preface

This book sets out to furnish the interested reader with information, more substantial in range than is commonly available, on a vital element of modern British history. Despite the importance of this element, recently underlined by the declarations of British governments that the situation in Northern Ireland is 'an emergency threatening the life of the nation',[1] it remains marginal to most English perceptions. This book has been written in the belief that the dimensions of the present crisis have been established by the relationship of government and resistance over the last century. It makes no pretence, however, to interpretative originality; although it deploys a good deal of original material, it does so mainly in the hope of providing historical illumination. It tries to indicate the great wealth of Irish historical scholarship now available to the reader and multiplying year by year. As a historian, I have endeavoured to maintain a form of narrative order, to allow the evidence to speak as much as possible for itself, rather than drawing out or imposing explanatory structures. In Gibbonian terms, the subtitle of this book might be rendered as merely a record of 'crimes and follies'.

More than many histories, this is incomplete; not just because of the incompleteness of the source material, but because of the particular framework within which it is conceived. 'Total history' only happens once, and not subsequently. This account is restricted to violent relationships, to the reciprocal effect of government in Ireland and resistance to it. The two concepts exist, indeed, to a great extent in symbiosis. Government, especially before the vast expansion of state activity in the late nineteenth century, found its primary definition in the absence of resistance. Resistance may be a manifestation of different cultural or political forces, but its meaning is determined by government. Indeed

[1] See below, p. 400.

governments not only interpret such events, but by their consequent reactions can almost create them.[1]

'Government', or governing, as it appears here will not involve politics—the interplay of groups at the level of policy-making—so much as administration. Above all it will involve the administration of law and the maintenance of public 'order': the most direct interface between state and people. The persistent difficulty for British government in Ireland was the apparent necessity of 'coercion', of administration by force rather than by consent. The use of force in a polity whose ethos was 'constitutional' (or what would later be called liberal-democratic) and whose public standards were grounded on an image of consensus, always posed acute problems. Every abrogation of the 'constitution', from the suspension of Habeas Corpus in the mid nineteenth century to the Emergency Provisions and Prevention of Terrorism Acts of 1973 and 1974, has evoked the spectre of arbitrary government. Yet fear of executive despotism has always been overcome by a sense of outrage at resistance to the rule of law and order. The reader will necessarily want to ask whether the government's interpretation of such resistance as a public threat has always, or often, been correct.

'Resistance', it will be clear, is a loose conception encompassing not only the organized and politically conscious employment of violence but also inchoate forms of communal struggle. The tradition of violence in Ireland is unmistakably important. Without exaggerating its ubiquity (and I hope that this book does not do so), there is a necessity to explain the manner in which violent acts or threats continued for so long to be an acceptable supplement to, if not an actual substitute for, political dialogue. The commitment of the 'physical force party' to armed struggle, amounting at times to obsession, cannot be construed as a rational response to British domination, physical or cultural. The persistence of Fenian reasoning in face of a great deadweight of reality cannot be explained by the intellectual or even the

---

[1] C. Tilly, 'Collective Violence in European Perspective', in H. D. Graham and T. R. Gurr (edd.) *Violence in America: Historical and Comparative Perspectives*. (A Report submitted to the National Commission on the Causes and Prevention of Violence; New York, 1969), pp. 41-2.

emotional power of republican ideology, but only by an inheritance of communal assumptions validating its methods as much as its ends. Indeed its methods have, at times, appeared to be ends in themselves. At such points political violence becomes a strictly meaningless conception, because then violence is used not to short-circuit or accelerate the political process but to replace it altogether. In this sense one may agree with Hannah Arendt that 'violence is dumb'. Its persistence indicates the limitations of political talk.

Works of political science often have short historical introductions and long contemporary analyses. This book has the reverse. This may seem inadequate to those who complain that historical accounts, 'while providing interesting insights, stop short at the point where analysis *normally* moves into recommendations'[1] (my emphasis). But the insights which emerge in the light of historical information may at least be valued a little higher now than in the days when mechanistic theories of revolt and revolution held sway. This book certainly does not aspire to indicate solutions, much less to produce recommendations. A historical account can, however, demonstrate the way in which certain avenues of political choice have been closed off. Without such understanding it is unlikely that successful policies can be formulated. More unwelcomely, history may suggest that certain realities lie outside the scope of political manipulation.

The abstractions of politics, of which the concept 'political violence' is one, may take on a degree of reality within the universe of politicians and those who study them. But beyond that relatively tidy world, other systems exist. A mass of obscure local determinants govern the form and purpose of the social violence that is so often given political meaning by outsiders. The contribution of history to the study of a phenomenon such as political violence must lie in casting light on this sphere, as much as in the careful analysis of political thinking and executive action.

In work stretching over several years I have been assisted

---

[1] J. Darby, *Conflict in Northern Ireland: the Development of a Polarised Community* (Dublin, 1976), p. 213. This is, in general, one of the most lucid and useful analyses of the northern problem and of the range of theoretical explanations.

by many institutions and individuals. My indebtedness to other researchers will be very apparent. More direct assistance and advice has come from Col. Dan Bryan, Taylor Downing, David Harkness, Richard Hawkins, R. F. V. Heuston, E. J. Hobsbawm, Michael Hopkinson, F. S. L. Lyons, and Leon O Broin, as well as the staffs of the State Paper Office, Dublin, the Archive of University College, Dublin, and the Public Record Office of Northern Ireland. In addition to other help I have received unstinting hospitality from Aisling and Roy Foster, Dorothy and Len Lawley, and Alison and David Stancliffe. Discussion with my Special Subject students at Keele has helped to bring a measure of order to my approach. My research was assisted by grants from the University of Keele and the British Academy Small Grants Research Fund in the Humanities. Ivon Asquith has been an unfailingly tactful editor.

Keele
Easter 1983

Contents

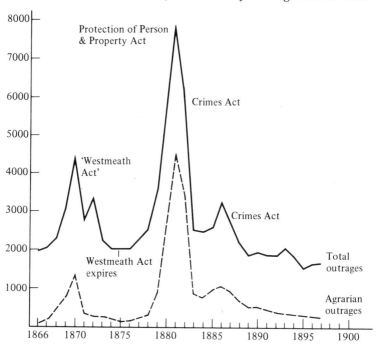

Royal Irish Constabulary: Returns of Outrages 1866–1897

Protection of Person & Property Act

Crimes Act

'Westmeath Act'

Crimes Act

Westmeath Act expires

Total outrages

Agrarian outrages

8000
7000
6000
5000
4000
3000
2000
1000

1866   1870   1875   1880   1885   1890   1895   1900

1
Resisters and Rebels

This is the 'cursed spite' of the relation between the two countries. Hedge-murder has been the only plan that the Irish peasant could contrive for resisting oppression. The Government cannot connive at hedge-murder: it passes a Coercion Act or a Crimes Act. This identifies the Government in the Irish mind with the oppressors. Hence, as a foreign observer put it, with every disposition to do what is best for Ireland, the English are forced into a situation in which the Irish will allow them to do nothing.

John Morley[1]

(i) *The nature of the problem*

The Irish propensity for violence is well known; at least to the English. And it was, of course, the English who conceived of the 'Irish problem'. For centuries, English writers, both eyewitnesses and more distant observers, remarked with professions of shock and horror upon the peculiarly cruel and anarchic nature of Irish violence. From Giraldus Cambrensis's chilling vision of a nation 'cruel and bloodthirsty' and a country 'barren of good things, replenished with actions of blood, murder, and loathsome outrage', to Barnaby Rich's assertion that 'That which is hatefull to the World besides is only beloved and embraced by the Irish, I mean civill warres and domesticall discentions', the English perspective was clearly drawn.[2] It was obviously political: Irish chaos evoked and validated an English civilizing mission which

---

[1] 'Irish Revolution and English Liberalism', *The Nineteenth Century*, Nov. 1882.

[2] While denouncing their 'abominable treachery' and adding for good measure that even their saints 'appear to be of a vindictive temper', Giraldus produced an extensive and often laudatory survey of Irish culture. His praise was, however, qualified in a way fundamental to English views of the Celt: 'Whatever natural gifts they possess are excellent, in whatever requires industry they are worthless' (Silvester Giraldus Cambrensis, *The Topography of Ireland*, in T. Wright (ed.) *The Historical Works of Giraldus Cambrensis* (London, 1863), 112–48).

brought with it control of a neighbouring island, whose
strategic position was increasingly critical to England. This
strategic imperative was never concealed, and never more
vital than during the unprecedented British dependence
on oversea communication in the nineteenth century. Yet
at the same time English perceptions of Ireland were increasingly informed by abstract ideas of progress and civilization. These took shape around a growing assumption—
not peculiar to Englishmen—that English society demonstrated the pattern of universal political and economic
progress.

A fundamental indicator of progress was growth in respect
for 'the rule of law' and decline in violent disorder. Until the
mid-nineteenth century, Irish disorder, while it may have
appeared to English eyes different in nature, had scarcely
been much different in scale from that endemic in the temple
of civilization itself, the home of that 'ungovernable people'.[1]
Subsequently, however, the contrast became noticeably
sharper. As J. L. Hammond put it in his great study of Gladstone and Ireland, from this time onwards violence in England 'melts away' whereas in Ireland it 'gathers force and
volume'. Following John Stuart Mill, Hammond attributed
this divergence to discrepancies in economic development.[2]
He saw English violence in the nineteenth century as a
response to transitional conditions—industrialization and
urbanization. The British economic and political system had
gradually solved these problems, but in Ireland the system
failed because Irish conditions were completely different.
The Irish agrarian society resisted the incursion of *laissez-
faire* economics. Irish violence and disorder were basically

---

[1] J. Brewer and J. Styles (eds), *An Ungovernable People. The English and their
law in the seventeenth and eighteenth centuries* (London, 1980). The substantial
body of research on English disorder mainly eschews any treatment of Ireland,
e.g. J. Stevenson, *Popular Disturbances in England of 1700–1870* (London,
1979), p. vi.

[2] J. L. Hammond, *Gladstone and the Irish Nation* (London, 1938),
12 ff.; cf. also John Morley's insistence on an 'agrarian revolution'—*The Life of
Gladstone* (London, 1903), Bk. VI, Ch. II. More recently T. N. Brown suggested
that 'assimilation of the economies of Ireland and England was completed in the
first quarter of a century following the Act of Union and its fruits were poverty,
bitterness and chronic violence' ('Nationalism and the Irish Peasant', *Review of
Politics* (Oct. 1953), 412).

a reaction against English law—above all the law of property which governed the holding of land.

English law was coupled with the utilitarian economic philosophy which reached its apogee in the early part of the century. The abstract laws which supposedly governed the spectacular success of the British economy were turned into new indicators of progress, and were taken to be automatically applicable to Ireland. Indeed, the intellectual orthodoxy was that England would be failing in its duty to civilization if it did not bring the Irish economy into line with its own. The same analysis was applied to Scotland: both areas were diagnosed as being victims of a Malthusian crisis resulting from low productivity and high procreation, and for both the cure was 'free trade in land'.[1]

As befitted a modernizing society, English land law was based on contract rather than custom. Such a basis was finally made explicit for Ireland in 1860 with 'Deasy's Act', which abolished the surviving customary rights of the Irish peasantry. This first Liberal attempt to legislate the Irish problem out of existence was expected to pave the way for real progress via the disappearance of the primitive, inefficient cottier.[2] The possibility that agrarian unrest in Ireland was caused less by poverty as such than by a deep structural social imperative to possess land was scarcely considered. A characteristic view from the side of modernization was put by a well-known commentator on the Irish land problem in a Cobden Club study of land-tenure in various countries. He was confident that the attitudes on which a system of peasant proprietorship (an idea then returning into economic vogue) might be based were

inconsistent with the mental activity of Irishmen. They are inconsistent with railways, penny postage, a cheap newspaper press, and national education. Men will follow where their interests lead them, and in general *it is not for a man's interest to be a peasant proprietor.*[3]

---

[1] W. L. Burn, 'Free Trade in Land, an Aspect of the Irish Question', *Tr(ans-actions of the) R(oyal) Hist(orical) S(ociety)*, xxxi (1949), 61–74; R. D. C. Black, *Economic Thought and the Irish Question* (Cambridge, 1960), *passim*.

[2] Hammond, op. cit. 13. On cottier cultivation, M. R. Beames, 'Cottiers and Conacre in pre-famine Ireland', *Journal of Peasant Studies*, ii, (1975), 352–3.

[3] The Rt. Hon. M. Longfield, 'The Tenure of Land in Ireland', in J. W. Probyn

Such pure utilitarianism was already on the defensive by the later 1860s. The publication of Mill's *England and Ireland* in 1868 was part of a dramatic volte-face by many intellectuals, who had begun to believe that the solution of Irish problems would be achieved not by forcing Ireland into the English developmental mould, but by recognizing the inherent characteristics of Irish society.[1] In this view it was England that was the exception: Ireland had to be compared with continental economies like those of France, Denmark, or Prussia.

A significant part in this Copernican revolution was played by the rediscovery of pre-Norman Irish law. The first volume of a collated and translated edition of the Brehon law tracts was published in 1865. One of its editors, W. N. Hancock, had advised the Liberals on the drafting of the 1860 Act, but by the end of the decade his attitude to customary law had been reversed.[2] This conversion was evidence of the power of Gaelic ideas over intellectuals of the post-romantic generation, which was to be further demonstrated later in the century. This almost visionary power stemmed in part from the revolutionary implications of the social system discovered by the researchers into Brehon law. It was a society

absolutely contradictory to (the principles) which we believe to be of universal application and primary necessity: a community without government or executive; without laws in the modern sense of the term; in which the individual had no rights save as a member of a family . . . ; firmly knit together, and regulated in the minutest details of everyday life by an undefined and unaccountable concurrence of all its members in certain inarticulate rules as to their conduct in the

(ed.). *Systems of Land Tenure in Various Countries* (London, 1875), 28–9 (emphasis in original).

[1] But practical results were small: these thinkers 'remained abstract even in denouncing abstraction' (J. Lee, *The Modernisation of Irish Society 1848–1918* (Dublin, 1973), 26). Cf. E. D. Steele, 'J. S. Mill and the Irish Question', *Hist(orical) J(ournal)*, xiii (1970); C. Dewey, 'The rehabilitation of the peasant proprietor in nineteenth-century economic thought', *History of Political Economy*, vi (1974).

[2] C. Dewey, 'Celtic agrarian legislation and the Celtic revival. Historicist implications of Gladstone's Irish and Scottish land acts 1870–1886', *Past and Present*, lxiv (1974) 43–9.

ordinary circumstances of life, the sum of which is expressed in the word 'custom'.[1]

The political as against the purely intellectual power of this vision—in which there was perhaps more than a tinge of fantasy—derived from the belief that a memory of this deeply un-English way of life survived amongst Irish peasants in the nineteenth century. It was this, it was suggested, which underlay a general repudiation of English law, a resistance which found expression in violence.

The idea of such an atavistic survival has received short shrift from most recent commentators, particularly from the foremost exponent of the view that Irish society was steadily modernizing after 1848.[2] But it offered a much better explanation than those previously current—the inherent savagery of the Irish—for a phenomenon which had been clearly recognized by contemporaries. There was, if not general repudiation, at least alarmingly widespread resistance to law and order as enforced by the administration in Dublin. To some extent, as will be indicated in the next chapter, this was simply a self-actualizing paranoia: the statesmen feared insurrection and saw conspiracy or disaffection everywhere, and their over-reaction often intensified violent resistance and the alienation of popular sentiment. But the resistance was not merely negative. It was rather the upholding of a different system of law or of social control.

If there has generally been less dispute about the incidence of Irish violence than about its meaning, the two are certainly not unconnected. To begin with, therefore, it is worth examining the scale of the problem. An often percipient writer has recently suggested that 'in the 1850s Irish agrarian relations were at a level resembling guerilla warfare. Landlords and agents carried arms as a matter of course: the peasants killed them when they could'.[3] Now, apart from the fact that the 1850s were a quite abnormally peaceful decade

---

[1] A. G. Richey, *A Short History of the Irish People* (Dublin, 1887), 35, quoted in Dewey, 'Celtic agrarian legislation', pp. 45-6.

[2] Lee has in addition raised the important question of the distinction between modernization and 'anglicization'. It could be thought that 'pre-Norman' might better be rendered as 'pre-modern'; the question then becomes whether Irish resistance was to anglicization or to modernization: Lee, op. cit. 139-40.

[3] P. O'Farrell, *England and Ireland since 1800* (Oxford, 1975), 167-8.

by nineteenth-century standards, the simplicity of the conflict thus sketched is too great. Although other writers on the agrarian struggle have spoken of 'insurgency', 'a recurring state of war between the authorities and rebellious peasants', 'a tradition of guerilla warfare', and so on,[1] these terms should not be taken to imply too much. Insurgency and guerrilla warfare are modern concepts which suggest the existence of a defined political objective if not a certain level of co-ordinated action and organization. It may be that, as another writer has put it, 'pre-famine Ireland was a remarkably violent country' in which people both individually and collectively 'robbed, raped, brawled and murdered'.[2] But this violence was only remarkable by the standards of an imaginary rural idyll. By those of an urban industrial society it was almost trifling. Comparison of crime figures in Ireland with those in Britain, after the police in both countries had begun to compile statistics of reported as well as prosecuted offences, tends at least to sustain the argument (common amongst nineteenth-century nationalists) that the 'normal' crime rate in Ireland was remarkably low.[3] The figures for outrage or 'abnormal' crime, in the worst years of the Tithe War were as follows:[4]

	1831	*1832*
Homicide	210	248
Robbery	1,478	1,172
Burning	466	571
Cattle maiming	293	295
Illegal notices	1,798	2,086
Illegal meetings	1,792	422
Attacks on houses	2,296	1,675

[1] J. S. Donnelly, 'The Whiteboy movement 1761–5', *I(rish) H(istorical) S(tudies)*, xxi (1978); *Landlord and Tenant in Nineteenth Century Ireland* (Dublin, 1973), 27, 39. J. Lee, 'The Ribbonmen', in T. D. Williams (ed.), *Secret Societies in Ireland* (Dublin, 1973), 29; G. Broeker, *Rural Disorder and Police Reform in Ireland 1812–36* (London, 1970), 10.

[2] S. Clark, *Social Origins of the Irish Land War* (Princeton, 1979), 66, 74.

[3] Reliable comparison is difficult, but it may be noted that in the later nineteenth century 'serious crime' ran at over 400 cases per 100,000 population in England and Wales. For the interpretative problems, V. A. C. Gatrell and T. B. Hadden, 'Criminal statistics and their interpretation', in E. A. Wrigley (ed.), *Nineteenth Century Society. Essays in the use of quantitative methods for the study of social data* (Cambridge, 1972). See also Ch. 2 below.

[4] Memo., Nov. 1880 (Bodleian Library, Harcourt MSS).

Some of these outrages were repulsively unpleasant. The 'houghing' and mangling of animals with scythes or blunt instruments consistently distressed law-officers; worse, though less frequent, was the 'carding' of humans, whose backs were lacerated with nail-studded boards.[1] But the most important thing about them was that they were put into a special category: 'special' or 'agrarian' crime was separated from 'ordinary' crime on the ground that its motive was to be found in the land struggle. At the height of the Ribbon disturbances of 1870 a grand total of 4,351 crimes were reported by the police outside Dublin, and 1,329 of these were judged to be agrarian. (Nearly half were threatening letters or notices or other forms of intimidation; offences of violence against the person totalled 49, against animals and inanimate property 59. There were 48 cases of 'demand of money' and 151 of 'levying contributions').[2] The basis for the classification of an offence as agrarian seems to have lain in combination to enforce resistance to law or to enforce another, illegal, law: it is here, with due allowance for the inadequacies of police procedure, that we must look for evidence of a violent challenge to authority.

The outbreak of 1870 provoked one Conservative MP to describe the county of Westmeath as 'a fortress . . . more successful than Metz, Strasbourg or Belfort'. In reply, Gladstone roundly condemned the use of 'exaggerated language', such as the phrase 'murder stalking abroad', to describe a mere handful of violent assaults.[3] Such alarmist exaggerations were, however, the commonest form of reaction to Irish disorder. The tendency of many subsequent writers has been to lump together all manifestations of violence as part of the Irish challenge. This is in a sense to hold that almost all violence is political, or at least that in Ireland any act

[1] P. J. Carroll, 'Notes for a History of Police in Ireland', N(ational) L(ibrary) of I(reland), MS 19486, p. 5.

[2] *Return of Outrages Specially Reported to the Constabulary Office*, S(tate) P(aper) O(ffice), Dublin, Crime Special MSS; P(ublic) R(ecord) O(ffice), London, CO 904 67. It is not always realized that the system of reporting agrarian incidents changed at least twice between 1865 and 1885; it is impossible to calculate exactly the shift introduced by the 1869 system or by the tightening of definitions in 1881. See P(arliamentary) P(apers), HC 1887 (140), lxviii.

[3] H(ouse of) C(ommons) Deb(ates), 3rd series, cciv, cc. 1173, 1187.

labelled a crime under English law could be seen as a political act, because the crime itself was politically defined. This would certainly be too capacious a definition of political violence, though it is true that almost all Irish violence, whatever its motive, had indirect political implications. Even inexplicable familial murders like those at Maamtrasna in 1882 reinforced the English image of the Irish. This image solidified in the Victorian period into the still sadly familiar prognathous ape-man, at once vicious and cowardly (at least if faced with a stiff upper lip).[1] While it is evidently impossible to quantify with any exactness the effect of racial attitudes, it is equally impossible to ignore the extent to which such assumptions permeate the records of Victorian public men. Their ubiquity and depth is arresting.[2] Saxon attitudes to 'the Celt' certainly furnished a basis for political rhetoric, and must also have conditioned the making of political decisions.[3] The impression of the Irish, first fixed by Giraldus, as 'light-minded' and easily swayed by fanatical agitators fed the recurrent English belief that conspirators, bandits, 'Thugs', 'gunmen', or 'murder gangs' were the sole cause of Irish resistance. This belief will be encountered time and again during this study.[4]

What the alarmist reactions of gentry and governments make plain about violence in Ireland is that the absolute level of 'crime' was considerably less important than the psychological construction placed upon each outbreak. This was true in a slightly different sense for the Irish people

[1] L. P. Curtis, *Anglo-Saxons and Celts* (Connecticut, 1968). S. Gilley, 'English Attitudes to the Irish in England 1780–1900', in C. Holmes (ed.), *Immigrants and Minorities in British Society* (London, 1978), criticizes Curtis's use of the term 'racial', but fails to modify the substance of Curtis's analysis. For a reasoned view see G. O'Tuathaigh, 'The Irish in nineteenth-century Britain: problems of integration', *Tr. R. Hist. S.* xxxi, (1981), 162.

[2] Cf. W. R. Jones, 'England against the Celtic fringe: a study in cultural stereotypes', *Cahiers d'histoire mondiale*, xiii (1971); more hysterically (and inaccurately), R. N. Lebow, *White Britain and Black Ireland* (Philadelphia, 1976); less schematically, C. Harvie, 'Ireland and the Intellectuals 1848–1922', *New Edinburgh Review* xxxviii/xxxix (1977); F. S. L. Lyons, *Culture and Anarchy in Ireland 1890–1939* (Oxford, 1979).

[3] Not always as 'unspoken assumptions'; see Lloyd George's remarks on 'Irish temper' in his Carnarvon speech (Notes, 19 Oct. 1920, Anderson MSS, PRO CO 904 188/1).

[4] Giraldus Cambrensis, *The Conquest of Ireland*, ch. XXXVII. Wright, op. cit., p. 323.

also. When a district appeared to be completely terrorized by a 'conspiracy', an 'association' or a 'secret society', there were seldom more than—as Gladstone pointed out—a handful of violent acts to be reported. Patrick O'Farrell has suggested that

A relatively low level of actual violence, or indeed none at all, can sustain a high level of fear and induce behaviour desired by extremists and destructive of social order and stability.[1]

Leaving aside the loaded final phrases (which rather reduce its general value), this is an important point; it was made in a more down-to-earth way in 1886 by the celebrated legal commentator Sir James Stephen.

A very small amount of shooting in the legs will effectively deter an immense mass of people from paying rents which they do not want to pay.[2]

Stephen's observation focuses upon the crucial question of the objectives for which a community may accept being coerced by 'extremists'. The threat of violence was always more common than its actual application, as any selection of statistics will indicate:[3]

	1867	1868	1869	1870	1871	1872
Total agrarian crime	123	160	767	1,329	373	256
Intimidation	53	72	480	624	195	144

The threat had its effect because of a fairly high expectation of retribution if it were ignored: in other words, it worked very much like what is ordinarily described as law. Like law, it also worked for the most part towards ends accepted by the community. This is what makes the last part of O'Farrell's assertion misleading. Much of Irish violence and intimidation in the nineteenth century was directed not by 'extremists' in any useful sense of the term, but by representatives of communities whose object was to maintain, not destroy, social order.

[1] P. O'Farrell, op. cit. 159-60.

[2] James Fitzjames Stephen, 'On the Suppression of Boycotting', *The Nineteenth Century*, cxviii (Dec. 1886), 773.

[3] *Constabulary Returns*. The steep rise 1868-9 reflected in part a new system of enumeration (see PP, HC 1887 (140), lxviii), which may itself have represented a 'moral panic'.

It has been said that Irish rural violence was 'politically illiterate'.[1] This will necessarily be true of much violent crime in any society, and especially in a pre-modern society where political awareness is limited. One of the major processes experienced by modernizing societies is that which may be called politicization: the process whereby the political system becomes accessible and comprehensible to the mass of the population, as against the governing élites which monopolize the traditional polity.[2] This process was, albeit irregularly, under way in nineteenth-century Ireland, and will be returned to later.[3] At this point it may be useful to look at the idea of 'political illiteracy', which may be accepted in so far as it does not imply political irrelevance, but rather a lack of capacity to formulate objectives in political terms. The violence of the agrarian secret societies, however primitive in intention and execution, had enormous political repercussions. The violence which habitually accompanied parliamentary elections, on the other hand, may paradoxically have been devoid of political meaning.

In an attempt to break down the aggregate of Irish crime figures, the triadic classification of collective violence proposed by Charles Tilly and others is perhaps helpful in drawing functional distinctions between various manifestations of violence. Tilly's categories are, in ascending order of sophistication, 'competitive', 'reactive', and 'proactive' violence.[4] The most elementary of these would certainly subsume the curious feature of early nineteenth-century Irish life called 'faction fighting'. The inarticulate struggles of groups bearing, in some cases, the names of families like Gallaghers and McGettigans (Donegal), or in others more obscure titles such as Gows and Poleens, Caravats

---

[1] By E. R. Norman, *A History of Modern Ireland* (Harmondsworth, 1973), p. 18. The views of Marx and Engels on agrarian violence were similar: P. Bew, *Land and the National Question in Ireland 1858–82* (Dublin, 1977), pp. 37–8.

[2] For a useful comparison see E. Weber, 'The Second Republic, Politics and the Peasant', *French Historical Studies*, xi (1980), 521.

[3] T. Garvin, *The Evolution of Irish Nationalist Politics* (Dublin, 1981). For an interesting perspective on politicization, K. T. Hoppen, 'Landlords, society and electoral politics in mid-nineteenth century Ireland', *Past and Pres.* lxxv (1977), 62–93.

[4] C. Tilly, *From Mobilization to Revolution* (Reading, Mass., 1978), 143–51; C., L., and R. Tilly, *The Rebellious Century* (London, 1975), 48–55.

and Shanavests, or Philibees and Drins (or Doirins: in fact members of the Sheehan family of Bantry, Co. Cork), have bewildered contemporaries and historians alike.[1] Beginning in Co. Tipperary around the turn of the century, they spread rapidly and were ubiquitous in the 1820s. Thereafter they continued sporadically, the last recorded fight being at Cappawhite, Co. Tipperary, in 1887. W. R. LeFanu, in his memoir *Seventy Years of Irish Life*, recalled the moment in 1829 when the Reaskawallahs of his native Limerick marched out in full pomp 'six deep, in military order, with music and banners', forming a procession nearly two miles long, for a reconciliation with their opponents, the Coffeys of Newport.[2] This was in response to O'Connell's call for unity in the face of the English, and the response implies a degree of political awareness: at least a generalized sense of resistance to the foreigner. For the most part, however, faction fights were purely local, private conflicts. Their vicious character notwithstanding, it may be suggested without levity that they represented a form of communal recreation. Fights usually took place on special public occasions like fairs, race meetings, and 'patterns', which of course provided the opportunity for two bodies to come into collision, but which also established a certain ritual or formal basis for fighting. The grounds for giving allegiance to one group rather than another, where they were not obviously familial, were as obscure or idiosyncratic as are, today, the grounds for loyalty to football teams in Britain.[3]

The explosive growth of faction fighting in the first quarter of the nineteenth century was a demonstration of the energies dormant in the countryside—energies which could potentially be mobilized for a number of causes. David Fitzpatrick has written suggestively of the 'organizational density' of rural (as compared with urban) Ireland,

[1] There is a recent, sensational study: P. O'Donnell, *The Irish Faction Fighters of the Nineteenth Century* (Dublin, 1975). Superb contemporary pictures of the addiction are William Carleton's celebrated story, *The Party Fight and Funeral*; W. R. LeFanu, *Seventy Years of Irish Life* (London, 1893), 31-2.

[2] LeFanu, op. cit. 34-5.

[3] Clark, op. cit. 77, suggests that 'family loyalty was the strongest force drawing people to one side or the other', though as Carleton's stories indicate many other loyalties existed.

its capacity to sustain many nationalist organizations, in later years.[1] The suggestion that the countryside had greater capacity than the towns seems less paradoxical if one remembers that the tight traditional infrastructure of rural society remained, while the monotony common to pre-modern societies impelled people towards politics as a diversion.[2]

The violent occurrences which had more direct political relevance were those which would fall into Tilly's inelegant but useful antithesis of 'reactive' and 'proactive' action. Reactive activity is no longer private or obscure; it has clear public meaning. It is, however, defensive action, intended to preserve the status quo from immediately perceived changes. This sort of action was extremely frequent throughout Europe, including Britain, in the early nineteenth century. Sometimes it was couched in explicitly political terms, but more often it was in effect the defence of custom against politics itself—politics implying, by this time, the machinery of change. Certainly its effect did not depend on a grasp of political concepts (such as law and the state) or the use of political language. Proaction, by contrast, is the form of activity designed to bring about change, and is hardly conceivable without political awareness. Sam Clark has argued that, for instance, the approach to the state by Irish tenant-right organizations with the demand for *laws* altering the position of the tenant was 'clearly proaction'.[3] This may be accepted, though in the case of the Irish land struggle such proaction was, in an important sense, a *reaction* against an ancient confiscation (whether imaginary or real). It demanded little or nothing that was believed to be novel: a genuinely new idea like Davitt's proposal of land nationalization was almost universally repudiated. An interesting transitional form of activity can be observed in O'Connell's great campaigns for Catholic emancipation and Repeal of the Union. Although they demanded the restoration of lost

[1] D. Fitzpatrick, 'The geography of Irish nationalism 1910-1921', *Past and Pres.* lxxviii (1978), 132-3.

[2] Cf. C. M. Arensberg, *The Irish Countryman. An Anthropological Study* (London, 1937), p. 124.

[3] Clark, op. cit. p. 354.

rights rather than any new disposition of power, they created near-revolutionary modern organizations, and utilized a sophisticated blend of 'moral force' and the threat of violence. The Repeal association has indeed been called the 'only Western national movement organized in a coherent form before 1848 which was genuinely based on the masses'.[1] But not until the demand for a republic was systematically articulated by the Fenians did there appear a truly original political programme, if so hazy a symbol can be called a programme.

Organization as such is a vital condition of 'mobilization' as conceived by Deutsch, Tilly, and others. 'Modern forms of organization', Hobsbawm and Rudé also observe, 'have to be learned, like anything else.'[2] The more developed the political objective, the more sophisticated must the organization be. The growth of formal organizations constitutes an aspect of modernization, and in a sense the existence of political awareness and the capacity to organize are mutually dependent. None of these things, however, is necessarily associated with the use of violence. Indeed, modernist orthodoxy suggests that violent protest should die away as politicization increases, as greater scope is provided for the exercise of political pressures through the institutional framework. Such would be the consensus explanation of the decline in violence in Britain under the impact of mid-century reforms, coupled, in ways not precisely measurable, with the creation of more efficient law-enforcement machinery.[3] Even if the organic metaphor, employed by Harold Perkin, of social progress from 'immaturity' through 'adolescence' to the full maturity of consensus in the later nineteenth century be rejected (in favour, perhaps, of the

---

[1] By E. J. Hobsbawm, *The Age of Revolution* (London, 1962), ch. 7.

[2] E. J. Hobsbawm and G. Rudé, *Captain Swing* (rev. edn., London, 1973), p. 254.

[3] As against L. Radzinowicz's view that affluent, competitive societies have produced greater criminality (*Ideology and Crime* (London, 1966)), and bearing in mind that the 'dark figure', the real total, cannot be calculated, it seems clear that a decrease in serious crime occurred in later nineteenth-century Britain: V. A. C. Gatrell, 'The Decline of Theft and Violence in Victorian and Edwardian England', in Gatrell *et al.*, *Crime and the Law. The Social History of Crime in Western Europe since 1500* (London, 1980).

hard-bitten view of ubiquitous 'social controls' producing a merely 'operational' consensus), the phenomenon remains remarkable.[1]

It was not so in Ireland. There, violence continued to be used as an auxiliary to, or even as a substitute for, modern political dialogue. If the absolute level (or 'volume') of violence did not increase to the extent suggested by Hammond, its impact (or 'force') certainly did, and became the more striking as England was pacified. The rest of this chapter will look at the groups or organizations which employed violent methods in the period before the Land War, under the two broad headings 'reactive' and 'proactive'. They may be seen more humanly as 'resisters' and 'rebels', or given contemporary labels: Ribbonmen and Fenians. How were they organized? What were their aims? And why were they violent?

(ii) *Ribbonism*

> . . . being, like most of those in his situation, fond of drinking, dancing, and attending fairs. In short, he became a Ribbonman, and consequently was obliged to attend their nightly meetings.
>
> William Carleton[2]

> But they have stopped from their labours and are now in a state of desperation and frenzy; the lower orders of the county Leitrim in general are sworn Ribbond men so that my own tenants living on my own property will no longer assist me against them—indeed I should not consider my life safe now amongst them.
>
> R. J. Lloyd[3]

The Ribbonmen stood in succession to a number of rural secret societies or 'associations', bearing names like Defenders, Rightboys, Carders, Rockites, and Terry Alts. To them

---

[1] Cf. H. Perkin, *The Origins of Modern English Society 1780–1880* (London, 1969), pp. 340–7; A. P. Donajgrodski (ed.), *Social Control in Nineteenth-Century Britain* (London, 1977); Gatrell, op. cit. p. 257.

[2] *The Party Fight and Funeral. Traits and Stories of the Irish Peasantry* (new edn., Cork, 1973), iv. 28.

[3] R. J. Lloyd to J. King, November 1815: F. S. L. Lyons, 'Vicissitudes of a middleman in county Leitrim 1810–27', *IHS* ix (1955).

all may be applied the generic title Whiteboys: to the communities from which they sprang they were just the 'boys'.
Some contemporaries, and later analysts, called them more
exotically 'banditti', which well conveys their negative
aspect.[1] They were proscribed because they resisted the
government's law. They were not, however, rebels. They had
no hope, and probably no conception, of overthrowing the
state. At the same time, to say of them, as is often said,
that their objects were economic rather than political is
to say too little, unless it is made clear that the economics
involved had a strong ethical foundation. The 'moral economy' is, in at least one sense, a deeply political construct.[2]
A not unperceptive observer, the British military commander
in Ireland at the time of the last great 'Ribbon' manifestation
in 1870-1, regarded it as 'very evident that the possession
of Irish land, on a sort of social principle, by the lower
classes is the aim of the Irish confederacies'.[3]

These confederacies he saw as the fundamental cause of
the Irish problem: an expression of 'the resistance of the Irish
to British Conquest & their ill will to English Rule & Law'.

The Irish could not oppose the English openly & in the field—but
they could & have, since the Conquest, opposed their Rule & Law by
popular combinations & confederacies, which if they were not so
general might be called conspiracies.[4]

The term Ribbonism has more recently been objected to, as
being too narrow and specific to be applied to the gamut
of agrarian secret-society activity. Whiteboyism is undoubtedly
a better general term, but the significance of the Ribbon
label in the nineteenth century is, in part, that it was so
widely and indiscriminately used by the authorities.[5] It is

[1] For a modern usage, G. Broeker, *Rural Disorder*, p. vii and *passim*; for a
criticism, Lee, 'Ribbonmen', p. 31. Cf. also Garvin, op. cit., 34–52.

[2] On legitimacy underlying collective action, E. P. Thompson, 'The moral
economy of the English crowd in the eighteenth century', *Past and Pres.* 1 (1971),
78 ff.

[3] Gen. Ld. Strathnairn to Duke of Cambridge, 19 May 1869, Rose MSS,
B(ritish) L(ibrary) Add. MS 42825, f. 177.

[4] Ibid.

[5] One of the strongest objections has come from M. R. Beames; for the indiscriminate usage cf. Broeker, *Rural Disorder*, p. 12. On Ribbonism generally,
see the assessment in T. Garvin, 'Defenders, Ribbonmen and others: underground
political networks in pre-famine Ireland', *Past and Pres.* xcvi (1982), 133–55.

no doubt true, though it is impossible to produce direct evidence, that magistrates exaggerated the role of 'secret societies' in the commission of individual 'outrages'.[1] The government certainly exaggerated the scope of the Ribbon movement. Yet in the long perspective the distinctions conveyed by specific names appear less significant than the broad similarities of all the agrarian 'associations'. Their activities span the period from around 1760 and 1850 with only one major interruption—the years of heavy repression, with the government wielding martial law powers, between 1798 and 1806. In the 1850s, as has been remarked, a dramatic decline set in, and lasted (with the equally dramatic exception of the 1870-1 Westmeath disturbances) for something like a quarter of a century.

The associations which sustained agrarian resistance were secret groupings bonded by ceremonies of initiation and oath-taking. The precise form of the oaths, whilst it fascinated contemporaries, was probably less important than the moral effect of oath-taking itself. On the basis of surviving records it would be impossible to produce a comprehensive catalogue of oaths and their regional patterns, though such an undertaking would be extremely interesting. The nearest that has been reached to a full survey was the first, and still most substantial, account of rural disturbances, published by George Cornewall Lewis in 1836. Even he, who, as will be seen, was concerned to distinguish between Ribbonism and Whiteboyism, admitted that 'in some cases, it seems that the Ribbon oath directed against Protestants has been used for swearing in Whiteboys, or at any rate has been combined with the Whiteboy oath'.[2] Clearly there existed many forms of oath, some differing only in the names used ('to be true to Captain Thrasher's laws'), some in substance. Often the difference in substance was due to variation in the length—some running to twelve or more points—rather than the tenor of the oath.[3] These variegated forms spread across Ireland by routes which were, naturally, all but invisible.

---

[1] Donnelly, *Landlord and Tenant*, p. 27.
[2] G. C. Lewis, *Local Disturbances in Ireland* (London, 1836; new edn., Cork, 1977), p. 133.
[3] Ibid. pp. 135-6.

A respondent from Co. Clare told a House of Commons inquiry in 1824 of an oath which had been introduced from Co. Galway and which differed from the already extant 'Ribbon oath'. 'I consider the Ribbon oath a more political oath; I think the other was more for local objects.'[1]

These were certainly local groupings, though the territory covered by a nominal 'association' could be large.[2] This was because one of the inducements, or pressures, put upon countrymen to join the association was its massive power. Sheer geographical scale helped in this, though it could not produce the sort of co-ordination which was often believed to exist. Activity was, indeed, not entirely parochial: it was usually performed at a distance of ten or twelve miles from a group's place of residence, and a readiness to travel 'ten miles on foot or twenty on horseback' at short notice was an important point in many oaths. But this was to shield participants from immediate identification rather than to allow substantial disposable forces to coalesce. If, as a recent authority has suggested, considerable portions of southern and western Ireland were effectively 'under the domination of peasant "armies" ' between 1813 and 1816 and again between 1819 and 1823, these terms must be construed loosely.[3] Normally, 'moonlighters' operated in the small bands common to most 'primitive rebels'. Usually though not invariably they were nocturnal, because night provided not only camouflage but spare time. In the 1820s, largish nightly meetings were held to plan activities: one of the ways in which the alarming Insurrection Act of 1822 was held to have succeeded was in the restriction of such meetings.[4] But as soon as such tight controls were relaxed, meetings once again became ubiquitous.

Out of a multitude of possible examples, one report from

---

[1] Ibid. 134. Cf. Spencer to Gladstone, 30 Mar. 1869, on a 'much-used form of oath' which Spencer judges 'a most revolting document' (BL Add. MS 44306).

[2] Lord Spencer insisted on the purely local character of agrarian crime in the remarkable Ribbon eruption in Westmeath; this was 'in some respects a cheering symptom', but 'the suddenness with which a quiet county may become infected is very startling' (Gladstone, 9 Mar. 1870, loc. cit).

[3] Broeker, *Rural Disorder*, p. 10.

[4] Evidence of Mr Becher (or Beecher), Co. Cork (Lewis, *Local Disturbances*, p. 187).

the mid-century period will be examined here. The famine years were not, as has frequently been suggested, a time when misery reduced the rural population to inertia or abject submission.[1] In October 1847 the military commander at Charleville, Co. Cork, found the situation rather different.

I find (the country) to be much disturbed by a set of men who, taking advantage of the times, make rapid excursions in parties of from 6 to 30 through the Country, breaking into and plundering the better sort of Farm Houses. These men are generally from the adjoining county of Limerick. They are all armed . . . their attacks are made by day as well as by night, and so rapid are their movements that it is almost impossible for Military or Police to catch them, unless through private information from one of themselves . . . The better Farmers are most anxious to have these parties put down, yet they would sooner surrender their arms and property than give any information to the authorities.[2]

This report fixed several aspects of rural 'disorder' which recur with sufficient frequency to be called general features: the elusive bands; the inability of the law-officers to obtain information, especially from those suffering depredations; the seizure of arms. Although the report attempts to brand the group as common thieves, it admits later that the 'men of character' within it take nothing but arms. After a series of arms raids in the neighbouring county, Kerry, the police suggested that 'it is supposed that this disarming is a precaution preliminary to plunder.'[3] This suggestion was disingenuous, or plain stupid. The fact was that the impulse to seize arms wherever possible was one of the most commonly observable rural tendencies, and was to remain so through the next two generations. It was the seizure of the means of physical resistance rather than of plunder.[4]

An important aspect of the Charleville report concerns the target group—the 'better farmers'. While it is not possible

---

[1] See E. Strauss, *Irish Nationalism and British Democracy* (London 1951), p. 106; J. W. Hurst, 'Disturbed Tipperary 1831-1860', *Eire-Ireland*, ix (1974), 47 ff. The most extreme condemnation of the 'epidemic of national cowardice' during the famine is Michael Davitt, *The Fall of Feudalism in Ireland* (London, 1904), pp. 47-8, 145, 258.

[2] Col. Creagh to Mil. Sec., Dublin, 27 Oct. 1847, PRO HO 45 1793.

[3] Constabulary report, 7 Dec. 1847, loc. cit.

[4] As Lewis observed, 'possession of arms is in general the first object aimed at' (*Local Disturbances*, p. 80).

to be absolutely clear on the subject, recent research has done a great deal to define the social groups from which the secret societies mainly sprang. The original Whiteboy movement was overwhelmingly concerned with the disabilities of the landless and near-landless; its primary grievance was the price of conacre, the mode of land-holding whose insecurity amounted to a gamble.[1] In the early nineteenth century this gamble took on an increasingly desperate, *va banque* character, and the friction between cottier-labourers and farmers intensified. On the basis of agrarian crime statistics in one of the most disturbed counties, Limerick, in the first six months of 1846, one recent historian has written of 'guerilla warfare maintained by labourers against farmers in an attempt to control conacre rent and reduce potato prices'.[2] Detailed research in Tipperary has not altogether borne out this view, suggesting rather that the dominant cause of the most serious rural violence lay in the struggles of farmers themselves over the occupation of land.[3] Cornewall Lewis observed that disturbances in general 'appear to prevail most where the peasantry are bold and robust . . . and where the land is productive' (as in Tipperary, such a storm-centre of disorder). However, he also argued that the transition to pasturage had a crucial effect: in Ireland it 'has never been completed, and it is to prevent its completion that the Whiteboy combinations have principally been organized'.[4]

In any case, the famine wrought great changes in the rural class-structure, linked with the consequent expansion of pasture and the decline of tillage. The cottier-labourer group was forced into a parallel decline, and a somewhat different set of grievances played an increasing part in generating Whiteboy/Ribbon activity: those of tithe and rent. These were the overriding concerns of the tenant farmers who emerged after the famine as the dominant social group. Even in the 1830s the 'Tithe War' rapidly escalated into perhaps

[1] Donnelly, 'Whiteboy movement', pp. 34-5; but on conacre cf. Beames, 'Cottiers and Conacre', pp. 352-3.

[2] Lee, 'Ribbonmen', p. 29.

[3] M. R. Beames, 'Rural conflict in pre-famine Ireland: peasant assassinations in Tipperary 1837-1847', *Past and Pres.* lxxxi (1978).

[4] Lewis, *Local Disturbances*, pp. 90, 6-7.

the most ferocious confrontation of the century.[1] The political implications of resistance to the payment of tithes to a church to which the mass of the population did not belong are obvious—perhaps too obvious.[2] It may be suggested that resentment against the economic demands of the tithe was merely aggravated, rather than created, by the fact that the recipient church was 'alien'. Certainly there was resistance also in homogeneously Protestant England. The Irish tithe war was carried on by highly traditional methods, especially those of secret societies enforcing the 'unwritten law'.

As has been remarked, these societies were not rebels in a political sense: they were intensely conservative in most respects, as Cornewall Lewis saw. Their violence was primarily a response to 'active interference, either actual or apprehended' rather than to mere suffering, which they patiently endured.[3]

There is a conservative feeling even in combinations to resist the law; the persons concerned have a limited purpose in view, and do not seek for indiscriminate plunder; they desire not a general sack, but a new tenure of property; they wish to substitute one government for *another*, but not to produce *anarchy*.[4]

'Government' here should be read in general rather than specific terms; the conservatism involved makes it misleading to follow the terminology of the authorities in describing what they saw as 'disorder'. One must add that 'anarchy' is a loaded word too. Lewis used it like a conservative, as a term of abhorrence, but if it is simply taken to mean hostility to government by the state, and preference for what Herder called *Zusammenwirken* or Proudhon *association* (or what some modern socialists call *autogestion*), then Irish society was surely deeply anarchic. The concept of the state appears to have remained alien to it.

The 'substitute government' and its 'unwritten law' were

[1] For a good short account of its development see C. Gavan Duffy, 'Ungrateful Ireland', *Nineteenth Century*, lxxxii (Dec. 1883).

[2] Broeker, *Rural Disorder*, p. 10, concluded that 'aside from opposition to tithe for primarily economic reasons, the role of religion in formulating banditti goals seems to have been minor'.

[3] Lewis, *Local Disturbances*, pp. 90-1.

[4] Ibid. p. 173.

admirably simple, rugged, low-level constructs. Its paramount demands were that landlords should not levy unjust rents and that no man should take over a farm from which another had been evicted. In this way the control of landlord behaviour was attained indirectly through violent sanctions applied against more vulnerable people, the tenants and lower legal officers. The Special Commission in Queen's County in 1832 heard that the associations had

always had objects connected more or less with land. The preamble to the Irish Act of 15 and 16 George III almost describes the present state of the country. Associations have been formed for regulating the prices of land, attacking houses, administering oaths, delivering threatening notices, taking arms, taking horses at night and returning them again in the morning, taking away girls, murders of proctors and gaugers, preventing exportation of provisions, digging up land, destroying fences, houghing cattle, resisting the payment of tithes, and other outrages . . . [1]

The enforcers of the 'law' in Tipperary in the 1830s and 1840s were bands of three to seven men, armed mainly with pistols, though occasionally with blunderbusses. They operated most frequently in the winter months from October to January. Some of them carried out their 'crimes' on behalf of others they did not know at all.[2] This, as Cornewall Lewis saw, gave them their peculiar significance:

The criminal who acts with these views, is as it were an executioner, who carries into effect the verdict of an uncertain and nonapparent tribunal . . .

He distinguished between these 'intimidatory' crimes, whose effect was intended to be public and demonstrative, and ordinary crimes carried out for private motives. The former were prevalent, possibly accounting for what he and many other observers saw as the 'singular cruelty' with which the associations operated.

. . . the offenders undertake . . . to give their opinion the weight of the law of the state by arming it with sanctions as painful as those employed by the criminal law.[3]

[1] Maryborough Special Comm., evidence of Matthew Barrington, ibid. p. 88.
[2] Beames, 'Rural conflict', pp. 85-6.
[3] Lewis, p. 77.

Opinions have differed over whether such cruelty formed part of the peasant character. Michael Davitt sought to exculpate the mass of the peasantry by suggesting that 'many outrages of a shocking kind' were committed by small off-spring groups such as the 'Lady Clares' and later the 'Molly Maguires', and 'unjustly fathered upon the larger society'.[1] More recent commentators have argued variously that 'passive resistance was a method of protest ill-suited to the peasant temperament', and that 'the Irish peasant was remarkably slow to resort to violence': the brutality of carding, it has been said, so repelled the peasantry that it had to be abandoned if the societies were to retain popular support.[2] It is a fact that carding declined dramatically as the century progressed, and less violent methods proved equally effective. But there were other forms of personal violence, and especially of violence towards animals, which remained in use. A whole range of retributive actions was available, and the system of terror was often so efficient that extreme violence was not necessary: the anticipation was enough to secure compliance. The effectiveness of the system was in large part due to its conservative character. Its customary bases were understood and substantially accepted by the community. None the less, it remains true that Ireland was distinguished from the rest of the British Isles, even in the first half of the century, by the preparedness of its rural societies to use assassination as a last resort.[3] The acceptance of these ruthless punishments, and indeed the preparedness of most Whiteboys or Ribbonmen to carry them out, was founded upon the impersonality of the action.

Agrarian secret societies should not, for the most part, be seen as organizations in any modern sense. Clearly some were better organized than others: one of the distinctions

---

[1] Davitt, *Fall of Feudalism*, p. 43.

[2] Broeker, *Rural Disorder*, p. 205. G. E. Christianson, 'Secret Societies and Agrarian Violence in Ireland 1790–1840', *Agricultural History* (1972), pp. 371–3, suggests that 'the great majority of peasants could not be coaxed into directly attacking their landlord, even when they suffered under the most deplorable of conditions'. This may not have been due to soft-heartedness, however.

[3] Beames, 'Rural conflict', p. 75; assassination being defined as 'the calculated, planned killing of a specific person for identifiable motives . . . in direct contrast to the random, spontaneous violence associated with the term "peasant *jacquerie*" '.

which Lewis drew between Whiteboys and Ribbonmen was the superior organization of the latter. Yet even Ribbonism, the most politically aware of all these groups, was regarded by the police—never people to close their eyes to evidence of conspiracy—as 'not united under any head'.[1] Contemporaries used the vaguer word 'movements'; and it may be suggested that the societies were muscular spasms rather than nervous systems. Their system was supplied by tradition and customary ideas. Their reaction was triggered by immediate stimuli: eviction, land-grabbing, enclosure, dearth. The adoption of a mythical leader's name—Captain Rock, Rory of the Hill, Captain Moonlight—supplied the exiguous organizational framework required. The 'boys' were driven by powerful collective controls akin to those found in existence by Arensberg and Kimball a century later.[2]

The social force which is most difficult to analyse, but central to the establishment of communal ideas, was religion. Ribbonism was an overtly Catholic movement, a direct descendant of Defenderism in the struggle against Protestant rural societies. Outside Ulster, perhaps, this had little relevance. Whiteboyism under its many names was non-sectarian, or so Cornewall Lewis maintained. He pointed out that the Roman Catholic clergy were unremittingly hostile to secret societies (and were indeed themselves occasionally victims of pressures aimed at lowering of fees), and that Catholic gentry were as much at risk as Protestants. He argued, with magnificent objectivity, that the fact that many Ribbon and Whiteboy oaths contained a pledge to 'wade knee deep in Orange blood' could not of itself be taken as evidence of sectarian animosity.[3] Yet it was impossible to deny that, if only because the overwhelming mass of the ordinary

[1] Dublin police report, Sept. 1841 (PRO CO 904 8).

[2] Cf. Lee's observation that 'the areas of widespread poteen-making and intense Ribbon activity rarely overlapped. They were not marginal men, but integral to the life of their communities.' Arensberg and Kimball were, however, wrong about the antiquity of some of the social controls they discovered: P. Gibbon and C. Curtin, 'The Stem Family in Ireland', *Comparative Studies in Society and History*, xx (1978).

[3] Lewis, pp. 125-6, 138-9. But at least one Ribbon catechism in the 1820s called explicitly for the regaining of 'all lost rights and privileges since the Reformation' (Statement of J. Kelly, 6 Dec. 1837, Secret Service MSS, PRO CO 904 7).

people were Catholics, Whiteboyism was Catholic. As was to be the case with more sophisticated and articulate nationalist organizations, even those under clerical ban and themselves overtly anti-clerical, Catholicism was implicit even where non-sectarianism was explicit.

(iii) *Fenianism*

> It is in that English parliament the chains for Ireland are forged.
>
> Jeremiah O'Donovan Rossa

Resistant Ribbonism was the despair of rebellious nationalists. While great efforts have been made to portray agrarian crime as a primitive form of nationalism in which the downtrodden Gaelic peasantry fought back against foreign landlords and an alien church,[1] the nationalist attitude has at heart been one of distaste. The squalid, greedy violence spawned by land-hunger muddied the shining cause of national freedom.[2] Classical Irish historiography discerns in the grim year 1848 only the forlorn hope of Young Ireland and its tragi-comic miniature 'rising' under Smith O'Brien. The enormous upsurge in rural crime, rising from 18,492 committals in 1846 to 38,522 in 1848 and 41,989 in 1849,[3] passes virtually unremarked. In this, there is a recognition of the important distinction between reactive and proactive violence. However trifling, quantitatively, may have been the actions of Young Irelander Confederates, or Fenians after them, their conscious political intent, and the articulate formulation of their objectives, gave them disproportionate significance. It was the occasional flashes of outright rebellion which gave indirect political meaning to the inarticulate turmoil of the peasantry.

Fenianism has been the object of intense and fascinated historical study, and even though there is not yet a single

[1] Cf. P. S. O'Hegarty, *A History of Ireland under the Union* (London, 1952), pp. 462–4.

[2] R. V. Comerford, *Charles J. Kickham. A Study in Irish Nationalism and Literature* (Dublin, 1979), pp. 149–54; cf. the attitude of Austin Stack, below, p. 380.

[3] Hurst, 'Disturbed Tipperary', App. C, p. 57.

full account of the movement, it would be superfluous here to attempt a survey.[1] It is necessary only to notice that the first signs of the new grouping became visible in 1858, and that it formed around survivors of the Young Ireland revolt ten years earlier. A County Inspector of the Irish Constabulary reported in November 1858:

> As to the prevalence of Ribbonism, there can be no doubt. But it is understood to be on a different principle from that which hitherto existed, inasmuch as they have neither signs nor pass words, and are under the designation of a 'Phenix Club'.[2]

A Belfast newspaper next month clarified the issue further:

> It is a gross error to confound the organisation of this 'Phoenix Club' and its ramifications, with the old Ribbon society. There is little doubt that the new organisation is entirely seditious, and made up out of the dregs of Young Irelandism.[3]

Yet another 'ism' was due to be added to the Irish catalogue. Fortunately, the ungainly 'Phoenixism' never appeared: within a short time the new body, which solidified rapidly amongst Irish emigrants in the United States, had adopted the name 'Fenian'.

In Ireland itself, interestingly, it went without a name for many months, or was simply known, then and later, as 'the organization' (a clear and significant statement of its structural uniqueness). In the end it adopted the celebrated title Irish Republican Brotherhood, though even then 'Republican' was sometimes rendered 'Revolutionary'. All this goes to show that names mattered little: the group occupied a more or less natural place in Irish political life, at least amongst the political class from which the leaders of 1848 had come.[4]

---

[1] The only general account is T. W. Moody (ed.), *The Fenian Movement* (Cork, 1968). Its excellent bibliography may be supplemented by that in B. MacGiollaChoille, 'Fenian documents in the State Paper Office', *IHS* xvii (Mar. 1969). Aspects of the movement are luminously conveyed in L. Ó Broin, *Fenian Fever. An Anglo-American Dilemma* (London, 1971), and T. W. Moody, *Davitt and Irish Revolution 1846–82* (Oxford, 1981).

[2] Report by County Inspector, Fermanagh, 20 Nov. 1858 (SPO Fenian reports, No. 1).   [3] *Daily Mercury*, 13 Dec. 1858.

[4] Cf. L. Ó Broin, 'Revolutionary nationalism in Ireland: the IRB, 1858–1924', in T. W. Moody (ed.), *Nationality and the Pursuit of National Independence* (Belfast, 1978); L. Ó Broin and T. W. Moody, 'The IRB Supreme Council, 1868–78. Select Documents', *IHS* xix (1975).

A perceptive, though hardly neutral, foreign observer later remarked that 'it was the name of Fenianism that was new, rather than the thing itself'.[1]

It bore clear marks of succession from Young Ireland, and, further back, from Emmet's conspiracy. Nationalist legend has strongly suggested that Fenianism was just another —and inevitable—manifestation of the 'phoenix flame', the immanent urge to national liberty; and metaphors of rebirth have been consistently employed by both traditional and less-traditional historians as explanations of the national movement. F. S. L. Lyons, writing of a later rebellion, put it thus:

> The embers of Irish identity had been subdued, they had not been extinguished; and out of them, as dedicated men blew on the coals, rose once more the deathless phoenix of independent nationality.[2]

Paul Bew, writing of the 1867 insurrection, says that its effect was to 'awaken' national sentiment. Such metaphors are a way of dealing with a phenomenon which has so far defied precise analysis: they rest on the romantic assumption of innate national consciousness.[3] It remains unclear, however, whether such consciousness was actually slumbering amongst the Irish people, or whether it was gradually but remorselessly constructed by intellectuals (as elsewhere in Europe) building on Herder's inspirational, revolutionary concept of *Volkstum*.

As against the perspective of continuity, it is useful to draw attention to what was novel about Fenianism. In the first place, the IRB was, much more than even the United Irishmen, an international organization with international awareness. Its foundation was indeed precipitated by the international crisis of 1858 which merged into the French–Austrian war of 1859.[4] Its founder, James Stephens, borrowed both political ideas and organizational methods from

---

[1] L. Paul-Dubois, *Contemporary Ireland* (Dublin, 1911), p. 75.

[2] F. S. L. Lyons, *Ireland since the Famine* (London, 1971), p. 21.

[3] P. Bew, 'Les Fenians et l'indépendance de l'Irlande', *L'Histoire*, xxxiii (1981), 20. For an extended, dispassionate historical analysis, D. G. Boyce, *Nationalism in Ireland* (London, 1981).

[4] R. V. Comerford, 'Anglo-French tension and the original of Fenianism', in F. S. L. Lyons and R. Hawkins (eds), *Ireland Under the Union* (Oxford, 1980).

the secret insurrectionist societies which abounded on the continent in the first half of the century. The notion of organization through 'circles' (which seems to have remained more notional than real) and the system of initiation rites were both derived, via Buonarroti, from European free-masonry. The links here were much closer than those which Young Ireland, its name notwithstanding, possessed with the Mazzinian societies. The all-important symbol of the Republic, the IRB's most distinctive contribution to the nationalist tradition, was plainly a French–American import, with no Irish roots deeper than the 1790s.[1] A further distinction, which became progressively more important in its implications, was that while the Fenians shared, outwardly, the non-sectarianism of Young Ireland and its illustrious forebear, the United Irishmen, even adding their own brand of anti-clericalism—expressed in the slogan 'no priests in politics' —they were predominantly Catholic in background. One recent writer has, indeed, suggested that 'in fact, the Fenians were hardly less Catholic than the Ribbonmen'. Charles Kickham, who wrote many articles condemning priestly inter-ference in politics, was a devoutly religious man. He established that willingness to defy the church, and indeed to break the sixth commandment, in the name of the sacred cause which has subsequently puzzled so many outside observers of Irish republicanism.[2]

The IRB, unlike Young Ireland, which was primarily a movement for publicizing the cause of nationality, was an oathbound secret society which, verbally at least, spurned mere words in favour of violence.

---

[1] Stephen's fellow-organizer, T. C. Luby, saw him as 'socialistically' inclined, though Luby was not much of a judge of such things: Luby MSS, NLI MS 331-3, quoted in Ó Broin, 'Revolutionary nationalism', p. 98. Cf. D. Ryan, *The Fenian Chief* (Dublin, 1967); Boyce, op. cit.

[2] E. D. Steele, *Irish Land and British Politics* (Cambridge, 1975), p. 30; cf. D. McCartney, 'The Church and the Fenians', *University Review* (1967), pp. 203-15; E. R. Norman, *The Catholic Church and Ireland in the Age of Rebellion 1859-1873* (London, 1965). For a sketchy treatment of the 'confessional nature of Irish nationalism', J. Newsinger, 'Revolution and Catholicism in Ireland, 1848-1923', *European Studies Review*, ix (1979).

Yes! up! and let your weapons be
Sharp steel and self-reliance!
Why waste your burning energy
In void and vain defiance
And phrases fierce but fugitive?
'Tis deeds, not words, that *I* weigh—
Your swords and guns alone can give
To freedom's course a highway![1]

The relentless grimness of Fenian rhetoric was established at the outset, and came to form a mental outlook almost entire of itself. Nobody expressed this more completely than O'Donovan Rossa, a founder member of the Phoenix Club. After his arrest in 1859 a letter was found in his home, declaring

I am every ready to do my utmost to promote the cause and acquire the reality of nationality . . . but . . . I don't believe the Saxon will ever relax his grip except by the persuasion of cold lead and steel.[2]

This simplistic symbolism was maintained into the 1870s, though steel was replaced by gunpowder (which Rossa, oddly, preferred to dynamite): in 1877 he promised that 'all the cities of England, if she do not let go her hold, must be laid in ashes'.[3]

In the meantime the IRB made its one attempt at open insurrection on the Blanquist model. The organization took off into sustained growth in the early 1860s, though, somewhat paradoxically, in view of its commitment to physical force, the event which catalysed its growth was a classic demonstration of non-violent, moral-force methods. The funeral of Terence Bellew McManus, a hitherto barely known national hero, in 1861 was stage-managed with a skill that was to become a vital aspect of Republican method.

At 1 o'clock the hearse which was uncovered and drawn by 6 horses moved off from the Mechanics' Institute followed by the processionists, the majority of whom wore black crape on the arm tied up with white

[1] Mangan, quoted in *Fenian Spirit* (Boston), vol. i, No. 3, 3 Sept. 1874: SPO, Fenian MSS, Police reports, No. 2.

[2] *Clare Journal*, 14 Mar. 1859, quoted in R. Kee, *The Green Flag. A History of Irish Nationalism* (London, 1972), p. 300.

[3] Circular sent by Rossa from USA, obtained by police at Limerick, 30 Apr. 1877: SPO, Fenian MSS, Police reports, No. 3.

tape and in addition about 250 wore green neck-ties. The procession
was preceded by several men on horse-back dressed in dark clothes and
turban-hats and each wearing a black scarf, some of whom wore medals
and were stated to have belonged to the Pope's Brigade. Each carried a
deal baton in his hand; others dressed and equipped in similar manner
rode on each side of the procession and took the control and manage-
ment of it . . . Behind the coach came 2 R.C. clergymen . . . then
followed the general processionists from 6 to 8 deep, headed by 3
bands playing the Dead March in Saul. They formed into sections,
each section being conducted and arranged by leaders who carried
white wands. In the centre were 8 men wearing large black sashes on
the front of which were inscribed in large white letters 'American
Deputation' . . . The great majority was composed of well-dressed
men, apparently small shopkeepers, tradesmen, and labourers . . . The
whole of these who composed the procession numbered between 7 and
8,000 persons and covered about a mile in length . . . when the procession was passing through Thomas Street, a cheer was attempted to be
got up, but it was suppressed by the leaders. All took off their hats
and caps when passing. It was stated that this was in consequence
of Thomas Street being the place where Emmet was executed.[1]

It is worth remarking, however, that the Dublin Metropolitan
Police, who made this report of the event, did not refer to
the Fenians, and clearly did not know they existed. The
secret organization had a head-start in laying its plans for
insurrection.

By 1864–5 the movement was making an impact on the
countryside, sometimes meeting opposition from Ribbon
societies. In County Monaghan, for instance, IRB leadership
was provided by an influential local man, James Blayney
Rice, who came from an old and respectable family and was
himself a former Ribbonman. The rank and file, however,
were from a distinctly different social group. Rice's men
probably totalled between thirty and fifty: those Monaghan
Fenians whose occupation is known included labourers, small
farmers, grocers' assistants or general dealers, assistant letter-
carriers, ex-soldiers, a butcher, a publican, a saddler, a
draper's assistant, a flax-buyer, a wool-buyer, and a hawker.[2]
Early in 1866 a constable of the Irish Constabulary reported

[1] DMP Report, SPO, CSO RP 1861/8418 (in RP 1877/3591), quoted *in
extenso* in MacGiollaChoille, 'Fenian documents', pp. 263–4.
[2] B. MacGiollaChoille, 'Fenians, Rice and Ribbonmen in County Monaghan,
1864–67', *Clogher Record* (1967), p. 236.

I have travelled through the supposed disaffected localities, namely, Toholland, Emyvale, Cavancope, and Curcaghan. As already stated, the poor labouring class only speak in favour of the Fenians—and now the R.C. bishop and the priests are condemning the movement from the altars in chapel, Sunday after Sunday.[1]

A recent authority has concluded that to begin with the Fenians drew their strength from rural social groups below the farmer class or from the declining artisans of the towns. Later, the movement helped to provide

in certain areas at least, some kind of leadership for forces hitherto fragmented, while at the same time encouraging a transient unity of interest between farmers and the relatively declining body of cottiers and landless labourers.[2]

But what did it offer? Its programme had from the start an air of vagueness. It had a very general basic standpoint: English rule was the cause of all Ireland's problems. This 'comfortingly simple analysis', as another recent writer has pointed out, was never contradicted either by Stephens or by the American Fenian leader O'Mahony.[3] Stephens may well have seen the intellectual inadequacy of the approach, and the *Irish People* certainly made some efforts to develop thoughts on land reform as a positive programme.[4] But the simplicity of the Fenian explanation gave it great power. For Charles Kickham, president of the IRB Supreme Council in the 1870s, there was a mystical connection between the solution of the land problem and the securing of national independence.[5] The bases of the demand for national independence were surprisingly little discussed. Very few Fenians showed any interest in national culture, especially language, as a foundation of national sentiment. Stephens seems to have assumed that Irish identity rested on something other than the Irish language, while O'Leary shared

[1] Report of Const. Kennedy, SPO Fenian MSS F701: loc. cit. 230.
[2] K. T. Hoppen, 'National Politics and Local Realities in Mid-Nineteenth Century Ireland', in A. Cosgrove and D. McCartney (edd.), *Studies in Irish History* (Dublin, 1979), p. 214.
[3] M. Gallagher, 'Socialism and the nationalist tradition in Ireland 1798-1918', *Éire-Ireland*, xii (1977), 76.
[4] Bew, *Land and the National Question*, pp. 38-40. The *Irish People* ran for two years, until suppressed by the government.
[5] Comerford, *Kickham*, p. 146.

the widely held attitude (itself instrumental in the dramatic decline of Gaelic speech) that the language was a hindrance rather than an asset in the modern world.[1]

Fenian publicity, above all the *Irish People*, repeatedly declared peasant proprietorship to be the ideal, natural, and inevitable solution. This was in fact proclaimed by the 'Provisional Government of the Republic' in 1867.[2] However, leaders like Kickham and O'Leary were intolerant of agrarian class struggle, and continued to see open insurrection as the only acceptable method. To put it simply, they fudged the connection between the land problem and the 'national question': Kickham, as his biographer remarks, 'could never admit, even to himself, that nationalism might be grounded on mere grievances'.[3] They were much less radical on this issue than the Young Ireland publicist James Fintan Lalor, though it was to him rather than the other Young Irelanders that subsequent republicans owed the greatest debt. Lalor's short burst of brilliant writings laid the basis for seeing the solution of the land problem not as a product but as the motor force of independence. While recognizing that 'It is never the mass of a people that forms its real and efficient might. It is the men by whom that mass is moved and managed', he saw that a mass movement must be founded on 'some question possessing the intrinsic strength which Repeal wants'—in other words, appealing to public opinion in a way that nationalism did not.[4] With unusual realism he held that 'the land question contains, and the legislative question does *not*, materials from which victory is manufactured'.[5]

Lalor was not, however, committed to the Fenian *leitmotiv* of physical force. His 'Proposal for an Agricultural Association between the Landowners and Occupiers' was

[1] John Devoy, however, contended that O'Leary was unusual amongst Fenians in this: *Recollections of an Irish Rebel* (New York, 1929), pp. 261–5.

[2] K. B. Nowlan, 'The Fenian Rising of 1867', in Moody (ed.), *Fenian Movement*, p. 30.

[3] Comerford, *Kickham*, p. 152; O'Leary, *Recollections*, pp. 37, 142.

[4] J. F. Lalor, 'Clearing the Decks', *Irish Felon*, 22 July; 'To the Confederate and Repeal Clubs', ibid., 1 July 1848: L. Fogarty (ed.), *Collected Writings of James Fintan Lalor* (Dublin, 1918), pp. 107, 92.

[5] Lalor to d'Arcy McGee, 30 Mar. 1847 (ibid., p. xxxiv).

almost Saint-Simonian in tone. His most stirring exhortation. 'To the Irish Confederate and Repeal Clubs' of July 1848, advocated struggle, but by means of what he christened 'moral insurrection'. This sophisticated technique (directly prophetic of the Sinn Féin programme in the twentieth century) he outlined as consisting:

    i. In refusal of obedience to usurped authority.
    ii. In maintaining and defending such refusal of obedience.
    iii. In resisting every attempt to exercise such usurped authority, and every proceeding adopted to enforce obedience.
    iv. In taking quiet and peaceable possession of all the rights and powers of government, and in proceeding quietly to exercise them.
    v. In maintaining and defending the exercise of such rights and powers, should it be attacked.[1]

Lalor perceived that in this process passive resistance might have to become active resistance. But in that case its defensive nature would add to its strength, both moral and physical.

To make it successful, your fight must be a *defensive* one. The force of England is *entrenched* and *fortified*. You must draw it out of position; break up its mass; break its trained line of march and manœuvre —its equal step and serried array. You cannot organize, or train, or discipline your own force to any point of efficiency. You must, therefore, disorganize, and untrain, and undiscipline, that of the enemy; and not alone must you *unsoldier* it—you must *unofficer* it also; nullify its tactique and strategy, as well as its discipline; decompose the science and systems of war, and resolve them into their first elements. You must make the hostile army a mob, as your own will be; force it to act on the *offensive*, and oblige it to undertake operations for which it was never constructed.[2]

Although Lalor was, like most of his contemporaries, still bound to the assumption that irregular forces must necessarily be untrained peasant mobs, he produced here a striking exposition—among the earliest and most lucid—of the principles of guerrilla warfare.[3]

It has been held that the Fenian leaders, when they launched

---

[1] Lalor to d'Arcy McGee, 30 Mar. 1847 p. 83.

[2] Ibid. pp. 80-1.

[3] Perhaps the only work to be compared with Lalor's is Mazzini's *Rules for the Conduct of Guerrilla Bands*—equally without practical effect, in spite of its technical nature.

their long-postponed but still premature rebellion in 1867,
did in fact intend to use guerrilla methods. But whatever may
have been in the minds of American Civil War veterans, local
Fenian leaders showed little conception of it.[1] James
Stephens's naïve idea that it was possible to acquire, along
with other masonic mysteries, 'those secrets by means of
which an indisciplined mob can be most readily and effectually
matched against a mercenary army' would seem to have
found its most authentic expression in a seventy-page pamphlet called *The Military Resources of Ireland*, by 'Charles
Beggs', which went into its third edition at the reduced price
of sixpence in 1858.[2] This grandiose tract declared that
Ireland could, if properly organized, produce a million fighting men. The Irish terrain gave great advantages to the
natives, and disadvantaged such expensive material as artillery. Indeed, 'Beggs' produced the comforting argument that
such things were nowadays useless—'the maintenance of
artillery, as an arm of military service, but symbolises the
military folly of the age'—and the same went for cavalry
(here, of course, he was closer to the truth). 'Beggs' did
discuss—briefly, on his final page—such modern gewgaws as
Minié and Enfield rifles, but the body of his pamphlet was a
sustained paean to that most Irish of weapons, the pike.

The chief and primary arm of Ireland's military force must be composed of pikemen, whose armament and equipment are so cheap and
simple that the very poorest man can at all times stand armed and
equipped.[3]

[1] The claim of a guerrilla plan is based on a letter of T. J. Kelly, 19 Mar. 1867:
F. D'Arcy, *The Fenian Movement in the United States* (Washington, 1947),
pp. 240-1. Such also seems to have been the proposal of J. McCafferty, veteran
of Morgan's cavalry: Ó Luing, *Fremantle Mission*, pp. 2-3. The commander-
designate, Cluseret, who had experience of Garibaldi's campaign of 1859-60 as
well as the American Civil War, and was to go on to become *Délégué de Guerre* in
the Paris Commune, left a curious *pièce justificative* which damned Irish drunken-
ness, Catholicism, and faith in the pike, but suggests that open warfare was
envisaged (especially in his demand for 'ten thousand armed men'). G. Cluseret,
'My Connexion with Fenianism', *Fraser's Magazine*, repr. *Littel's Living Age*,
cxiv (1879), pp. 353-65.
[2] Ryan, *Fenian Chief*, p. 48: C. Beggs, *The Military Resources of Ireland, with
a system of armament, plan of organization, and mode of warfare, adapted to the
circumstances of the country* (Dublin, London, and New York, 1858); SPO
Fenian MSS, Police reports, No. 2.
[3] Ibid. pp. 18, 66, 20.

His standpoint was admirably democratic: all criticisms of the pike were the work of 'despotic or oligarchical governments' which feared its 'simplicity, invincibility, and cheapness'. This was morally attractive, but much less attractive (if put into practice) was a passage showing how two ranks of pikemen could successfully *attack* an enemy armed with modern rifles.[1] The actual outcome would be ghastly to imagine.

In fact, of course, the real argument was moral rather than technical. Like a later school of French military writers, the author believed that *élan* would overcome everything else. Cold steel was essentially a rhetorical weapon, an adjunct to

the grandest poetry of the soul, and the sweetest anthem of the heart —the sacred and soul-elevating language of liberty; that spirit-moving sentiment which evokes inspiration, and sends the floating flag of freedom in triumph through the foeman's adamantine ranks and opposing forests of blazing steel . . .

Irresistible as the ocean in its might, in quick-moving cataclysms of ordered waves of bristling steel, our pike columns fiercely advance; now levelled lines of pikes gleam, charging in the gloom of night; heedless of the groans of their expiring foes, over ground slippery with their gore, these chivalric columns advance . . . these serried lines of blazing steel . . . when the stars commingle their descending rays with the well-won wreaths of victory, gently hovering around the green standards of our fatherland.[2]

Pleasant though such writing-table fantasy may have been, something more was needed in 1867. Something more, even, than John O'Mahony's declaration at the Fenian Congress of January 1865 that 'this Brotherhood is virtually at war with the oligarchy of Great Britain', the Congress acting as the national assembly of the Irish Republic while 'our organized friends in Ireland constitute its army'.[3] And though the pike was to remain a central Fenian symbol, as celebrated in the ballad 'The Rising of the Moon', and was to be carried as late as 1916 and even 1920, Fenians in the 1860s made attempts to get modern firearms. They were only moderately successful in this, and a more promising line of activity was

[1] C. Beggs, *The Military Resources of Ireland* pp. 24, 26.

[2] Ibid. pp. 31, 48.

[3] Proceedings of the 2nd International Congress of the Fenian Brotherhood, Cincinnati, Jan. 1865: D'Arcy, op. cit. p. 47.

'military Fenianism'—the swearing into the IRB of large numbers of regular troops in Irish regiments. The dramatic possibilities created by this policy were, however, removed by energetic suppression by the military authorities after 1865. Thereafter, many believed that the plan for the 1867 insurrection turned on an attempt to seize the armoury at Chester Castle by a sudden coup.[1] The attempt was indeed prepared, but aborted at the last moment: the end of a series of misadventures which cumulatively doomed the whole rebellion. Inappropriate military methods set the seal upon this. The most successful, and indeed prophetic, operation carried out in 1867 was an attack on the Constabulary barrack at Kilmallock, Co. Limerick (which was to be the site of the most spectacular assault on a police barrack in 1920).[2]

The power of Fenianism, however, resided as much in rhetoric as in facts. Military disaster meant little in itself. Its opponents failed to realize this as they exulted over the fiasco. The Chief Secretary, Lord Naas, declared that the Chester affair 'shows what a ludicrous set of snivelling cowards the Fenians are'—if they had only marched boldly up to the Castle no one could have stopped them[3] (a criticism to be repeated fifty-one years later). 'I gave the Fenians credit for more power of combination', commented Lord Kimberley; 'What can be more contemptible than their attempt?'[4] It is true that after 1867 the idea of physical force, construed as the bodily ejection of the English from Ireland, went into a kind of suspended animation. The last Fenian raid on Canada in 1870 effectively ended the open war declared in 1865. The Supreme Council's 'Address to the People of Ireland' in January 1870 even condemned arms raids—'those silly exploits fit only to excite the enthusiasm [of] unthinking boys', which did 'great injury to our cause

---

[1] The armoury contained 30,000 rifles and was weakly guarded. The plan to seize it appears to have been tangential to the rising, however, and in part an effort to salvage Fenian honour: Ó Broin, *Fenian Fever*, p. 126.

[2] Barely mentioned in most accounts of 1867, but dramatically highlighted in R. Anderson, *Sidelights on the Home Rule Movement* (London, 1906), pp. 66–7.

[3] Naas to Under-Sec., n.d. 1867 (Larcom MSS, NLI MS 7593).

[4] Kimberley to Larcom, 18 Feb. 1867 (loc. cit).

while the resulting advantages, if any, are utterly contempt-ible'—and recommended a policy of attempting to obtain control of local bodies such as 'corporations, town commis-sioners, &c, as a means of increasing the power and influence of the Irish Republic'.[1] But such hesitant Lalorism did not herald the abandonment of physical force. It was rather replaced by a symbolic, or one might even say rhetorical, use of violence. O'Donovan Rossa's move from steel to powder signified the adoption in fact, albeit not in theory, of ter-rorism; or what contemporary anarchists called propaganda of the deed. This was an activity structurally akin to the 'public crime' of the Whiteboys, but differing in intention. T. P. Thornton's useful analysis of terrorism suggests a division into two species, 'enforcement' and 'agitational' terror. These correspond in effect to reaction and proaction. Both are the application by small groups of a small degree of violence (much less than is normal in actual warfare) to the 'resonant mass' of the general public, whose reaction measures the effect of the armed propaganda.[2] The weakness of Thornton's treatment of 'enforcement' terror—which is in any case very sketchy—is that it is restricted by the common view (shared by Thornton) that the function of terror is 'disorientation'.[3] Thus, enforcement terror amounts, for him, to governmental counter-terror: the whole scope of communal violence is removed from his analysis. Neverthe-less, his approach helps to underline the formidable task which the Fenians took on in passing from traditional agrarian terror towards the direct application of force to British public opinion.

In fact, considering their weakness, and the low level of British public interest in Irish matters, they were rapidly and astonishingly successful. The desperate rescue of the Fenian prisoners at Manchester in September 1867 and the subsequent execution of the 'Manchester Martyrs', followed in December by the dreadfully bungled, destructive explosion

[1] SPO Fenian MSS, 6450R; Moody and Ó Broin, 'IRB Supreme Council', p. 310.
[2] T. P. Thornton, 'Terror as a weapon of political agitation', in H. Eckstein (ed.), *Internal War* (New York, 1964). Cf. H. E. Price, 'The strategy and tactics of revolutionary terrorism', *Comp. Stud. Soc. Hist.* xix (1977), 53.
[3] Thornton, op. cit. 74.

under Clerkenwell prison wall, though not conceived in any theoretical sense as terrorist acts, had far greater public impact than the attempted rebellion. Coming, as John Stuart Mill put it, like a thunderbolt from a clear sky, Fenian violence on the mainland led to a major political reappraisal. This fact found its most notable expression in the words of W. E. Gladstone at the inception of his first ministry and his partial programme of Irish reforms.[1] These words are none the less important for having been frequently quoted: their importance derives from the fact that they were spoken by a political party leader, whatever their intended purpose.

In my opinion and in the opinion of many with whom I communicated, the Fenian conspiracy has had an important influence with respect to Irish policy; but it has not been an influence in determining, or in affecting in the slightest degree, the convictions which we have entertained with respect to the course proper to be pursued in Ireland. The influence of Fenianism was this—that when the habeas corpus Act was suspended, when all the consequent proceedings occurred, when the tranquillity of the great city of Manchester was disturbed, when the metropolis itself was shocked and horrified by an inhuman outrage, when a sense of insecurity went abroad far and wide . . . when the inhabitants of the different towns of the country were swearing themselves in as special constables for the maintenance of life and property —then it was when these phenomena came home to the popular mind, and produced that attitude of attention and preparedness on the part of the whole population of this country which qualified them to embrace, in a manner foreign to their habits in other times, the vast importance of the Irish controversy.[2]

John Devoy, a steady opponent of terror strategy, was surely right to say that they 'proved a stronger argument in favor of physical force—and even of Terrorism—on the part of Ireland . . . than any Irishman ever made'.[3] The public panic

---

[1] J. Vincent, 'Gladstone and Ireland' (British Academy, 1978), points out that Gladstone's 'mission' was more a media event than a deep interest, and discounts 1867 as a turning-point in his views. But see Gladstone's worries about imperial security, 22 Oct. 1866: H. C. G. Matthew (ed.), *The Gladstone Diaries*, (Oxford, 1978), vi. 473; and Dec. 1867; E. D. Steele, 'Gladstone, Irish Violence, and Conciliation', in Cosgrove and McCartney, op. cit., 268.

[2] Hansard, 31 May 1869; Morley, *Gladstone*, i, 875-6. Derby later wrote that though this speech had often been censured as unwise, 'to me it has always seemed a gain that the exact and naked truth should be spoken' (*Nineteenth Century*, lxvi (Oct. 1881), 483).

[3] Devoy, *Recollections*, p. 250.

of 1868 seemed to demonstrate the effectiveness of random violence, though its real significance was scarcely greater than that of the earlier 'garrotting' panic. At the same time a very different process of reaction established the position of the Manchester 'Three' as Irish martyrs of quasi-religious status,[1] cementing Fenianism within the popular Catholic culture.

(iv) *Ulsterism*

> Protestantism and loyalty do not mean in Belfast what they mean in London and Manchester. Here they represent religious enlightenment and the equality of political parties. In Belfast they mean simply and nakedly the ascendancy of one creed and one set of principles.
>
> *Daily News*, 20 Aug. 1872

Most analyses of Irish questions, however they deal with everything else, detach 'Ulster' for separate treatment. No matter how clumsy this device may seem, it is difficult to avoid. The North is *sui generis*; the 'isms' of others sit awkwardly on it. To justify this separate treatment it may perhaps be defensible to propose 'Ulsterism' as an analytical concept—or even indeed 'Belfastism'.[2] The structure of actions and expectations connected with political violence in Belfast, and to a lesser extent in other northern Irish towns, exists nowhere else. Perhaps the less inelegant and neologistic 'Northernism' might serve, to point up the regional nature of the distinction. Rural Ulster, too, differed in important respects from the rest of Ireland; the best-known, and most relevant to the problems discussed at the beginning of this chapter, being the so-called 'Ulster custom' of tenant right. Indeed, rural Ulster played a crucial part in the institutionalization of violence. It was there, particularly in Co. Armagh, that Peep o'Day Boys, Oakboys, and Steelboys fought with the Catholic groups called Defenders as well as

[1] The *Irishman*, 27 Nov. 1877, referred to the anniversary of the Manchester executions as the 'Feast of the uncanonized', adding the prayer, 'In nomine Patris et Filii | Et Spiritus Sancti—swearing me | To watch and wait, and foster my hate | To walk in the red paths of the Three'.

[2] 'Ulsterism' was adopted by the geographer M. W. Heslinga in his remarkable study, *The Irish Border as a Cultural Divide* (Assen, 1971), e.g. p. 55.

with landlords.[1] Above all it was there, out of a complex of economic and demographic changes, that the Orange Order developed.

The emergence of this institution has lately been subjected to the questioning analysis that befits so intractable a phenomenon, but it remains impossible to escape from the crude foundation of the northern problem—the existence of a substantial Protestant population. Had the settler community not retained, by whatever process, its religious segregation, the sort of conflicts which would have developed in the nineteenth century would surely have been those more normally associated with modernizing, industrializing societies. Whether the retention of separate identity was a psychological means of justifying conquest and confiscation is a question requiring too extensive an investigation to be touched on here.[2] All that must be observed is that religion remained a polarizing force, or at least symbol, effectively hobbling the development of class consciousness. But if modernization, in an attitudinal sense, failed to occur, its mechanical concomitant, industrialization, was dramatically in evidence. Paradoxically, indeed, it played an important part in sustaining religious segregation. It was not the struggle for land that divided the Armagh community.[3] It appears to have been rapid developments in the linen industry that destabilized the fairly delicate set of status balances between Protestant and Catholic groups.[4] Still, the essential structural elements were the approximate numerical equality of the two sides, coupled with the mental preparedness to see themselves

[1] On the much-misunderstood custom see Christianson, 'Secret societies', p. 370; Donnelly, *Landlord and Tenant*, p. 21. P. Gibbon, 'The origins of the Orange Order and the United Irishmen', *Economy and Society*, i (1972), 152, suggests that 'the principal political legacy of the Oakboys was anti-landlord armed insurrection (i.e. military or quasi-military attempts to destroy or to paralyse for a prolonged period the prevailing system of administration)'. Cf. A. T. Q. Stewart, *The Narrow Ground. Aspects of Ulster 1609–1969* (London, 1977), pp. 116–18.

[2] The perspectives developed in studies of 'frontier' cultures may provide a line of explanation; Gibbon, 'Orange Order', p. 155—though Gibbon's argument remains speculative and tendentious at many points.

[3] Stewart, op. cit. p. 129.

[4] Gibbon, 'Orange Order', pp. 154-9; *The Origins of Ulster Unionism. The Formation of Popular Protestant Politics and Ideology in Nineteenth Century Ireland* (Manchester, 1975).

as 'sides'. Without a rough demographic balance, the celebrated 'siege mentality' of the northern Protestants (and in this state of mind Presbyterians early identified with Episcopalians) could not have been formed in quite the same way.

The physical geography of siege was most starkly shaped in Belfast. The city's rapid growth in the early nineteenth century was, 'at first, experienced as a Catholic invasion'.[1] The two groups settled for the most part in distinct areas, which they still inhabit. Between these are the 'shatter zones' where violence has persistently erupted. The first riots took place in 1812, and represented, in the view of one of Ulster's most perceptive historians, 'the transfer to the urban environment of well-established patterns of violence'.[2] Like other things in Ulster history, these patterns seem to have been frozen in time: the basic form of the Belfast riot altered scarcely at all over the next hundred years and more, though its technology became more formidable. It was the open, quasi-ritual confrontation of faction-fighting rather than the guerrilla technique of the agrarian secret societies. This form probably derived in large measure from the Ulster-Protestant tradition of 'banding', established before the eighteenth century.[3] The habit of public banding for the maintenance of 'order'—in effect the Protestant ascendancy, invoked in Protestant parlance as the 'constitution' which guaranteed 'freedom, religion, and laws'— was a crucial organizational resource. It enabled the protestant gentry to mobilize the Volunteer movement in the late 1780s to obtain a Protestant Irish parliament. The success of this mobilization underlined the political function of armed force: as Grattan himself observed, Magna Carta, the foundation of English ideas of public liberty, 'was not attained in Parliament but by the barons armed in the field'.[4]

If it is true that, as David Miller's highly original study

[1] O'Farrell, *England and Ireland*, p. 165.

[2] Stewart, *Narrow Ground*, p. 140.

[3] For a brilliant sustained analysis of public banding, D. W. Miller, *Queen's Rebels. Ulster Loyalism in Historical Perspective* (Dublin, 1978).

[4] And like the American settlers Protestants maintained into the nineteenth century a belief in the right to bear arms: S. E. Baker, 'Orange and Green. Belfast 1832–1912', in H. J. Dyos and M. Wolff (edd.) *The Victorian City: Images and Realities* (London, 1973), ii. 807.

of Ulster 'loyalism' suggests, Protestant agrarian violence 'constituted a plea to the landlord class to restore the traditional order'—that is, the order in which idealized feudal relationships between Protestants governed the economic system—then the Volunteer movement can be seen as a sort of surrogate for this.[1] It reaffirmed the 'special relationship' between the Protestant lower classes and their social superiors. The Orange Order went on to institutionalize this function on a permanent basis. In 1857 a Belfast newspaper offered a jaundiced but percipient view of the 'Orange party' bands:

They have grown up, and increased with the prosperity of the town, in which they have always had 'a local habitation and a name'. Their old ascendancy habits inspire them with confidence in themselves. They have been a dominant faction, and thus became ably organised and skilfully disciplined . . . Their union has been maintained through the organisation of their lodges; they are better educated than their Romanist antagonists—have a greater spirit of independence—are more accustomed to the use of firearms—stand firmer together—and have always the confidence and superiority inspired by victory about them.[2]

At about the same time, the Lord Chancellor of Ireland held that 'the Orange Society is mainly instrumental in keeping alive . . . excitement' and that, while the government believed it had been finally suppressed in the late 1820s

it still appears to remain an extensively organised body, but with some changes of system and rules, under which it is alleged to be free from any legal prosecution. However that may be, it is manifest that the existence of the society and the conduct of many of those who belong to it, tend to keep up through large districts of the north a spirit of bitter and factious hostility . . . and to provoke violent hostility and aggression.[3]

The argument over the primacy of economic or theological hostility in shaping the Ulster Protestant outlook has been in

---

[1] Miller, op. cit. p. 53. On the continued assertion of special social equality in the Order, R. Harris, *Prejudice and Tolerance in Ulster. A Study of Neighbours and 'Strangers' in a Border Community* (Manchester, 1972), pp. xii–xiii.

[2] *Belfast Mercury*, 25 Sep. 1857 (NLI MS 7624).

[3] Ld. Chancellor to Ld.-Lieutenant Co. Down, 3 Oct. 1857 (loc. cit.). The Select Committee on Orange Institutions in Great Britain had found the order 'dangerous to the peace of Her Majesty's subjects' (PP, HC 1835 (605)) (xvii).

progress for a long time, and has of course intensified in the last decade. There seems now to be some tendency towards giving more serious consideration to the religious issue than has been common in the twentieth century.[1] In examining the behaviour of nineteenth-century Protestants, there can be little doubt that their religious sense underpinned their whole world-view; this included, naturally, their view of Roman Catholics. There was nothing peculiar to Ulster, or even to Ireland, in this. English anti-popery became notably intense in the nineteenth century. The response of working-class Dublin Protestants to the Repeal issue, which has recently been analysed, well illustrates the vision of politics as a struggle between good and evil. Like that of the Ulstermen, their loyalty to England was conditional. The Dublin Protestant Operative Association and Reformation Society declared roundly in 1843, 'Who cares a fig for the "integrity of the British Empire" if it be not the Empire of immortal truth?' —in other words, the ascendancy of Protestantism.[2] The DPOA had also reached the conclusion, significant for the future, that no physical force in Ireland was stronger than that of the Protestants.

The main thing that prevented Dublin from becoming like Belfast was the isolation and numerical weakness of its Protestant population. Street preaching, a major trigger for public disturbances, was pursued there as aggressively as in Belfast. But in Belfast, and to a lesser extent in Derry, Protestants could assert and test their strength by means of regular ritual displays.[3] The celebration of the apprentice-boys' action, and of the battle of the Boyne, called forth great quasi-military marches, for which the Orange Order provided the organizational basis. Periodically, other less spectacular challenges could be issued through the device

---

[1] For interesting approaches to this, F. Wright, 'Protestant ideology and politics in Ulster', *European Journal of Sociology*, xiv (1973); K. Heskin, *Northern Ireland: A Psychological Analysis* (Dublin, 1980), pp. 23–37; also R. P. C. Hanson, 'It *is* a Religious Issue. Some Drastic Proposals for an End to the Miseries of Irish Sectarianism', *Encounter*, lv (Oct. 1980).

[2] *Two Addresses to the Protestants of Ireland*, No. II, DPOA and RS (Dublin, 1843), 60; J. Hill, 'The Protestant response to repeal: the case of the Dublin working class', in Lyons and Hawkins, *Ireland Under the Union*, p. 49.

[3] Heslinga, *Irish Border*, pp. 60–1.

of 'drumming'. All these displays were, on the most charit-
able view, tactless and lacking in political judgement, or in
preparedness to treat politics as having to do with compromise and consensus rather than elemental confrontation.
'Where you could "walk", you were dominant.'[1] In fact,
for ten or fifteen years after the suppression of the Orange
Order, the Protestants were unable to dominate the 'Protestant city'. Catholics were demographically in the ascendant,
growing rapidly to over one-third of the urban population, and also held the political initiative through the Repeal
movement. After 1850, however, a steady Catholic decline
set in. Far from reassuring working-class Protestants, this
seems to have stirred them into reasserting control; whilst
the more sophisticated organizational structure created by
Catholics during the Repeal period increased their power
of resistance. When rioting was renewed in 1852 the intensity
of violence was perceptibly greater than before: firearms
were used for the first time, and the traditionally rural
response of house-burning, hitherto a minor element in
urban riots, became a persistent feature enforcing physical
segregation.[2] The riots of 1864 began in the 'shatter zone'
of Sandy Row, whose atmosphere was conveyed in a telegram sent within a few hours of the initial disturbances.

The town is in a very disturbed state. The mob wrecked the National
school and other houses in Brown St. A large number of navvies are in
town: they came in contact with the Orange party about an hour & ½
ago and had a regular battle, and were with difficulty separated by the
police. Every portion of the disturbed districts is lined by police with
fixed bayonets. The military has been called out and are at present
under the command of Mr Lyons J.P. parading the Orange districts.
Great rioting is expected. The disturbed districts are literally crowded
by men, women, girls & boys all carrying large bludgeons, pitchforks,
hatchets &c.[3]

The level of disorder reached a half-hour mutual fusillade
of musketry, profoundly shocking the English press.[4]
Altogether 316 people were injured in rioting that lasted

[1] Baker, 'Orange and Green', p. 790. Cf. F. Boal, 'Territoriality in Belfast',
in C. Bell and H. Newby (edd.), *The Sociology of Community* (London, 1974).
[2] Ibid. p. 797.
[3] Belfast Police telegram, 8 Aug. 1864 (Larcom MSS 7626).
[4] *The Times, Irish Times*, 22 Aug. 1864.

from 8 to 22 August. Eleven of these were killed.[1] The evidence would suggest that the participants were overwhelmingly working-class: out of 118 casualties whose occupations were listed, only 2 were 'gentlemen' and 3 shopkeepers, as against 36 labourers and 33 mill-workers, mechanics, carpenters, and porters.[2] The trigger for the outburst was agreed by all observers to have been the laying, in Dublin, of the first stone of the O'Connell monument. The Orangemen had responded to this by a demonstration at which O'Connell was burned in effigy. While not as irrational and evanescent as the triggers often discovered by Lefebvre and other observers of crowd behaviour, the disproportion between proximate cause and final effect was a measure of the deep-seated tensions of the north.

By this time the government had retaken special powers to prevent provocative displays. But the new Party Processions Act ran into obstinate resistance, and was weakly enforced. In the aftermath of the 1864 riots, the senior official of the Irish government wrote with apparent unconcern,

the practice in the North has been not to interfere with or prevent the marching and drumming of the Orangemen, but to take down the names of the parties and to summon them afterwards. In truth they were sinking into little more than something between Guy Fawkes and a Carnival.[3]

Although rather optimistic (in 1872, when the Party Processions Act was despairingly repealed, the worst riots since

---

[1] Statistical Report of Injuries Sustained during Riots in Belfast, 1864 (Larcom MSS 7626). Of the 316, 212 received contusions or lacerations; 98 gunshot wounds; 5 stab-wounds. The other injury was diagnosed as 'mania caused by fright'. Cf. Dublin Castle report, PRO HO 45 7649/2.

[2] Statistical Report. The 118 occupations included: 36 labourers, 13 policemen, 11 millworkers, 8 carpenters, 8 mechanics, 6 porters, 3 shopkeepers; 2 gentlemen. Cf. the overwhelming proletarian predominance in breaches of the Party Processions Act (e.g. reports for Co. Antrim, 1869, SPO Unregistered MSS).

[3] Note by Sir T. Larcom, 26 Aug. 1864 (HO 45 7649). Cf. 'Instructions for the Guidance of Magistrates in Suppressing Party Processions, 13 Vict. c. 2', Larcom MSS 7624. The English view was put concisely in Peel to Larcom, 17 Aug.: 'I do not understand why people have not as much a right to burn O'Connell in effigy in one place, as to glorify his memory in another, and it is clear that it is not for O'Connell's sake, for as Ld Palmerston observed to me yesterday, "I should think they have forgotten him long ago", that the subscribers to his ugly statue have revived this stupid agitation which has extended to Belfast' (Larcom MSS 7626).

1864 destroyed over 250 houses and drove out 857 families), this last observation is not without interest.

Collective violence has habitually been looked upon as disorder, both literal and metaphorical: an aberrant social dysfunction or, indeed, disease. Charles Tilly has gone some way towards shifting this perspective by stressing the normality of violence, particularly in pre-modern societies.[1] In a specifically Irish context, it has recently been suggested that 'on an overview of Irish history, it is hardly too much to say that violence, or incipient violence, was the normal condition in which society existed'.[2] The writer of these words tends, like many people, to see violence as negative; he is reluctant to accept the view of a modern Jesuit that men are too squeamish and easily shocked—'they take exception to violence, although violence is one of the ways in which life bursts forth'.[3] Yet it is important to consider whether some forms of violence are 'incurable' because they are not symptoms of social disease, but mechanisms of social adjustment and integration. To some extent a modern society defines itself by the absence of serious combat within its frontiers, or by (following Weber) vesting in the government the monopoly of the legitimate use of violence. Other societies have, however, had more flexible definitions (especially if they were not concerned to analyse themselves *qua* societies). The modern state is intolerant of anarchy, which is more or less its anti-principle, but many human beings appear to like it. Especially if they have not been fully politicized, they prefer the communal, local rather than central, regulation of communal life.

It is hard to look at some of the manifestations of Irish collective violence, especially the clearly structured faction fight and sectarian riot, without seeing in them some element of carnival. Although governments and political modernizers condemned Belfast riots as unacceptable methods of conducting political disputes, Belfast Protestants continued to meet for parades, because these had positive communal

---

[1] e.g. 'Collective violence in European perspective', in H. D. Graham and T. R. Gurr (edd.), *Violence in America* (New York, 1969).

[2] O'Farrell, *England and Ireland*, p. 161.

[3] J. Danielou, *Prayer as a Political Problem* (1967), q. ibid. p. 175.

value. They were first and foremost a celebration and affirmation of Protestant identity; only consequentially were they a challenge to combat with the Catholic community.[1] In a wider sense, for both Protestants and Catholics, 'riots and revivals were the emotional release in an impoverished working-class culture where politics and religion were the only respectable activities'.[2] Even less gaudy and extravagant forms of collective violence may usefully be brought within the framework of functional social controls. English 'rough music' and French *charivaris* alike represented the controlled application of communal pressures, which could in certain circumstances spill over into violence.[3] It may be suggested that the powerful integration of the Irish rural community (remarked, albeit in the framework of rather recent developments, by Arensberg and Kimball as late as the 1930s), coupled with the power of the Catholic church (which underwent a remarkable revival in the nineteenth century), normally rendered internal regulation by such methods unnecessary.[4] Energy—and anger—in defence of communal values were turned overwhelmingly to the land issue. In Belfast, by contrast, whose population suffered all the well-known problems of rapid urbanization and industrialization, fighting may have been one of the few ways in which an originally rural identity could be preserved. The sectarian divide was too functional to be permitted to disappear.

[1] Though the *Saturday Review*, 24 Aug. 1872, held that 'the assertion of the principles in which they suppose themselves to believe is comparatively unattractive unless a profession of faith serves the collateral purpose of an insult and a challenge'.

[2] Baker, 'Orange and Green', p. 806. Stewart, *Narrow Ground*, p. 153, suggests cautiously that 'the Orange summer revels would appear to be the most visible and colourful part of a much more complex, and largely concealed, structure of ritual social behaviour which has not yet been satisfactorily explained'.

[3] E P. Thompson, ' "Rough Music": le Charivari anglais', *Annales: Économies, sociétés, civilisations*, xxvii (1972); N. Z. Davis, 'The reasons of misrule: youth groups and charivaris in sixteenth-century France', *Past and Pres.* 1 (1970).

[4] D. W. Miller, 'Irish Catholicism and the Great Famine', *Journal of Social History* (1975), pp. 81-94.

(v) *Law and the habit of violence*

> What statesman would shape his policy by the wild and passionate aspirations of the very men whom he is striving, by just laws, to educate into a respect for government and property?
>
> G. C. Brodrick[1]

In describing the tough reaction of the Irish authorities to outrage and 'disorder', one of the most lucid of modern Irish historians has suggested that

> It is very doubtful if, once the habit of violence had established itself, a policy of conciliation and concession would have been any more successful; but it was a policy that the landlords never entertained. They met force with force.[2]

The importance of this reaction, and its reciprocal effect on the intensity of violence in Ireland, will be returned to in the following chapters. Here it is worth noticing that such a characterization of the 'habit of violence' is not unusual. Another recent historian has talked of the 'disposition towards violence' fostered by the Oakboy–Steelboy tradition. Yet another holds that 'the normalizing of violence in Ireland was a direct product of the English refusal to attend to Irish grievances unless they were expressed violently'.[3] This is to say too little and too much. It attributes too much political, modern, proactive intent to Irish violence; and it underestimates the level of violence natural in pre-modern societies. The same writer observed in an earlier work that 'a concentration on politics and nationalist agitation neglects a vital fact'—that 'Ireland and the Irish were not politically modern'.[4] This is surely a crucial point. There is nothing abnormal about violence as a means of expressing grievances in pre-political societies. What is abnormal is the use of violence as a means of political communication in a modern society. Much of the Irish violence which disturbed nineteenth-century England was

---

[1] The Hon. George Charles Brodrick, 'The Irish Land Question', *Recess Studies* (1870).

[2] J. C. Beckett, *The Anglo-Irish Tradition* (London, 1976), p. 82.

[3] Gibbon, *Origins of Ulster Unionism*, p. 152; O'Farrell, *England and Ireland*, p. 163.

[4] P. O'Farrell, *Ireland's English Question* (London, 1971), p. 2.

not political in its own terms, but English perceptions were conditioned by the circumstances of a society already substantially modernized.

The tendency to attribute political significance to Irish 'disorder' was closely connected with widespread English assumptions about law and about Irish attitudes to it. A. V. Dicey, in his remorseless exposition of *England's Case Against Home Rule*, accepted that there was 'discord in Ireland between the law of the land and the law of the people', though he maintained that Irish opposition to the law of the land 'never has been general opposition to the law'.[1] He instanced agrarian wars in France and Belgium which had 'no connection whatever with national, or even it would seem with general political feeling', to support this view. With classical contractarian aplomb he was even able to cite the anti-rent war in New York in 1839–46 as evidence of the way in which the law could be hated 'not because it was "foreign", but because it enforced the obligation of an unpopular contract'.[2] If certain English laws offended, they could and should be cast out.

The great jurist was, however, unusual in denying a deeper social significance to the Irish resistance to law. Others were —and some indeed remain—aware of a disturbing Irish tendency to treat the law not as a manifestation of abstract 'justice' but as a manipulable vehicle of group interest. A Whitefoot oath of the 1820s contained the undertaking

I sware I am to Bear My right arm to be Cut of and trow over the left shoulder and nailed to the traples Door of Armagh before I will lay or betray or go into any Court to prosecute a Brother, known him to be such.[3]

Maria Edgeworth distinguished the attitude of 'an Englishman who expects justice' and used the phrase 'I'll have the law of you', from that of 'the Irishman who hopes for partiality', whose threat was 'I'll have you up before his honour'.[4]

---

[1] A. V. Dicey, *England's Case Against Home Rule* (London, 1886), pp. 119, 94–5.

[2] Ibid., 105.

[3] HC Committee of Inquiry, 1832, quoted in Lewis, *Local Disturbances*, p. 136.

[4] C. Maxwell, *Country and Town in Ireland under the Georges* (Dublin, 1949), p. 182.

Less wryly, Henry Inglis recorded the authentic Anglo-Saxon shock after observing the 1834 summer assizes: 'To save a relation from punishment, or to punish anyone who has injured a relation, an Irish peasant will swear to anything.'[1] A more recent study came to the conclusion that 'clan feeling' made the administration of law according to Anglo-Saxon concepts extremely difficult in Ireland.[2]

Some contemporary observers, notably the English press, went further in distinguishing certain peculiarities of the Irish criminal sense. One newspaper in 1860 contrasted the general English hostility to crime, and above all to murder—in which even 'classes hostile to the police' assisted them in their investigations—with Ireland, where '*The* feature of Irish murder is the sympathy of the people for the perpetrator'.[3] Generally, as A. T. Q. Stewart has recorded, outsiders' views of the Irish have noted 'their capacity for very reckless violence, allied to a distorted moral sense which magnifies small sins and yet regards murder as trivial'.[4]

By the 1870s the Irish had created the impression of being 'banded against all order, law and government'.[5] Once again it is worth stressing that it was not so much the level of violence as its perceived anarchic nature which provoked English reactions. Indeed, in 1871 *The Times* admitted that

[1] H. D. Inglis, *A Journey Throughout Ireland in the Spring, Summer, and Autumn of 1834* (London, 1838), i. 162; though he was careful to add, 'although in swearing falsely, the Irish peasant wishes to defeat the ends of justice he does not do so, merely because he hates justice and the law, but because he thinks he is bound to save his relation, or any one of his faction'. Cf. Carleton's ironic 'Essay on Irish Swearing', *Traits and Stories of the Irish Peasantry* (London, 1846), i. 203-19; also M. MacDonagh, *Irish Life and Character* (London, 1899), pp. 141-3.

[2] Brown, 'Nationalism and the Irish peasant', p. 406. On the absence of a Gaelic conception of public loyalty (cf. MacDonagh, loc. cit.), Lord Naas found when he tried to give the newly-'Royal' Irish Constabulary a Gaelic motto meaning 'Honour and Loyalty' that, according to his expert informant, there was no Irish word conveying loyalty to the monarch as embodiment of the state, as distinct from personal fealty: Larcom MSS 7619.

[3] *Weekly Packet*, 30 Oct. 1860 (ibid. 7620).

[4] Stewart, *Narrow Ground*, p. 113.

[5] *Saturday Review*, 26 Mar. 1870. Ten years later Lord Derby cautiously suggested ('I do not wish to lay stress on an argument which may seem invidious') that the 'peculiar misfortune of Ireland—agitation accompanied by violence', was also shown by Irishmen in America where they had no special grievances; and that the 'unfortunate propensity' might be due 'to an inherited custom of regarding and treating Government as an enemy' ('Ireland and the Land Act', *Nineteenth Century*, lvi (Oct. 1881), 486).

Westmeath, the centre of Ribbon activity, was tranquil: 'but what is the nature of that tranquillity?'—it was 'the tranquillity of a society paralysed by terror':

the appearance of order . . . is deceptive. Its real meaning is not that law is supreme, but that law is dethroned. Society is inverted . . . [1]

In the comparatively trouble-free mid 1870s the English press continued to insist that 'the crimes of Ireland are those which constitute not so much a war against morality as against society', and that 'the question between British crime and Irish crime is not one of degree but of kind'.[2] Discussing the latest coercion bill, the *Spectator* held that

It is perfectly true, no doubt . . . that England is a far more dangerous country to live in, so far as regards the violent outbreak of individual selfishness, brutality, and lust, than Ireland. But then no class is put into fear, as a class, by the violence of these outbreaks.[3]

It was thus, as Cornewall Lewis had seen earlier, the public nature of Irish violence which raised it to the political sphere. Whatever its intention, the English government could not fail to see it as a challenge.

[1] *The Times*, 13 May 1871.
[2] *Evening Standard*, 23 Mar. 1875.
[3] *Spectator*, 27 Mar. 1875.

2

Powers That Be

Who would govern Ireland must have much patience.

Sir Thomas Larcom

(i) *Government*

> We the undersigned Magistrates usually attending the Petty
> Sessions of Nenagh, having assembled to consider the recent
> dreadful attempt on the life of Mr. R. Bayley, deemed it
> our duty at this crisis to inform your Excellency that
> to such an extent has the lawless spirit of assassination
> advanced in this District and so completely inadequate are
> the existing powers of the law to check this frightful
> system, that it is wholly out of our power to discharge
> with advantage to the public our very responsible duty
> as Magistrates or as Ex Officio Poor Law Guardians.
>
> Co. Tipperary magistrates, November 1847[1]

The most outstanding quality of the administrative and
judicial infrastructure of nineteenth-century Ireland was
its weakness. Disraeli, in his celebrated 'Pope and potatoes'
speech, put 'the weakest executive in the world' as one of
the four cardinal elements of the Irish problem. A high civil
servant later wrote of Dublin Castle in the 1860s as 'a government *pour rire*'.[2] It is by now almost a truism that the
Union of Britain and Ireland was more substantially breached
by the British government than by Irish nationalists during
its first century. At least, in many important respects, it
remained nominal rather than real. Ireland was a 'special
case'. A sequence of laws (not all repressive) passed by the
imperial parliament with application to Ireland alone bore

---

[1] Co. Tipperary magistrates to Earl of Clarendon, Nov. 1847 (PRO HO 45
1793).
[2] R. Anderson, *Sidelights on the Home Rule Movement*, p. 48. The most
sustained, if partisan, treatment is R. B. O'Brien, *Dublin Castle and the Irish
People* (2nd. edn., London, 1912). See also Ridgeway to Balfour, 28 Mar. 1891,
quoted below, p. 217.

dumb testimony to this.[1] The Irish government was unmistakably different. It had at its head a Lord-Lieutenant with executive powers, who also bore the exotic title of Viceroy. His government, the Irish executive housed in Dublin Castle, was controlled by his Chief Secretary, a minister who became in effect the main link between Britain and Ireland, often (though not invariably) being a member of the Cabinet, and crossing from Dublin to the Irish Office during parliamentary sessions.[2] Under him the Castle administration developed far-reaching controls, and implemented policies markedly more interventionist than were conceivable in Britain. Indeed, some have seen Irish policy at this time as a kind of experimental exercise, in which the government treated the sister island as a 'social laboratory' for testing modern state functions.[3] Certainly the centralization of governmental apparatus, whether approved or disapproved, was obvious to contemporaries: equally obvious, however, was the reason for that centralization. It was not that central government was overweeningly strong, but that the periphery was intolerably weak.

Although it has been suggested that the Anglo-Irish gentry gave a passable imitation of a ruling class, such was not the opinion of the government. Successive ministers would have agreed rather with the improving landlord James Grattan, who condemned even his Wicklow peers as 'ignorant, prejudiced, vulgar and brutal', and blamed the condition of the country in the 1830s on them.

The people in many places are insufficiently civilized, pursued by tithes, habituated to see a great military force and to think that the law depended upon them; for the most part unacquainted with an active magistracy or an efficient police, kind or indulgent landlords, or a respectable clergy.[4]

---

[1] See the interesting analysis by H. Walker, 'The Tendency towards Legislative Disintegration', in J. H. Morgan (ed.), *The New Irish Constitution* (London, 1912), pp. 388-411.

[2] The delicate and shifting relationship between the Chief Secretary and Lord-Lieutenant is charted in R. B. McDowell, *The Irish Administration 1801-1914* (London, 1964).

[3] Especially O. MacDonagh, *Ireland: the Union and Its Aftermath* (London, 1977).

[4] James Grattan's notebooks, NLI MS 5776, quoted in R. F. Foster, 'Parnell and his people: the Ascendancy and Home Rule', unpublished paper, 1980.

A similar denunciation came later from one of the landlords' most literate supporters, Standish O'Grady: 'Christ save us all, you read nothing, know nothing . . . Of you, as a class, as a body of men, I can entertain not the least hope; indeed who can?'[1] It must be admitted that the government in England was not always content with the performance of its own gentry. At the time of the 'Swing' riots, for instance, Lord Melbourne angrily rebuked magistrates who had shown an accommodating attitude towards the rioters.[2] But the situation in Ireland was perceived as far worse. Until stipendiary or resident magistrates were widely employed, incompetence, pusillanimity, and even corruption, were hallmarks of the local administration of justice.[3] The state of affairs in Belfast, where the challenges were most severe, was worst of all. In 1857 the Irish Lord Chancellor found it necessary to warn that no justices of the peace should be members of the Orange Order.[4] More seriously, perhaps, even amongst 'worthy and honourable men' there was weakness of judgement in dealing with mobs. An observer of the 1858 riots, demanding the extension of stipendiary magistrates to Belfast, told the Lord Chancellor:

Last night, I saw the most injudicious display. While in the neighbourhood of my church, there was really no large shew of people— little more than what is always seen on a fine evening when the mills are closed: the bugles were ordered to sound and a company of soldiers were sent running like Zouaves along the entire length of the street!
This is folly indeed. Surely the people will come out universally at the sound of bugles and tramp of armed men and so it was.
I gently remonstrated with poor William Lyons (the only magistrate

---

[1] F. S. L. Lyons, *Culture and Anarchy in Ireland 1890–1939* (Oxford, 1979), p. 34. Cf. the verdict of Under-Secretary Henry Drummond: 'Property has its duties as well as its rights; to the neglect of those duties in times past is mainly to be ascribed that diseased state of society in which such (agrarian) crimes take their rise' (O'Brien, op. cit. p. 49).

[2] E. Hobsbawm and G. Rudé, *Captain Swing*, pp. 219–20.

[3] It was thought, for instance, that local justices turned a blind eye to faction fighting, if the factions supplied labour for their estates: Inglis, *A Journey Throughout Ireland*, p. 162.

[4] Maziere Brady to Lord Londonderry (Lord-Lieutenant of Co. Down), 3 Oct. 1857 (NLI MS 7624). Brady's letter was published in the *Northern Whig* on 8 October, and his implication of Orange involvement in rioting was repudiated by the Grand Lodge of Ireland. I. Budge and C. O'Leary, *Belfast: Approach to Crisis* (London, 1973), p. 93.

present in that locality) and referred to the certain result of such exciting display. He, however, seemed to think it all right.[1]

In 1860 the Chief Secretary, Cardwell, wrote to Sir Thomas Larcom, the first man to occupy the henceforth pivotal post of permanent Under-Secretary at Dublin Castle,

I look upon the conduct of the Magistrates (in Belfast) as meaning that they will neither put the thing down themselves (i.e. the apprehended riot) nor allow of our doing so, if they can avoid it.[2]

Amidst the appalling riots four years later, the succeeding Chief Secretary, the younger Robert Peel, complained that 'the local magistracy have proved themselves miserably inefficient': while a shaken *Times* demanded that 'the strange apathy or timidity of the local authorities should be brought to severe account'.[3] Not insensitively, the newspaper suggested that the magistrates were either partisan 'or afraid to be labelled partisan'. It was a clear case for interference by the central government of Ireland.[4]

The problem was that from another perspective it could be argued that it was precisely the repeated intervention of a government armed with special powers which had weakened the authority of the local magistrates.[5] Even though the magistrates were usually the first to cry out for special legislation, the government's response reinforced their alarmism. The *Spectator* charged in 1875 that 'the habit of claiming almost despotic discretion has demoralized those who execute the ordinary law in Ireland'. It added, using Cavour's phrase, 'Any one can govern with a state of siege'.[6] This charge is worth considering in two main particulars. First, that the special legislation adopted year after year to maintain law and order in Ireland amounted to a 'state of siege' as understood on the Continent. And, secondly, that

---

[1] T. Drew to Lord Chancellor, 1 June 1858 (NLI MS 7624).

[2] E. Cardwell to Sir T. Larcom, 13 Dec. 1860 (T(rinity) C(ollege,) D(ublin) MS 1710/41).

[3] Quoted in *Irish Times*, 22 Aug. 1864.

[4] Ibid.

[5] This point was in fact made by Gladstone when he said that 'repeated innovations' in the law prevented men from 'looking to themselves': House of Commons, 2 Mar. 1871 (HC Deb. cciv, c. 1195).

[6] *Spectator*, 27 Mar. 1875.

the resulting mentality led the authorities to react excessively to any perceived challenge.

(ii) *Coercion*

> That we wish to impress upon Her Majesty's Government the absolute necessity of placing in the hands of the Lord Lieutenant of Ireland such powers as may enable His Excellency to proclaim districts where savage acts are perpetrated, as it is quite manifest that the common law of the land is not sufficiently stringent to subdue the combination that has so long prevailed & which so constantly prevents the possibility of detecting & convicting the base miscreants who are guilty of crimes more atrocious than are to be heard of in the most uncivilised parts of the world.[1]
>
> Roscommon magistrates, November 1847[1]

There is no doubt that the state of Ireland provoked a great deal of special legislation. During the first half-century of the Union, as J. L. Hammond pointed out, Ireland was governed under 'ordinary' English law for only five years.[2] Indeed the nineteenth century opened with Ireland under martial law imposed by statute, a state of affairs unique in British history.[3] The extraordinariness of the situation should not, however, be exaggerated. Until the 1820s there was no marked difference, in nature or frequency, between emergency legislation in Ireland and in Britain.[4] Powers taken by special legislation included restrictions on movement and on possession of arms (which were always more loosely controlled in Ireland than in England), suppression of organizations, meetings, and publications; the facilitating

[1] Resolution of meeting of Roscommon magistrates, 9 Nov. 1847 (PRO HO 45 1793).

[2] Hammond, *Gladstone and the Irish Nation*, p. 16.

[3] Martial law was declared by the Viceroy and confirmed by statute (39 Geo. III, c. 11 (I); 40 Geo. III, c. 2 (I); 41 Geo. III, cc. 14, 61; 43 Geo. III, c. 117). Such statutory imposition was unusual and was not to be repeated when martial law was declared in Ireland in 1916 and 1920: C. Townshend, 'Martial law: legal and administrative problems of civil emergency in Britain and the Empire, 1800-1940', *Historical Journal*, xxv. i (1982), 167-8.

[4] Richard Hawkins has outlined a fruitful conception of 'dynasties' of coercion laws, of which the first, from 1763-87, consisted of acts with strong likeness in purpose and form to the English Riot Act, the Waltham Black Act, and others. The next major dynasty sprang from the Insurrection Act of 1796 (36 Geo. III, c. 20 (I)), which shaped coercive measures for the next forty years.

of police searches; levying of compensation from localities; change in trial procedures; and, occasionally, suspension of Habeas Corpus. Each of these powers was temporary, as English standards required. This had several results. Psychologically, it assisted in the creation of a near-permanent atmosphere of crisis. Yet, at the same time, it did not help, and may even have hindered, the formulation of a concept of 'state of emergency' or 'state of siege'.[1] Certainly nothing so systematic as Cavour's term existed in Ireland.

Still, a pattern of divergence became unmistakable after the 1820s. The 'Swing' disturbances in southern England were dealt with under the ordinary criminal law, as consolidated and 'Benthamized' by Peel.[2] The Irish Tithe War, by contrast, called forth the drastic Suppression of Disturbances Act of 1833. This might be attributed in part to the undeniable fact that the Irish disturbance was more violent than 'Swing'. The infrequency of personal violence (as distinct from damage to property) in the latter, as also in the 'Rebecca' riots, is striking alongside even a single Irish incident—for instance, the affray at an auction of cattle seized for tithe at Newtonbarry, Co. Wexford, on 18 June 1831, where at least twelve or thirteen people were killed or severely wounded.[3] It would be difficult to argue in Ireland, as a commentator has argued of popular disturbances in Britain, that a great part of the violence in political life emanated from the authorities, whose action frequently turned peaceful protest into something much more alarming.[4] None the less, the response of the Irish authorities was scarcely moderate. The view of the Lord Lieutenant of King's County in 1834 was conveyed to the government in the following terms:

[1] Townshend, 'Martial Law', loc. cit.
[2] R. Hawkins's review of *Captain Swing, Historical Journal*, xii (1960), 716; Hobsbawm and Rudé, *Captain Swing* (2nd edn), p. xiv.
[3] G. H. Townsend, *Manual of Dates* (3rd edn., London, 1870), 705.
[4] M. I. Thomis, 'Aims and Ideology of Violent Protest in Great Britain, 1800–1848', paper delivered to conference on 'Social Protest, Violence and Terror', Bad Homburg 15–17 Nov. 1979. W. J. Mommsen (ed.) German Historical Institute *Bulletin*, iii (1980).

Lord Oxmantown truly observes that the combination established surpasses the law in vigour, promptitude, and efficacy, and that it is more safe to violate the law than to obey it.[1]

It was this sort of perception of fundamental challenge which put pressure on a reluctant Whig administration to sanction extreme countermeasures.[2] The Suppression of Local Disturbances Act, also called an Insurrection Act, and probably the first to be colloquially labelled the 'coercion Act', reinforced the powers of curfew and suppression of meetings contained in former Insurrection Acts with the power to try offences by courts martial established under military procedures. The object of this was to provide courts which would be proof against intimidation, and herein lay its proximity to outright martial law.[3] It was an admission that the normal legal process has broken down, or perhaps one should rather say had become paralysed. (The Newtonbarry incident just referred to was typical in that the coroner's jury was discharged without reaching a verdict.) This was a situation that was to be repeated at fairly frequent intervals, and while special tribunals were not to be resorted to until the 1880s, the development of the resident magistrate system gradually built such extraordinary courts into the ordinary judicial machinery. The RMs were a standing demonstration of the fragility of the law in Ireland: combining executive and judicial functions, they reminded foreign observers of French rather than British local authority.[4]

An interesting aspect of governmental response can be found in attitudes to 'political crime' and the treatment

[1] Lord Wellesley to Melbourne, 15 Apr. 1834 (PP, 7 July 1834, quoted in Lewis, *Local Disturbances*, p. 81.

[2] Lord Anglesey declared 'Ireland wants a Bonaparte' (as later officials were to wonder whether 'a Prussian' might be needed): A. D. Kriegel, 'The Irish policy of Lord Grey's government', *EHR* (1971), pp. 40–1; 'Tithe Agitation (Ireland) 1822–32', Cabinet memo., Nov. 1880 (Bodleian, Harcourt MSS 106).

[3] I. S. Leadam, *Coercive Measures in Ireland, 1830–1880* (London, 1881), provided the first and still most comprehensive review of the rationale and working of this and later repressive legislation. In fact the court-martial provisions were not used. Lord Spencer was later told that the Act—whose powers were in his opinion 'awful'—had never been put in force; its 'very severity' had had the effect of curbing disorder: Spencer to Gladstone, 28 Dec. 1869 (BL Add. MS 44306).

[4] RMs were first commissioned after the 1814 Act (54 Geo. III, c. 131) which

of political criminals. It was to become something of an English orthodoxy that there were none such on Albion's shore, and that special status for political prisoners likewise did not exist. They came close to existence in Ireland, however, at least until Balfour's time. Gladstone drew in general terms a distinction, which he felt was 'perfectly well understood', between 'ordinary' crime—'crime against individuals' —and 'offences against the state'.[1] He himself was concerned to prevent agrarian crime from being pushed into the latter category, but he made it clear that the weight of opinion went the other way. Of the status of the Fenian prisoners there was less doubt. The Lord Chancellor of Ireland, for instance, urged on the Lord-Lieutenant in 1869 that

> it might be considered whether with reference to those who might be retained in custody it may not be possible to mitigate the severity of their punishments, and treat them as political prisoners . . . Certainly the usages of former times and continental nations at present would seem to make the propriety of such an arrangement not wholly unworthy of attention.[2]

Earl Spencer, the weightiest of all Viceroys, gave this 'serious consideration', and pressed the policy on Gladstone. In October 1869 he argued that

> the treatment of the prisoners much affects the mind of the people. If as in France Prussia & Italy political prisoners (apart from those guilty of violence) could be held differently to ordinary criminals, the feeling here would be much softened.[3]

The major difficulty, as he acknowledged, was 'to define the men who would be so treated'. For this amongst other

---

gave the Lord-Lieutenant power to appoint magistrates to reside in such districts as he thought fit. The title was officially employed after the Act of 1853. By 1860 there were 72 RMs, on a stipend of £700 p.a.: McDowell, *Irish Administration*, pp. 114–5; W. H. Hurlbert, *Ireland Under Coercion. The Diary of an American* (Edinburgh, 1888), i. 25.

[1] House of Commons, 2 Mar. 1871 (HC Deb. 3s, cciv, c. 1186). Comerford, *Kickham*, pp. 79–99, gives an account of political imprisonment and suggests that a customary distinction was in practice drawn. But the experience of Davitt was rather different: see Moody, *Davitt*, pp. 154–6.

[2] O'Hagan to Spencer, 9 Jan 1869 (P(ublic) R(ecord) O(ffice of) N(orthern) I(reland), O'Hagan MSS D. 2777/8, f. 6).

[3] Spencer to Gladstone, 12 Oct. 1869 (BL Add. MS 44306, f. 161).

reasons, Gladstone never liked the idea. The Cabinet turned it down, but Spencer continued to maintain that special treatment would reduce public hostility. To him it was 'mere prudery to say that we cannot admit of the distinction between Political and ordinary crime'.[1]

Certainly Gladstone admitted it implicitly by his pressing concern for the release of the Fenian prisoners. Spencer saw this as political weakness, and continually resisted, maintaining that released Fenians would simply throw themselves back into mischief. Some 'selected' prisoners were released early in 1869, but the leaders were retained for political reasons. Their release would be 'dangerous in its bearings upon the public security', and would, in Spencer's view, 'make it very difficult to deal with any future sedition or conspiracy' because loyal men would have lost faith in the government's firmness and determination.[2] To the Irish Lord Chancellor, Spencer remarked that 'if much agrarian outrage took place immediately after release, the Govt. would be very seriously shaken' (although he maintained 'stoutly' to Gladstone that agrarian outrages had 'nothing to do with Fenianism').[3] On the other hand, political pressure was in any case being exerted by the widely based Amnesty Movement, which included the Catholic clergy, and it was this which impelled Gladstone towards release. Spencer reacted the opposite way, bristling at the 'improper tone' of public petitions like the Address of the Cork City Corporation, and seeing Amnesty meetings as 'Fenian demonstrations'.[4] Neither man's attitude to the release of prisoners was based on the seriousness of their crimes; politics dominated their response.

Spencer doubtless feared that if Fenian leaders were once released they would be beyond the reach of the law. The root

---

[1] Spencer to Gladstone, 25 Nov. 1870 (ibid., f. 333).

[2] Spencer to Gladstone, 22, 23 Sept., 12 Oct.; Gladstone to Spencer, 8 Oct. 1869 (ibid., ff. 139, 150, 154, 158). Morley, *Gladstone*, i, 931, notes Gladstone's keenness on release but does not indicate the issues involved.

[3] Spencer to Gladstone, 30 Mar. 1869 (BL Add. MS 44306, f. 99); Spencer to O'Hagan, 23 Sept. 1870 (O'Hagan MSS D.2777/8, f. 125).

[4] Gladstone to Spencer, 8 Oct. 1869, spoke of the need for 'sound arguments against release' in face of 'so considerable a movement'. See also Spencer to Gladstone, 22 Sept., appending Cork address (BL Add. MS 44306, ff. 154, 139).

of the problem was the undermining of English legal practice through the intimidation of witnesses and juries, and during his first Viceroyalty Spencer made efforts to tackle this root. At the height of the Ribbon crisis of 1871 he confronted the subject of jury-packing by Crown law officers.

> I for a long time believed that these accusations were the work of the enemy and that no ground whatever existed for an imputation which if extensively credited in the country must greatly damage the strength of the Law, and encourage that dislike of legal remedies which is so prevalent in the country.
>
> Now I understand that in Political and important trials the Sheriff takes care to secure the most loyal and trustworthy persons on the jury: he in fact selects the panel, and it happened that the same people repeatedly served on the Dublin juries when the political prisoners were tried.[1]

He believed that 'proof cannot be given to the idea (frequently I admit expressed) that Ireland is not fit for juries'. Yet despite this optimism, he was forced to admit two years later that the experience of his new Juries Act had been 'certainly rather unfortunate'.[2] He pointed, none the less, to the good results of juries in Dublin, holding to the progressive idea that 'as education, civilization, and love of law spreads' good juries would be produced, 'but it is obvious that the Act went before the Age'.[3] Such optimistic liberalism could be sustained during the 1870s as disorder gradually subsided. In the 1880s, unfortunately, jury trial was to prove as inadequate as ever before.

Spencer's attitudes display with pellucid clarity the Liberal capacity to combine faith in the essential good in the Irish people with determination to punish crime and vindicate the rule of law with an iron hand.[4] The Liberal coercive response is more interesting than that of the Tories because it was more agonized; yet Liberal governments more often than Tories found themselves abrogating the 'constitution' in its

[1] Spencer to O'Hagan, 23 Mar. 1871 (O'Hagan MSS D.2777/8, f. 152). On jury-packing, cf. O'Brien, *Dublin Castle*, pp. 129-34.

[2] Spencer to O'Hagan, 10 Mar. 1873 (PRONI D.2777/8, f. 222): 'change will be essential but I hope that it may be made in a way not to damage the principle of legal selection, instead of arbitrary selection by the sub-sheriff.'

[3] Spencer to O'Hagan, 24 Mar. 1873 (ibid., f. 223).

[4] See below, p. 103.

fundamental guarantee of individual liberty, Habeas Corpus. Although it was Lord Derby's government which had to deal with the Fenian outbreak in 1867, it did so under legislation already passed by the Liberals in 1866. It simply maintained the suspension of Habeas Corpus initiated by the Act of February 1866, an Act intended to last only six months, but later renewed.[1] (The effect of the arrests under this Act, totalling 756 by July 1866 when Lord Naas took over as Chief Secretary, was described by one official as 'magical'.[2]) The Ribbon crisis of 1870-1 posed particularly difficult problems, because it was so limited in area and so concealed in character. At the end of 1869 Gladstone tried to elicit from Spencer what he called 'characteristic' crime figures—

as showing the minimum of Irish crime and its attendant circumstances which may have been thought to justify exceptional restraints, or the maximum of these which may have been allowed to subsist without them.[3]

This remarkable move towards a definition of what might be called a coercion 'threshold', or an 'acceptable level' of violent crime, was stillborn. Spencer quietly missed the point, and levered the government into a strong Peace Preservation Act in 1870 containing his sovereign remedy, the power of magistrates to compel witnesses to testify during the investigation of a crime, before a case came to trial.[4] In addition various

---

[1] For the government's arguments in favour of suspension see Sir G. Grey's speech, 17 Feb. 1866 (HC Deb. 3s, clxxxi, cc. 667-81). Gladstone rejected Disraeli's contention that the government would have had sufficient powers had it not repealed the Act of 50 Geo. III (ibid., c. 717).

[2] Anderson, *Sidelights*, p. 59 n. According to a return drawn up by Anderson for Naas, the number in custody had dropped to 320 by August (when the Act was renewed) and to 73 by November. Naas, using these figures in the Commons on 2 Aug., held that 'a better effect even than that caused by the consignment of these persons to prison was produced immediately after the passing of that measure: for a number of persons who were known to be engaged in treasonable practices instantly left Ireland from the fear of coming under its operation' (Leadam, op. cit. 24).

[3] Gladstone to Spencer, 28 Dec. 1869 (BL Add. MS 44306, f. 206). Chichester Fortescue, introducing the Peace Preservation Bill on 17 Mar. 1870, said 'our standard has risen since 1847 and we are not prepared to endure a state of crime . . . which was considered inevitable in 1847'. But he did not specify the point to which it had risen.

[4] Spencer always maintained that the basic problem in law enforcement came before the intimidation of juries and witnesses, and lay in the impossibility of obtaining evidence on which prosecutions could be brought against

arrangements, such as the provision of military patrols and the establishment of a new detective training branch of the police were made. Spencer, however, was not sanguine about their effect.[1] Agrarian crime continued to be 'committed with almost entire impunity', and by early 1871 he was approaching despair.

> The necessity for fresh action is shown by the utter collapse of the law in the Westmeath district . . . The terrorism extends through all ranks of society and arrests ordinary transactions of business . . . This appears to me to be a great scandal, and to reflect most gravely upon Government.[2]

At last the government publicly confessed itself baffled by the challenge, provoking Conservative charges that they were trying to 'shirk the responsibility which attaches to them'. According to the Opposition, Westmeath represented 'a fortress of Ribandism, which sets the government at defiance, and (whose) garrison carries murder and rapine uncontrolled through a whole district'.[3] Gladstone, in reply, vehemently denounced this extravagance of language, pointing out that the disorder amounted to four murders and four attempted murders. The real problem was 'an extensive system of terrorism supported, in case of need, by personal violence'.

> It is easy, comparatively, to do what we did in 1866. In that year numbers of foreigners came into the country; large seizures of arms were made; multitudes of facts of a positive character that could be stated, in a clear and distinct form, were at our command . . . But that is not the character of the present situation.[4]

Gladstone warned that deep investigation must take place before the suspension of Habeas Corpus could be considered. His contemporaries, in his view, had lost 'that firm

---

agrarian criminals: Memo. on need for special legislation, 9 Mar. 1870 (BL Add. MS. 44306, f. 233).

[1] He had little faith in a 'detective system in agrarian cases': as for military assistance, he did not 'place much reliance on the success of these measures', but thought it 'right to try them' (ibid.). The inception of the celebrated 'crime special' branch was of recent date: MacGiollaChoille, 'Fenian documents', p. 278.

[2] Spencer to Gladstone, 6 Feb. 1871 (BL Add. MS 44307).

[3] Speech of Col. Wilson-Patten, 2 Mar. 1871 (HC Deb. 3s, cciv, cc. 1173, 1176).

[4] Ibid., cc. 1187, 1194.

intellectual grasp of the first principles of political liberty which was so great a characteristic of our forefathers'. The remedy must lie not in coercion but in restoring the healthy life of society:

Why is government easy in this country? Not, God knows, from want of criminal elements amongst the population, but from the vigorous and healthy tone of social life, which makes men of whatever class an ally of the law.[1]

This desirable state was to be achieved through the redress of real grievances; and Gladstone's government had to its credit at this point two major reforms, the disestablishment of the Church of Ireland and the first Land Act. Would these steps be reversed by a resort to coercion? Spencer, arguing for drastic repression in Westmeath to 'stop a scandal', believed not: the 'healing process which has had its good influences in other parts of Ireland' would continue.[2]

Spencer's conviction overcame Gladstone's scruples, and in June 1871 the Protection of Life and Property (Ireland) Act, known as the 'Westmeath Act', emerged. Its object was succinctly described by its full title: 'to empower the Lord Lieutenant or other Chief Governor or Governors of Ireland to apprehend and detain for a limited time persons suspected of being members of the Ribbon Society in the County of Westmeath, or in certain adjoining portions of the County of Meath and the King's County.[3] Here was the principle of internment; arrest on 'reasonable suspicion' and detention without trial. 'No writ of Habeas Corpus shall issue to bring up the body of any person so arrested or committed or detained.'[4] The reasoning behind the measure was that if a society was being terrorized, this was due to the activity of terrorists; if this small group could be removed, normality would reassert itself. This way of looking at the problem established an important pattern, which has been well characterized by Patrick O'Farrell as the English habit of 'setting up a sharp division between the men of peace

---

[1] Ibid.

[2] Spencer to O'Hagan, 16 Feb. 1871 (O'Hagan MSS d.2777/8, f. 146).

[3] 34 Vict. c. 25. The Act also continued the Peace Preservation (Ireland) Act, 1870.

[4] Ibid., s. 8.

and the men of violence': it had the effect of 'isolating, in English minds, the men of violence from the real, majority Ireland, and of elevating violence and those who used it into the entirety of the Irish problem'.[1] Perhaps few responsible English minds simplified the problem quite so drastically. The illusion, if so it was, derived in great part from liberal principles which found resonant expression in the words of Joseph Chamberlain.

When it is said that it is contrary to Liberal principles to suspend the safeguards of liberty, I say that liberty is a mere phantom unless every man is free to pursue his inclinations, to consult his interest within and under the protection of the law.[2]

At first, moreover, Spencer's belief in the efficacy of a suspension of Habeas Corpus appeared to be vindicated by the result—a dramatic decline in the level of agrarian crime.[3] There does indeed seem to be little doubt that the 1871 Act struck terror into the secret societies, and a few exemplary arrests discouraged active participation for the time being.

Was this response excessive? Although some radical observers saw even the 1870 Act as putting parts of Ireland under 'state of siege', it is hard to accuse Gladstone and Spencer of alarmism.[4] The intense legalism of the Irish government served as a brake on the application of unnecessary force.[5] It is

---

[1] O'Farrell, *England and Ireland*, p. 157. *The Times* drifted in this direction in 1867 when it held that 'We are confronted by a gang of reckless criminals, who respect no laws, human or divine . . . We must crush them at any cost': N. McCord, 'The Fenians and public opinion in Great Britain', *University Review* (1967), 234.

[2] Liverpool speech, 25 Oct. 1881 (Hammond, *Gladstone*, p. 251).

[3] See graph, p. xiv. But, as Isaac Leadam pointed out in his careful analysis, the number of variables involved in measurement, and the contradictory nature of some shifts in crime levels, make it questionable in this as in other cases 'whether any positive conclusion can be arrived at' (*Coercive Measures*, pp. 5, 27, 29).

[4] Cf. Louis Blanc, quoted in the *Spectator*, 19 Mar. 1870. The *Freeman's Journal* protested that 'short of a complete abrogation of all personal liberty in Ireland no Bill could go further than does the present one, and indeed we would be inclined to view a total suspension of the Habeas Corpus Act with less repugnance'.

[5] W. H. Hurlbert professed surprise that, unlike the USA, Britain seemed unprepared to take truly drastic action to save the state. 'To await the results of slow judicial prosecution is to allow crime to be consummated', as a member of Lincoln's Cabinet had said (*Ireland Under Coercion*, p. 8). It is certainly remarkable to find Cardwell asking Larcom whether the imposition of arms controls might not be charged against the government as 'excess of use of power' (11 Aug. 1860; TCD MS 1710/41).

possible to understand the view of an English newspaper that 'the plain reason why we are compelled to use exceptional legislation in Ireland is that in Ireland the crimes are exceptional'.[1] Englishmen believed that if the same crimes were committed in Yorkshire they would be met by the same sort of legislation. Yet the English perception of 'exceptional' crime was clearly conditioned by England's own political culture. The relative novelty, and perhaps fragility, of the culture of 'equipoise' (to use W. L. Burn's celebrated label) kept alive middle-class fears of regression, leaving a predisposition to sense betrayal or rejection of civilized values. An emotional expression of this was the outcry of the Liberal *Newcastle Daily Chronicle* after the Clerkenwell explosion:

English liberalism . . . cannot grasp a hand which smells rank with the blood of her children, slaughtered in the mere wantonness of fanaticism. Quite as little can it have fellowship with those who smile approval on a spirit so sanguinary.[2]

Adherence to 'civilized' English values made it difficult to accept Irish protests on their own terms. Even after the publication of Mill's *England and Ireland*, few could fully accept the implications of Arthur Young's old question, 'Where *manners* are in conspiracy against *law*, to whom are the oppressed people to have recourse?'[3] Dicey, contemptuously dismissing the 'folly of popular declamation' against coercion, confidently asserted that English law was founded on universal morality. The law condemning a sinner, 'though it may excite temporary outcry, can rely on the ultimate sanction of the popular conscience'.[4]

Unlike some commentators, however, Dicey fully realized the nature of the circumstances which caused the law to be denounced as 'coercion'. Their moral peculiarity was that those condemned as criminals saw themselves as being in the right (as even habitual criminals in England did not), and

---

[1] *Standard*, 23 Mar. 1875.

[2] 16 Dec. 1867 (McCord, 'Fenians and public opinion', p. 235).

[3] A. Young, *A Tour in Ireland . . . made in the years 1776, 1777 and 1778* (Dublin, 1780); quoted in Lewis, *Local Disturbances*, p. 42.

[4] A. V. Dicey, *England's Case Against Home Rule* (London, 1886), pp. 115-6.

others agreed with them.[1] These circumstances would have to be altered by reform, but reform must be coupled with strong government—not necessarily the same thing as coercion. Dicey believed that if the powers erratically and transiently granted by special legislation were built into the criminal law of both Ireland and England on a permanent basis, they would become much less contentious. His wish was to be only partly fulfilled in the 1887 Crimes Act, and perhaps for that reason his prognostication was not to be entirely borne out.

English perceptions of reasonable or necessary action could not rely in Ireland on the fundamental acceptance which would make such action effective. Even minimal coercion was consistently provocative, and the administration was generally perceived as a resolute opponent of the rural population's primary requirement, the secure holding—not necessarily ownership—of land. One of the most succinct statements of the case against coercion, not simply as a series of special laws, but as a permanently entrenched structure, was delivered in the House of Lords by Lord Wodehouse in 1864.

The landed proprietors are supported by the force of the United Kingdom in a position which, I am convinced, if Ireland stood alone, they could not possibly maintain, and this country is strictly responsible for seeing that its military force is not applied in perpetuity to save the landlords from measures which they have neglected to provide and which otherwise might be forced upon them.[2]

The duty of maintaining the law of the land fell to the armed forces of the Crown; and pre-eminently the Irish Constabulary, which effectively presented the public face of government in Ireland. The efficiency of this body determined the administration's ability not only to implement such rarefied measures of repression as the Westmeath Act, or to crush such overt manifestations of disaffection as the Fenian rising, but also to guarantee, day by day, the service of writs and the functioning of the civil law.

---

[1] Dicey, *England's Case Against Home Rule* p. 112. Cf. Anderson's discussion of 'ordinary law' and 'coercion' (*Sidelights*, pp. 174–7).

[2] Quoted in Pomfret, *Struggle for the Land*, p. 69.

(iii) *Police*

Who governs Ireland? Larcom and the Police.

(popular witticism of around 1860)[1]

Surveying the government's failure to eradicate the local disturbances which had culminated in the 1830s, Cornewall Lewis charged that

The statute-book has been loaded with the severest laws; the country has been covered with military and police; capital punishment has been unsparingly inflicted; Australia has been crowded with transported convicts; and all to no purpose.[2]

The publication of this indictment coincided with the establishment in its final form, by Drummond's Act of 1836, of the Irish Constabulary.[3] It was something of an exaggeration to say that before this the country had been 'covered with police'. The development of police forces in Ireland was sporadic and unsatisfactory. The deepest problem was one to which a sympathetic and expert commentator drew attention in the late nineteenth century, that whereas the English parish constable 'represents the principle of minute local government carried down from days long anterior to the Norman conquest', the police system in Ireland 'has not so grown with the growth of the people'. The Irish police were at root a foreign importation, introduced at first for the benefit of English settlers within the Pale.[4] To this weak foundation was added administrative incoherence. The baronial police established in localities (baronies) in the eighteenth century, and known to the people as 'Barneys', were unsystematically organized and recruited only from Protestants.

Attempts to create a uniform structure were defeated by the Irish parliament, which held to English ideas of

---

[1] Anderson, *Sidelights*, p. 49.

[2] Lewis, *Local Disturbances*, p. ix.

[3] J. A. Gaughan (ed.), *The Memoirs of Constable Jeremiah Mee, RIC* (Dublin, 1975), pp. 232-4.

[4] H. A. Blake, 'The Irish Police', *The Nineteenth Century* (Feb. 1881), pp. 386-7.

resistance to despotic, French-style police forces.[1] Even Peel's 'Peace Preservation Force', which bequeathed the deathless sobriquet 'Peelers' to all subsequent Irish police, was of limited efficiency because of its lack of cohesion. In effect it was a set of forces in 'proclaimed' districts, each operating in its own way, but resembling militia troops rather than civil bodies. One such force was described by a witness (in Maryborough) as follows:

[The commander of the Leinster peace preservation force, Major Nicholson] wore a dark blue jacket, closely braided in front with round black silk cord, and small buttons; red cuffs and collar, red and gold lace girdle, and tall beaver cap and feathers, with crescent Turkish-shaped scimitar. Of the men, ten wore scarlet cloaks over their uniform, reaching down over their horses' tails, brass helmets and plumes, 'Waterloo' on the helmets; ten were in hussar uniforms . . . Ten were in a uniform which I cannot now describe, but sitting behind them on pads were voltigeurs with short rifles resting on the thigh. These voltigeurs were made to dismount and remount occasionally by their eccentric commander.[2]

Indeed, regular troops and militia furnished the main forces of order until the 1830s. Only gradually did a constabulary emerge. Inspector-Generals were appointed in each of the four provinces in 1822, and the police were increasingly employed in attempts to control faction fighting. Inevitably the relationship between police and community was based at first on pure force; and violent affrays such as those at Castlepollard and Carrickshock, Co. Meath, in 1831 set a pattern that would be hard to break. When the Irish Constabulary took definitive shape in 1836 there was no question of its being an unarmed civil police.

In fact the constabulary became one of the most dramatic administrative innovations in Irish government. Its difference from the English county constabularies, which were also gradually taking shape, was remarked from the start. It resolved the long argument between local and centralized forces in favour of the latter—the continental model of

[1] S. H. Palmer, 'The Irish police experiment: the beginnings of modern police in the British Isles, 1785–1795', *Social Science Quarterly*, lvi. 3 (1975), 410–24.
[2] q. Blake, 'Irish police', p. 387.

'gendarmerie'.[1] This was a state police, commanded from Dublin (though the capital itself remained outside its control, with a separate unarmed police force) by a single Inspector-General. At local level its novelty was apparent in the creation of new police districts to replace the old baronies. The outward signs of this new structure were the 1,400 police posts, always known as 'barracks', which were placed at the centre of the new sub-districts. They were sited if possible in existing towns or villages (in which case ordinary houses were rented, and were distinguished from other habitations by a fourteen-inch long black iron sign with the word 'Constabulary' and a crown and shamrock picked out in white).[2] The exigencies of rational geography, however, often led to their appearance as lone buildings at remote crossroads.

The size of the force, and its structure of command, became fixed in the decade after 1836. Its strength rose from around 7,500 in 1838 to 8,500 in 1840, and reached 12,358 in 1850 before settling down around 10,000.[3] This represented a rough doubling of police density in the countryside—though the force was distributed on a rather odd system which allocated a mere 176 police to the large county of Donegal and 224 to the small county of Louth. Appropriately, however, the largest allocation was to Tipperary (1,030) and the second largest to Galway (704).[4] The appointment of constables, which had previously rested with local magistrates, was transferred to the central command; and in order to neutralize intimidation of their families, it became fixed practice that constables were never stationed in their county of origin. What remained of local involvement—though this was due to Treasury parsimony—was the requirement that counties should pay half the cost of these forces.

Two major reforms, in 1839 and 1845, led to the creation

---

[1] T. Bowden, *Beyond the Limits of the Law* (Harmondsworth, 1978), p. 168; MacDonagh, *Ireland*, p. 35.

[2] Any embryonic artistic licence in this matter was quashed by an order of 1 Nov. 1844 (PRO HO 184 111).

[3] R. Curtis, *The History of the Royal Irish Constabulary* (Dublin, 1869), *passim*.

[4] Table of forces, ibid. pp. 88-9.

of a reserve of 200 constabulary in Dublin (housed in some elegance in Phoenix Park, where their parade-ground evolutions drew crowds of sightseers) under the command of a Deputy Inspector-General,[1] and to the acceptance by the government of full financial responsibility for the constables on permanent station. The cost of this 'fixed quota', over £1m. per year, was thenceforth borne by the Consolidated Fund, with the exception of the reserve if and when it went on active duty. If 'extra force' was sent to a disturbed county, half the cost of this was charged to the locality.[2] Alongside these major changes, the command hierarchy was modified in detail, largely by way of reducing the number of Deputy Inspector-Generals and Provincial Inspectors. The eventual effect was to tighten centralization, leaving no intermediate authority between the Inspector-General and the thirty-five County Inspectors (Cork, Galway, and Tipperary had two each).

The duties of the force expanded in parallel with the expanding activity of the state, at its most rapid in mid-century. As early as 1838 constables were used to make inquiries ('privately and discreetly, so as to avoid creating an erroneous impression as to the object for which they are made') into the size of the potato crop relative to previous years.[3] In the 1840s a Registry of Householders was compiled.[4] By the 1860s the Constabulary's ordinary duties included the collection of comprehensive agricultural statistics, census work, the serving and collection of poor-law election notices, collection of an ever-widening range of 'returns', the escorting of prisoners (previously done by the army), customs duty, weights and measures inspection, factory inspection, and the enforcement of extensive new laws governing fishery and liquor control.[5] In 1865 a register of prostitutes was commenced.[6]

---

[1] Later as Assistant Inspector-General, when the two Deputies were pared down to one.

[2] 2 & 3 Vict., c. 75; 9 & 10 Vict., c. 97.

[3] IC Circular order, 17 Dec. 1838 (HO 184 111).

[4] Circular, 11 Sept. 1844 (ibid.).

[5] H. J. Brownrigg (Inspector-General, Irish Constabulary), *Examination of some Recent Allegations concerning the Constabulary Force of Ireland, in a Report to His Excellency the Lord Lieutenant* (Dublin, 9 Apr. 1864), 73–4.

[6] Circular, 8 Mar. 1865 (HO 184 113).

The modern state's obsessive attitude to the collation of statistics was made manifest through the Irish Constabulary from its inception. As the 'red tape', for which the force became a byword, mounted up, an impossible burden of work was placed on the Inspector-General, and perhaps still more upon the County Inspectors. The latter were almost literally 'inspectors' rather than commanders. In the view of a magistrate in the early 1880s, these senior officers were reduced by the sheer volume of reports required from them to the level of transmitting-clerks.[1] In many cases, by the time an officer reached the rank of County Inspector he was 'past his work' and most of his individuality had been knocked out of him.

Every possibility of an officer acting upon his own responsibility seemed to have been carefully guarded against . . . It was a system centralized to the last degree.[2]

The same tightness of regulation applied to the lower ranks also. Every aspect of life, from marriage to the cut of pockets, was controlled with a parsimonious fussiness bordering on the absurd.[3] This was frequently to produce grumbling, and occasionally open discontent.

Centralization did have its defenders. When Henry Blake observed that

the sub-constable in the wilds of Donegal will answer the same questions in the constables' daily examination as to his knowledge of police duties, get up at the same hour, parade at the same time, and fold his barrack-bedding in exactly the same pattern as his brother stationed in the quiet glens of Wicklow or the troubled city of Cork,[4]

he argued that this uniformity, together with the constabulary's meticulous system of reporting, made it possible to transfer men from one trouble-spot to another without dislocation. However, it is easy enough to see why

---

[1] Blake, 'Irish police', p. 396; C. D. C. Lloyd, *Ireland under the Land League: a Narrative of Personal Experiences* (London, 1892), p. 36.

[2] Ibid. pp. 56-7.

[3] Consider, e.g., the instructions on modification of sheet-iron bedsteads (to be carried out 'without expense to the public'), on the use of 'Marder's jet' for blacking, and on the sewing-up of side pockets: Circulars, 17 Aug. 1839, 5 Dec. 1860, 4 Oct. 1861 (HO 184 111-13).

[4] Blake, 'Irish police', p. 393.

many contemporaries, not all of them hostile nationalists, thought the force 'too military' (the complaint repeated with increasing frequency after the middle of the century). Robert Curtis in his *History of the Royal Irish Constabulary*— itself full of military dry humour—felt that these complaints became noticeably stronger after the force was rearmed with the long Enfield rifle and sword-bayonet. ' "Look at that fellow swaggering up the street," people would remark, "with his long sword almost tripping him up at every step. I should like to see him in pursuit of an active chap who had committed a murder." '[1] But it was probably true also that, as Curtis added, 'the "military appearance" of the constabulary was "the head and front of their offending" '.[2] Even so there were those who did not disavow the constabulary's military nature. Clifford Lloyd cheerfully described it as 'an army of occupation upon which is imposed the performance of certain civil duties'.[3] The *Morning Post* was still speaking defiantly in 1920 of the RIC as 'a semi-military force, armed and drilled and concentrated in those little barrack forts that are the blockhouses of Imperial rule in Ireland'.[4]

To others these qualities were politically undesirable. The most sustained public attack on the constabulary occurred in the mid-1860s, and was begun by the Tipperary grand jury at the spring assizes of 1864. The jury complained to the government that

for some years past the constabulary had become more and more a military force, and in exact proportion as that system had been established, their usefulness and efficiency as a domestic force had been weakened and impaired.[5]

It specifically instanced 'their recent equipment with a heavy and delicate weapon' (i.e. the long Enfield) which reduced their capacity to pursue delinquents; and, still worse, the military organization of the headquarters structure, which cut off local police from the magistrates, and indeed from

---

[1] Curtis, *History of RIC*, p. 100. [2] Ibid. p. 104.
[3] Lloyd, *Ireland under the Land League*, p. 51.
[4] C. J. C. Street, *The Administration of Ireland, 1920* (London, 1921), p. 274.
[5] Curtis, *History of RIC*, p. 103.

each other, since communications between police stations followed a triangular route via central headquarters.[1] Similar criticisms were voiced by judges at quarter sessions in Roscommon, Cavan, and Limerick. The Inspector-General was impelled to produce a substantial vindication of his force. In a detailed analysis of 'allegations' against it, running to over one hundred pages, he endeavoured to defend its centralized organization by demonstrating that the earlier diffuse magisterial control had been quite unsatisfactory. He suggested that some people

possibly, may fail to see the essentially *civil* character of the constabulary, looking at them only as members of an organized force, having a certain amount of military appearance—thus, confounding a *disciplined* with a *military* body.[2]

Brownrigg denied that his force had a 'military spirit'. Strict discipline was necessary in an armed force of such size, the more so as its members were dispersed in small groups outside the direct supervision of their officers; yet that discipline was not 'martial law' (by which he meant military law) but a civil code whose heaviest penalty was dismissal.[3] Constables, he held, did not see themselves as soldiers. On the contrary, they had a most unsoldier-like propensity for putting down roots in their localities, and were often difficult to shift when the central system demanded it.[4]

In spite of this pamphlet, or perhaps because of a certain lack of impact in its presentation, criticisms continued. For instance, alongside the splenetic attacks of the Dublin *Mail*, objecting to

'officers' of Constabulary, who write up over their own room wherever they happen to be together in two's or three's 'officers' mess'—who never get leave of absence, but are 'on furlough'; who 'march' to a place where a Fenian or sheepstealer is to be apprehended, and would not run after an offender for the world, lest the dignity of the Force should be lowered,[5]

---

[1] Ibid. pp. 103-9 for this and other instances of legal criticism of the police.
[2] Brownrigg, *Examination*, p. 21.
[3] Ibid. p. 27.
[4] Ibid. p. 23.
[5] NLI MS. 7619; cf. the collection of press criticisms in MS. 7620, esp. *Londonderry Sentinel*, 24 Aug. 1860.

there was the more measured view of *The Times*:

The Irish Constabulary resembles, indeed, a continental *gendarmerie* far more nearly than is consistent with our habits of local self-government. It is doubtless a great anomaly from this point of view that a force more or less analogous to our own rural police should be under the immediate control of the Executive, maintained almost entirely at the expense of the Imperial Exchequer, drilled like soldiers, armed with Minié rifles and sword bayonets, and yet employed in collecting agricultural statistics, getting in returns for the census, and detecting illicit stills.[1]

By 1866, when this was written, *The Times* was prepared to admit that 'no part of our expenditure yields a better return' even though 'no statesman would undertake to justify the policy on principle'. Such pragmatic undermining of Victorian public morality was due to the fear of Fenianism. Only two years earlier the same newspaper had scoffed that the ability of the Irish police to put down open rebellion was of no account alongside the fact that 'they are not policemen' for ordinary purposes.

We might as well, when we go partridge shooting, carry spears and rifles, for fear of an attack from a mastodon or a swoop from a pterodactyl, as march out our policemen in battle array to catch pickpockets. The English pleiosaurus and the Irish rebel are extinct.[2]

After 1867, fiasco though it was, such levity was silenced.

None the less, the armament of the police, though it was vindicated in that transient flurry of violence, involved very serious issues. As has been observed, the fact of their carrying firearms went unquestioned from the outset. Yet it was already accepted in Britain that armed forces should be under the special discipline of military law. This issue was nearly raised in 1862 when the new rifles were being supplied to replace near-useless muskets: the War Office suddenly began to insist that Irish policemen should undergo the same training as Volunteers, on the ground that rifles were 'not required for police duty'—it was 'only *quâ* Volunteers that the Constabulary ought to have them'.[3] The point was not pressed, however. Some doubt remained over the sort of

---

[1] *The Times*, 6 June 1866.
[2] Ibid., 18 Apr. 1864.
[3] Cardwell to Larcom, 22 Jan. 1862 (NLI MS 7617, f. 71).

firearms the police should carry. When the *Mail* protested against the arming of constables with rifles, pointing to the uselessness of eighty police riflemen against 'a handful of blackguards' in the streets of Cork, it merely reflected the concern of ministers.[1] Edward Cardwell, then Chief Secretary, told the Under-Secretary, Sir Thomas Larcom, in January 1860 that the War Office could supply the IC with the long Enfield rifle but not the short one as originally requested, adding 'I said I feared the long one would be an inconvenient thing for the men to carry', but suggesting that the long model might be accepted temporarily for practice.[2] Larcom, with an ingrained grasp of Horse Guards bureaucracy, disapproved: 'I fear that if they once arm us with the long Enfield, we shall never get them exchanged.' He preferred to wait until carbines were available, and mentioned the possibility of using Lancaster rifles instead. 'Our men often carry their pieces under their coats—& slip about unobserved. They might as well try to pocket a duck gun as a long Enfield.'[3] The Commander-in-Chief was also unhappy with the idea, asking 'are you really prepared to arm them with a weapon which will shoot five or six people at once?'.[4] Once again it seems that these questions were side-stepped. The rearmament went ahead against the wishes of the Irish authorities, apparently because of Treasury demands for standardization.[5]

In the end, the normal police weapon was to become the Snider, and later the Martini-Henry carbine, handier and shorter-ranged than the service rifle. These breech-loading guns were none the less lethal, and as such could be more often a liability than an asset to a policeman. The danger that police would be prevented from taking effective action by the same fear of lethal consequences as inhibited soldiers was recognized, but no solutions were proposed. The whole problem of armed forces in confrontation with the ordinary population, as will be seen later, is the sudden and dramatic

[1] *Dublin Evening Mail*, 27 Mar. 1863.
[2] Cardwell to Larcom, 19 Jan. 1860 (NLI MS 7617, f. 44).
[3] Larcom to Cardwell, 21 Jan. 1860 (ibid., f. 45).
[4] Cardwell to Larcom, 1 Feb. 1861 (ibid., f. 68).
[5] Brownrigg, *Examination*, p. 106.

transition from the threat to the reality of fatal violence. The leap is so great that except in the last extremity it cannot reasonably be made. Crowds cannot be controlled by gunfire. Nor, as the *Mail* pointed out, can criminals be apprehended by it.

General Lord de Ros, who took a strong professional interest in the operation of the IC, argued in 1857—before the rearming with the Minié rifle—that the force should be substantially disarmed. His candid analysis of its *raison d'être* was that of

interposing between a population in a state of almost insurgency & the Military force, a body of men formed, & to a certain degree trained, on military principles; but yet so connected with the Magistracy & Civil Authorities, as to remove some of the outward appearance of depending on Troops for the government of Ireland.[1]

He suggested that the force had now succeeded in its object to the extent that there had been a 'decrease in personal and barbarous violence' (partly due, he allowed, to improved relations between landlords and tenants as a result of legislation which meant that landlords were no longer driven to 'all manner of shifts' to protect their property rights). Henceforth its style should be brought closer to that of the English rural police—stationed in smaller groups, and carrying truncheons, or at most concealed pistols, rather than muskets.[2] Brownrigg's response to such suggestions was that, whilst police stationed in towns did in fact normally carry truncheons only, for rural detachments service weapons were vital. The IC, 'having arms, are rarely assailed; without arms, the case would be very different'. Its powerful weaponry had secured for it a 'prestige' which alone enabled it to perform its duties (together, for instance, as the Inspector-General carefully pointed out, with those previously performed at great trouble and cost by the Revenue Police) economically. To disarm the force 'would be to essentially alter its character and undermine its prestige'. As for the use of batons, so frequently advocated for crowd control,

[1] Memorandum on the Irish Constabulary Force by Lord de Ros, Feb. 1857 (NLI MS 7617, f. 8).
[2] Ibid.

any person who is acquainted with the character and propensities of the country people must see that the interference of Policemen armed with *sticks* in a popular assembly would be simply an invitation to oppose them with similar weapons; frequent collisions between the baton men and the people would be the inevitable result, which could only be put an end to by the armed party, perhaps not without a resort to serious extremities.[1]

The Inspector-General conceded that one day, when Ireland's social problems had been solved, the constabulary might be disarmed. But while they remained armed, they should be properly armed—with bayonets as well as rifles—and well trained in the use of their weapons.[2]

The Fenian crisis, as has been said, silenced many critics of the armed police. 'The parrot cry "too military" at its loudest cackle', Larcom noted, 'changed suddenly in 1866 and 67 and was succeeded by "hurrah for the brave force!" ' Their exemplary loyalty and discipline sufficed in most cases to disperse the Fenian bands with a single volley of rifle-fire.[3] In token of appreciation, the prefix 'Royal' was added to their title—the greatest honour the government could conceive, though one which would do little good to the constabulary itself in the future. The public ceremony conferring the new title in Phoenix Park on 6 September 1867 was a grand affair; but as the *Freeman's Journal* pointed out some years later, the flood of praise for the RIC was 'unaccompanied by any more solid tribute'.[4] Titles and badges were cheaper than pay-rises. A sub-constable's pay remained at around 15 shillings a week, while his already heavy duties were being constantly increased.[5]

[1] Brownrigg, *Examination*, pp. 22, 25.

[2] Ibid. p. 26.

[3] According to Lord Strathnairn, however, their record was not entirely without blemish. During the 'Kerry affair' of February 1867 the local constabulary abandoned their barracks precipitately. Ó Broin, *Fenian Fever*, pp. 131-2.

[4] *Freeman's Journal*, 3 July 1872.

[5] By the 1880s the pay of sub-constables had risen to 20-24s. a week; that of constables to £72 p.a., and of head constables to £90-£101. Sub-inspectors earned £250-£450, County Inspectors £500-£650, Assistant Inspector-Generals £600-£800, and the Deputy Inspector-General £1,000. The salary of the IG remained at the level originally fixed in the 1830s, £1,500, still thirty times that of the lowest rank (Blake, 'Irish police', pp. 391, 393). These rates actually fell for some officers by the end of the century: District Inspectors ranged from £125

As euphoria died away in the later 1860s it became necessary once again to think about the suitability of the force for
its normal civil duties. In 1868 instructions were issued on
the use of firearms, enjoining once more the need to guard
against the slightest possibility of their misuse (though
adding, in line with military orthodoxy, that if fire had to
be opened on a crowd it must be aimed and not overhead,
since the latter endangered the innocent bystander). Significantly it was ordered that half of each police patrol should
be armed only with their sword-bayonets.[1] This was the
beginning of a series of attempts to mitigate the violence of
the modes of control available to the RIC, and to provide
a graduated scale of responses to various forms of disorder.
The 1872 RIC Code required that at 'riots, elections or any
other occasions of excitement' at least one-third of the police
should carry truncheons only. The opening of the land war
brought the well-intentioned expedient of supplying
buckshot as well as ball cartridges, the former to be used
in all but the most desperate circumstances.[2]

These good intentions did not succeed in placating public
hostility. Buckshot had rather the reverse effect. Part of
the reason for this was that the question of armament,
though it subsumed major aspects of the RIC's nature and
role, was not the whole problem. The pressure to 'normalize'
—one might almost rather say 'civilize'—the force involved
consideration of its everyday function of policing society.
This was a matter both of ethos and of technique, and it was
not clear which, if either, of these was more basic. There

(3rd class) to £330 (1st class), County Inspectors from £350 to £450 (*RIC List
and Directory*, 1898). But the guarantee of a pension remained one of the force's
strongest attractions.

[1] *Dublin Daily Express*, 6 Aug. 1868 (NLI MS 7619). Cf. the earlier instruction
that men with loaded arms 'should be duly warned of the necessity of being
peculiarly circumspect in the use of them. They should always bear in mind that
any injury inflicted by any individual of the Establishment . . . must of course
be followed by solemn inquiry, the consequences of which cannot fail to be most
serious to those who shall be found to have transgressed' (Circular, 16 Mar.
1841; HO 184 111).

[2] R. Hawkins's introduction to 'An Army on Police Work, 1881-2: Ross of
Bladensburg's Memorandum', *Irish Sword*, xi (1973), 80–1, provides a lucid survey of this process and points out that the adoption of buckshot was 'a make-
shift' whose results were unsatisfactory.

was general agreement that the exemplar of successful policing was the London Metropolitan force, which had attained
by the 1860s a great moral authority in the capital through
'persistent firmness and resolution, coupled with temper
and moderation'.[1] But was moderation the result or the
cause of this success? Had the Metropolitan force created,
through superior technique, circumstances which could be
improved upon by subsequent moderation, or was moderation the essence of the technique? If the latter, the outlook
for the RIC was not bright, for even superhuman 'tact and
firmness' could scarcely begin to establish a dialogue with
warlike Irish crowds, or make headway in criminal investigations through the wall of silence put up by the rural community. In an instructive if less than amicable discussion of
police technique between Lord de Ros and Sir Duncan
McGregor, Inspector-General during the constabulary's
formative years from 1838 to 1858,[2] de Ros stressed the
need to break through the barrier of terrorism which paralysed the ordinary population.

It must never be forgotten that intimidation is the grand secret of the
Irish assassin,—that he himself is a coward, & that any unusually
vigorous or unexpected display on the part of the Executive has invariably produced among the peasantry . . . a counter-intimidation of the
most remarkable kind. They become terrified & bewildered—they
exaggerate the danger that besets them, & best of all, they dare no
longer run the risk of harbouring & assisting the malefactors.[3]

This attractive theory, grounded in part on Saxon ideas of
Irish character, was often to be repeated (not always with the
same candour) in the following seventy years. How was the
formula of mild counter-terror to be implemented? De Ros
suggested a system of intensive patrolling in the military
manner. What was needed, he said, was skill combined with
stealth: it was no good clumping about the roads as the constabulary did.
  McGregor's reaction to these and other suggestions was

---

[1] Lord de Ros to Lord-Lieutenant (Lord Wodehouse), 20 Mar. 1865 (Larcom
MSS, NLI MS 7627, f. 22).
  [2] McGregor's attitudes are politely but revealingly illustrated in Curtis, *History
of RIC*, pp. 47–58 ff.
  [3] Lord de Ros to Lord-Lieutenant (Lord Clarendon), 15 Dec. 1847 (Larcom
MSS, NLI MS 7617, f. 1).

predictable. Though himself a military officer (he had come to the IC from commanding a regiment), like a large proportion of his officers, he perceived the honour of his force to be at stake. He observed stiffly of de Ros's first memorandum, 'I cannot really discover any really useful or practicable suggestion in it which has not been enjoined in my *detailed* printed instructions on the same subject' (although in his own general orders six months earlier he had stated that 'in several counties' patrolling was 'either wholly neglected or only partially performed').[1] He denied that military patrols furnished an object for study, since they consisted

of detachments each under the command, if possible, of an officer, seldom if ever deviating from the high roads—& intimating by the noise of their footsteps, &c, their approach at considerable distances.[2]

No criminal had yet been arrested by them, and their only useful purpose was to 'afford confidence to the peaceably disposed in disturbed districts'. McGregor objected that the idea of small patrols combing the countryside intensively ignored the physical limitations of the police force: the average number of men available for patrol duty at each post was only five, the average area they had to cover was 18 square miles.[3]

The Inspector-General rejected de Ros's criticism of the system of 'personal protection'—the employment of constables in twos or threes to guard threatened ('obnoxious') individuals, which de Ros regarded as a waste of police strength. Its justification was the fact that only three protected persons had been attacked in the last ten years. Still more important was the issue of the 'disposable or detective police'. McGregor misunderstood de Ros as criticizing his deployment of detective police generally, though in fact de

[1] Circular, 15 May 1847 (HO 184 112).
[2] Notes by Sir D. McGregor, 1 Jan. 1848 (NLI MS 7617, f. 2). Cf. 'Inspector General's Orders on Patrolling', Circular, 9 Feb. 1841 (HO 184 111).
[3] Notes by Sir D. McGregor, loc. cit. Later in his reply he said that even if the army were to agree to disperse its strength in patrols, 'I very much doubt whether either Military or Police Officers could possibly accomplish the object which Lord de Ros seems to think so easy of attainment'. With an average strength of 28-9 men per 100 square miles, any 'network' would have to be so loose that assassins could pass through it with ease.

Ros believed that McGregor had made a great improvement by having four or five provincial detective centres rather than a single centre in Dublin. Rather, McGregor's system was to select four or five men in each county, regardless of rank,

most distinguished for their respectability & ingenuity in tracing crime, who under ordinary circumstances continue to perform the usual duties at their respective stations, but on the occurrence of any heinous ourage . . . are directed to proceed in disguise to the scene of the crime, and endeavour by every legitimate means to discover the perpetrators.

Perhaps unsurprisingly, these investigators had not had much success. The basic problem facing the constabulary was that they were

required to discharge their onerous duties with all the delicacy demanded of our jealous English constitution amidst a population a vast majority of which is either determinedly & systematically opposed to the laws, or so intimidated from various causes as to refuse to the Authorities even the slenderest clue to the apprehension of the most atrocious criminals.[1]

This plaint somewhat missed the point, as de Ros was concerned with how the system of intimidation could be overcome. He returned to the attack by declaring that the military patrols belittled by McGregor were not the sort of patrols he was advocating. They were 'parade marches', intended to support police patrols and give general confidence.

The sort of patrolling I mean is that which was pursued during the riots in Kent and Sussex in 1830, when, with comparatively few troops, the face of the country was so perambulated, that all attempt at outrage was entirely paralized [*sic*] & order restored immediately.[2]

De Ros protested that he had never said that such an intensive system could be applied across the whole of Ireland at the same time. Rather, a series of limited areas would be successively saturated. There was no uniform basis for calculating the necessary strength: in some parts of Ireland one policeman was enough for twenty square miles, in others 'you almost need one for twenty square yards'.

This dispute, full as it was of unnecessary misunderstandings, pre-echoed recurrent friction between the two arms

[1] Ibid.
[2] De Ros to McGregor, 23 Jan. 1848 (NLI MS 7617, f. 4).

of the Crown forces. It ended politely enough with McGregor regretting that de Ros thought him annoyed, and acknowledging that de Ros's efforts had been instrumental in obtaining the funds needed for developing the detective police.[1] But de Ros remained a close critic of the Irish police. As we have seen, he advocated civilianization in 1857, and may have spurred Brownrigg to issue immediately on his succession to McGregor as Inspector-General a general order which established the bases of modern police work. This order, called by an establishment newspaper 'the most important document ever issued by the Police authorities in this country',[2] instructed County Inspectors not to allow their officers and men to confine their attention to serious outrages, but to 'pay due regard to larcenies, and other offences of a *minor* character'.

And it cannot be too strongly inculcated, that the *prevention* of offences is of even more importance than their detection and punishment; and that the absence of crime, in any locality, is held to demonstrate the most clearly the efficiency of its police.[3]

Discussion of the effectiveness of any police force, whether measured by this criterion or by the ratio of convictions to reported crimes, is notoriously difficult. Opinions of the RIC were to fluctuate throughout the rest of its history, but there was a noticeable tendency at any time to hold that the force was a pale shadow of its former self—a view which intensified at successive crises, in 1880, 1912, and 1919. At the same time its detective skills were staunchly defended, not only in Brownrigg's 1864 pamphlet but also in more popular works like Curtis's anecdotal *History*—which prefigured later adventure-packed accounts like *Tales of the RIC*—and in Blake's article in the *Nineteenth Century* magazine in 1881.[4] Brownrigg's attempted vindication remained the most ambitious, drawing parallels with

---

[1] McGregor to Clarendon, 28 Jan. 1848 (loc. cit.).

[2] *Dublin Daily Express*, 9 Dec. 1858.

[3] IG General Order, 1 Dec. 1858 (NLI MS 7620).

[4] Also R. Curtis, *The Irish Police Officer* (London, 1861), and *Curiosities of Detection* (London, 1862). Blake, 'Irish police', p. 395, presents a statistical table of RIC conviction rates for 1879—he admitted that for 1880 they would 'not be so favourable to the force'—showing an overall rate of 59.3 per cent.

England and Wales. His statistics suggested, first, that the crime rate in Ireland was less than a third of that in England and Wales; and, second, that the Irish Constabulary—in spite of the peculiar difficulties of the Irish situation—achieved arrest and conviction rates not markedly at variance with those in England.[1] The peculiar difficulty was, as always, that the efforts of the police to trace offenders were 'not only unaided but systematically baffled' by the general public. Brownrigg remarked rather testily that

> while many Magistrates, and a large portion of the public, would seem to be impressed with the notion that the Police should be able, as if by intuition, to lay their hands on the perpetrators of (agrarian) crimes as soon as committed—those very gentlemen and landlords have rarely found themselves in a position to render help in the matter; and not-withstanding all the facilities they possess, through their agents, bailiffs and numerous tenantry, they have not in a single instance that I can call to mind after an experience of thirty-three years, been able to detect any crime of an agrarian character, or been able to afford the Constabulary any useful hints for the discovery of the perpetrators.[2]

He did recognize that some duties (such as patrolling to stop road nuisances) created public ill-will which 'often prevents information being given that would otherwise be had'. He never permitted himself to ask, however, whether the fact of the constabulary's being armed also played a part in raising this obstacle.[3]

In the view of some critics, particularly in the press, the constabulary's militarism was at fault not simply in this way but in a tendency to select recruits on grounds of physique rather than intelligence. (And to promote officers according to seniority rather than aptitude.) It was agreed by all that the constables in their smart rifle-green uniforms looked as impressive as guardsmen; but their amiable slow-wittedness was legendary. Even Lord Spencer was not above fulminating against the stupidity of hapless sub-constables

---

[1] Brownrigg, *Examination*, pp. 61–2.

[2] Ibid. pp. 59–60.

[3] Ibid. p. 101. Brownrigg refuted the allegation that the long rifle and bayonet were a physical impediment, citing the case of a constable who succeeded in chasing and arresting a malefactor—though the latter drew the policeman's bayonet and wounded him. He did not consider the moral repercussions of the weapons.

who so consistently proved unable to effect the arrest of agrarian criminals.[1] No doubt it is true that the force attracted few brilliant men, and it may be that its excessive rigidity stifled those few. In these matters it was not very different from the English police, however. At root, popular resistance was always the critical factor. And whilst resistance, even violent resistance, to policing had not been unknown in England, it survived and even intensified in parts of Ireland.[2] Nationalist denunciations of the force on political grounds, as an 'army of occupation' and 'the eyes and ears of Dublin Castle', could only sharpen the divide.

(iv) *Policing Belfast*

> The town is practically again under martial law. The military and police hold the streets as though they were invaded by a foreign foe.
>
> *Freeman's Journal*, 19 Aug. 1872

Inevitably, some of the most powerful strictures on police effectiveness concerned the problem of Belfast. The 1864 riots drew from Lord de Ros his last major assessment of police technique, a good deal more moderate than the denunciations heaped on the executive by *The Times*. In the opinion of the latter, 'in any other country' the method of restoring order would have been 'perfectly simple'.

A strong body of police, aided by a few cavalry, would have marched through the more turbulent streets, clearing them as they passed. Every person would have been warned to keep indoors and all crowds in any part of the town would have been dispersed with firmness, but without any unnecessary violence.[3]

Instead of this edifying vision, *The Times* saw the police employed in making miniature charges and 'arresting ring-leaders', or placing themselves between contending factions and trying to keep them away from each other. 'This imbecile

---

[1] See Spencer to O'Hagan, 25 Feb. 1869 (PRONI D.2777/8, f. 17).

[2] On English resistance cf. R. D. Storch, 'The plague of the blue locusts: police reform and popular resistance in northern England, 1840-57', *International Rev. of Soc. Hist.* xx. 1 (1975). It must be remarked that actual violence against police was uncommon in Ireland; see below, p. 150.

[3] *The Times*, 21 Aug. 1864.

method of dealing with mob violence', it snorted, 'has been condemned by repeated failures in former cases.'

De Ros held that the riots, with their alarmingly high incidence of gunshot injuries, had been a shocking failure of public order: 'a full week passed before order was restored, & even then, the small number of rioters captured shewed the weakness with which the law had been vindicated.' Such a failure made further disturbances more likely, and was particularly unforgivable because Belfast was inherently an easy city to occupy and control, given the correct techniques. Once again he looked to English examples:

Those who were employed (both Police & Military) in the different disturbances of London, from Queen Caroline's funeral Riot, in 1820, to the last occurrence of the kind in 1848, will recollect the extraordinary manner in which the late Duke of Wellington devoted his attention to the intricate & difficult details of posting Troops in support of the Police of London (for such support & not Military action alone was always the prominent character of his arrangement).[1]

The essence of the perfect arrangements in 1848 had been close co-operation between the Commander-in-Chief and the chief of police. What should be done in Belfast, de Ros argued, was for two staff officers to make a study of the best ways of cutting communications and preventing collision between crowds—by judiciously located troop centres and by the use of special plain-clothes officers to convey messages unobserved.[2]

The idea of depending on troops for the maintenance of order in cities, though it could not be escaped, was becoming less and less attractive. What was possible in 1848 might be undesirable by 1870. Yet the manifest failure of the Belfast authorities in 1864 called for some major change. The obvious target was the city's independent police force. Shortly after the riots, Larcom was writing that the only way of preventing 'all processions of magnitude', and if possible of abolishing the Orange Societies altogether, was by 'placing Belfast under Police Magistrates and a Government Police like Dublin'.

---

[1] De Ros to Wodehouse, 20 Mar. 1865 (NLI MS 7627, f. 22).
[2] Ibid.

At present the County Magistrates around and in the Town act in the Town Court, and on occasions of riot, and there is a Borough Police of 150 men, who are said to be wholly inefficient. They certainly are useless in a case like that in question.[1]

This view was sustained by an investigation into the riots, which concluded that the demonstrations 'could have been easily prevented if the local Police had been sufficiently active and vigilant'—and less partisan: 'Many members of that Force reside in Sandy Row—yet it is almost impossible to get information as to the doings of the people in that district.'[2]

The Town Council's protest that they had made efforts to remodel the police, and had even sent a deputation to consult with the London force in 1858, was passed over.[3] Sir Robert Peel, who at the height of the riots had blithely maintained that he did not understand 'why people have not as much right to burn O'Connell in effigy in one place as to glorify his memory in another', quickly came to agree that the 'miserably inefficient' local police and magistrates had 'allowed tumult to get out of hand before they could make up their minds to act' and must be 'replaced by our more efficient constabulary'.[4] Predictably, though, when it came to providing barracks for that efficient force, Peel worried that the change would be 'attended with a good deal of ultimate expense to the public'. Only after a debilitating struggle did the Treasury (under that paragon of good housekeepers, Gladstone) agree to meet the costs involved in the new Constabulary Reform and Belfast Police Bill.[5]

---

[1] Larcom to C.-in-C. Ireland (Sir George Murray), 26 Aug. 1864 (PRO HO 45 7649). In fact the strength of the Belfast police was 161, of whom five were Roman Catholics.

[2] Sub-inspector, Belfast, to IG, 27 Feb. 1865 (NLI MS 7627).

[3] Commission of Inquiry, evidence of Ald. W. Mullan, 17th day, 2 Dec. 1864.

[4] Chief Secretary to Under-Secretary, 17, 19 Aug. 1864 (NLI MS 7626); cf. same to same, 1 Mar. 1865 (MS 7627).

[5] Eventually 28 & 29 Vict., c. 70. The Treasury's resistance reduced Larcom to near-despair: he wrote to Burke on 4 May 1865, 'That the Treasury insist upon the Borough paying the whole of the cost of the extra men, is a case of that mere innocence of all knowledge of the subject, so common in London as to anything connected with Ireland'. He could not get the Treasury to understand that using the police reserve in Belfast actually saved government money, since it had to bear the whole cost while the reserve was at Phoenix Park. He refused, however, to reduce the costs by removing the charge for extra pay to magistrates. 'Poor Bill

The Act, passed in June 1865, furnished a basic force of 130, to which the Lord-Lieutenant could add an extra force of up to 320. The 'free quota' was provided at imperial expense, and the borough had to bear half the cost of the extra force. A similar arrangement was made for Londonderry in 1885.[1]

But the effect of the change was less than miraculous. In August 1872 the city again erupted in massive violence, and the unfortunate RIC seemed almost to augment rather than quash it. No fewer than 73 of them were wounded, 12 very severely, and one was killed. By 15 August—the sixth day of rioting—there were 420 RIC and 80 auxiliaries, together with artillery, cavalry (50 men of the 4th Dragoon Guards), infantry (321 men of the 78th Highlanders) and militia (the Antrim Rifles) in the city; yet rioting continued for another week. The end came only with general exhaustion and a tremendous deluge of rain, which 'emptied the streets more effectually than the thousands of military and police'.[2] The Lord-Lieutenant, Spencer, wearily surveying the wreckage, was reduced to the dismally familiar litany of 'regret that more vigour was not shown at the outset in stopping the riots'. He proposed to increase the permanent RIC force to 650 and to create a 'Commissioner of Belfast Police', who was also to be a town magistrate. If disturbances were apprehended in future the mayor should convene the magistrates with the senior military and police officers, and plan preventive action in good time.[3]

The fact was that Belfast produced challenges which overstretched the loose British administrative machine. Repeatedly the constraints on hasty or excessive action ingrained into the British system of government produced hesitation; and the system itself was ruptured by the impossibility of eliciting compromise within the divided population. Little of the

---

—little Bill!', he wryly concluded, 'What it will be by the time it passes I cannot guess. But whatever mischief Parliament, or Treasury, or other focus of ignorance, may impose, is easier borne than the self inflicted folly of castrating it ourselves by such a step.'

[1] McDowell, *Irish Administration*, p. 143.

[2] *The Times*, 23 Aug. 1872. The *Freeman's Journal*, 22 Aug., exaggerated police and troop strength to 1,500 and 2,000 respectively.

[3] Lord Hartington to Mayor of Belfast, 6 Jan. 1873 (NLI MS 7631).

violence was directed against the state or the law as such, except in so far as the 'rule of law' still represented, to Catholic and Protestant alike, the defence of the political *status quo*—the Protestant ascendancy. Yet the law dissolved as Protestant ships' carpenters drove Catholic navvies into the mudflats of 'Slob-land' and picked them off with musket fire. Time after time it seemed that order had collapsed so utterly as to throw the state on its last recourse, martial law.[1] This recourse might at least have supplied the consistent and expeditious decision-making so conspicuously absent in Belfast. But the inhibitions evoked by this menacing concept were such that chronic social breakdown was preferred to the threat to liberty implicit in an overt system of military control in emergencies.[2] Even Belfast did not, in English eyes, call for a 'state of siege'.

(v) *Emergency powers and the martial law problem*

> The military measures applied to Ireland, in so far as they have come under my observation, have been of the nature of temporary expedients to ward off some pressing evil (supposed to be temporary likewise) . . . and after having escaped, as I trust we may hope to do, from the existing cause of apprehension, it will be found when in a few years hence, another occurs, that nothing solid has been done against the permanent insecurity.
>
> Sir George Murray[3]

That government in Ireland depended on military force, not simply in the general sense that is true of all government, but on an immediate, almost day-to-day basis, was hardly open to dispute. Whilst this dependence naturally became less marked after the creation of the armed constabulary, it did not disappear in the way that had been hoped. Yet no constitutional doctrine governing the conduct of crises which required the use of regular military forces was permitted to emerge. An atmosphere of uncertainty and apprehension permanently enveloped the matter. Aversion to the domestic employment of troops was deeply rooted in the English

---

[1] e.g. *Evening Post* report, 22 Apr. 1857 (NLI MS 7624).

[2] Cf. C. Townshend, 'Martial law', pp. 174-6, and *passim*.

[3] Gen. Murray to Lord FitzRoy Somerset, 31 Jan. 1844 (PRO WO 80/9).

public mind. It gave rise to a feeling that because a doctrine
of emergency powers—such as existed in most continental
states—was morally undesirable, it was practically unnecessary also. When the Lord Chief Justice maintained that
martial law was repugnant to the English law, and had been
abolished by the Petition of Right, he gave expression to a
general confidence that such things were not needful on
Albion's shore: a modern society would solve its problems
in more enlightened ways.[1] The result of this attitude was
confusion amongst those responsible, under commission and
under common law alike, for the maintenance of 'law and
order'. The irresolution and vacillation so often reproved in
Irish magistrates was due in great part to this. Delay permitted an increase in violent disorder, and could lead in turn
to an excessive application of force when troops were finally
sent in.

It was, as has been observed, quite easy for Irish disorder
to go beyond the power of the ordinary law to restrain it.
Likewise it overwhelmed, periodically, the physical resources
of the civil authorities. Military headquarters at Kilmainham,
Dublin, whose main responsibility was the training of recruits
for overseas drafts, was repeatedly pressed to parcel out its
forces on alien and demanding duties. In 1848 the army
provided 2,898 parties of troops to aid the civil power—
patrolling, escorting prisoners, guarding buildings, enforcing
the execution of writs, quelling riots, and evicting tenants.[2]
This alarming wave of activity receded in quieter times. The
total fell to 441 parties by 1850 and to 39 at the end of that
peaceable decade. But in the 1860s renewed and novel alarms
commenced. Fenianism posed at one level a direct military
threat which could be met by conventional methods, but at
the same time it was assiduously burrowing into the muscula-
ture of the army itself, creating the possibility that in the
final emergency the military arm might be paralysed. This
unpleasant prospect was countered by vigorous action.
A new Commander-in-Chief, Sir Hugh Rose, celebrated for
the storming of Jhansi and the pursuit of Tatya Tope in
1858, initiated a widespread investigation, and, as he later

---

[1] See below, p. 95.
[2] Return of parties furnished (Kilmainham MSS, NLI MS 1226).

told Lord Spencer, crushed military Fenianism by 150 courts martial.[1]

My predecessor Sir George Brown was a very fine gallant old soldier, but he was under the same delusion as several Indian Generals who to the last maintained that it was impossible that the British uniform could cover a traitor.

Rose was under no such illusion. Never a man to underestimate his own achievements, he told the government in 1867

that officers, prudent and experienced men, are of opinion that if there had been a rising in 1865, before Military Fenianism had been properly dealt with, something disagreeable might, and would, probably, have occurred.[2]

Even after his action, for which he was elevated to the peerage as Lord Strathnairn, considerable apprehension remained. The Fenians' own military forces might not be very formidable but they could cause severe problems to the small detachments which the civil authorities were always demanding. The tension between the military requirement—for training and disciplinary as well as operational reasons—that forces be concentrated, and the civil demand for what amounted to supplementary (and free) police, was to be permanent. In 1866 it even drew in the Prime Minister as arbitrator.[3]

Constabulary officers, with military pretensions if not military backgrounds, seem to have understood this better than magistrates. McGregor had used as an argument against de Ros's scheme of intensive military patrols the assertion that

it is not probable that, knowing the character & habits of our Soldiers Sir E. Blakeney would allow the Troops to be scattered over the

---

[1] Strathnairn to Earl Spencer, 26 Dec. 1869 (BL Add MS 42826, f. 70).

[2] Gen. Lord Strathnairn's report to the Cabinet, 7 June 1867 (PRO WO 32 6000).

[3] Lord Derby to Lord Naas, 3 July 1866 (Derby MSS 153/3) quoted in Ó Broin, *Fenian Fever*, pp.. 105-7. Though balancing judiciously the points that 'some risk must unquestionably be run rather than have extensive districts wholly without military protection; on the other hand, you must be firm in resisting importunities for local protection to such an extent as will seriously compromise the safety of small detachments, and fritter away your military force so as to make it useless as an army', Derby came down in favour of eliminating any risk of 'sudden surprise and consequent destruction of a single company of the Queen's troops'.

Country in Light Infantry order, for the purpose of searching for unknown assassins.[1]

In 1866 Strathnairn resisted a series of demands for small forces, and made it clear that since the police had not been 'trained to arms' he could not rely on them, 'further than as good scouts to give the first notice of danger'. He believed that

in the opinion of the Government the state of this country is very critical; that an outbreak which will take effect·in all parts of the country . . . is probable.

Under these circumstances the Commander of the Forces again ventures to draw the attention of the Government of Ireland to the positive danger to the Army, and therefore to the State . . . which accrues from the small detachments under young and inexperienced leaders—an expedient which materially affects the discipline, prestige, power and safety of Troops.[2]

It was, of course, the Civil War experience of the American Fenians which created a potentially serious military hazard. Even if no large forces were brought over, there would be dreadful risks, as Strathnairn pointed out to Lord Naas:

Nothing would create such a panic amongst the loyal supporters of the British Government as the destruction of a Detachment of regular Troops, and yet it is indisputable that this inauspicious occurrence is liable to happen if Detachments are placed in several of the localities required by the Government.[3]

The Chief Secretary reassured him that the government was very anxious to fall in with his ideas and to strengthen posts wherever possible, and at the same time the Under-Secretary, Larcom, took the unusual step of issuing commissions of the peace to a number of military officers in Cork 'to enable them to act as Magistrates with the Troops on any emergency when it may not be practicable to obtain the services of one of the ordinary magistrates'.[4] This certainly seemed to indicate a new approach.

As the year 1867 broke, the most prominent military

[1] McGregor to Clarendon, 1 Jan. 1848 (NLI MS 7617, f. 2).

[2] C.-in-C. to Chief Secretary, 3 Dec. 1866 (Kilmainham MSS 1059).

[3] Ibid.

[4] Chief Secretary to C.-in-C., 7 Dec.; Under-Secretary to Maj.-Gen. Bates, OC Cork Division, 5 and 11 Dec. 1866 (loc. cit).

problems were still traditional ones. At the Waterford election, for instance, the troops were pelted with bottles and stones by a 'determined' mob while assisting the police.[1] But increasing tension and alarm were unmistakable by February. The commander of the South-Western Division, Brigadier-General McMurdo, issued calming orders on the 9th:

Care to be taken that no retaliation is committed by the Troops (nothing short of self-defence will justify it). *Forbearance* will cause the hostile feeling to subside, and redound to the credit of the Regiment.[2]

As the attenuated uprising began, full instructions for military commanders 'in time of open rebellion' were issued by the Chief Secretary.[3] They were scarcely needed, however, nor were the military 'flying columns' which were immediately established when isolated detachments were withdrawn. Larcom explained to one apprehensive landlord that

Our tactics are changed with the change of circumstances . . . standing detachments in the towns was a defensive measure . . . it had the effect of calming the extravagant alarm which some months ago was felt in many localities.

Now we assume the offensive. Lord Strathnairn is forming flying columns each of which will be able to move quickly from place to place & disperse the armed bodies wherever they come together.[4]

Yet the idea of having military commanders as magistrates does not seem to have worked, notwithstanding Strathnairn's belief that he had 'obtained from the Government very good law opinions, enabling the Troops to act, use their arms, against insurgents'.[5] Complaints about the failure of magistrates recurred. A military report of the action near Templemore, Co. Tipperary, early in March, illustrates the nature of the clashes involved.

---

[1] Military Secretary to Under-Secretary, 1 Jan. 1867 (loc. cit.).

[2] Note, 9 and 18 Feb. (loc. cit.).

[3] 'Instructions to Officers in command of parties of Troops in time of Open Rebellion or Insurrection against Her Majesty the Queen', being a letter from Lord Naas to Gen. Lord Strathnairn, 8 Mar. 1867 (loc. cit).; Memo. on Arming of Special Constables, and on Powers and Duties of Magistrates, 11 Mar. 1867 (Larcom MSS, NLI MS 7594).

[4] Larcom to Earl of Devon, 10 Mar. 1867 (NLI MS 7594). Similarly, Strathnairn explained to Hartington that the withdrawal of isolated detachments to form flying columns was 'reculer pour mieux sauter' (9 Mar. 1867; Strathnairn MSS, BL Add. MS 42823, f. 134).

[5] Strathnairn to Bates, 8 Mar. 1867 (ibid., f. 128).

We came upon a party of between sixty and seventy men, some armed with guns and some with pikes. Upon perceiving us they left the road and took to the country, and got behind a large bank. I proceeded to take them in flank. Upon seeing the intention they broke away. Mr Gore Jones ordered the police party, ten in number, to fire—but would not allow me to fire. The police fired one volley at I should think between 400 and 500 yards upon which they ran away and dispersed through the fields.[1]

Commenting on this, a flying column commander claimed that 'had the military been permitted to take a more decided action, the best results would have happened, probably the capture of the whole body of Fenians'. Strathnairn put it even more strongly: a 'capital opportunity' had been lost by 'weak measures', and the magistrate was not a fit person to be in charge of troops in such times.[2]

On 14 March Strathnairn reverted to the idea of swearing in officers as magistrates, suggesting that three of them be held in readiness in Dublin, to start at a moment's notice for any of the neighbouring counties. The flying columns pressed on in spite of inadequate directions ('the country people will not show the way to troops, and police are apparently not expected to') and severe suffering in the wintry weather.[3] A general review of their activities drawn up in early April suggested that insurrection had been prevented around Killarney and Limerick in February; a body of insurgents had been surrounded by three columns at Tallaght Hill and ninety-three had been captured; and a Fenian force had been driven from the fort of Bally-hurst near Tipperary, and one of its leaders captured. Strathnairn, using a form of reasoning which was to reappear in later years, held that although only three or four of the seven flying columns had been called upon for 'any marked action', they had all had a 'good effect'. The Thurles, Tipperary, and Waterford columns had made long, rapid surprise marches, often through six feet of snow (the Waterford column had

[1] Report of 31st Reg., 5 Mar. 1867 (Kilmainham MSS 1059).

[2] Report of Maj.-Gen. Bates, 7 Mar., note by Strathnairn, 9 Mar. (loc. cit.); Strathnairn to Naas, 9 Mar. 1867 (BL Add. MS 42823, f. 130).

[3] Military Secretary to Under-Secretary, 14 Mar.; also Strathnairn to Secretary of State for War, 17 Mar. 1867, requesting 'extraordinary' field allowance for his officers (Kilmainham MSS 1059).

spent an unenviable time scouring the Galtee mountains).[1]
He pointed to the important psychological effect of frequent small patrols, which had forced the Fenians to go into
hiding, and shown the superior power of the government.

Their sudden appearance in different parts of the country where
Troops have rarely been seen; their patrols, by day and night, combined so as to surprise and surround bad districts often in the worst
possible weathers; the search of houses, and arrest of suspected parties
which the Police, without their aid, had been unable to effect, have
produced the best possible impression in reassuring the loyal and over-
awing the disaffected.[2]

Regrettably, 'good' and even 'the best' effects were never
to be susceptible to clear definition or measurement. The
idea of 'overawing' the people, common in military ideas
of crowd control,[3] could not approach the clarity of conventional military criteria for victory in open combat. It was,
moreover, potentially double-edged: it could produce short-
term compliance at the price of longer-term hostility. These
facts combined to reinforce political disquiet about handing
power to the military, even in serious emergency. When
the military were finally called on to act, they were seldom sure what legal restrictions were placed upon their
actions, or how far these actions would be defended by the
government.

This was because of general uncertainty—amongst lawyers
as much as statesmen—over the administrative resort known
as 'martial law'. In common-law terms this might more
correctly, and usefully, have been labelled the 'law of necessity', since it was based on the duty of the government to use
force 'to repel force' and to maintain order if the ordinary
processes of law had broken down because of war or insurrection. (As has already been seen, the Inspector-General of
the IC confused 'martial law' with the military law governing
the armed services under the Mutiny Acts, and this was a
common error.) The term 'martial law' focused the self-

---

[1] C.-in-C. to Under Secretary, 4 Apr. 1867 (loc. cit.).
[2] C.-in-C. to Secretary of State for War, 12 Apr. 1867 (Kilmainham MSS
1060). He added that wear and tear would have to be made good at the soldiers'
own expense, and asked for a compensatory allowance to be made.
[3] On this theory, Hawkins, 'An Army on Police Work', pp. 78 ff.

conscious English aversion to militarism. In 1867 this aversion generated a fierce public controversy, led by the brightest lights of the Victorian intellectual establishment—Hill, Huxley, Carlyle, Kingsley—over the use of martial law by Governor Eyre in Jamaica two years earlier.[1] The 'Jamaica case' seemed to manifest a public determination to curb executive power: even in civil crisis, individual rights must take precedence over the preservation of the fabric of society. And although, curiously, all the prosecutions brought against those who had allegedly abused their power were rejected by juries, their arguments resonated.

The Irish press was particularly keen to report the comments made by the Lord Chief Justice on the use of martial law in Ireland in and after 1798.[2] He held that the Act of Indemnity that had been passed to cover the actions of Crown servants in this period proved that the Crown did not have the right to carry martial law into effect except through Act of Parliament.[3] Cockburn's further assertion that martial law had been abolished by the Petition of Right, though not accepted by the eminent lawyer on whose opinion Cockburn's charge to the grand jury in *R.* v. *Nelson and Brand* was based,[4] had a straightforwardness that inevitably increased its currency. By July 1867 we find Major O'Reilly rising in the House of Commons to draw attention to 'the law as laid down by the Chief Justice of England', and declaring it to be 'unquestioned and unquestionable' that no British subject could be subjected to martial law.[5] W. E. Forster, taking a less absolutist but still extreme interpretation, held that the Crown had not the power to suspend the law without parliamentary assistance. All these views, by concentrating on the issue of royal prerogative, missed the crucial common-law point that martial law was not brought into effect by executive action, but was made an unavoidable necessity by the failure of the ordinary law.

---

[1] Townshend, 'Martial law', p. 169.

[2] *R.* v. *Nelson and Brand*, report in *Freeman's Journal*, 15 Apr. 1867.

[3] On the indemnity issue, Townshend, 'Martial law', p. 177.

[4] That lawyer was Sir James Stephen. See his *History of the Criminal Law of England* (London, 1883), i, 207.

[5] HC Debates, *The Times*, 3 July 1867.

It was really no more and no less than what a government must do when it had no means of governing other than by direct force.[1]

The atmosphere of excitement and scandal surrounding the Jamaica affair undoubtedly impressed on the Cabinet the need for more than usual caution. Although the Fenian crisis rendered acceptable the idea of giving magisterial powers to military commanders, there was no move to use martial-law methods to bypass the rickety judicial system. Nor were the administrative problems involved in using troops resolved in any satisfactory way. The whole complex of questions concerning the use of force in a liberal polity—not simply the confusion over the theory and practice of martial law as such, but the related mental and physical constraints and inhibitions affecting the domestic deployment of soldiers—which may be called 'the martial law problem', was a permanent underlying feature of Anglo-Irish relations. British rule in Ireland so often found itself paralysed because it could neither operate on English principles (because it did not have sufficient public co-operation) nor abandon English principles and govern by the direct application of force. It had to preserve the show and rhetoric of 'civilization'. As Dicey wrote, 'Every government must be true to its principles, and a democracy which played the benevolent despot would suffer demoralization'.[2]

Demoralization in a less exalted sense, however, was the resulting lot of those charged with the enforcement of the law at a more concrete level. How were soldiers to cope with violently hostile crowds, for instance? The advice of the Irish Law Officers was that

Her Majesty's troops, in execution of their duty, may use the force necessary to overcome any resistance to them in the execution of that duty, and if such resistance be of a nature that renders it necessary for their defence and the protection of themselves or their comrades to fire upon their opponents, they are at liberty to use their fire-arms against the persons who attack them with stones or other missiles, or otherwise.[3]

[1] As even opponents of *droit administratif* like Hallam and Dicey made clear.

[2] Dicey, *England's Case*, p. 132.

[3] Opinion of Irish Law Officers, 2 July 1867 (WO 32 6001).

In case the word 'liberty' might conduce to laxity, they added 'But in the exercise of this right great caution and forbearance must be used, and they should not fire unless in great extremity'. It was perhaps unreasonable to expect from lawyers any more precise instruction, but concepts like necessity and extremity were a good deal easier to put on paper than to use as rules of conduct in action. Military officers were only too well aware that brother officers had been court-martialled or indicted in the criminal courts for failing to adhere to the fine line which separated excessive and inadequate force.[1] They could not even be certain that a court, sitting in judgement on their actions after the event, would accept in principle that the circumstances had necessitated the 'meeting of force with force'.[2] They did not have the mental training of lawyers, or the ingrained attitudes of policemen. Yet they were repeatedly thrown in the teeth of violent disorder and left to shift for themselves.[3]

Not long after Lord Naas's instructions were issued in March 1867, Strathnairn found that the lawyers were beginning to query them. The Judge Advocate-General felt that they should have been submitted to the English Law Officers as they 'involved such important questions of civil right as well as military duty'. Strathnairn protested that now his officers were 'placed in the most disagreeable predicament of being doubtful how they are to act under the difficult serious circumstances, for which the instructions were to provide'.[4] The whole point was that in emergencies there

[1] Most notably after the Bristol riots of 1831.

[2] Few put their dilemma as trenchantly as Sir Charles Napier: 'But as things are, the soldier has all the responsibility, while, at the same time, no precise power is confided to him, no line of conduct defined for his guidance. . . . His thoughts dwell upon the (to him) most interesting question, "shall I be *shot* for my forbearance by a court-martial, or *hanged* for over zeal by a jury?" . . . When a riot has taken place and all is over; when every thing is known: when fear, danger, confusion, hurry, all are past: then come forth the wise, the heroic, the patriotic, "How undecided the officer was", exclaims the first; "he ought to have charged at once" cries the second; "That redcoated butcher must be hanged", says the third' (*Remarks on Military Law and the Punishment of Flogging* (London, 1837), p. 47).

[3] Indeed, uncertainty over military powers extended down to ordinary guards on government property, who did not know if they had the right to arrest trespassers before the police arrived: C.-in-C. to Under-Secretary, 22 Dec. 1869 (Kilmainham MSS 1304).

[4] C.-in-C. Ireland to C.-in-C. Whitehall, n.d., 1867 (WO 32 6001).

was, in the nature of things, no time for the extensive analysis of legal issues from first principles, which is why soldiers (not only in Ireland) repeatedly asked for clear instructions to be drawn up in advance. In this case, it was not until January 1868 that the English Law Officers reached the conclusion that the March 1867 instructions applied in any case to 'troops not accompanied by a magistrate' (i.e. not called out in aid of the civil power) 'meeting with persons in open rebellion', and that they did not see that any other instructions were needed. Shortly afterwards, with incredible shortness of sight or memory, they added the further caution:

We do not know under what peculiar circumstances the Irish instructions of 1867 were framed and issued, but we would suggest that similar instructions should not be issued in England unless there is deemed to be a possibility of Troops coming into collision with civilians acting in numbers and with force in treasonable or felonious enterprises.[1]

The nature of the emergencies envisaged should be defined, they said, if instructions were desired—an apparently reasonable demand which was, in fact, merely a bureaucratic reformulation of the common-law precept that action must suit the necessities of each individual case. There was to be no permanent codification of emergency powers.

Nor was there to be any remission of military involvement in the maintenance of order after 1867. The 1868 elections and the 1872 Belfast riots were the most striking manifestations of still-endemic social violence, to which the army struggled to find responses. At Waterford in 1868

The rioters selected four cross roads, as the position best suited for the attack (on) cavalry escorting a long line of voters on cars.

The gaps, leading from the roads into the fields, had all been built up and heaps of large pointed stones piled up carefully for the assault of the troops along the road; obstacles were also placed in the road to prevent the passage of the escort, and as soon as it made its appearance at the cross roads, it was brought to a stand still by the obstacles, and received with volleys of stones from behind the enclosures bordering the roads. The cavalry unable to jump the enclosures were in many cases seriously hurt. The voters decamped from the cars

---

[1] Opinion of English Law Officers, 7 Jan.; further opinion, 17 Jan. 1868 (loc. cit.).

across the country at the first volley of stones, and refused to proceed to the Poll.[1]

Strathnairn concluded that this defeat was due to the use of cavalry without accompanying infantry ('on the requisition of the magistrates', inevitably), and henceforth a balance of arms—cavalry for maximum psychological effect, infantry to provide viable protection—was sought.[2] Yet though techniques might be susceptible to improvement (and the techniques used in Belfast under Strathnairn's less competent successor, Lord Sandhurst, in 1872 were demonstrably bad) the underlying problems could not be altered. After the violent clash at the Drogheda election, Strathnairn observed that 'troops had to endure the greatest and wanton outrage' simply because they were 'obeying orders and performing an unpopular duty'.[3] And as he grimly remarked to Larcom, 'when soldiers with arms in their hands are thus assaulted, it cannot be wondered at that retaliation, with all its regrettable consequences, should ensue'.[4]

The only effective way of avoiding this was to keep military forces concentrated, and deploy them only in such strength as would deter the biggest and most hostile crowd. Military pressure for such a policy seems to have been answered in 1869-70 by the re-formation of flying columns. According to Larcom's successor, Burke, these were not designed

for the purpose of making any military display throughout the country, which His Excellency considers, under present circumstances, would be highly injudicious, but solely to have troops in readiness to move at a moment's notice wherever their services may be required by the magistrates to act in support of the civil power in suppressing any disturbance, seditious meeting, or procession, or any attempt at an insurrectionary movement.[5]

---

[1] C.-in-C. to Secretary of State for War, 4 Sep. 1868 (loc. cit.).

[2] On military action at elections see D. N. Haire, 'In aid of the civil power, 1868-90', in F. S. L. Lyons and R. Hawkins, *Ireland Under the Union*, pp. 122-5.

[3] C.-in-C. Ireland to C.-in-C. Whitehall, 21 Nov. 1868 (BL Add. MS 42825, f. 177).

[4] C.-in-C. to Under-Secretary, 21 Mar. 1867 (Kilmainham MSS 1059).

[5] Circular to RMs, 9 Dec. 1869 (SPO, CSO RP1870/10814, quoted in Hawkins, 'An Army on Police Work', p. 78). (The columns were usually composed of some 300 infantry and 30 cavalry with 2 guns.)

The blithe disavowal of the 'display' function, earlier held to be their primary virtue, suggests that the reconstituted columns were mainly a sop to military prejudices. Still, it was simply not practicable to use troops in battalion strength at all times. The root problem had always to be faced, and it was put with feeling and clarity to the parliamentary committee of inquiry into elections in 1869 by General Mc-Murdo. He urged the need to remedy

one of the worst defects that a military system can be subject to in its relations with the people, viz. the habitual and reckless employment of troops armed solely with deadly weapons.[1]

He depicted the reaction which normally resulted: the provocation of an already 'excited populace', 'stimulated by the fact (well known to all) that soldiers dare not use their weapons'; so that the troops were at the mercy of the crowd 'till the extremity of violence has been reached'. At that point the magistrate would order the troops to act, and they had then only one course of action—to open fire.

In short, McMurdo said, when confronted by riot 'the effectiveness of the armed soldier suffers inversion of its normal state, while his liabilities are increased in alarming proportion to the immunity enjoyed by the citizen'. The present system of employing troops for crowd control was 'remarkable for its stupidity as for its severity'; its outstanding defect was

the absence of a due gradation in the employment of physical force; in other words, because no other form of organized force is brought to bear . . . between the defeated efforts of the police and the fatal action of the military.[2]

McMurdo's proposed solution, however—the arming of two-thirds of the troops on riot duty with batons rather than rifles—was unsatisfactory. It side-stepped the real issue of the proper role of military forces in civil crises, besides offering no persuasive evidence that baton-armed soldiers would be more effective than constabulary. If it had been implemented it would certainly have drawn the army deeper into ordinary policing, a further blurring of roles which

[1] Haire, op. cit. p. 129.
[2] Ibid. p. 130.

could not have been useful on either side of the civil–military boundary.

Sir John Michel, Commander-in-Chief in Ireland from 1875 to 1880, was surely right to urge in unambiguous form the classic view of the parameters within which the army could sensibly function in the suppression of disorder.

It does not appear to the Commander of the Forces advisable to use the military as a police force.

Sir John Michel considers that the troops should never be brought into contact with the people until after the police have been employed and failed.

The regular Troops are a repressive not a preventive force and should only be used in support (not in place) of the civil power.

When so employed they should in all cases be placed under cover and never called therefrom except when the police have failed, and then for the purpose of taking immediate and decisive action.

To employ troops, in a state of inaction, in the presence of a mob whom no civil force is endeavouring to repress, appears to the Commander of the Forces a grave mistake.[1]

But mobs, however formidable, were not to remain the only form of challenge to authority for which a method of control had to be found. After 1879 renewed agrarian agitation was accompanied by a new style and scale of diffused resistance which was to tax the authorities' resources still more severely.

(vi) *Law and order*

My firm belief is that the influence of great Britain in every Irish difficulty is not a domineering and tyrannizing, but a softening and mitigating influence; and that were Ireland detached from her political connection with this country . . . it might be that the strife of parties would there burst forth in a form calculated to strike horror through the land.

W. E. Gladstone[2]

The composite concept 'law and order' is one of the cornerstones of Anglo-Saxon political structures. Its weight and gravity are such that to label it a slogan seems to verge on irresponsible levity. It is, however, employed as such more

---

[1] DAG to Lord-Lieutenant, 10 Aug. 1877 (Kilmainham MSS 1069).
[2] HC Deb. 3s, clxxxi, c. 721, 17 Feb. 1866.

often than it is subjected to detached analysis.[1] The siames-
ing of the two distinct ideas is an assertion of belief in their
reciprocal validation: order is validated by justice; and law,
the attempt to implement just relations between men, is
validated by consensus—expressed in compliance, the
absence of resistance or disorder. The common-sense view
would be that they are the two sides of the same coin. In a
'healthy' society this may be true; indeed, the equation may
form a definition of such a society. But when disruption
occurs the coin has to fall on one side or the other. The
Governor Eyre controversy was very much about which side
should be uppermost, and not all could accept Huxley's
radical argument that order must, if necessary, be sacrificed
to legal principle. For the two sides are not really equivalent.
Order is the fundamental principle, and law, notwithstanding
its accretions of abstract notions of justice, functions primarily as an expression of the impulse to order.[2] Especially
was this the case in Ireland, which was in the last analysis
being governed in answer to a British strategic imperative
rather than any imagined duty to the people.[3]

Unfortunately, abstract justice was seen as an integral
part of English law (as *ius* and *iustitia* had been seen as
inseparable in Roman law), with the social corollary that
since the English framed and obeyed just laws, Englishmen must be naturally just. If, therefore, the enforcement
of the law provoked disorder, as it appeared to do in Ireland,
the fault lay in English eyes not with the law but with
the people. While Dicey certainly recognized that the
strength of law, and indeed the authority of governments,

---

[1] John Morley remarked that orators loved to use Irish issues to display
'all the grand common-places of their art', such as 'Law and Order' versus 'Reconciliation of the People' (*The Times*, 22 Sep. 1891): D. A. Hamer, 'The Irish
Question and Liberal Politics, 1886–1894', *Hist. J.* (1969), p. 512.

[2] The alternative legal formulation is simply 'peace': in Blackstone's words,
'peace is the very end and foundation of civil society'. For a luminous discussion
see Gatrell, 'Theft and violence', p. 254; and the penetrating analysis in A. P.
d'Entrèves, *The Notion of the State* (Oxford, 1967), 153–5.

[3] This important question deserves more space than it can be given here; it
certainly underlay the Tory policy of 'constructive unionism' and continued
to affect British policy into the submarine age. For a traditional survey cf.
C. Falls, 'Northern Ireland and the Defence of the British Isles', in T. Wilson
(ed.), *Ulster Under Home Rule* (Oxford, 1955), pp. 79–90.

stemmed not from physical power but from popular acceptance—

Laws derive three-fourths of their force not from the fears of law-breakers but from the assent of law-keepers; and legislation should, as a rule, correspond with the moral sentiment of the people. The maxim *quid leges sine moribus*, though it should always be balanced by the equally important maxim *quid mores sine legibus*, is one which no legislator dares neglect with impunity[1]—

his acceptance of this relativist perspective lacked the relish and conviction of his characteristically magisterial pronouncement that 'laws ought to be not only strong but just'.[2] Abstract justice should rule, and the English had a plain duty to enforce order in Ireland on the basis of just laws, even if Irish opinion repudiated those laws and that duty. The same point was put at the end of a more progressive, sophisticated analysis by Lord Spencer.

The Irish masses had been so long trodden down & crushed that they accepted without much argument measures & acts which their rulers imposed upon them.
  They have gradually been relieved & when they first feel their feet . . . they not unexpectedly break out in unreasonable demands etc.
  As they lose the impulses which caused them to fall to their knees, they will be on the road to greater independence of character.
  In the meanwhile however a heavy responsibility rests on the Executive to protect life & property which during the process of Reform stands in certain places in very great danger.[3]

So English governments rolled up their sleeves and dedicated themselves to the Sisyphean task of maintaining, or 'restoring', order in Ireland. They insisted that the Irish should follow the rules of 'civilized' political discourse, so well embodied in the British constitution. Even Liberals who cared deeply for Ireland could not tolerate political

---

[1] Dicey, *England's Case*, p. 114.

[2] Ibid. 104. Though it should be observed that not long before this Dicey had inveighed, in the American journal *The Nation*, against 'The prevalence of lawlessness in England', and cited as a major instance the 'constant suggestion' by modern Tories that 'the one thing needful' for Ireland was martial law (2 Aug. 1883, p. 96). This, of course, Dicey saw as the abnegation of 'the restrained and just force of law'.

[3] Spencer to Gladstone, 28 Dec. 1869 (BL Add. MS 44306, f. 200).

crime, or negotiate with extremists who used 'unconstitutional methods'.[1] Yet they never really answered the
question, How can you force men to be reasonable? Does
not the use of force destroy rather than promote reasonable-
ness? When Gladstone fumed that the 'resources of civilization had not yet been exhausted' in the battle against agrarian
violence, those resources were nothing more than military
force and repressive laws denounced in England itself as
unconstitutional. Gladstone disliked them, and disloyal Irishmen could scarcely be expected to regard them as a blessing.
'Every government must be true to its principles'—but to
vindicate the rule of law and order in Ireland, the government had to abandon its principles. This created a dilemma
from which it was never completely to escape.

[1] Conservatives naturally charged that Liberal pusillanimity over 'coercion'
encouraged Irish lawlessness. Cf. the extended critique in P. G. Cambray, 'Law
and Order', ch. VIII of *Irish Affairs and the Home Rule Question* (London,
1911), pp. 142–71.

3
Land War

I may notice a singularity in the use of popular language which has lately become common and which is most significant . . . It is the constant use of the word 'war' in reference to every sort of popular movement which would formerly have been called 'agitation' . . . the Irish disturbances are a 'land war', a 'rent war' . . . The title of Salvation and other armies, and the language which they consider appropriate to their functions, is a standing hint that those who conduct them mean to make bad people good by some sort of forcible means; and this use of language shows how ready people are in the present day to fall into what Hobbes called 'the monstrous confusion between power and liberty.'

Sir James Stephen[1]

(i) *Harvests and homesteads*

The mass of small tenants, who were the main support of the movement, understood very little of the land problem beyond the question of rent and the dread reality of eviction. There could be no ignorance upon these powers of landlordism in Ireland, but otherwise the people generally were the enemies of the system by force of Celtic instinct more than by any process of independent thought or conviction.

Michael Davitt[2]

The series of events which are generally known as the land war form a pivotal point in the development of modern Ireland at several levels. Fundamentally, and incontrovertibly, the land war created a revolution in land tenure: it forced the British government first to invert the legal relationship between landlord and tenant, and finally to deploy state funds and machinery to bring about a substantial transition

---

[1] Sir J. F. Stephen, 'On the Suppression of Boycotting', *The Nineteenth Century*, cxviii (Dec. 1886), 772.
[2] *Fall of Feudalism*, p. 164.

to peasant proprietorship. More generally, and debatably, it focused the political awareness of the previously unpoliticized rural population, and created a new consciousness of collective strength. Specifically, this involved the growth of new organizational forms (the Land League and, less immediately, the 'Parnellite' party) and the adoption of sophisticated methods of struggle, such as communally co-ordinated witholding of rent, and social sanctions against opponents—ostracism, or 'boycotting'. Alongside such ostensibly non-violent methods, there was an upsurge in agrarian crime, especially in intimidation and violent offences. By early 1880 in the Headford district of Galway

the injury to property includes cases of great brutality in the maiming of cattle, plucking of sheep, and their destruction by smashing the legs with stones and twisting them nearly off. The assaults on houses include night visits and administering unlawful oaths that the full rent should not be paid; attempts to murder by firing bullets through the windows in the direction of the bed, one case in which the shot was fired directly at the person, and cases in which the inmates have been 'carded'.[1]

The connection between this traditional form of resistance and the modern organizational structure of the Land League has for a century been a matter of dispute—at first the fierce disputes of national politics and state trials, later the less public but not always passionless disputes of historians.

The formative impact of the land war was as great as that of the famine itself. The careful scholarly dissection which it is now receiving is hardly premature; but, in the manner of such investigations, complexities are now being revealed which threaten to disintegrate the event altogether. When approaching revolutions (or alleged revolutions), the first step in historical revisionism is usually to pick out and stress —perhaps overstress—elements of continuity rather than rupture. It is true that over the *longue durée* some changes appear increasingly insignificant, and the absence of deep structural change is often striking. Contemporary understanding and estimation of events is frequently defective. And yet a reinterpretation which flattens contemporary

---

[1] H. A. Blake, Galway W. Riding, report 19 June 1880 (BL Add. MS 44624).

awareness of a distinct event or a decisive juncture is surely inadequate. The land war has not yet, certainly, been overrun by the levelling stream which has submerged the landmarks of the French Revolution, but the meteorological signs of an impending downpour are present.[1]

Here it will only be necessary to consider these historiographical developments in their bearing on a handful of critical issues. The most important of these are the place of violence in the land agitation, and the relationship between the 'land question' and the 'national question'—the economic and political forms of conflict. In one sense the function of violence is readily understandable, and was pithily expressed by William O'Brien: 'Violence is the only way of securing a hearing for moderation.'[2] Although British statesmen protested that this was not so—that if anything the reverse was the case—the political history of the nineteenth century unquestionably bore out the dictum. Observers comprehended, even if they deplored, the blurred, ambiguous, but ever-present link with elemental violent forces which deepened the political power of O'Connell and later of Parnell. Parnell himself declared at the start of his political career that 'No amount of eloquence could achieve what the fear of an impending insurrection—what the Clerkenwell explosion and the shot into the police van had achieved'.[3] Such a tribute from a parliamentarian to the physical-force organizations was to become rarer after the Phoenix Park assassinations. The organizations themselves were to go into a lengthy decline. The effect of agrarian violence, however, remained marked, even if it was unamenable to control. The difficulty is to determine its cause. Was it a blind reaction to economic distress? Was it a traditional mode of social regulation? Or was it, as the 1888 Special Commission alleged, the work of a criminal conspiracy which terrorized the people into acquiescence in its political aims? Were the likely political effects of

[1] Especially in the combative revisionism of Paul Bew's *Land and the National Question*; see also P. J. Drudy (ed.), *Ireland: Land, Politics and People* (Cambridge, 1982).

[2] M. McDonagh, *Life of William O'Brien*, quoted in C. C. O'Brien, *Parnell and his Party 1880–90* (Oxford, 1957), p. 69.

[3] Speech at Navan, Sept. 1875 (*United Ireland*, 5 Oct. 1895).

rural violence intended or understood by those who used it?

The traditional picture of Irish rural life, that is to say the picture painted by nationalists and tenant leaders, was one of total rather than relative deprivation. At least in the loosely defined 'west', an area approximating to the old province of Connacht, the mass of the people lived on the verge of starvation and eviction. The latter fate was, in the peasant view, equivalent to the former: physical survival might be bought through moral death—the loss of a self-respect which centred on land-holding—or emigration. Lack of security in the possession of homestead and income was, in this view, due primarily to a system of land-tenure in which parasitic landlords removed crippling quantities of wealth from their estates, and often from Ireland altogether. Landlords rack-rented, evicted at will, confiscated improvements made by tenants, and failed to make improvements themselves. The mass of the people lived literally on the margins: of the productive land as well as of survival. Thus an economic crisis such as the harvest failure and price collapse of 1878-9 triggered the resistance born of desperation.

This plain black-and-white picture mediated some important realities. In addition it reflected (where it did not actually create) a folk-attitude to reality which had its own importance. None the less, it has not proved satisfactory to modern analysts. In the first place, political scientists became increasingly sceptical about the apparently common-sense connection between desperation and resistance. They noticed that outright starvation produced paralysis rather than rebellion, since it destroyed the cohesion on which effective action depends. Even the crude low-level combinations of the Irish countryside might be subject to this law, and an apparently sophisticated response such as the land war would be most unlikely to emerge in conditions of disaster. Without falling into the excessively mechanistic conclusions originally propounded with Davies's 'J-curve' of 'rising and declining satisfactions', it is reasonable to assume that any movement which can be usefully characterized as rebellion or as a collective challenge to the government can only grow out of a prosperity sufficient to provide the resources for struggle. These resources include the mental capacity to organize, as well as the economic and human material for organization. Attitudes and ideas are as important as money, but what is probably most important of all is experience. Mobilization is difficult, as Charles Tilly has said.[1] It requires favourable circumstances. If the mobilization is to result in revolution, this is more likely when popular expectations have been rising for some time before being subjected to a sudden, possibly temporary, set-back.[2]

Secondly, detailed studies of the post-famine economy provided numerous indications that Ireland fitted the J-curve pattern remarkably well. Instead of the grim traditional picture of unrelieved poverty and eviction, investigators began to see an effective readjustment of the Irish agricultural economy and a marked improvement in living standards after the famine.[3] This improvement was maintained through the 1870s up to the crisis at the end of the decade. Moreover, it has been demonstrated that 'rack-renting' was more mythical than real by this time: although some estates did see massive rent increases, the average was well below what one recent authority estimates as the 'potential rental capacity' of the land.[4] Not only this, but the level of absenteeism amongst landlords was below 25 per cent in 1870,[5] while a study of the proportion of evicted tenants who were subsequently restored to their holdings either as tenants or as caretakers has shown that the extent of dispossession was enormously

---

[1] D. Snyder and C. Tilly, 'Hardship and Collective Violence in France, 1830 to 1960', *American Sociological Review*, xxxvii (1972), 526. Although in his most recent work, *From Mobilization to Revolution* (1978), Tilly concentrates almost exclusively on quantifiable material resources.

[2] However, the multiple-regression analysis of statistics by A. W. Orridge, 'Who Supported the Land War? An Aggregate-Data Analysis of Irish Agrarian Discontent, 1879–1882', *Economic and Social Review*, xii (1981), fails to confirm either the J-curve or the variants of the modernization thesis.

[3] The leading 'optimistic' reappraisal was B. L. Solow, *The Land Question and the Irish Economy 1870–1903* (Cambridge, Mass., 1971). Reappraisal has continued in the work of W. E. Vaughan, cited above and below.

[4] Vaughan, 'An assessment of the economic performance of Irish landlords, 1851–81', in Lyons and Hawkins (eds.) *Ireland Under the Union*, pp. 175 ff.

[5] S. Clark, *Social Origins of the Irish Land War*, pp. 157–9. This is the strict figure for absentees, i.e. those outside Ireland.

exaggerated.[1] Whilst these conclusions may underestimate the degree to which the original serving of a process of eviction was as provocative as the outcome, or to which atypical landlords played a disproportionate part in popular demonology, they show that objectively the situation out of which the crisis grew was not chronically disastrous. As one of the foremost revisionists has said,

The incidence of agrarian violence is inexplicable if the only cause sought is harsh behaviour on the part of landlords. The existence of turbulent groups amongst the tenantry prepared to make trouble on any pretext was equally important.[2]

Admittedly, even on under-rented estates, rents formed a large proportion of tenants' outgoings, and the fear of arbitrary increases and evictions may have contributed to what was undoubtedly chronic under-investment. The 'cheerful' or 'optimistic' reinterpretation of the post-famine economy may in its turn be substantially modified. Still, its most recent critic has gone no further than to say that 'it may well be' that the standard of living experienced by those who survived the famine did not markedly improve.[3]

Finally, it may be remarked that the worst violence occurred as a rule not so much at the time of maximum economic disruption and distress, as after the restoration of stability, in 1880-1.[4] The intensification of agrarian crime was, however, subject to marked local variations. As Joseph Lee has pointed out, Mayo was eighteen months ahead of Kerry in what he calls the 'agitation calendar'.[5] This fact was related to the significant economic differences between the west and the south-west, but it may also have been due to the differential spread of 'agitation' (whether or not one identifies this with 'conspiracy').

The question is how this agitation spread, and this question is linked with the fundamental question of the nature of the land war. Was this in fact a 'collective challenge' of a group

[1] Solow, op. cit. p. 54-7.

[2] Vaughan, 'Landlord and Tenant relations', p. 220.

[3] C. Ó Grada, 'Agricultural head-rents, pre-famine and post-famine', *Economic and Social Review*, v (1974), 391.

[4] J. S. Donnelly, *The Land and the People of Nineteenth Century Cork* (London, 1975), p. 377.

[5] Lee, *Modernization of Irish Society*, p. 83.

—in the first instance an alliance of labourers, small tenants, shopkeepers, publicans—aiming at the redistribution of power in the country?[1] If so we might expect to find agrarian crime intensifying, not spontaneously in response to immediate economic dislocation, but according to the growth of the challenging organization, the Land League. Such indeed was the belief of the administrators of Ireland in the early 1880s, and in particular of the RIC, on whose information the government (and the British conservative press) depended. Such, as has been said, was the belief of the Special Commission which investigated the connection between 'Parnellism and crime' at the end of the decade.

There was no shortage of evidence to sustain this belief. The Special Commission assembled a daunting mass of material which, even when rendered down into a popular edition, could be taken as forming a comprehensive indictment.[2] To take a single example of this material, the report drawn up by the West Cork RIC analysing outrages in Ballydehob ran to fourteen printed pages, commencing with the report of a speech by Parnell at Cork on 5 October 1879, in which he said 'The good landlords will reduce their rents, but what will the bad landlords do?' When voices shouted 'Shoot them', neither Parnell nor anyone on the platform rebuked the expression. The report then listed a number of speeches in 1880 and 1881, including Parnell's declaration at Cork on 3 October 1880 that ' "We are determined to take the power of governing Ireland out of the hands of the English Parliament and people, and transfer it to the hands of our own people" . . . (Cheers.)'. According to the RIC, the surrounding countryside was 'remarkably quiet and peaceable' before the establishment of the Land League in Ballydehob on 12 September 1880. Thereafter notices began to appear such as 'Notice No. 1 to farmers':

Notice is hereby given that any farmer who has not paid rent yet, not to pay more than Griffith's valuation. If they do they are sure to

---

[1] Clark, *Social Origins*, ch. 8.
[2] *Reprint of the . . . proceedings . . . under the Special Commission Act 1888*, 12 vols. (London, 1890); edited extracts in Liberal Unionist Association, *Parnell Commission Report* (London, 1890).

be visited by Rory, junior, who is supplied with Notter's powder and ball. He is expected on Wednesday next to meet Sam Jago, agent.

(Notter was a local magistrate who had threatened that 'the people should get powder and ball'.) Not until May and June next year, however, were attacks actually made—on, amongst others, Notter—including one by a massive crowd of people, allegedly totalling 5,000, assembled by the blowing of horns and 'in response to various horsemen riding through the country', on the police barrack at Skull. The most sustained local campaign seems to have been that against Robert Swanton and his son George, both JPs: the former was shot at and lost an eye in May, and the latter was shot at in June. Amongst a series of threatening notices signed by 'Rory of the Hills' or 'Captain Moonlight', was one found on 31 July which declared (very irregularly written on an old envelope),

> One thing more I have to say
> Is to shun those peelers without delay
> And not to give the country say
> That you should be a traitor
> Robert, George, and Daly too!
> Woe be to them, for I am true,
> A Croppy-still for ever.
>
> GEORGE
>
> You'll go.[1]

Despite its crude execution, such a notice carried a definitely political message.

The form of reasoning employed by the RIC and the Special Commission to demonstrate the direct link between the Land League and outrage was too inferential to be conclusive.[2]

---

[1] SPO, Dublin, INL MSS, No. 10. Richard Daly, mentioned here, had a house burned in Oct. and this less elegant notice posted: 'Dear Richardeen, I am going to pay you a small compliment that is only too well due to you, you pimping, soupcapping, bastard! Take my word, as sure as God is in heaven I will stain my hands in your blood . . . Yours truly, Captain Moonlight & Co.'

[2] See the discussion of the League's criminal record in Bew, *Land and the National Question*, pp. 150-1, and section (iv) below; also the thoughtful general analysis of agrarian crime in Garvin, *Evolution of Irish Nationalist Politics*, pp. 73-8.

In his incisive analysis of outrage in Kerry, which became one of the three most disturbed counties (the others being Mayo and Galway) late in 1880, Joseph Lee argued that although the idea of 'conspiracy' looked more tenable there than in Connacht, this was superficial.[1] The timing of the intensification of outrage was governed by the slower onset and recovery of crisis in dairying, the economic foundation of the southwest. The crucial precondition for the explosion was demographic: the result of a dramatic increase in age at marriage, coupled with a 2 per cent increase in population during the decade 1871–81. This produced an abnormally large group of discontented single men, consigned to the status of 'boys'.[2]

This point is undoubtedly important. It is not altogether unlikely that 'moonlighting' functioned as a form of outdoor relief for this group. A still more detailed study of county Cork has revealed similar conditions, and added the perspective of sexual frustration to that of social inadequacy in explaining willingness to go 'out' with agrarian bands.[3] This may bear some relationship to the persistent cruelty of agrarian outrages, which impressed many observers, not all as unsympathetic as Samuel Hussey.[4] The notorious land-agent's observation was, however, not entirely malicious—

It is a curious thing that the Irish and the Italian are the two most poetic and most sensitive races of Europe, and are also the two which exhibit the greatest indifference to the sufferings of dumb animals.[5]

The humane and sympathetic J. L. Hammond suggested that Ireland merely suffered from an inadequate urban base for the civilizing influence, and remarked that Davitt, 'who had the strongest dislike of the mutilation of animals in the agrarian war, had lived as boy and young man in a town'.[6]

[1] Although there seems to be some discrepancy in the use of the term 'conspiracy': Lee is prepared to attribute importance to the 'outstanding local leadership' of Tim Harrington, editor of the *Kerry Sentinel: Modernisation*, pp. 79–84.

[2] But not labourers, who played no positive part in the Land War: Orridge, op. cit. 222–3.

[3] Donnelly, op. cit. pp. 249–50.

[4] e.g. B. Becker, *Disturbed Ireland*, pp. 79–80.

[5] S. M. Hussey, *The Reminiscences of an Irish Land Agent* (London, 1904), p. 221.

[6] Hammond, *Gladstone and the Irish Nation*, p. 43. For instances of English abhorrence see J. Marlow, *Captain Boycott*, pp. 226–7.

The deep bedrock of agrarian violence can probably not be attributed either to conspiracy (at least in the common definition of the term) or to immediate economic crisis.[1] The most resonant of all acts of violence in this period was the assassination of the Earl of Leitrim and two of his retainers in Co. Donegal on 2 April 1878, long before the failure of crops or the crisis in butter markets, and before the foundation of the League. Lord Leitrim's intentions have been subsequently shown to have been honourable, in so far as his programme of evictions was designed to rationalize landholdings on his huge estates and to prevent another famine, but he was regarded as a 'bad landlord' in the classic mould. His killing, though it was in one sense a social act—the killers were widely known to the community, and were sheltered from 'justice'—appears to have been primarily an act of personal vengeance. Even Davitt accepted that the assassination was due not to a general hostility to landlordism but to a specific belief that Leitrim had dishonoured a tenant's daughter.[2]

Notwithstanding this, it is impossible to mistake the significance of the Land League. At the national (that is to say, country-wide) level its novelty was dramatic. Some of this novelty may be seen in the distinction drawn by Davitt at the Westport meeting on 8 June 1879: 'Instead of "agitate, agitate", the cry of the present should be "organize, organize".' From the government's standpoint, as will be seen, it certainly appeared as the 'challenging collectivity' that it has been recently labelled. But this perspective can hardly have had much immediate relevance to the peasantry who joined the organization, for whom it performed more limited functions. Even Clark's analysis, which determinedly propounds the idea of a collective challenge for power at national level, shows that throughout the life of the Land League economic demands dominated its programme.[3] The great slogans which formed a crucial part of the League's working

[1] Bew, *Land and the National Question*, p. 32, stresses the wide range of tenant demands.

[2] Davitt, *Fall of Feudalism*, pp. 142-3.

[3] Clark, *Social Origins*, pp. 297-9; see also P. Bew's further thoughts in 'The Land League ideal: achievements and contradictions', in Drudy (ed.), *Ireland*, p. 81, on 'the level of consciousness of the small men'.

methods were calculated to have the most straightforward attraction: such as Parnell's call at the Westport meeting to 'Hold a firm grip of your homesteads', and the great cry 'Hold the harvest!' which arose in mid August 1880.

Without losing sight of its novelty, it is important to stress that the Land League, in its local manifestation, was in many ways just the biggest and most successful of the old 'associations'. There was little that was new about its methods: meetings, the demand for rent reduction (to 'Griffith's valuation', itself a standard of some antiquity by 1880) enforced by intimidation, directed primarily at recalcitrant tenants, rather than landlords or even agents.[1] The mass of threatening letters and notices which formed a large proportion of agrarian offences reported by the RIC were usually traditional in sentiment and signature, even if Rory, Captain Moonlight, or Bombshell sometimes declared their alliance with Parnell—who was rapidly transformed into a quasi-legendary figure for the 'hillside men'. The 'witnessing' of evictions by popular assemblies and the use of violence against process-servers were likewise traditional; as was the extraordinary formalism of the separate female and male participation in the 'battle' of Carraroe.[2]

The effect of the land war in 1880 was obtained through the intensification of old methods of struggle rather than the development of new ones; but the impact could be near-total, at least in the early stages. For instance, a Mayo resident magistrate reported in June 1880

I regret to state that I never remember lawlessness to have assumed anything like its present proportions in my district; this after over six years' residence here: Houses fired into at night; combination against rent paying, and where rent is paid it is almost done on tenant's own terms or sought to be so; threatening letters almost innumerable; where evictions take place the evicted restored to their former holdings within a few hours by an irresponsible body . . . the combination against process serving general, so much so that the process server has to be accompanied by a large force of police; on two occasions, where some processes for rent were to be served, I had to attend with 100 police and two sub-Inspectors; even with this large force stones were thrown at the police.[3]

---

[1] Clark, op. cit. pp. 309–26.
[2] Davitt, op. cit. pp. 213–18.
[3] J. T. M'Sheehy to Chief Secretary, 20 June 1880 (PRO CAB. 37/2).

The main evidence of modernization in the land struggle lies in the decline of the most awful tortures such as carding, and the growth of ostracism, the most widely publicized of land-war methods. The Land League, which earnestly disclaimed any connection with violent crime (indeed Davitt held that 'many of these acts' were perpetrated by enemies of the League, while many more were bogus), saw moral force as a powerful replacement for, or supplement to, the physical force which many ex-IRB men like Davitt had abandoned as inadequate. Ostracism was the most effective manifestation of this. At the Ennis meeting on 19 September 1880 Parnell was able to reply to the habitual cries of 'Shoot him' with his 'better way' of putting offenders into 'moral Coventry':

depend upon it if the population of a county in Ireland carry out this doctrine, there will be no man so full of avarice, so lost to shame, as to dare the public opinion of all right-thinking men within the county and to transgress your unwritten code of laws.[1]

It may be, as has recently been argued, that the role of the 'boycott' during the land war was exaggerated by Land League propaganda, and that its effectiveness was more mythical than real.[2] In a sense this merely underlines its publicity value, of which Leaguers were profoundly conscious. But ostracism was not an entirely new method— nor indeed was it entirely non-violent. Davitt was aware of many precedents; he also, interestingly, tried to distinguish between ostracism directed against land-grabbers—which had previously been known as 'social excommunication'— and that applied to a landlord or agent. (These latter were presumably already excommunicated on religious grounds, and partially so on class grounds.) His view was that the term 'boycott' should only be used of the second form of ostracism.[3] The connection between ostracism and violence was indirect but pervasive. It was adumbrated in a straightforward way by Parnell (in America, where he spoke to an audience which

---

[1] Police reporter's account; F. S. L. Lyons, *Charles Stewart Parnell* (London, 1977), p. 134.
[2] Bew, *Land and the National Question*, pp. 221-2.
[3] Davitt, *Fall*, p. 274; on the history of ostracism see pp. 279-82.

demanded a hard-hitting manner of speech) as early as December 1879:

> Well, it may be accepted as an axiom that you cannot effect a social revolution by dealing with it with kid gloves. Of course, if any farmers have burned the crops of their neighbours, or destroyed their cattle, because they have paid their rent, those farmers are not only wrong, but they are fools, for they have to pay the cost . . . But a certain amount of pressure from public opinion, which in such cases is apt occasionally to manifest itself in unpleasant ways, must be brought to bear upon those who are weak and cowardly.[1]

Public opinion, which often incorporated private or factional feuds, could be rough. Yet outright violence was often unnecessary, because the anticipation of punishment was enough. Non-violence could function admirably with communal controls that were essentially defensive; an outright challenge to the government by these means, however, required a level of control and sophistication that was seldom present at this stage. More common was the sort of hopeful archaism displayed at a meeting near Balla, Co. Mayo, in November 1880—intended as a demonstration against an eviction (at Loonamore) which was not in the end carried out, it turned into an address by Parnell on the subject of non-violence. His audience had arrived as follows:

> About 2½ p.m. at least 4000 persons were seen approaching . . . in military order and under control of leaders—it was the largest and most formidable gathering I have yet seen in this district. They moved in a remarkably compact and military organized form—marched well in fours . . . had fewer imitation pikes &c. than usual, but were nearly all armed with stout sticks . . . Their demeanour struck me and many others present as much more determined than on any former occasion —and much more under the control of the persons directing their movements[2]—

and was halted by a bugler on horseback. Old patterns of behaviour persisted: if the people were mobilizing, it was according to 1798 precedents. Bernard Becker, a journalist who analysed the west in some depth at this time, and who witnessed the Boycott affair, was quite clear about the limits of their political awareness.

---

[1] Interview in *New York Herald*, 21 Dec. 1879: *Parnell Commission Report*, p. 18.

[2] Maj. Wyse, RM, Report, 23 Nov. 1880 (SPO, CSO RP 1880/12061).

Very few in Mayo, and hardly anybody at all in Connemara, seem to take any account of Home Rule, or of any other rule except that of the Land League. The possibility of a parliament on College-green affects the people of the West far less than the remotest chance of securing some share of the land. If ever popular disaffection were purely agrarian, it is now, so far as this part of Ireland is concerned.[1]

(ii) *New departures*

> The numerical strength of the strongest revolutionary organization by no means measured the strength of the feeling for complete independence. Millions of Irishmen who were and are separatists in conviction would on no account become members of a secret society.
>
> Michael Davitt[2]

The spontaneous action of the rural population, recreating the sort of turmoil which had appeared in the 1830s and in 1870, would inevitably have had political effects. Violent expression of 'grievances' would have brought some measure of redress, though by now the government had reached the limit of the sort of redress which could be envisaged within the traditional English view of the law of contract. When Parnell declared in September 1880 that 'the measure of the land bill next session will be the measure of your activity and energy this winter', he was in one sense stating the obvious. However, the fact that this incitement to agitation was spoken by a man already marked as a dominant figure in constitutional politics transformed the political impact of rural disturbance. Hitherto such disturbance had for the most part been inarticulate, if not altogether disorganized or directionless. Now it was politicized from the top. All agrarian 'crime', no matter by whom it was carried out or for what object, was taken to be part of a political challenge—to make Ireland ungovernable on British terms, or at least landlord terms. The inchoate and violent land struggle was adopted by vocal, determined political groups which had previously treated it with caution: the Fenians and the parliamentarians.

[1] *Disturbed Ireland: being the letters written during the winter of 1880–81* (London, 1881), p. 85.
[2] *Fall of Feudalism*, pp. 119–20.

The Fenian movement had been becalmed since the end of the 1860s. This was true not only of the organization in Ireland, but also of the powerful Fenian movement proper in the United States. Indeed, the latter gave way to the fissiparous tendency which has so often damaged Irish nationalist groupings. A brief revitalization caused by the arrival of released Fenian prisoners in 1871 involved the attempt by the 'Cuba Five' to establish a new organization, the Irish Confederation, whose Directory would co-ordinate all nationalist endeavours. But after holding an apparently successful first annual convention in 1872 the new group suddenly collapsed. Its members drifted back into the Fenians or the home rule movement, and henceforth the most vital Irish American grouping was to remain the Clan na Gael. Founded in 1867 by IRB men who had decamped from Ireland when Habeas Corpus was suspended, it was remarkably successful in maintaining secrecy in its early years. Not so the Fenians, who had been penetrated by the British amateur spy (not, as he has often been called, an 'informer') Henri Le Caron, whose information wrecked the second Fenian attempt at an invasion of Canada in 1870.[1] The final raid into Manitoba in 1871 ended this ill-conceived mode of action. More successful, though markedly less ambitious—or more realistic—was the Clan na Gael's rescue of six prisoners from the penal colony at Fremantle, Western Australia, using the whaling vessel *Catalpa*.[2] Thereafter the Clan's thinking drifted further in a nautical direction, and it made a remarkable contribution to the development of naval technology by funding the experimental Holland submarine. (The Clan's pioneering record in military technology was to be maintained some fifty years later when it assisted at the birth of the Thompson sub-machine-gun.) But the hoped-for Fenian navy never became an operational prospect.[3]

Of greater eventual importance was another breakaway

[1] H. Le Caron, *Twenty-Five Years in the Secret Service* (16th edn., London, 1893) pp. 81–99.

[2] S. Ó Luing, *Fremantle Mission* (Tralee, 1965), provides a full account, unfortunately citing no sources.

[3] D'Arcy, *Fenian Movement in the United States*; K. R. M. Short, *The Dynamite War* (Dublin, 1979), p. 35 ff., on submarine developments.

movement, whose inspiration was the Phoenix Society veteran O'Donovan Rossa. The master-concept of this group was 'skirmishing', outlined thus in the *Irish World*:

We are not now advising a general insurrection . . . But we believe in action nevertheless. A few active, intrepid and intelligent men can do so much to annoy and hurt England. The Irish cause requires skirmishers. It requires a little band of heroes who will initiate and keep up without intermission a guerrilla warfare—men who will fly over land and sea like invisible beings—now striking the enemy in Ireland, now in India, now in England itself, as occasion may present.[1]

This early example of the manipulation of the idea of guerrilla warfare towards a system of sporadic terrorist attacks is of some significance for the future. For the time being, however, Rossa's establishment of a 'Skirmishing Fund', in March 1876 was not followed by any immediate action.[2] Still, John Boyle O'Reilly was brought back into the physical-force fold, admitting in 1878 that movements outside constitutional agitation were necessary in order to compel British attention. Use of the knife and the bullet was regrettable, but the blame lay with the 'merciless country that has filled Irish hearts with hatred and violence towards her'.[3]

An even more thoroughgoing intransigence continued to mark the leadership of the IRB in Ireland during the 1870s. It was personified in the president of the Supreme Council, Charles Kickham, partially incapacitated by the effects of a youthful gunpowder accident. Kickham's deafness and increasing blindness symbolized his detachment from the real world of politics and economics (a detachment shared, however, by the robust John O'Leary). The Supreme Council's doctrinaire rigidity was increasingly unsatisfactory to the more practical-minded members of the brotherhood, and from 1873 onwards a development of great political importance began to occur. John O'Connor Power, a senior IRB man, moved openly towards the new Home Rule League and stood for parliament in 1874. Still more remarkably,

---

[1] *Irish World*, 4 Dec. 1875, quoted in Short, op. cit. 38.

[2] Substantial sums were in fact paid from the fund for the development of the Holland boat: ibid. 43.

[3] Boston *Pilot*, 21 Sep. 1878; O'Reilly had earlier lost faith: D'Arcy, *Fenian Movement*, pp. 386, 398.

Joseph Gillis Biggar, elected for Cavan as a Home Ruler, was subsequently sworn into the IRB and co-opted on to the Supreme Council.[1]

The emergence of what has recently been labelled 'neo-Fenianism'—a loose entity which amounted to a tendency rather than a splinter group—involved not only a *rapprochement* with parliamentarianism, but also a commitment to the land struggle. The traditionalists Kickham and O'Leary saw this latter as a selfish and sordid grab by the tenantry at the expense of other classes—the landlords as well as the 'labourers and mechanics'. Kickham, indeed, regarded the agrarian campaign as wicked, and was to denounce the Land League agitation as Whiteboyism.[2] The fact that many IRB men took a more sympathetic, or less idealist, attitude was attested by the appearance of the term 'Ribbon Fenianism' to denote links between the two organizations in some localities in the 1870s.[3] The most striking deviation from hard-line Fenianism was the 'New Departure' of 1879. This series of negotiations drew its main impact from the recognition by Fenians, especially John Devoy's American movement, of the validity of constitutional methods when controlled by a man such as Parnell. As Republicans were once again to do in the 1920s, some Fenians now decided that it was possible to take the oath required to sit in parliament without being guilty of treason to the Republic. T. C. Luby explained to O'Leary that Parnell's agitation was 'not supplicatory like O'Connell's, not to say Butt's': it was 'aggressive, semi-belligerent . . . He wrests Irish rights against the will or wish of those forced to concede him. I efface myself for the public good.'[4] This was in 1882, by which time Parnell's stature was unmistakable. Devoy's recognition of

---

[1] T. W. Moody, *Davitt and Irish Revolution 1846–82* (Oxford, 1981), p. 129; Moody and Ó Broin, 'IRB Supreme Council', pp. 290–2. Comerford, *Kickham*, p. 124

[2] Comerford, pp. 146–54, suggests that Kickham's objection to the League was that by presuming to seek a solution to the land question prior to independence it challenged his belief that one objective was unattainable without the other; and, perhaps more fundamentally, 'he could never admit even to himself that nationalism might be founded on mere grievances'.

[3] Bew, *Land and the National Question*, p. 42, points out that this was never a systematic process.

[4] Luby to O'Leary, NLI MS 5926.

Parnell's potential early in 1879 was characteristically perceptive, though the credit for this must go primarily to
Davitt, who built the main bridge between the physical-
force and moral-force mentalities.

Davitt's evolution seems, by his own account, to have
been quite rapid. He first met Parnell in 1877, and in May
of the next year he was still expounding the idea of a revolutionary vanguard even more select than the IRB:

Heretofore the plan had been to recruit members anyhow and anywhere, and then, with the boast of a 'very strong' body numerically,
to think of obtaining weapons with which to arm the members. Better
to make the accumulation of arms a prior consideration of the swearing-
in of men under conditions which scarcely suggested a common-sense
protection against unsteady or disreputable elements.[1]

But this 'reorganized society' was not to confine its activity
to conspiracy and arms, with 'only the eternal expectation
of a Russian or American war with England as the forlorn
hope of an Irish Republic'. It should operate on the constitutional front, making an appeal to 'all men of separatist
principles', to create a parliamentary party of high calibre
which, if it were thwarted at Westminster, might return to
Ireland as the nucleus of national resistance. This vision,
adumbrating the Sinn Féin doctrine later derived by Arthur
Griffith from his study of the Hungarian struggle against
Austria, was far from being Parnell's way. For this reason
amongst others, the New Departure, shadowy and disputed
in its particulars, was not the blueprint for the agitation of
1879-82. As the historian who has done most to illuminate
the negotiations and their consequences has said, although
there were connections between the New Departure and the
Land League, 'the relationship was not that between a plan
and its execution'.[2]

However, as is so often the case, illusion did perfectly
satisfactory duty for reality. The idea of a broad nationalist
coalition, or what would later be called a 'front', was out-

---

[1] *Fall of Feudalism*, p. 111.

[2] T. W. Moody, 'The new departure in Irish politics, 1878-9', in H. A. Cronne
et al., *Essays in British and Irish History* (London, 1949); cf. Bew's 'modifica-
tions' of this conclusion, op. cit. pp. 72-3; and Moody, *Davitt*, ch. VII, which
underlines the intiative of Devoy.

wardly attractive, logical and impressive. In the nature of
things it was also temporary, and its cohesion while it
lasted depended to a great extent on its very vagueness.
As Davitt himself recognized, there was nothing really new
about the combination of moral and physical force; nor was
it possible to define the relationship clearly.[1] What had
altered was that 'extreme nationalists' were no longer prepared to provide constitutionalists with strong arguments
through futile efforts at revolution which 'purchased penal
servitude for themselves'.

The division of penalty and concession was too one-sided to be always
encouraging to the men of action, and the time had come when greater
gains might hopefully be counted upon from a rational policy of
making the open movement more revolutionary in aim and purpose,
if not in method, and . . . trying to interrupt the order which had
hitherto obtained in alternate Irish movements by combining both,
as far as practicable.[2]

In all this, the demoralization of the physical force group
was more obvious than was the specific content and direction
of the 'common-sense plan of semi-revolutionary action'.
Frustrated Fenians who refused to retreat into Rossa's
perpetual embittered defiance could take comfort from the
sense of action generated by the dynamic Parnellite party.
The political weight of the latter, stemming from success
in the 1880 general election, was in turn strengthened by
its indeterminate but universally credited link with the men
of violence.

The Land League performed the function of front-
organization with overwhelming success. There was some
genuine fusion of parliamentary, agrarian, and insurrectionist groups in the personnel of the local League branches,
and from the start these displayed a consciousness somewhat
wider than the bounds of the disputed fields. It appears that
few, if any, rural branches were formed on the basis of
specific estates, in spite of the League's advice.[3] The Land

[1] *Fall of Feudalism*, pp. 116-22.

[2] Ibid. pp. 122-3.

[3] This is one of the most interesting conclusions suggested by the research
of Clark, *Social Origins*, p. 294. See also 'The social composition of the Land
League', *Irish Historical Studies*, xvii (1971), and 'The political mobilization of
Irish farmers', *Canadian Review of Sociology and Anthropology*, xii (1975).

League's infrastructure was moulded primarily by a larger structure based on the Catholic church, and branches were formed around the parish or half-parish. Not only this, but the lower clergy were involved in the League in ways which would have been inconceivable with earlier, 'anarchic' agrarian combinations. Neo-Fenians and priests shared platforms at Land meetings without undue strain: the latter either realized that they could not afford to repudiate a movement so sweeping without damaging—perhaps destroying—their influence over public opinion; or abandoned with some relief the hostility which they had been obliged to maintain towards agrarian or 'Mazzinian' secret societies. For the duration of the land war the Catholic church broke with conservative views of the Land League as anarchy or communism made manifest. This extraordinary volte-face may, indeed, have been a tacit recognition that the League had passed beyond the threshold of illegal challenge and become in effect the legitimate political authority, the source rather than the breaker of law.[1]

The position of the church in the land war has been extensively examined in recent years by Emmet Larkin: nowhere was its reaction more concisely expressed than by Bishop MacEvilly of Galway in the early months of the agitation.

Whether the priests will it or no, the meetings will be held. Their people will assemble under the pressure of threatened famine to expound their wrongs to landlords and government; if the priests keep aloof these meetings will be scenes of disorder; if the priests attend they will keep the people attached to them.[2]

From this time the Catholic clergy were essentially followers rather than leaders of public opinion: their acquiescence in the great movement beyond their control merely disguised

---

[1] E. Larkin, 'Church, State and Nation in Modern Ireland', *American Historical Review*, lxxx (1975), 1263, is the most forceful if infelicitous expression of this view. Cf. also *The Roman Catholic Church and the Creation of the Modern Irish State 1878-1886* (Philadelphia, 1975). It is notable, though, that even the anti-Fenian Cardinal Cullen spoke of 'those who had an earlier right to the land' than that of the landlords: E. D. Steele, 'Cardinal Cullen and Irish Nationality', *IHS* xix (1975).

[2] J. MacEvilly to Kirby, 11 Dec. 1879: Larkin, 'Church, State and Nation', p. 1265.

the limits of their power, and kept some Fenians and 'God-less nobodies' out of positions of 'leadership' in the League.[1]

At the same time, the church's accommodation with the League vitally enhanced the strength—if hardly the modern-ity—of the organization. As a result partly of this and still more of Parnell's dramatically increasing political stature (itself dependent in part on clerical acceptance, but mainly on the charisma of the combative new parliamentary group), the League began to appear as more than a resistance move-ment. Contemporary observers frequently spoke of it as a 'rival government', indeed, in some areas, the only effective government. The novelty of this should not be overstated: earlier writers had spoken of the unseen government of the 'associations' which enforced the unwritten law. Moreover, the efficiency and organizational depth of the League can easily be overestimated. One of its most acute observers and critics, Anna Parnell, whose Ladies' Land League came to the fore after the League was suppressed in 1881, found that the local organization had been practically non-existent in some areas. The concentration on a few 'monster meetings' was a cover for slapdash methods, and absence of real day-to-day commitment.[2] But it would be perverse to deny that the alignment of forces in 1870–80 created revolution-ary possibilities which exceeded even those inherent in the emancipation movement. Not until after 1882, perhaps, was there to be a fully political focus and an overtly political machine. Yet the mere existence of a national—in the sense of supra-local—organization fronted by national*ist* politicians was bound to stretch the perspectives of local groups. A con-ceptual expansion, which some recent writers have seen as the creation of a new consciousness, was almost inevitable. The League fostered, where it did not articulate, the identi-fication of basic local demands with wider political issues, which in themselves lacked much meaning for the peasantry.[3]

---

[1] For a brilliant discussion of the function of the church in relation to social modernization see D. Miller, 'Irish Catholicism and the Great Famine', *Journal of Social History* (Fall 1975).

[2] 'The Tale of a Great Sham', Anna Parnell MSS, NLI MS 12144; see the lucid discussion in R. F. Foster, *Charles Stewart Parnell: The Man and his Family* (Hassocks, 1976), pp. 260–83.

[3] Larkin, op. cit. 1263; Lee, op. cit. 94–6, 100.

'Land to the tillers' might carry in varied if unspecified ways the abstract principle of national freedom.

The League did not set itself to become an embryo state: in particular it had no mechanism for controlling the use of violent sanctions on which much of its coercive power rested.[1] But its very existence altered the implications of even uncontrolled violence. The resulting situation has been sensitively outlined by Sam Clark; 'because farmers did more than commit outrages, outrage itself became more effective; they were now able to make clear why they were angry and to leave no room for doubt [as to] why outrages were being committed'. Agrarian crime, as well as being a method by which the decrees of the Land League were enforced, also meant that 'the government could ignore demands made by the League only at its peril, and at the peril of every land-lord and land agent in the West of Ireland'.[2] Undoubtedly this is how the government saw the matter. The peril, however, did not arise from any direct challenge to the state. There was no threat of insurrection or invasion such as had permitted alarm about the insubstantial manifestations of 1803, 1848, or 1867. It was the derogation of law, the unenforceability of the royal writ, which constituted the gage which the government could not avoid picking up. The direct personal peril to land agents and process-servers meant, in abstract political terms, the breakdown of law and order.

(iii) *Protection of person and property*

That we beg to call the attention of the government to the new phase into which the land meetings have entered. That now they are held for the purpose of terrorism wherever ejectments are to be executed and to denounce individuals where farms are taken after being given up even where voluntary by their former occupiers. That these cannot be

---

[1] It is doubtful whether agrarian outrage was co-ordinated as is suggested in Clark, 'Political mobilization', pp. 488, 493, where it is taken to amount to 'rebellion', Lyons's atmospheric concept 'penumbra of outrage' (*Ireland since the Famine*, p. 160), may be preferred. But cf. Garvin, op. cit. 77–8.

[2] Clark, 'Social composition', p. 464.

considered legal or constitutional meetings and we now call
upon the government to stop them.

Petition of magistrates meeting in Castlebar, 30
December 1879[1]

The Land League challenge solidified in the dying months
of Disraeli's last administration. The man who had once
encapsulated with un-British perception the fundamental
problem of the British–Irish relationship—who had admitted
that in any independent country the remedy for the defects
in the Irish economy and government would be revolution—
was no longer capable of any imaginative response. Conservatives had run out of patience. Salisbury, surveying the Irish
problem since the union, testily wrote that

The internal history of Ireland has been a continuous tempest of agitation, broken by occasional flashes of insurrection. The legislation of
the period has been a continuous stream of concession.[2]

Goschen, in a revealing comment, was to brand Irish home
rule as 'bastard nationalism'. It was the issue of separation,
which now seemed to be fusing with the endemic land crisis,
that sharpened English reactions. Even radicals who wanted
to do the best for Ireland jibbed on this issue. Bradlaugh,
who had helped to draft a Fenian proclamation against landlordism in 1867, was clear by the 1870s that 'If Britain is to
hold any place in the world at all, it cannot afford to lose
Ireland'.[3] Bright felt the same: as Gladstone observed to
Granville in 1869, there was a 'very large residuum of John
Bull in him'. By 1881 Bright was openly engaging in a sort
of Mancunocentric mockery of the laziness of Irish workers.[4]

These great issues of status and strategy were less apparent
in 1880 than the perennial issue of law and order, though the
two were connected in Britain's self-image as a world guaran-
tor of law and civilization. It was the undermining of the

---

[1] SPO, CSO RP 1880/581.

[2] 'Disintegration', *Quarterly Review* (Oct. 1883), p. 585.

[3] *National Reformer*, 10 Oct. 1871: F. D'Arcy, 'Charles Bradlaugh and the
Irish question: a study in the nature and limits of British radicalism, 1853–91',
in A. Cosgrove and D. McCartney (edd.), *Studies in Irish History*, p. 246.

[4] Hammond, *Gladstone*, pp. 213, 241. He wrote to Sarah Bright, 16 Jan.
1881, 'We have not only a *foreign* element among us, but a *rebel* party, with
whom we must reckon' (K. Robbins, *John Bright*, p. 242).

'rule of law'—rather than the rule of Britain—which automatically became a political challenge. As Forster declared in 1880,

We feel bound to carry out the law . . . with any exercise of force however severely [evictions] may press upon this distressed people. So long as I remain where I am, and that law exists, it will be my hard duty to enforce it, because nothing can work so much harm in Ireland as to allow the law to be disobeyed or disregarded.[1]

However, behind this abstraction the nature of British law in Ireland was changing. The old emphasis on contract had, in the eyes of landlords at least, been severely shaken by Gladstone's first Land Act. It was to be unmistakably wrecked by the second in 1881. (This process was not to be confined to Ireland, though the Act re-emphasized Ireland's status as a 'special case'; the erosion of the traditional canons of English law was to go on henceforth in defiance of Dicey.) Coincidentally there appeared in the Irish executive an increasingly noticeable reluctance to rush with horse and foot to assist every landlord in the enforcement of the letter of every last right, regardless of the political consequences. Landlords, in fact, were beginning to be seen less as the *raison d'être* of English law than as a major barrier to its acceptance by the mass of the Irish people. The long-term implications of this incipient change of attitude were to be enormous.[2] For the time being, however, British governments, imprisoned by their own principles, had little freedom of manœuvre. Even if the ruthless enforcement of landlord rights no longer seemed politically attractive, or altogether safe, those aspects of the law which had been traditionally asserted could not be suddenly abandoned. The RIC might always have taken an easy-going attitude to petty crime (in fact it was at one with nationalists in pretending that it did not exist), but it had guaranteed the service of writs and the enforcement of ejection processes. However the statistics may be interpreted, there was undoubtedly a steep rise in

[1] HC Deb. 3s, ccliii, col. 1125.
[2] On the origins of the change see R. Hawkins, 'Liberals, land and coercion in the summer of 1880: the influence of the Carraroe ejectments', *Journal of the Galway Archaeological and Historical Society*, xxxiv (1974–5), 50.

the rate of evictions in 1878-80.[1] The normal responses of the administrative system were being triggered.

The problem which confronted the Liberal ministry from the summer of 1880 onwards was in the first place how to mitigate the upsurge of violent crime apparently provoked by evictions. The Cabinet's early decision to 'try the experiment of governing the country under the ordinary law' was probably made easier by the fact that outrages had gone into seasonal decline.[2] As against 30 Land League meetings and 118 agrarian outrages reported in the first quarter of 1880, there were 14 and 82 in the second.[3] The League was still effectively confined to Connacht, at least until Archbishop Croke's nationalistic speech at the end of May. Any tendency to increased agitation in Munster and Leinster seems to have been more than offset by the hopes attached to Gladstone's new government. A degree of goodwill was evident even before the establishment of the Land Commission under Lord Bessborough at the end of July. During the summer, as the League ramified more comprehensively, attention was effectively focused on a Compensation for Disturbances Bill based on a proposal brought forward by O'Connor Power and accepted by the Cabinet as a way of defusing the eviction crisis.

The bill was the first important action of the new Chief Secretary, W. E. Forster, whose imprint on the land war was to be indelible. The 'Stage Yorkshireman' was thrust agonizingly into the cleft of the Liberal dilemma over the handling of violence in Ireland. Although his apparently immaculate Liberal pedigree was perhaps more blemished than was generally thought, especially in respect of the 1870 Education Act which fortuitously bore his name, he attempted

[1] Taking into account families readmitted as 'caretakers' the number of final ejectments in 1880 was 1,056. Although such figures are not available for the 1870s (HC 1881 [C. 185], lxxviii; HC 1881 (2), lxxvii), it seems clear that readmissions do not dramatically modify the overall pattern of increase: 1877—463; 1878—980; 1879—1,238; 1880—2,110.

[2] T. Wemyss Reid, *Life of the Rt. Hon. W. E. Forster* (London, 1888), ii, 240. Local peace officers were divided on the issue of a new Coercion Act; cf. Hawkins, 'Gladstone, Forster, and the release of Parnell', p. 429; 'Carraroe ejectments', *passim*.

[3] Hammond, *Gladstone*, p. 191; but see the larger totals reached by the Dublin *Evening Mail*, quoted in Marlow, *Boycott*, p. 225.

to find solutions that accorded with Liberal principles.[1]
(Indeed, the attempt to find solutions was at this time a
Liberal principle in itself.) He was, however, hampered by a
heavy sense of his own political powers. Gladstone's private
secretary, who raged privately that the 'wretched bill' had
already done 'incalculable harm to the party', predicted that
Forster

> will upset the coach sooner or later, depend upon it. He is vanity itself;
> honest no doubt and exceedingly able, but without a particle of tact
> or taste; a very 'bear' in manners and a 'bull' in measures. I sometimes
> wish we were rid of him; and this is the man who 6 years ago was
> pitted against Hartington for the leadership![2]

The self-confidence that vibrates in his communications was
typical of the English statesman, the acknowledged legislator
of the world. Admirable in principle, it could rapidly turn
to obstinacy in practice, with catastrophic consequences if
judgement should prove mistaken.

Forster took the overwhelming rejection of the bill by the
House of Lords on 2 August as a personal affront. The event
was undoubtedly of much greater importance than the Lords
appear to have realized. Joseph Chamberlain's terse pronouncement, 'The Bill is rejected, the civil war is begun',
was barely over-dramatic. A truly unparalleled upsurge of
agrarian outrage followed: the connection was inescapable.
Out of the extraordinary total of 2,585 outrages in 1880,
no fewer than 1,696 were recorded in the last quarter of the
year.[3] Impressive though these numbers might be, it was
not simply the quantity that caused alarm. Parnell's Ennis
speech and the astounding Boycott case had established
a new system of control, which was used to back up the most
unacceptable of all acts of defiance, the creation of Land
League courts. To have met this state of things, Forster's
biographer wrote, not by any attempt to vindicate the

---

[1] Both Davitt and O'Brien were careful to pay tribute to the nobility of
Forster's intentions—so that his failure pointed up the dysfunctionality of English
rule in Ireland: e.g. W. O'Brien, *Recollections*, p. 292.

[2] Edward Hamilton's diary, 5 Sept. 1880: D. W. R. Bahlman (ed.), *The Diary
of Sir Edward Walter Hamilton 1880–1885* (Oxford, 1972), i, 46.

[3] The figures for County Cork, previously a fairly quiet area, ran: first quarter
—10; second—12; third—30; fourth—237. The real increase began no earlier
than the end of October: HC 1881 (12), lxxvii. 619.

authority of the law, but by the simple concession of the League's demands, 'would have been justly regarded as tantamount to a surrender on the part of the Government to the forces of disorder'.[1] But Forster made a further effort to deal with the situation by prosecutions under the ordinary law. He explained his reasoning to Gladstone on 8 October; while doubtful of the chances of success with a Dublin jury, something had to be done to 'make it clear that we did not mean to let Parnell's law be put in place of *the* law', and to show that the Liberals were not encouraging outrage so as to justify a strong land bill. 'Administratively . . . we are doing all we can—have proclaimed Mayo and Galway, and asked military authorities to fill barracks in these counties'. If the prosecutions failed, 'we shall be driven to a special session for the suspension of *Habeas Corpus*', but at least 'we should be able to tell Parliament that we had done what we could with our present powers'.[2]

Forster looked forward to Lord Spencer's advice based on his experience with the Westmeath Act. At the same time the opinion of RIC County Inspectors was sought, and emerged strongly in favour of the suspension of Habeas Corpus (or more vaguely a new 'coercion act').[3] Spencer visited Ireland, primarily on education business, and concluded that the state of parts of the country was 'extremely dangerous'.

It may be true that on former occasions when fresh powers have been given to the Irish Government, murders and attempts to murder have been more numerous, but I cannot admit that life has been in greater danger in the last twenty-five years especially in 1869 than it is at the present time.

Remedial measures were clearly necessary, but at present it was not clear exactly what they should be. It would take some months to draw up properly considered reforms.

I have however a strong opinion that the Irish should not be encouraged in the view which has unfortunately always, in former years as in the

---

[1] Reid, *Forster*, ii, 255.

[2] Ibid. 255–8. Yet Hamilton perceived that 'A state trial of that kind leads to a disagreeable dilemma. If it succeeds, those prosecuted become martyrs. If it fails they become heroes' (diary, 13 Oct. 1880). This may have reflected Gladstone's view, as an indeterminate number of Hamilton's cogitations did.

[3] Reports, Oct. 1880 (Bodleian, Harcourt MSS 39).

present year, been urged upon them, that the more they agitate and the more startling the results of their agitation are made, the more likely will they be to obtain what they desire. For the [future *added*] good of Ireland the Restoration of Order should precede Remedial measures.[1]

This significant pronouncement delineated a major axis of the Liberal response. Spencer wanted to use force to drive a wedge into the connection, brought to a head in the Land League, between physical force and moral force, and between violence and reform. He added that while fully sharing Bright's view that force was no remedy—'if you put the word Permanent before remedy'—he saw 'great danger for the future if force is never to be used alone'.

The 'force' referred to by Liberal ministers was nothing so dramatic as military government; nor, as we have seen, was there any clearly defined idea of a state of emergency which could be brought into being. Force meant, essentially, the suspension of Habeas Corpus: the short-circuiting of the legal system to permit arrest and imprisonment without trial. The belief that this would have a real effect in restoring order was based on a number of assumptions which were revealed as the Cabinet grappled with the issue in November. Lord Cowper, Forster's nominal chief as Lord-Lieutenant, put the nub of the case for internment thus:

The sudden imprisonment of some of those who are known to instigate or to commit [agrarian] crimes would strike general terror in a way that nothing else would, for no man would know how far he was suspected or whether his own turn might not come next.[2]

Cowper was confident that the police, 'in many districts' at least, had a list ready of those who were 'at the bottom of the mischief', and in all places could 'probably pick out somebody to make an example'.

If this sounded a rather shaky basis on which to abrogate the constitution, the Viceroy was on more solid ground when he argued in conclusion

Speaking in the cause of liberty, it seems to me that to be constantly giving just a little more power to the Government than is given by

[1] Spencer to Gladstone, 22 Nov. 1880 (BL Add. MS 44308, ff. 74–9).
[2] Ld.-Lieutenant, memo. for Cabinet, 8 Nov. 1880 (PRO CAB. 37/3, No. 67).

the common law is more demoralizing than to pass a really stringent measure for a short period and on a great emergency.[1]

Gladstone resisted the idea of Habeas Corpus suspension, however, believing that some form of special legislation on incitement to break contracts and mischievous speeches would suffice.[2] To this Forster returned the objection that such legislation would be even opposed by English radicals as well as the Irish. Moreover, he wrote to Gladstone on 8 November, outrages were now beyond the League's control, so that measures against the League itself were not altogether relevant.

The actual perpetrators and planners are old Fenians or old Ribbonmen or *mauvais sujets*. They would shrink into their holes if a few were arrested. Only we want men.[3]

This was the crucial assumption around which Forster's coercive policy was built. It marks the first clear formulation of the theory by which governments tried to bridge the gulf between 'law' and 'order'. Coercion, unconstitutional repression, could be justified if the government believed that opposition was not widespread among the people, but fomented by a small group of 'terrorists' (later 'gunmen' or 'murder gangs'). The use of repressive force might then be expected to produce moderation rather than intensified resistance, if it succeeded in neutralizing or destroying this small group.

The fullest exposition of Forster's reasoning appeared in a Cabinet memorandum of 16 November, a long document which deserves to be read in its entirety to absorb its atmosphere of agitated discomfort. At its root was the 'humiliating confession' that the Irish government was 'not protecting life and limb, to say nothing of property'. In other words, it was failing in its primary function as a government. Actual homicides might be fewer than during the disturbances of 1830-2: this was due to the strength and efficiency of the

[1] Ibid.
[2] A. B. Cooke and J. R. Vincent (edd.), 'Herbert Gladstone, Forster and Ireland 1881-2', part II, Select Documents, XXVIII, *IHS* xvi (1972), 75. Gladstone's memo. in Morley, *Gladstone*, Bk. VIII, Ch. IV. Cf. also Hawkins, 'Gladstone, Forster', p. 430.
[3] Reid, *Forster*, ii, 265.

police force, which could not, however, 'prevent secret individual outrages'. Armed guards saved, with difficulty, seventy to eighty men from probable murder, but constant patrols failed to prevent outrages.[1] Amidst the reign of terror in the countryside, law-breakers and not the law inspired fear.

> Large as is the police force, we have strained its strength to the utmost, and it takes months to train a policeman. We might pour in some thousands of soldiers and occupy the disturbed districts as though they were an enemy's country, but these secret outrages are as difficult to deal with as guerilla warfare. I fear no troops will prevent them, and the work is one for which our young soldiers are singularly unfitted.[2]

Amidst such overwhelming gloom, only suspension of Habeas Corpus offered the government any hope of fulfilling 'its first duty of protection to the person'. It had worked in Westmeath in 1871, and though there was 'no secret society now so clearly planning outrages as the old Westmeath Ribbon Society', he was certain that 'the principal perpetrators and planners of these outrages are known by the police, and that they themselves are well aware that they are known and *"reasonably suspected"* '. He believed that 'A few arrests would at once check outrages'.[3]

On this declaration of faith a cold douche of scepticism was immediately poured by Chamberlain, the leading anti-coercionist in the Cabinet apart from Gladstone (with whom he was unfortunately unable to co-operate). 'It is really impossible', Chamberlain acutely protested:

> to suppose that the arrest of thirty subordinate agents, as proposed by Mr. Forster, would immediately stop threatening letters and the assaults on life and property which are rife all over the country. It would be like firing with a rifle at a swarm of gnats.[4]

But Chamberlain's anti-coercionism was too radical for the majority of the Cabinet, resting as it did on the premise that

---

[1] Forster noted that in Galway there was one policeman for every 47 adult males and one soldier for every 97, yet 'no man could safely take an evicted farm'.

[2] Chief Secretary, memo., 16 Nov. 1880 (PRO CAB. 37/4, No. 71).

[3] Ibid.

[4] Minute to Gladstone, 18 Nov. 1880 (BL Add. MS 44125, ff. 48-9): J. L. Garvin, *Life of Joseph Chamberlain* (London, 1935), i, 338.

the only way to restore respect for law was to remove the injustice which provoked disorder.

The tenants of Ireland are universally in a state of excitement under which anyone of them, in face of provocation, may take the law into his own hands. The remedy must be one which affects all—not the arrest of individuals when a whole nation has more or less escaped from the ordinary respect of the law. The condition has been brought about by an unjust law—or by a law which under the exceptional circumstances of the country has practically worked injustice, and the only remedy is the alteration of the law.[1]

Something had to be done, in the view of the majority, while the planned reforms were maturing and taking effect.[2] The failure of the 'state trials', anticipated by Forster, and given the most resounding publicity by the League, made some repressive legislation inevitable.[3]

Forster returned to the subject in a letter to Gladstone on 7 December, where he analysed the chain of impunity on which the power of the League was based.[4] Finally, another substantial Cabinet memorandum on 15 December, whilst admitting that it was 'impossible to overrate the objections, both in principle and in administration' to the proposed legislation, argued that it was justified by the fact that at present the government could not fulfil its first duty, and by a reasonable belief that no less arbitrary exceptional powers would be effectual. He reiterated his objection to a stronger law against the Land League.

It is true that the Land League has stimulated men to commit these outrages, but its principal leaders have not planned or perpetrated them themselves. The actual criminals are old Ribbonmen and old Fenians and Mauvais sujets, and, though they are also generally members and local leaders of the League, I do not believe that they are now under the control of Parnell and his parliamentary friends.[5]

[1] Ibid.

[2] Though Harcourt, later the foremost coercionist, trod warily at this stage, thinking 'coercion would be fatal to the Government and the party' (Hamilton's diary, 19 Nov. 1880).

[3] On the trials, Davitt, *Fall of Feudalism*, pp. 286-95; O'Brien, *Parnell and his Party*, pp. 55-6.

[4] BL Add. MS 44157, ff. 35-8, quoted *in extenso* in Hawkins, 'Gladstone, Forster', pp. 431-2. As Hawkins observes, Forster's stress on the League was not quite in line with his main argument. This confusion of thought became more serious later.

[5] Chief Secretary, memo., 15 Dec. 1880 (BL Add. MS 44625, ff. 94-6).

In effect, Forster's argument was the reverse of Chamberlain's. The anti-coercionists held that outrage was due to the power of the League, which stemmed from the inequity of the land law; Forster argued that the power of the League depended on the impunity with which outrages could be committed. Once again he asserted his belief that

> upon the proclamation of the worst districts—say the two counties of Mayo and Galway—a few arrests would at once check outrages; as before, some of the worst perpetrators and planners would decamp, and the others would be seized by a most wholesome fear.[1]

These, then, were the principles on which the new 'coercion act', the Protection of Person and Property (Ireland) Act of 2 March 1881, was founded. Henceforth, for eighteen months, those 'reasonably suspected' of incitement or participation in any act of violence or intimidation 'tending to interfere with or disturb the maintenance of law and order' could be arrested and detained without trial.[2] These alarming powers were intended to restore to the government its essential quality—monopoly of the legitimate use of force.[3] The protection of life and property was simply a test of this power.[4] But was Forster right to believe that his Act would do this? His belief in the efficacy of arrest was certainly shared by Davitt.[5] Still, the working of the Act would depend on the capacity of the government's agents at local level—above all the Royal Irish Constabulary. From the start there was some doubt whether the new powers could be turned against individual 'planners and perpetrators' with the

---

[1] Chief Secretary, memo., 15 Dec. 1880 (BL Add. MS 44625, ff. 94-6).

[2] Act for the Better Protection of Person and Property in Ireland, 44 Vict. c. 4, to expire 30 Sept. 1882. This was followed by a new Peace Preservation Act (44 Vict. c. 5, 21 Mar. 1881) to last until 1 June 1886. Primarily an Arms Act, it showed once again the sporadic and unsatisfactory nature of arms control in Ireland.

[3] Cf. the similar but non-Weberian formulae used by Sir James Stephen, 'Suppression of Boycotting', pp. 767-9.

[4] Hawkins has suggested ('Gladstone, Forster', pp. 434-5) that the two issues can be seen as separate, though it must be the case that capacity to protect life is a primary measurement of the 'strength of government'.

[5] 'If the HC is suspended the whole movement would be crushed in a month and universal confusion would reign' (Davitt to Devoy, 16 Dec. 1880: W. O'Brien and D. Ryan (edd.), *Devoy's Post Bag*, ii, 22-4).

sort of precision suggested by Forster.[1] Many RMs had to be prodded to produce more than a handful of names, and the eventual bag of 955 detainees[2] undoubtedly included a large number of League leaders who were not suspected of complicity in actual crime but whose behaviour had caused excitement and an atmosphere of disturbance. Such a wide interpretation did not exceed the very loose terms of the Act, but it stretched its original intention as construed by the Cabinet.

The inability of the RIC to put their fingers on those directly responsible for outrage was, in the opinion of many observers, an inevitable function of its militarized paralysis. It still lacked a proper detective branch, and its efforts in this direction were if anything reduced by the Act. In Clifford Lloyd's view the force stopped exerting itself to detect criminals, 'it being thought quite sufficient to "suspect" them'. This behaviour was reinforced by the steady deterioration of public support, never at the best of times a plentiful commodity. As H. A. Blake sharply put it, the fundamental problem was that

not one in five hundred of the community, be he gentleman or peasant, looks upon the commission of crime upon another as a matter affecting anybody but the Government.[3]

The Government was certainly aware of this problem, although baffled by it. Gladstone continued to worry, as he had in 1870, over the absence of the spirit of self-respect and self-defence which in other societies made ordinary citizens support the law.[4] Forster confronted the issue in a letter of July 1881.

The greatest of all Irish evils is the cowardice, or at best the non-action of the moderate men; and, indeed, this is the best, if not the sole argument for Home Rule. Sensible, moderate Irishmen let things

[1] In fact it transpired that the police were unable to pin-point suspects after outrages: Reid, *Forster*, ii, 312-13. Cowper complained to Harcourt that 'the police led us quite astray'. A. G. Gardiner, *Life of Sir William Harcourt*, p. 433.

[2] 425 of them arrested for 'interference' in the payment of rent, 131 for boycotting: Memo. on Protection of Person and Property Act 1881, 9 Dec. 1887 (Balfour MSS, BL Add. MS 49808).

[3] Blake, 'The Irish Police', p. 392.

[4] Hammond, *Gladstone*, p. 245.

alone and let them get from bad to worse, because they know that at a certain point we English must step in and prevent utter anarchy.[1]

Gladstone returned to the point in conversation with Hamilton at Hawarden in November, mystified by the fact that

The constabulary never seem to be in the right place. It is astonishing that no one who commits these outrages is ever arrested. It shows an alarming state of demoralisation throughout the Irish community, which excites Mr. G.'s gravest apprehensions. Unless a country is governed by Martial law, it is impossible that the Executive should do everything.[2]

This interesting gloss points to an aspect of the situation which the government could never bring itself to accept. It was in effect already governing Ireland under 'martial law' in so far as jury trial had been bypassed. Admittedly, there were no military tribunals in place of defunct civil courts, and no military governors. But towards the end of 1881 Forster created a new species of executive officer out of the old resident magistracy. On 15 December he briefed three of the most successful RMs, H. A. Blake, C. D. C. Lloyd, and Capt. The Hon. T. O. Plunkett, for new responsibilities as 'Special Resident Magistrates' in charge of groups of the most disturbed counties.[3] Two other officers were later added and a total of twelve counties were grouped into the five special areas.[4] On the 28th, Forster issued formal instructions, though these were never clear or public enough for the role of the SRMs to be fully understood.

The actions of these special magistrates—'commissioners' would have been a more accurate term[5]—varied considerably. The most energetic of them was Clifford Lloyd in Limerick, who revelled in the very imprecision of his powers (which tended, in the British tradition, to paralyse others) and was unafraid of making enemies (which he did with some

[1] To Lord Ripon, 17 July 1881: Reid, *Forster*, ii, 330.

[2] Hamilton's diary, 23 Nov. 1881 (Bahlman, i, 186).

[3] Lloyd, *Ireland Under the Land League*, p. 229.

[4] R. Hawkins, 'An Army on Police Work, 1881-2. Ross of Bladensburg's Memorandum', *Irish Sword*, xi (1973), 114-15 n. 25.

[5] They were in fact so called when first referred to by Hamilton in his diary 30 Dec. 1881, where he posed the inevitable question 'Why was this not done sooner?'. According to Lloyd (op. cit. 229), the title 'commissioner' was objected to by Crown law-officers and the 'misleading and faulty designation' adopted in its place.

thoroughness). Lloyd firmly declared in his memoirs, *Ireland Under the Land League*, that

To send persons for trial before a jury was but to advertise the weakness of the law; and as my object was to assert its strength, I avoided this course during my magisterial administration at Kilmallock.[1]

Faced early in 1881 with 'a state of affairs recognised to be bordering upon civil war, and much more difficult to deal with', in which the 'Land League committee was able to rule by means not at the disposal of the Government', Lloyd had taken the dramatic and assertive action normal to district officers in colonies far from the seat of imperial power. Believing it necessary to 'dethrone' the League committee, he proceeded to the arrest of the turbulent local priest, Father Sheehy, on 20 May, assisted by columns of troops from Limerick, Kilfinan, and Charleville. Sheehy and other members of the committee were placed on the train to Naas amidst extraordinary scenes of popular hysteria.[2] Reactions to Lloyd's administration were inevitable: no fewer than sixteen parliamentary questions about his conduct were put down by Irish MPs during 1881. Most of them concerned accusations that Lloyd dispensed summary justice in his own house, refused to accept bail, and dispersed crowds with the cheery paraphrase of the Riot Act, 'if you don't be off at once I will have you shot down'. T. P. O'Connor called him 'atrociously cruel and despotic', and asked 'how could moderate counsels be expected to prevail with a population exasperated with the conduct of magistrates like Mr. Clifford Lloyd?'[3] In the long term, the barrage of criticism does appear to have induced the government to terminate Lloyd's public career.

Fear of such a fate no doubt played its part in the less unrelenting activity of Lloyd's fellow-magistrates. Lloyd himself observed that

Many of the resident magistrates believed that they were not clothed with any more general authority than the local justices possessed. If the Government had orders to give, they were prepared to execute

---

[1] Lloyd, op. cit. 72.
[2] Ibid. 88–9.
[3] HC Deb. 3s, cclxv, cols. 894–5, 25 Aug. 1881.

them; but it was in their opinion no part of their duty to initiate action for the maintenance or restoration of order.

Clearly Lloyd's interpretation of necessary preventive action was unusual, and was part of the stretching of the 1881 Act away from mere punishment of offences already committed, and towards action against those suspected of being about to commit crime.[1]

Lloyd's energy was particularly noticeable in his intensification of day-to-day public security arrangements. Effectively these fell into two categories, patrolling and personal protection. Both required an increasing participation by the regular military forces, a process which met with some resistance from the military authorities. A dismal foretaste of military duties in aid of the civil power was provided during the Boycott affair, when 500 infantry and three squadrons of cavalry were sent to protect the saving of the unfortunate Captain's harvest. The sufferings of the military force from weather and forced marches were compounded by inefficient staff-work.[2] At a more exalted level, the familiar struggle between military demands for concentration and civil demands for dispersion recommenced. The establishment of flying columns on the 1867-9 model was, of course, not unattractive to the soldiers, and this was done by mid 1880.[3] Nine columns were in existence in January 1881,[4] but since no overt opposition coalesced which they could fly towards, they were gradually stood down and

[1] Lloyd, op. cit. 99; cf. Hawkins, 'Gladstone, Forster', p. 437. However, Earl Grey took the view that suspension of Habeas Corpus had always been used as a preventive and not a punitive measure, 'to enable servants of the Crown to disorganize treasonable or seditious conspiracies by seizing and detaining the leaders' (*Ireland* (London, 1888), pp. 221-2).

[2] e.g. Becker, *Disturbed Ireland*, pp. 123, 130-1.

[3] C.-in-C. Ireland (Sir John Michel) to C.-in-C. (Duke of Cambridge), 17 Aug. 1880 (Kilmainham MSS, NLI MS 1304): 'The Government here (which means Mr Forster in England) are of opinion that a cordon of posts about the disturbed districts, and 3 flying columns are imperatively demanded. In a military point of view, if there were to be a strong outbreak, of course this (I mean the cordon) would be a most unmilitary proceeding . . . but . . . as long as I can keep up the bodies in sufficient strength to occasionally help the Civil Power, and yet keep a sufficient reserve to hold each barrack safe: I shall feel myself bound to answer the Government demands.'

[4] SPO, CSO RP 1881/12928, 23100, 26578.

detachments were sent off to more mundane tasks. By May, the Commander-in-Chief was complaining that

> the ill-feeling towards military . . . is gradually becoming general throughout districts wherein soldiers have been employed in aiding the Civil Power . . . Unless some immediate and strong measures are taken to suppress stone throwing at the Military and constabulary most serious results must ensue.[1]

By 'serious results', he meant retaliation. In the event, however, no disastrous reprisals occurred, though the strain and provocation increased still further. The Lord-Lieutenant was worried that the stoning of troops showed that they were not being correctly employed:

> a certain amount of this may be unavoidable, but troops in my opinion should never be brought face to face with the mob unless they are intended to act. It is not fair upon the troops and it diminishes their moral effect upon the people. The Police should if possible be employed in preference as they can use their batons, which they are not afraid to use, and which inflict just the right sort of chastisement.[2]

Cowper pointed out that the nature of the challenge appeared to be changing; in the previous autumn, individual assassination had been the great danger, but now in addition there was the possibility of 'a sudden overwhelming, by sheer weight of numbers, of small bodies of police and military'. One such catastrophe 'might actually be the beginning of a small civil war' which could not be ended without great bloodshed.[3]

Whatever their fears, the Irish authorities could do nothing but keep on 'pegging away'.[4] Throughout 1881 the military commitment increased. Troop strength had been raised to 25,062 at the start of the year as against 19,027 in July 1880.[5] In June, two-thirds of Clifford Lloyd's 'overawing forces' were still composed of police; by the end of the year they were almost entirely military, with some ten police sent from divisional headquarters so as to avoid using local

---

[1] C.-in-C. Ireland (Sir Thomas Steele) to Ld.-Lieutenant, 18 May 1881 (Kilmainham MSS 1304).
[2] Cowper to Gladstone, 9 June. 1881 (BL Add. MS 44470).
[3] Ibid.
[4] Forster to Harcourt, 6 June 1881 (MS Harcourt 81).
[5] H. Gladstone notes (Visc. Gladstone MSS, BL Add. MS 46110, f. 86).

forces already fully stretched by constant patrol and protection duties. Forster told the Home Secretary in June, 'H.R.H. [the Duke of Cambridge] is in strange ignorance of the situation if he supposes we can keep the soldiers out of sight—the police are worked nearly to death and we have to send soldiers with them'.[1]

The military authorities endeavoured to restrict the army's involvement in every possible way, short of actually refusing assistance required by magistrates. The employment of troops was governed by a set of general orders issued in 1870, of which a slightly revised version was to be reissued in 1882.[2] These defined the purposes for which troops could be required by magistrates, sheriffs, or sub-sheriffs to aid the civil powers as being primarily to oppose armed insurrection; to suppress and disperse treasonable meetings; to preserve the public peace, and prevent or suppress riot and disorder; to search for arms; to escort judges, prosecutors, and witnesses to Crown Courts; to escort prisoners in civil custody so as to prevent their rescue or escape; to escort voters at elections; and 'to patrol any district' (in the 1870 instructions, 'any district named by a magistrate'). The fourth of the original purposes, search for arms, was omitted from the revised version.[3] The delicate problem of command of military parties on these duties was left unresolved. An opinion of the Attorney-General in 1851 was 'communicated' for the 'instruction' of officers, reading as follows;

The Deputation from the Sheriff does not confer on the Magistrate any special authority over the Troops, nor can it be said with accuracy that any one of the Magistrates whether a Resident Magistrate or a local Justice, has the general or chief Command.

When there is a Resident Magistrate on the spot, I recommend the Officer in charge of the Troops to look to him for directions. As a general rule, this will be safe; but in the event of any conflict in the Orders of the Magistrates, the officer commanding the Troops must

---

[1] Forster to Harcourt, 4 June 1881 (MS Harcourt 81).

[2] *General Orders for the Guidance of the Troops in Affording Aid to the Civil Power in Ireland* (Dublin, 1870, 1882; PRO WO 32 6329).

[3] *General Orders* (1870), pp. 15–17. The other puposes were to 'protect stranded vessels from plunder', 'prevent the country-people carrying away turf, sea-weed and other property' (omitted from the 1882 version), 'to attend on Coroner's requisition', 'to attend on Rate-collectors &c', and 'to attend as guards over gaols'.

exercise his discretion, and on his own responsibility determine which he will obey.[1]

This relationship remained in force throughout the land war. The expanding reliance of the civil authorities on troops never led to the direct involvement of soldiers in judicial or administrative affairs. The expedient of giving magisterial powers to certain commanding officers, experimented with in 1867, was not reverted to, and an idea that troops might be attested as police or special constables was rejected by the government as illegal.[2]

None the less, the involvement of troops under the wide and vaguely defined powers of the special RMs could be very close indeed. An unusually full picture of the process can be obtained from a remarkable memorandum drawn up, at Lord Spencer's instigation, at the end of 1882.[3] This details the administrative arrangements made to streamline requisitions for 'protection parties' once it became clear that every single sheriff, every process-serving, and every eviction, impounding, or forced sale would have to be accompanied by a strong military force. These perpetual rain-swept marches were usually more wearying than dangerous to the troops. Herbert Gladstone's observation of an eviction at Erne in December 1881 was typical; fifty RIC were accompanied by 150 men of the 36th Rifles, and though the people were 'defiant and demonstrative . . . the force present was far too strong to allow of anything like violence'.[4] When exceptions occurred, however, the results could be appalling. At Ballaghadereen, Co. Mayo, which had been one of the first districts to suggest an increase in the number of regular troops,[5] an inadequate force of constabulary under

---

[1] *General Orders* (1870), p. 19, (1882), p. 18.

[2] Childers to Spencer, 2 July 1882 (Spencer MSS); Hawkins, 'Army on Police Work', p. 82. Even the C.-in-C.'s call (to WO, 5 Jan. 1881: Kilmainham MSS 1072) for military authorities to be given 'a power adequate to their responsibilities in emergencies', equal to that held by commanders in 1867, fell on deaf ears.

[3] By John Ross of Bladensburg, 'military adviser' at Dublin Castle: copies in PRO CO 904 187/1, original in SPO CSO RP 1883/2214; printed with rich annotation in Hawkins, 'Army on Police Work'.

[4] H. Gladstone's diary, 1 Dec. 1881: Cooke and Vincent, op. cit., part I, p. 543.

[5] D. Harrel, RM, to Chief Secretary, 19 June 1880 (PRO CAB. 37/2).

a sergeant was employed at a process-serving in April 1881. The police, harassed by an excited crowd, panicked and opened fire. Even though they were loaded with the new buckshot ammunition, they killed two men. The crowd fell furiously on them, and stoned the sergeant to death; his men fled to escape a similar fate.[1]

The 80th Foot, which had in fact sent a detachment to Ballaghadereen in January, was not unusual in furnishing a force which set out from Dublin for Cavan by rail in midwinter 1880–1:

It then marched seven miles to Killashandra to the north-west, where it spent the night, and at 7.30 the next morning the detachment of forty-two escorted wagons to Glebe House and unloaded them. Still moving in the same direction it marched to Ballinamore, having covered eighteen miles during the day, and after another start at 6 a.m. took six hours to march to Carrick-on-Shannon, a further nineteen miles.[2]

The military authorities were driven at times to complain of troops being sent on long harassing marches without real necessity. They were also, sometimes, taken advantage of, being used for instance as cattle-drivers when sheriffs had failed to provide themselves with proper staffs for impounding stock. However, it has to be added that troops themselves could on occasion be a threat to law and order. In November 1881, for instance, an Irish regiment behaved like a mob in face of a police detachment, waving their rifles and shouting 'buckshot!'; and one of the worst breaches of the peace in Galway city in 1882 was a fight between two traditionally hostile regiments, the 84th and the Connaught Rangers.[3]

The greatest strain, as always in such operations, fell on the junior officers, as may be seen from a typical report by a subaltern of the South Staffordshire Regiment in Tralee in January 1882.

---

[1] Davitt, *Fall of Feudalism*, p. 316.

[2] Digest, 80th Foot, Staffs. Regt. Museum, Whittington, Cf. W. L. Vale, *The South Staffordshire Regiment* (London, 1969), p. 202–3, on problems of training under these circumstances.

[3] C.-in-C. to Under-Secretary, 4 Jan.: Report of Capt. Collingwood, Maryborough, 29 May 1881 (Kilmainham MSS 1072): Becker, *Disturbed Ireland*, pp. 123, 130–1.

He was in charge of the patrol on 14th Jan, and at 8.45 p.m. while patrolling at the corner of Denny St. and Castle St. he heard a row some distance off. He immediately went down with his portion of the picquet and found the other portion, in charge of Sgt. S. Carter 2/S.S. Regt and Sub. Const. McLeherty, engaged in taking a civilian to the Bridewell, and being prevented from doing so by a large mob which had collected. He had to hold the street to allow the picquet to escort the prisoner to the Bridewell, and while engaged in doing so one of the men of the picquet Pte. Fellows 2/S.S. Regt. received a severe contusion on the right side of the head from a brick thrown by one of the mob. On reaching the Bridewell the crowd was so threatening that he placed his men across the street with fixed bayonets. After remaining there some time his attention was called by the sub Constable to the state the civilian prisoner was in & whom he found had a slight wound on his left side—he stated he had been wounded by a soldier, but when and how he could not say. When the excitement had somewhat subsided he (Lt. Freer) perceived that Sgt. Carter in charge of the other portion of the picquet was drunk. He placed him under arrest . . . he also confined two others of his portion of the picquet who were drunk . . . The Constable in charge of Sgt. Carter's portion of the picquet was under the influence of drink . . .[1]

The most ubiquitous form of military action during the land war was patrolling, either separately or in co-operation with the police.[2] General orders laid down that the object of patrols was to arrest illegally armed parties, to prevent houses being broken into by persons searching for arms,

and not only to apprehend Criminals thus disturbing the country, but to strike a terror in the locality. So as to prevent crime being perpetrated, and to give confidence to the well-disposed, and those possessing Arms, to defend their houses.[3]

Such operations were effectively the sole offensive means open to the authorities, and great hopes were entertained of their success. An RIC circular of December 1880, explaining to local police that Queen's Regulations prevented military patrols from operating in a strength of less than twenty men accompanied by an officer, pointed out that

police officers, being aware of the hours and routes which the military are patrolling will have at their disposal the policemen which would

[1] Report of Lt. Freer, 2nd S. Staffs. Regt., 14 Jan. 1882 (Kilmainham MSS 1073).

[2] Bladensburg's memo., s. 3.

[3] *General Orders* (1870), pp. 37–8.

otherwise be required to watch that particular locality . . . and it cannot be doubted that the presence of military thus moving through the country will not only have a good effect in giving confidence to the law-abiding, but produce a deterrent effect on evil doers.[1]

The imprecision of this phraseology—'moving through the country' and 'having a good effect'—was to echo through many later attempts at peace-keeping, and indicates a certain operational weakness. The size of military patrols was the first problem for the police, who would have preferred them to be smaller and less visible. The military claimed that even regulation-sized patrols seriously interfered with training. By midwinter of 1881–2 an angry resident magistrate was complaining that military patrols which went out three times a week at 10 a.m. and returned at noon, whose movements were 'perfectly known', were 'perfectly useless'. He advocated halving their size to ten, increasing their number, and sending them out at irregular hours, especially after dark. Soon afterwards the commander in chief permitted 'Local Authorities' (i.e. RMs) to reduce the strength of military patrols at their discretion. The range of infantry patrols (restricted by the General Orders to four hours at two miles per hour) was also to be extended where desired by the use of cars.[2]

This more flexible attitude on the part of the military allowed resourceful magistrates such as Colonel Forbes, Henry Blake, and Clifford Lloyd to develop schemes of close control based on intensive patrolling. The Cabinet was informed of Forbes's system in a memorandum in April 1882—essentially it involved the maximum possible number of patrols of varied strengths going out mainly by night (most outrages having been found to occur between nightfall and midnight), and either converging on a predetermined spot or lying in ambush.[3] Lloyd moved towards the ambitious idea of a network of small posts linked by frequent patrols,

---

[1] RIC Circular, 16 Dec. 1880 (CSO RP 1883/2214).

[2] Mil. Secretary to Under-Secretary, 19 July 1881; RM Mullingar, report 8 Jan. 1882 (Kilmainham MSS 1304; RIC Circular, 19 Jan. 1882, CSO RP 1883/2214). The Royal Artillery claimed that their horses and waggons had already been misused for this purpose in 1881: Kilmainham MSS 1073, letter-book pp. 104–5; 4th Bde. RA to OC Tps. Limerick, 28 Nov. 1881, SPO RP 1881/44053).

[3] Col. Forbes's memo., 9 Apr. 1882 (BL Add. MS 44160, ff. 143–4).

and as part of this policy he made novel demands on the army. To begin with he called for 600 troops to act in groups of three to six men to relieve RIC on personal protection duty (protecting threatened individuals on a permanent basis). The Commander-in-Chief objected that he could not find so many men, but eventually agreed. Then he asked for selected veteran soldiers to act in small parties with police. The Commander-in-Chief was 'most opposed to any troops being employed except as soldiers', and there were legal problems over placing soldiers under the control of civilians. Eventually an auxiliary force was enrolled from the army reserve, and, in addition, pending its arrival soldiers were allocated for special service duties

on the understanding that the men shall remain under the general command of their officers, that a commissioned officer and a certain number of NCOs should accompany the soldiers into the districts to which they are ordered, and the usual relations existing between officers and men be as far as possible maintained.[1]

The system had been stretched to its limits—some soldiers would have said beyond them—in the attempt to hold the campaign under the control of the civil authorities. Although martial law as such had not been resorted to, Lloyd's administration seemed to have approached the course earlier disavowed by Forster, of 'pouring in some thousands of soldiers and occupying the disturbed districts as though they were an enemy's country'. The question remained whether troops could achieve the government's objectives, and whether these objectives had been correctly conceived. Even if the Land League could be overpowered, was this the way by which law and order could be restored?

---

[1] Bladensburg's memo., s. 4. This states, not altogether correctly, that Steele 'agreed at once' (but see Steele to Under-Secretary, 5 Jan. 1882, Kilmainham MSS 1073). The total of troops so employed was:

Capt. Plunkett's Division (W. Cork, Kerry)	26
Col. Forbes's Division (Mayo, Roscommon, Sligo)	53
Capt. Butler's Division (Westmeath, Leitrim, Longford)	50
Mr. Lloyd's Division (Limerick, Clare)	224
Mr. Blake's Division (Galway, King's, Queen's)	134
Capt. Slacke's Division (Tipperary, Wexford, E. Cork)	88

(iv) *Land League to National League*

> In (the League's) hands must be the plan of campaign.
> Whoever moves without their orders is a deserter. Whoever
> thwarts them by disjointed individual action is an *enemy*.
>
> *United Irishman* 17 September 1881

To begin with, it looked as if all the government's efforts
were to be unavailing. The apparent power and unity of the
Land League continued to grow. So did outrage, which, in
Gladstone's phrase, 'dogged its heels'. The total number of
agrarian crimes leapt to an unexampled 4,439 in 1881, and
though this figure may be somewhat too high (the results of
a rather loose method of multiple counting, particularly
for incidents of intimidation, which were reckoned at no less
than 2,191), it was on any count striking. Certainly, the first
three quarterly totals were not as appalling as that for the
end of 1880. The drop in the quarterly figure (excluding
intimidation cases) from 717 then to 369 in the first quarter
of 1881 was thought to be due to the impact, and even the
pre-echo, of the Coercion Act.[1] But in Clifford Lloyd's
opinion this effect was thrown away through the tardy and
weak application of the Act. The delay, due to Forster's
determination to be seen to review carefully every individual
case before authorizing arrest,[2] was followed by the 'political'
treatment of the men arrested—in fact they were imprisoned
as first-class misdemeanants—who were held under what
Lloyd saw as 'luxurious conditions'.[3]

Inevitably, the Act lost its alarming effects with time,
as Forster himself admitted in July.

> As to secret outrages, the first effect of the Protection Act was very
> good; but the fear was soon discounted, and I have had to put the Act
> into much more active operation, and, indeed, to arrest right and left;
> and at last I am stopping the outrages.[4]

The quarterly figure for April–June was up to 622; for July–
September it dropped somewhat to 525; but in the final
quarter it rose again to 732. In June Lord Cowper produced

---

[1] Hamilton's diary, 7 Feb. 1881.
[2] Reid, *Forster*, ii, 306-11.
[3] Lloyd, *Land League*, pp. 210-11.
[4] To Ripon, 17 July 1881 (Reid, *Forster*, ii, 330).

a cheerless 'statement of our position here' in which he presented a view of the Land League's role rather different from that held previously by Forster.

> It must be remembered that the Land League has now taken very deep root throughout the country; and that Fenians, Ribbonmen and bad characters of every description take advantage of its organization and are enrolled in its local branches. If the restraining influence of the Central Body were withdrawn and the local branches driven to become secret societies, crime—particularly assassination—might increase.[1]

The Viceroy thus portrayed the League, almost as Davitt did, as reducing violent crime, and was apprehensive about the consequences of suppressing it. At the same time he believed that the failure to prevent Land League meetings 'has been and will be fixed upon as the chief error of our administration'. Yet, as he bemusedly admitted, even if the meetings had been suppressed, outrages would have continued and would possibly have increased—'we should have been accused of sitting on the safety valve and it would have been said that if we had allowed a free expression of opinion and a constitutional agitation all would have been well'. Still, as it was now a question of realities and of deciding who should be arrested for 'incitement to violence', Cowper's view was that at present 'everybody who takes a leading part in the Land League, does by the very fact of so doing incite to outrage'.[2]

Certainly, naked violence seemed to be moving closer to the forefront of the conflict between the League and the government. This conflict was still in a sense indirect, mediated through landlords and the civil law. A study of the crime statistics in 1881, and throughout the land war, does not sustain the idea that a prototypal guerilla struggle was already being waged. At least, there were few violent crimes which could be seen as purely political, rather than economic, in content.[3] In 1881, when 'agrarian' crime represented 57 per

---

[1] Memo. by Ld.-Lieutenant, 9 June 1881 (BL Add. MS 44470).

[2] Ibid.

[3] RIC Statistics of Crimes Specially Reported to the Constabulary Office (PRO CO 903). The RIC developed no category of 'political' crime; the tendency was to regard 'agrarian' crimes as an index of political disturbance.

cent of the total (the highest so far: see Table I), the proportion of homicides labelled 'agrarian' was only 47 per cent (see Table II). Forty-nine per cent of 'aggravated assaults', and 63 per cent of incidents of 'firing at the person' (Irish assassins had something of a reputation for missing, whether through infirmity of purpose or malfunction of firearms often hidden in damp places), were agrarian; but for 'cutting and maiming the person' the figure was only 13 per cent. This seems to sustain the idea that crude personal violence was in decline as an agrarian mode.[1] (Only a single case of rape, out of a total of 19, was accounted agrarian—and this remained the only agrarian case in the whole decade, out of a total of 186.) The figure for arson, 55 per cent, was closer to the proportion of agrarian crime as a whole, while that for maiming of animals, at 57 per cent, matched it exactly. Where agrarian crime decisively preponderated was in the area of intimidation (76 per cent) and the specialized acts of 'administering unlawful oaths' (84 per cent) and 'taking and holding forcible possession' (94 per cent). The low incidence of purely political crimes may be indicated in the figures for seizure of arms and assaults on the police, actions which would be the basis of any direct attack on the state. In spite of Dillon's belligerent assertion in America in May 1880 that

It will be our duty, and we will set about it without delay, to disorganize and break up the Irish Constabulary that for the past 30 years have stood at the back of the landlords bayonet in hand,[2]

at 29 and 27 per cent respectively, such actions were well below average, and the figure for assaults on the police is an exception to the general run. Such assaults showed a fairly consistent, and rather surprising, general decline from the 1870s through to the 1890s, and the agrarian component was running at zero until 1879, when it appeared as 6 per cent, rising to 15 per cent in 1880 before dropping back to zero from 1882 to 1884 (see Table III).

---

[1] According to official figures used in T. P. O'Connor, *The Parnell Movement*, pp. 393–4, there was only a single instance of 'carding' between February and October 1890.

[2] *Parnell Commission Report*, p. 30.

TABLE I

Totals of Outrages in Ireland

Year	Agrarian	Total	Percentage agrarian
1867	123	2,021	6
1870	1,329	4,351	30
1875	136	2,001	7
1879	863	3,500	25
1880	2,585	5,669	46
1881	4,439	7,788	57
1882	3,433	6,628	51
1883	870	2,535	34
1884	762	2,453	31
1885	944	2,683	35
1886	1,056	3,251	35
1887	883	2,270	39
1888	660	2,182	30
1889	534	1,895	28
1890	519	1,934	27

TABLE II

Outrages in 1881

Crime	Agrarian	Total	Percentage agrarian
Murder	17	36	47
Firing at person	66	104	63
Aggravated assault	101	205	49
Cutting, maiming person	13	99	13
Arson	356	647	55
Maiming cattle	155	273	57
Taking forcible possession	65	69	94
Intimidation: letter or notice	2,191	2,862	76
Other intimidation	415	542	76

None the less, the language of violent confrontation was creating its own meanings. The Parnellite leadership now reached a peak of rhetorical intransigence as it cemented its moral ascendancy over a movement that appears to have been far shakier and more riven with discord than even

TABLE III

Assaults on Police

Year	Agrarian	Total	Percentage agrarian
1870	nil	58	—
1871	nil	31	—
1872	nil	112	—
1875	nil	23	—
1879	3	47	6
1880	12	81	15
1881	24	89	27
1882	nil	29	—
1883	nil	15	—
1884	nil	12	—
1885	7	20	33
1886	4	33	12
1887	11	45	24
1888	1	23	4
1889	3	21	14
1890	1	6	17

Parnell thought.[1] The second Land Act threatened to break it up. In March a violent speech by John Dillon stung the Home Secretary into declaring

We have heard the doctrine of the Land League expounded by the man who has the authority to explain it; and to-morrow every subject of the Queen will know that the doctrine so expounded is the doctrine of treason and assassination.[2]

J. L. Hammond ruefully commented on the fact that parliamentary obstruction, which outraged English ideas of responsible conduct, and led, in the introduction of the 'guillotine' (equally exotically labelled *clôture* in the first instance), to a major and irreversible change in the British constitution, was Parnell's speciality. But Parnell was treading close on a different form of confrontation. In May 1881, speaking to the man he thought was a senior officer of the Clan na Gael and certainly intending his words

[1] Parnell wrote privately that the movement was 'breaking fast' at the time he was arrested, but if Bew is correct it had always been riven with contradictions, and its momentum depended—in Anna Parnell's word—on sham.

[2] Gardiner, *Harcourt*, i, 427.

for an American audience (though in fact they went straight to Anderson, the head of secret intelligence at the Home Office), he declared that he had long since ceased to believe that anything but the force of arms would accomplish the final redemption of Ireland. He saw no reason why, 'when we [presumably the Americans] were fully prepared', an open insurrection could not commence, and he went carefully into the question of resources; so at least reported his interlocutor, the spy 'le Caron'.[1]

The British did not take the possibility of open insurrection seriously in 1881. Surprisingly level-headed over this, they nevertheless saw the aggressive obstructionary tactics of Parnell and the torrent of agrarian crime as two aspects of an equally grave threat. Parnell's deft speech in the Commons on 17 January, in which he dissociated himself from violence and argued that peasant proprietorship would make possible an alliance of all classes to obtain legislative independence 'in a rational and peaceable way, without any violent revolution in my opinion, without jingle of arms', failed to convince.[2] Ten days later Gladstone gave his reasons for linking the Land League with crime, and though his over-simple assumption that, but for the League, disturbance should have died away as distress diminished was rebutted by Sexton in a famous speech, Sexton's own reasoning was unlikely to silence opponents. (His use of average figures for county areas was particularly dubious.) The atmosphere of confrontation sharpened almost daily. It culminated in February in the unprecedented mêlées in the Commons following Forster's announcement of the arrest of Davitt. Parnell's confidential flourish of revolutionary rhetoric in May has to be seen in the light of his firm rejection of revolutionary action at this critical juncture.[3] The idea of withdrawing the Irish MPs *en bloc* from parliament and establishing a focus for resistance in Ireland was directly advocated by radical tenant leader Andrew Kettle, and had ostensibly been accepted by Parnell.

---

[1] Le Caron, op. cit., 174-5. Anderson was recognized as an alarmist, though (Lewis Harcourt's diary, 23 Jan. 1881, Harcourt MSS 347).

[2] Bew, *Land and the National Question*, pp. 151-2.

[3] O'Connor, *Parnell Movement*, pp. 388-417; O'Brien, *Parnell and his Party*, pp. 59-64.

But Parnell's own preferences obviously lay in keeping up the fight at Westminster: in Ireland the parliamentarians ran the risk of being swamped by, or absorbed into, an extra-parliamentary—indeed anti-parliamentary—body which might move in unattractive directions. The struggle against the Coercion Bill created a new nationalist epic, and restored the ascendancy to the parliamentarians. The atmosphere during the passage of Forster's coercion bill was inevitably bad, but the government hoped that its new land measure would mend the situation (although Forster gloomily wrote in March that he was '*very* melancholy' about it: 'Very few persons will understand it and those who do will denounce it').[1]

The reaction of the Irish politicians was hostile, displaying a verbal intransigence which does not seem to have been demanded by opinion within the Land League,[2] and which may have been a compensation for their sense of failure over the Davitt affair. Admittedly the government might have foreseen that even a generous measure of reform which had been prefaced by such a contentious measure of repression would face an icy welcome. None the less, Bright and Chamberlain, in particular, responded to the criticism with increasing bitterness against Irish 'ingratitude'.[3]

The much-discussed policy of 'testing' the bill emerged in the end as a means of papering over cracks in the League that multiplied as tenants discovered what the new legislation had to offer, pushed along by the successful actions of the Property Defence Association. There was, as has been seen, a decline in crime figures for the autumn, though the total remained formidable. Edward Hamilton surely reflected his masters' frustration when he wrote 'one does not see what can be done further, unless it be to govern Ireland by martial law, and this would require Parliamentary powers which simply would not be given'.[4] Gladstone's own bitterness

[1] To Harcourt, 6 Mar. 1881 (Harcourt MSS 81).

[2] And which may not have been entirely honest: Bew, op. cit. pp. 162-3; O'Brien, op. cit. 67.

[3] Hamilton echoed hostility to home rulers as 'a set of ruffians absolutely unfit to have a share in the government of any country', 14 Sept. 1881 (Bahlman, i, 168).

[4] Diary, 2 Oct. 1881, (ibid. p. 172).

against Parnell drove him to the stunning peroration of his speech at Leeds in October:

If it shall appear that there is still to be fought a final conflict in Ireland between law on the one side and sheer lawlessness upon the other, if the law purged from defect and from any taint of injustice is still to be repelled and refused, and the first conditions of political society to remain unfulfilled, then I say, gentlemen, without hesitation, the resources of civilization against its enemies are not yet exhausted.[1]

This extraordinarily intense expression of the fundamental English attitude was all the more striking in the mouth of an 'anti-coercionist'. Gladstone was escorted home from the Cloth Hall by a torchlight procession, the streets of Leeds 'packed, in spite of drizzling rain, with dense throngs cheering vociferously'; the following day he was fêted again in similar style.[2] There could be little doubt of English opinion.[3] A fortnight later, Chamberlain delivered a speech of almost equal significance at Liverpool, in which he declared,

When it is said that it is contrary to Liberal principles to suspend the safeguards of liberty, I say that liberty is a mere phantom unless every man is free to pursue his inclinations, to consult his interest within and under the protection of the law.[4]

The Land League, by the imposition of its dictates, had become 'a tyranny as obnoxious to liberals and liberalism as any other form of despotism'.

In between these two speeches, Parnell was arrested, having responded with even greater verbal violence against the 'pretending champion of the rights of every other nation except those of the Irish nation' who was now 'prepared to carry fire and sword into your homesteads, unless you humbly abase yourselves before him and before the landlords

[1] Morley, *Gladstone*, ii, 301 (misdating the speech); on 'the violence of the threat', Hammond, *Gladstone*, p. 249.

[2] Hamilton's diary, 11 Oct. 1881.

[3] A year later, out of office, Forster was cheered at Bradford when he explained his reasons for using 'force, if force were necessary, to prevent open resistance—(cheers)—open resistance to the law (cheers)' (*Leeds Mercury*, 8 Dec. 1882).

[4] Hammond, *Gladstone*, p. 251.

of the country'. More threateningly, though less frequently quoted, he also declared that

The Irishman who thinks that he can now throw away his arms, just as Grattan disbanded the volunteers in 1789, will find, to his sorrow and destruction, when too late, that he has placed himself in the power of a cruel and perfidious enemy.[1]

Echoing his earlier language, Gladstone announced that this arrest was the first step 'towards the vindication of law and order' and of 'the first elements of political life and civilisation'. As Morley later put it, 'the arrest of Mr. Parnell was no doubt a pretty considerable strain upon powers conferred by parliament to put down village ruffians; but times were revolutionary'.[2] At the time, however, as a radical anti-coercionist, Morley produced a convincing analysis of the spiral of violence and political alienation. Only violent agitation, he wrote, could bring Irish issues to English attention. But the English, disgusted by violence, and fearing to appear to give way to force, struck at the agitators at the same time as redressing grievances.

Then comes the vexatious conclusion. The Irish are more provoked by the application of force than they are gratified by the extension of justice. The English are then in turn disgusted by what they consider to be ingratitude.[3]

The final throw of the Land League leadership was the 'No Rent Manifesto' issued from Kilmainham gaol on 18 October. Though this fell flat in the countryside, it provided the government with a reason for at last suppressing the Land League as an organization two days later. Suppression was accomplished with surprising ease—'we are getting on well' Forster reported on 25 October, while stoutly maintaining that 'the proclamation of the Land League would have done little had it not been preceded by the arrest of the central leaders and accompanied by that of the local

---

[1] Speech at Wexford, 9 Oct. 1881 (Lyons, *Parnell*, pp. 167–8).

[2] Morley, *Gladstone*, ii, 302.

[3] *Pall Mall Gazette*, 21 Oct. 1881 (D. A. Hamer, *John Morley* (Oxford, 1968), p. 129).

leaders'.[1] This was doubtless so. But as Lord Cowper had feared, the suppression of the League organization rather aggravated than curtailed rural violence. According to Parnellite legend, at dinner after the Wexford speech, Parnell, discussing policy in the event of his arrest, observed with deliberation 'if I am arrested, Captain Moonlight will take my place'. Whether apocryphal or not, this remark was an accurate expression of the trust that national political leaders could place in the permanent presence of inchoate local violence.

Conditions on the ground rapidly deteriorated. By mid November previously quiet districts had become disturbed: in Cork, the police lived 'as in an enemy's country'. In Limerick 'intimidation largely prevails, and rents do not come in at all'.[2] Violent crimes, especially murders and attempted murders with firearms, showed a definite increase during the winter.[3] Whether the League had exercised discipline as Professor Lyons suggests, or had merely diverted energies, it is clear that 'agrarian anarchy', centrifugal in force, welled up in its place.[4]

The crushing of the Land League had certain beneficial effects for Parnell. In the following year, after his release from gaol under an accommodation with the government, the terms of which have ever since been matter for dispute, he was able to establish a new organization. The Irish National League—though many officials continued, accidentally or deliberately, to call it the 'Land League'—was built very much more in Parnell's image. It was more overtly political, and was fashioned into the party machine for the increasingly homogeneous parliamentary body which took shape around the leader, demonstrating its power in co-operation with the Catholic clergy for the first time in the general election under the new franchise in 1885.[5]

---

[1] To Harcourt (Harcourt MSS 81). A few days earlier he had been talking about working through Ireland 'county by county with an overwhelming force of police and a flying column' (H. Gladstone's diary, 19 Oct. 1881, Cooke and Vincent, p. 531).

[2] Ibid., 17 Nov., 4 Dec. 1881, pp. 540, 544.

[3] Cases of murder and firing at the person rose from 1 and 12 in July–Sept. 1881 to 8 and 34 in Oct.–Dec., and to 6 and 27 in Jan.–Mar. 1882.

[4] Lyons, *Parnell*, p. 177.

[5] P. Bew, *C. S. Parnell* (Dublin, 1980), p. 61; O'Brien, *Parnell and his Party*, pp. 126–33; Garvin, *Evolution of Irish Nationalist Politics*, pp. 78–84.

(v) *Terrorism*

> . . . he could not believe that the Irish race was as badly
> off as the Russian race. They had all seen what Hartmann
> had done, and, if the present constitutional course that
> they were pursuing in Parliament did not succeed in getting
> the rights they wanted for Ireland, he thought that Ireland
> would be able to produce another Hartmann, probably
> with a much better result.
>
> Joseph Biggar[1]

The British authorities, as has emerged, had used the term
'terrorism' widely in their assessments of the breakdown of
law in Ireland. The apparently systematic, and obviously
effective, application of intimidatory violence by anonymous,
amorphous agrarian 'secret societies' was indeed seen as their
most striking and dangerous characteristic. This estimate of
the mechanism—if not of the power—of rural groups may
have been a little distorted, especially when it was extended
to the Land League.[2] Subsequent writers have tended on the
whole to treat the official perception of rural terrorism as
rather hysterical. Norman Palmer put it urbanely when he
suggested that the great majority of the Irish tenantry 'did
not need to be terrorized into adopting a policy which
appealed so obviously to their own interests'. As has been
seen, the English legal commentator, Sir James Stephen,
observed at the time that 'a very small amount of shooting in
the legs will efficiently deter an immense mass of people
from paying rents which they do not want to pay'.[3] Certainly the payment of 'Griffith's valuation' was an attractive
policy, but it must be doubted whether even such an
attraction coupled with the power of communal pressure
was sufficient to induce rather than coerce everyone. As
contemporary accounts make clear, most rural communities
were riddled with recidivists, who feared the consequences
of falling foul of landlords and the law. Although solidarity

---

[1] Joseph Biggar's speech of the Parnell Banquet, Cork, 21 March 1880 (Parnell
Comm. Rep., p. 22).

[2] e.g. in Forster's declaration that it was 'the first agitation I have ever seen,
the main strength of which was to obtain its end not at the ballot box . . . not by
public opinion, but by terrorism to individuals' (*Leeds Mercury*, 8 Dec. 1882).

[3] Palmer, *Irish Land League Crisis*, ch. IX, *passim*; Stephen, 'Suppression
of Boycotting', p. 773.

could help to convince some of these waverers that the policy would actually succeed, and that they would not suffer punishment by the government, it never worked entirely. Many of the crimes which the government saw as part of the system of terrorism were clearly designed to make the fear of punishment by the 'unwritten law' greater than fear of the landlords' law. Even those which were not so intended generally had this effect. Violent acts carried out as part of familial vendettas were 'agrarian' in so far as they concerned the possession of land, and though they did not bear the wider meaning—of hostility to landlords and land law— often read by the authorities into that term, they were equally part of a situation in which the threat of direct personal violence took the place of the orderly settlement of disputes through legal channels.

Unquestionably intimidation was an important, ingrained element of rural life. It was, as has been suggested earlier, 'enforcement' terror; basically conservative in intention, and unpolitical in its level of consciousness. In the 1880s, however, there began to appear a new and distinctly political form of terrorism, a strain of modern revolutionary or 'agitational' terror, announced by attempts to blow up the Mansion House in London and Liverpool Town Hall in May and June 1881. 'Fenian' terrorism (as the government called it, though it was denounced by the most authentic Fenians, John O'Leary, T. C. Luby, and John Devoy)[1] was undoubtedly politically aware, and employed new methods. Dynamite, one of the latest marvels of science, was used to create sensational outrages that would resound through the national and even the international media. But what were these shock-waves intended to accomplish? It is hard to detect amongst Skirmishers, Clan bombers, or Invincibles the sort of passionate belief in terrorism that distinguished their Russian contemporaries. Biggar's throw-away reference to the man who made the first attempt on Alexander II's life would nowadays, perhaps, be pounced upon by eager analysts to demonstrate the existence of a network of international terrorism. But Irish terrorists seem to have made no deep

[1] And by Davitt. See his discussion of the 'desperate and criminal attempts' of the dynamiters, *Fall of Feudalism*, ch. xxxv.

or systematic theoretical study of the new mode of action. They did not manifest the 'irrationality' which, in the persuasive view of a recent writer, underlay the belief of the *narodovol'tsy*.[1] Nor was their strategy consciously provocative—that is to say intended to force the British government into unpopular reactions. Such provocation has formed the intellectual basis of many modern revolutionary terrorist campaigns, but the Irish revolutionaries believed that the government had already lost all Irish sympathy. Its rule was based on force, and had to be confronted by force.

The rationale of the bombing campaign initiated by O'Donovan Rossa was in fact quite straightforward. It was the only way of engaging Britain with physical force, given that no insurrection was possible for the time being. This point was put with perfect clarity in 1883 in a secret memorandum of Clan na Gael:

We cannot see our way to an armed insurrection in Ireland this side of some great Foreign War with England. But in the meantime we shall carry on an incessant and perpetual warfare with the power of England in public and in secret.[2]

More crudely, it may be seen as a rhetorically inflated extension of already familiar patterns of violence. The most obvious element in Rossa's own outlook was that of revenge; the punitive use of violence was enunciated by him at the outset: in the *Irish World* in 1876 he threatened that if a Skirmisher were hanged, the minister who ordered the execution would be killed and the town in which the hanging took place would be burned. Davitt's threat in 1882, that 'the world would hold England responsible for the wolf-dog of Irish vengeance bounds over the Atlantic at the very heart of the power from which it is now held back by the influence of the Land League', was akin to this. Ten years later Rossa's approach remained the same; though tempered by disillusioning experience to the aim of 'doing something to hurt England before I go'. There is little suggestion here of any real hope that revolutionary changes could be effected by terrorism itself. Nor is there evidence of much careful

---

[1] W. Laquer, *Terrorism* (London, 1977), pp. 34–8, 69–70.
[2] Sept. 1883, quoted in Short, *Dynamite War*, p. 155.

thought about the possibly counter-productive effect of some forms of attack.

The most sophisticated critic of the terrorist impulse amongst Fenians was Devoy, a close friend of the man who led the Clan na Gael campaign in the early 1880s, William Lomasney. Lomasney himself intended to avoid taking life, especially innocent life, with his bombs, but Devoy tried to warn him that the Irish temperament would upset his calculations of 'bloodless terrorism'. 'When the Irish blood was up, there would be loss of life, the campaign would go on with increasing violence, and the pious British government with its control of views and propaganda would see that the world was duly shocked.'[1] In fact, although Lomasney was a purist of terrorism, it is hard to see how his version could have been expected to go on generating fear, let alone sufficient fear to force the government into policies desired by the Clan. Rossa's bloodthirstiness was in some ways more credible, but in execution it was let down by technical incompetence. Nor was Rossa tempted by the powerful and dangerous new explosives; he stuck to gunpowder.

Rossa's failures left the cutting edge of the bombing campaign in Lomasney's hands. The Clan organization was fairly efficient, and as with the Holland submarine earlier, was eager to experiment with new technology. With more courage than technical skill they mixed and transported awesome quantities of nitroglycerine, and, aided by a patchy police special branch and an ineffective customs service, found little difficulty in completing the preparatory stages of their projected attacks.[2] The final point of detonation was harder to achieve, and several attempts ended in failure or disaster —most notably the ambitious plan of the Gallagher team in 1883, and Lomasney's own death during his attempt to blow up London Bridge in December 1884.[3]

A considerable number of the bomb attacks, however, were carried out successfully. Their effect in inducing terror,

[1] D. Ryan, *The Phoenix Flame* (London, 1937), p. 226. On his attitude to terrorism and terrorists, ch. 11, *passim*.

[2] Records of customs searches 1884-7 (PRO HO 144, Closed files, A34848B).

[3] There is a highly detailed account in Short, *Dynamite War*, chs. 5-8.

though loyally sustained by Devoy, was problematical. As with subsequent campaigns, the impact lessened with time. It would probably have been impossible to recreate the mass-hysterical reaction which followed the Clerkenwell explosion in 1867. The first series of explosions did produce considerable shock, amongst the government as much as the public—and most importantly upon the Home Secretary. Harcourt's reaction was all that could have been hoped for by the Skirmishers had their policy been one of provocation. In March he rushed in a new Arms Act, extending the power of police search, against the views of Gladstone, Chamberlain, and Bright. Although he wrote complacently to the Queen in June 1881, after the abortive attempt on Liverpool Town Hall, that he had 'watched this business most intently now for more than six months', and 'the more I learn of it the less it alarms me', his alarms were soon renewed by the discovery of a number of bombs (or 'infernal machines' in contemporary parlance) buried in barrels of cement arriving at Liverpool. At the same time, the news of President Garfield's assassination reached him. This, in his view, confounded 'those who have been disposed to ridicule our alarms and condemn our proceedings'.[1]

The following year matters were no better. There were successful dynamite attempts, but the Phoenix Park assassinations created 'great alarm as to what the desperadoes may do next'; London was 'full of threatening letters and rumours of all kinds'.

The attempted explosion at the Mansion House was a Fenian scare of the old clumsy kind. I made it a reason for having all the Irish quarter in London beat up [i.e. patrolled] last night. My police report very little Fenianism in London, but of course it may be imported any day from either America or Ireland . . .[2]

By April 1883, when the Gallagher group were arrested, Harcourt was writing to Gladstone 'There can be no doubt that we are in the midst of a large and well-organized and fully equipped band who are prepared to commit outrages all over the country', and insisting that a new Explosives

---

[1] To Granville, 3 July 1881 (Gardiner, *Harcourt*, i, 430).
[2] Harcourt to Spencer, 14 May 1882 (ibid. 442).

Bill be rushed into law. Sir Charles Dilke commented sharply that 'Harcourt thought himself a Fouché', and the *Annual Register* observed that even the most panic-stricken members of society 'were somewhat taken aback by the headlong zeal of Sir William Harcourt to protect society at the expense of parliamentary procedure'. The Explosives law was pushed through its three readings in an hour and a half on 9 April, and only the slothfulness of a royal official prevented the consent being given on the same day—Harcourt raging that the psychological impact of the law had been blunted.

Controls on explosives were undoubtedly important, but the government set its sights impossibly high by aiming to prevent bomb attacks altogether. E. G. Jenkinson, head of the newly created Dublin Castle intelligence section, never had the courage to tell his superiors that this was impossible. He explained that 'it is most difficult to get proof against these men'—the police had to wait 'till they carry out one of their wicked schemes and even then detection and conviction are most difficult'. He lamented 'it is horrible to think that we have such devils in the midst of us, and are not able to come down on them', but added 'We shall never completely stop this "dynamite" war till we stop the supplies from America, and prevent Rossa's missioners from taking up their abode in England & Ireland'.[1] In May a special investigating officer, Major Gosselin, was appointed, with a roving commission to co-ordinate the work of the RIC political branch in Britain.

Gosselin was for a while the repository of many hopes; Jenkinson felt 'he understands these Irish scoundrels, and can *talk* to them', and Harcourt no doubt expected wonders.[2] The investigation focused on Birmingham, and a mass of hot but tantalizingly inconclusive information served to increase the tension. A wave of reprisals was expected in December after the hanging of O'Donnell, the 'executor' of the invincible informer Carey. According to Edward Hamilton, the CID chief Howard Vincent 'says that threats are very rife', though Hamilton himself calmly discounted alarmist rumours. 'With

---

[1] To Harcourt, 29, 31 Mar. 1883 (Harcourt MSS 103).
[2] Jenkinson to Harcourt, 7, 10 May, 11 Aug. 1883 (loc. cit.). On Gosselin's working methods see Gosselin to Harcourt, 22 Aug. 1883 (Harcourt MSS 105).

these scoundrels "the unexpected" is generally the order of the day.'[1] Harcourt could not accept this; in January he insisted on giving a reluctant Gladstone police protection, and declared that 'the "Dynamitists" are more than ever active and are bound to assert themselves so as to make a show for the O'Donnell "Vengeance Fund" money'. By early February the Home Secretary was 'more alarmed than ever', believing that 'we are on the eve of some terrible demonstration'.[2] He had just received a disappointment in being told by Gosselin that all his plans in Birmingham had failed so far and that he had 'nothing but bad news'.[3] At last, in April 1884, Gosselin achieved a great *coup* by arresting John Daly in possession of several brass cylinder grenades, 'most terrible weapons' in Jenkinson's opinion.

They are meant to be thrown by hand, and it was Daly's intention to come up to London, and to throw them at a group of Cabinet Ministers. If he could not find any good opportunity for doing this, he intended to throw a bomb from the Gallery of the House of Commons on to the front bench where Ministers sit.[4]

This half-baked plan was the measure of Daly's expertise, in spite of his sophisticated devices; he had been under intensive police surveillance for some time before his arrest, and was in a 'funk'.[5] He had clearly been betrayed, and it seemed that the police had the measure of the Fenian terrorist organizations. Yet on 30 May the most extraordinary of all the attacks was successfully brought off. Two minor explosions, one at the Junior Carlton Club where five people were injured, were accompanied by a devastating blast under the detective department at Scotland Yard itself. Incredibly, there was a public urinal built into the corner of the block, and it had been left open in spite of all the alarms and warnings. Jenkinson as usual bewailed the 'confusion and want of system at Scotland Yard',[6] but a night of frenzied searching discovered another, unexploded bomb near Nelson's column in Trafalgar Square.

[1] Hamilton's diary, 17 Dec. 1883.
[2] Ibid., 23 Jan., 4 Feb. 1884.
[3] Gosselin to Harcourt, 29 Jan. 1884 (Harcourt MSS 105).
[4] Jenkinson to Harcourt, 12 Apr. 1884 (Harcourt MSS 104).
[5] Short, *Dynamite War*, pp. 173–81.
[6] To Harcourt, 31 May 1884 (Harcourt MSS 104).

As it reached the end of 1884 Gladstone's government, battered by the struggles over the new franchise, had also to acknowledge that it had been unable to defend the country against terrorist attacks. Harcourt's obsession with Fenianism had caused a Cabinet crisis (when he insisted that Home Office control over the London Metropolitan police be built into the Municipality Bill). Gladstone, seeing the Liberal reputation being steadily undermined by Harcourt—who once told the Cabinet, according to Dilke, that coercion was like caviare, 'unpleasant at first to the palate, it becomes agreeable with use'—had refused to treat Fenian plots 'as a permanent institution of the country'.[1] Yet it appeared that, as long as 'Fenians' of whatever variety so chose, attacks would continue. In December 1884, Jenkinson wrote miserably to Harcourt

I have been dreadfully despondent since I saw you yesterday, because I could not help noticing how disappointed you were at our want of success in dealing with these dynamitards.[2]

He explained defensively that 'in a war such as this there must be some reverses', but admitted that he was 'not satisfied' with his work: 'on the contrary, I am very much dissatisfied'. He was continually thinking how he could do better, but 'under present circumstances' could not see how he could do more. This was due in part to the terrorists' method of operating, in small groups of three or four trusted men who could not be 'got at'; in part to the 'great jealousy of me and my Irish staff' in England.

The English detectives are utterly useless in this particular kind of work, and it is quite impossible to establish any system because there is no central authority over the police.[3]

The unhappy Jenkinson was soon squeezed out by both the British and the Irish police systems. With chilling if predictable governmental unconcern, his services were dropped as soon as the immediate crisis passed. After the death of Lomasney, the bomb campaign died away of its own accord, and no long-term preparations were made to cope with another.

[1] Gardiner, *Harcourt*, i, 426, 483-5.
[2] 10 Dec. 1884 (Harcourt MSS 104).
[3] Ibid.

Despite the primitive nature of their expectations, the Irish American operations of the 1880s must be seen as an early example of modern political terrorism. The Clan may have been overstating the case when it maintained, late in 1883, that the efforts of the brotherhood had 'settled the legal status of new mode of warfare', and 'compelled England to recognize a new epoch in the art of war', but both the limitations and the achievements of the campaign have to be viewed in a novel framework. Such was not the case with the most celebrated of all acts to which the label 'terrorist' was applied: the Phoenix Park murders. The assassination of Forster's successor, Lord Frederick Cavendish, and the Under-Secretary, T. H. Burke, in May 1882, was carried out with cold steel by a secret society, the Invincibles, which belonged more to the agrarian world than to Fenianism.[1] Several attempts had previously been prepared against Forster, and the chance success of this one depended on the amazing carelessness of police and officials, not least of Burke himself. It is doubtful whether its executors had any clear political intention—such, for instance, as the wrecking of the Kilmainham initiative. Yet its political impact was probably greater than that of any other terrorist act of the 1880s: it led to a radical shift in government policy, the abandonment of a nascent attempt at normalization, and the return to coercion, with, effectively, the permanent amendment of the criminal law.

(vi) *Prevention of crime: the reign of Lord Spencer*

> The public opinion of England is satisfied of the absolute necessity of repression and is most grateful to you for what you have done and will aboundantly support you in all you may think it necessary to do.
>
> Sir William Harcourt[2]

The much-discussed Kilmainham initiative brought a crisis

---

[1] Despite the claims of P. J. P. Tynan, *The Irish National Invincibles*; on the incident, T. Corfe, *The Phoenix Park Murders* (London, 1968), pp. 135 ff. Kickham, condemning the political imbecility as well as the gruesome violence of the killers, said that if they were Fenians they were 'Fenians seduced by the Land League' (Ryan, *Phoenix Flame*, p. 223).

[2] Harcourt to Spencer, 2 Jan. 1813 (Harcourt MSS 41).

in the Irish administration, forcing the resignation of both Cowper and Forster. The critical issue was the release of the most distinguished state prisoners, and above all Parnell. It turned on the question of their involvement in 'crime' and the likely effect of their release. As early as September 1881, before Parnell's arrest, Lord Spencer wrote from Aix-les-Bains to advise Gladstone that 'the detention of a number of men arrested under exceptional legislation is a great misfortune in view of the encouragement of good feeling towards the English Government in Ireland'. But since large-scale releases would be seen as a Parnellite victory and would discourage the few citizens who had supported law and order, releases should be gradual.[1] This optimistic argument accorded with Gladstone's ideas, but Forster held out against the release of the major leaders unless they pledged themselves to oppose violence. He refused or failed to see the constitutional impropriety of locking up opposition MPs and demanding obedience.[2] Gladstone, on the other hand, was personally discomfited when his opponents gleefully reminded him of the bad old days of the government of Naples.

Forster produced a major memorandum on the Irish situation in April 1882, but even before then rumours of his fall were current.[3] He admitted to the Cabinet that rents had generally been paid to date, with important exceptions such as the Mitchelstown estates, and that there was 'no open resistance to the law'. The Land League had been 'put down', and the Ladies' Land League (which Forster enjoyed mocking in public) was no substitute. Even boycotting was partly in decline 'mainly owing to the arrests of respectable "Boycotters" as suspects'. The Land Act was working, and 'poor cottier tenants are beginning to

[1] Spencer to Gladstone, 12 Sept. 1881 (BL Add. MS 44308, f. 151).

[2] Hammond, *Gladstone*, pp. 266 ff., argued persuasively that Forster had been 'so demoralized by the use of his arbitrary power that he had ceased to think of his prisoner as a man with rights that a Constitutional Government had to keep in mind'.

[3] Hamilton accused him of having lost his nerve as early as Dec. 1880. On 26 Mar. 1882 Lewis Harcourt heard that Spencer would not work with Forster, and his father fumed 'We shall never do anything with that country till both Cowper and Forster are out of it' (Diary, Harcourt MSS 350).

see that their only hope is in emigration'. So far, Forster said, 'the condition is hopeful, but on the other hand the outrages continue'. Indeed, as has been seen, they were worsening in respect of serious crime. The total of homicides and attempted killings in the last six months was 'alarming and unprecedented', and something would have to be done to make evil-doers fear punishment and to obtain public support against crime. Forster had tried his utmost 'to stimulate or create in localities some organization for mutual protection, but hitherto without effect'. He now recommended collective fines as a way of appealing to self-interest, and a special legal commission to replace jury trial. (He hinted that a military tribunal might be better, but 'would not get through the House'.)[1]

This stern document caused a revolt, and the Cabinet carried out a *coup* at the beginning of May by ordering the release of the suspects. The sudden reorientation is well reflected in the diary of Herbert Gladstone, then in Ireland and a keen believer in collective fines as the way to restore the effectiveness of law. On 22 April he recorded firmly that 'To yield a hair's breadth from what is the true and honest course, in order to make terms with men denounced by the government as criminals is impossible'. On 3 May he was trimming fast:

> The question of course arises ought you to deal with men you have accused of crime? . . . But a nation is involved, seeing that three-quarters of Ireland is ready to follow Parnell. It is obvious that the course we have been pursuing on the lines of the Coercion Act is hateful to the Irish, disliked by nearly everyone in England, and ineffectual in stopping outrage.[2]

The day before, Forster had resigned, and the so-called Kilmainham 'treaty' had secured from Parnell a promise not only to discourage outrages but also to co-operate with the Liberals in the cause of reform.[3] Parnell was released, and

---

[1] Cabinet memo., 21 Apr. 1882 (BL Add. MS 44160, f. 139).

[2] Cooke and Vincent, 'Herbert Gladstone', part II, pp. 78, 82.

[3] Lyons, *Parnell*, pp. 196-207; J. Enoch Powell, 'Kilmainham—the Treaty that Never was', *Historical Journal*, xxi (1978), 949-59. The American journalist W. H. Hurlbert held that the British shift was precipitated by US demands for trial or release of nationals held under the 1881 Act: *Ireland Under Coercion*, i, 21.

Davitt also on 5 May. A new Irish government was announced: Lord Spencer and Lord Frederick Cavendish, the latter's name being received by the House of Commons with 'no little derision'.[1] There was surprise that a position of 'such transcendent importance' had not gone to a political figure of greater weight, and it may be that Gladstone's curious choice was one of the more noticeable results of the distraction he was under throughout this period from the Egyptian crisis.[2] Cavendish's death affected Gladstone more directly than would have that of any other minister, and paved the way for an ironic return to Forsterian coercion.

Spencer's policy of control was, however, substantially different from Forster's. With Cavendish's successor, G. O. Trevelyan (Dilke having refused the job unless it carried a seat in the Cabinet),[3] he was 'determined not to revert to Forster's measures or to their spirit, nor to slide into military rule, nor to become the partisans of the Orangemen'.[4] Spencer specifically rejected the idea of martial law, which Harcourt felt was the only recourse left, throughout the crisis and acted with a calm resolution which confirmed his standing as a 'Roman'.[5] He was, however, strongly critical of the Dublin Castle system, especially the police and the magistracy. He recognized that any new Coercion Act would be pointless unless the local machinery existed to enforce it. Shortly after the assassinations he explained to Gladstone that it would be necessary to bring some distinguished and experienced officer over to take charge of the 'Magisterial Executive' and to help the heads of the police in trying to ferret out murderous groups; adding with rare sagacity

[1] Hamilton's diary, 5 May 1881.

[2] A. Ramm, *The Political Correspondence of Mr Gladstone and Lord Granville 1876–1886* (Oxford, 1962), p. xxiii.

[3] For which he was haughtily condemned by Hamilton, though his demand was sound and not merely ambitious. Even Trevelyan, who behaved impeccably in 1882, found that exclusion from the Cabinet made his position impossible.

[4] G. M. Trevelyan, *Sir George Otto Trevelyan. A Memoir* (London, 1932), p. 112.

[5] Morley's judgement: Hammond, *Gladstone*, p. 349. The idea of martial law had evidently passed through ministers' heads: in Dec. 1881 Chamberlain felt it necessary to tell Gladstone that 'of course martial law is out of the question' (Garvin, *Chamberlain*, i, 346). For Harcourt's reaction, Lewis Harcourt's diary, 7 May 1882 (Harcourt MSS 350).

'If I cannot strike a telling blow I shall remain quiet for it is weak to beat the air merely for effect'.[1] Next day he added that the case he had against the police was 'overwhelming', and later warned that 'the magistracy the RM's I mean need to be weeded with no sparing hand'.[2]

A graphic picture of local failure was supplied at this time by a friend of Hamilton's who returned in April from a visit to Clifford Lloyd, characterizing

the landlords as a parcel of funks, and the magistracy . . . as hopelessly rotten and equally cowardly and cowed. The magistrates decline to convict even in the face of evidence, and the constables naturally become disheartened. One magistrate out of sheer fright went and signed a petition for the release of a suspect whom he knew to be a leader of the intimidation party of his own district . . . Compton says he never could have believed without seeing how great is the effect of threatening letters. To them he greatly attributes the state of collapse and the success of the agitation.[3]

Herbert Gladstone noted that Spencer was most struck by the 'deficiencies in the organisation of the constabulary and police . . . and *this Forster has all along put aside and refused to deal with*'[4] (Gladstone's emphasis). The greatest problem was the impossibility of obtaining information—once again, allegedly due to Forster's lack of interest in building up a specialized service.[5] Spencer brought in a military expert, Col. Brackenbury, to take over the co-ordination of intelligence. According to Brackenbury's assistant, Major Alfred Turner, Brackenbury had been intended to become Inspector-General of the RIC, but quickly saw that 'the powers of this official were much too restricted to enable him to work any general good'.[6] He prepared a substantial memorandum analysing the nature of political crimes and of the agencies needed to deal with them.

[1] Spencer to Gladstone, 7 May 1882 (BL Add. MS 44308, f. 224).

[2] Spencer to Harcourt, 8 May (Harcourt MSS 39); to Gladstone, 11 May 1882 (BL Add. MS 44308, f. 242).

[3] Note of letter from W. Compton (Hamilton's diary, 16 Apr. 1882).

[4] H. Gladstone's diary, 8 May 1882 (Cooke and Vincent, 'Herbert Gladstone', part II, p. 83).

[5] Hamilton's diary, 9 May 1882.

[6] Maj.-Gen. Sir A. E. Turner, *Sixty Years of a Soldier's Life* (London, 1912), p. 55.

Political and agrarian crimes are solely and entirely promoted by secret societies. The police in Ireland is now dealing with the symptom of the disease; it is not dealing with, and is powerless to deal with, the secret source of the disease.[1]

Secret societies had to be penetrated by a secret intelligence organization, and Brackenbury undertook to achieve this if he were given sole and absolute control, with power to co-ordinate agents from the RIC and DMP. Brackenbury was at length gazetted Assistant Under-Secretary for Police and Crime, Gladstone having jibbed at the intended (but more accurate) title and post of 'Chief Special Commissioner'. The large sum of £25,000 a year was painfully wrung from a reluctant Treasury and First Lord, but restricted to two years. Spencer, who backed Brackenbury to the hilt in all his demands, protested that it was

absurd to expect to root out Secret Societies in 2 years. The agrarian & Fenian Societies are too old & are too deeply rooted in the country to disappear in 2 years.[2]

In the end, although the Cabinet disliked Brackenbury's statement that he intended to give effective legal immunity to informers and agents who infiltrated secret societies and had to commit crimes,[3] the operation was satisfactorily launched, and Spencer reposed great confidence in it. (He wrote to Harcourt that it was 'a case of "Trust me all in all or trust me not at all". As we have chosen him for the place the words of the song should be followed'.[4])

Within a few weeks, however, Spencer's good humour had turned to fury: Brackenbury attempted to get a place on the staff of General Wolseley (who had originally recommended him for the Irish post) for the Egyptian expedition, and Spencer icily dismissed him.[5] He was succeeded by Jenkinson,

---

[1] Memo., 31 May 1882 (Spencer MSS, quoted in R. Hawkins, 'Government versus Secret Societies: the Parnell Era', in T. T. Williams (ed.), *Secret Societies in Ireland*, pp. 104–6.

[2] Spencer to Harcourt, 18 May 1882 (Harcourt MSS 39).

[3] Loc. cit. Harcourt commented on Brackenbury's memo. at length to Spencer, 12 June, partly quoted in Gardiner, *Harcourt*, i, 446.

[4] 18 June 1882 (Harcourt MSS 39).

[5] Turner op. cit. 56–8. Spencer told Harcourt on 19 July that Brackenbury had behaved 'quite infamously' and urged the Secretary of State for War not to

who, despite Spencer's fulsome praise, never possessed the same energy or power. Most importantly, he never succeeded in establishing the single agency for co-ordinating information, in England as well as Ireland, which he believed to be vital.[1]

While this crucial groundwork was beginning, the government was preparing its new law, designed to fulfil Harcourt's desire to 'exercise to the utmost the powers of repression'.[2] The Prevention of Crime (Ireland) Act was passed in July 1882 after a moderated parliamentary struggle by Parnellites who were forced, in the wake of the Phoenix Park murders, to admit the inevitability of some such measure. Yet it was not just the renewal of traditional coercion: it was in some ways wholly new. It established a style in criminal law amendment which was to be perpetuated with the 1887 Crimes Act. It was certainly as drastic as the measure planned by Cowper and Forster.[3] Although it restored Habeas Corpus (the 1881 Act remained in force until August 1882, and Spencer considered making further arrests under it, but repeated that 'as yet information has been wanting: it is only a sign of weakness to arrest for the sake of appearing to be vigorous'),[4] it abrogated the right of trial by jury. Cases of treason, murder, and assaults on dwelling-houses were to be tried by special tribunals of three judges, if the Lord-Lieutenant believed that an impartial trial could not be obtained under the ordinary law.[5] Spencer's tenaciously held belief in Irish juries[6] had at last been undermined: he felt that the 'very audacity' of the Phoenix Park crime

employ him in 'any post of distinction'. He was banished to an artillery depot and only rescued by Wolseley in 1884. In 1886 he became Director of Military Intelligence.

[1] Jenkinson, memo., 22 Mar. 1883; to Harcourt, 10 Dec. 1884 (Harcourt MSS 103, 104).

[2] Hammond, *Gladstone*, p. 302.

[3] Giving, in the view of L. P. Curtis, 'many Irishmen direct experience of what amounted to martial law'—surely an overstatement (*Coercion and Conciliation in Ireland, 1880-92* (Princeton, 1973), p. 15).

[4] To Gladstone, 2 July 1882 (BL Add. MS 44309, f. 51).

[5] Act for the Prevention of Crime in Ireland, 45 & 46 Vict., c. 25, Part I.

[6] Repeated as late as 1881: to O'Hagan, 10 May (O'Hagan MSS D/2777/8, f. 246).

would 'if possible still further paralyse jurors'. On 8 May he recorded, 'Mr. Blake SRM told me today that he would not trust a jury of RMs at this moment'.[1]

Another major novelty of the Act was its attempt to define the crime of boycotting. This was not at all easy: the law could not, at its most basic, compel people to be sociable to each other. But it now defined as a criminal any person who

Wrongfully and without legal authority uses intimidation or incites any other person to use intimidation, to or towards any person or persons with a view to cause any person or persons, either to do any act which such person or persons has or have a legal right to abstain from doing, or to abstain from doing any act which such person or persons has or have a legal right to do

or towards anyone who had done/not done anything which they could legally do/not do. It defined 'intimidation' as

any word spoken or act done in order to and calculated to put any person in fear of any injury or danger to himself, or to any member of his family, or to any person in his employment, or in fear of any injury to or loss of his property, business or means of living.[2]

Such offences were to be tried by courts of summary juris-diction. This provision was highly unpopular with Liberals, who disliked the idea of vaguely defined crimes (of which treason was a still weightier example) being tried without jury. Gladstone was unhappy with the whole idea at first, as Harcourt struggled to get his stern requirements accepted by the Cabinet. Only on 8 June did the Prime Minister come out 'in full force against Boycotting'.[3] But he spoke with massive conviction on the subject during the Commons debate on the bill:

The evil, which there is in boycotting, dwells more or less in the breasts of most men—the question is, what is the amount of the evil? In Ireland

---

[1] Spencer to Gladstone, 8 May 1882 (copy, Harcourt MSS 39).

[2] 45 & 46 Vict., c. 25, Part III. Harcourt refused to accept the Irish MPs' demand that incitement be omitted from the clause.

[3] Gardiner, *Harcourt*, i, 441. Critics felt that 'these clauses enormously increased the powers of the special magistrates . . . who had already shown that they were not to be trusted with the more limited powers already conferred on them' (Lord Eversley, *Gladstone and Ireland. The Irish Policy of Parliament from 1850-1894* (London, 1912), p. 222).

it is a great and serious evil, limiting most unduly the liberty of action of men, and seriously endangering the peace and order of the country.

As a system, Gladstone repeated, it was 'a monstrous public evil, threatening liberty and interfering with law and order'.

The provision over which Harcourt failed, to his indignation, was his demand that the powers of the police to make night raids and searches be extended. Harcourt believed such powers to be vital, and when Spencer showed that he did not share the belief, he reproved him for being

a little *weak kneed* about the right of search. I don't think we shall have serious difficulty with it in Parliament and I attach the greatest importance to the power of going in to any cabin on a hill side at night and seeing who is in it. I make great use of this practice in the bad haunts of London.[1]

Spencer's attitude was vital, since Gladstone took refuge in the 'principle' of not passing into law any power that Spencer was willing to forgo.[2] This power was thus omitted, leaving Harcourt to fume against the disastrous 'couleur de rose view in which Gladstone persists in looking at the state of Ireland' and which produced the conciliatory Arrears Bill. He hoped that this would be defeated: 'the sooner the end comes the better, for this Government is not fit to govern Ireland.'[3]

Notwithstanding the Home Secretary's pique, the Liberals continued to govern Ireland for three years, practically the whole lifespan of the Crimes Act. Lord Spencer's administration gave every appearance of being remarkably successful. He tackled first of all the administrative machinery itself, having found

evidence of tension in all departments of Executive. A disposition to take the harshest action even when not necessary. It is not easy to relax this while maintaining perfect firmness, but we are aiming at that.[4]

[1] Harcourt to Spencer, 29 May 1882; also 8, 17, 21 June (Harcourt MSS 39).

[2] Gardiner, *Harcourt*, i, 448.

[3] To Hartington, 9 July 1882 (loc. cit.).

[4] Spencer to Gladstone, 11 June 1882 (BL Add. MS 44309). Brackenbury simultaneously denounced the 'administrative chaos' and over-centralization of Dublin Castle: to Hamilton, 20 June (Bahlman, i, 290).

He appointed a commission to look into the role of the special RMs and their relationship with the RMs, and took steps to remove the judicial function of the former and to separate the executive and judicial duties of the latter,[1] so as to enable them to sit on the new tribunals of summary jurisdiction. Harcourt felt that

The present status of the RMs seems essentially vicious as an administrative arrangement. From one point of view they are head-policemen and in another point of view they are judges. It would surely be far better to make the present RMs exclusively heads of Police executively and appoint a new set of men better selected for the purpose to act judicially.[2]

But while Spencer admitted that out of eighty-one RMs only twelve clearly had legal qualifications (one of them being Clifford Lloyd, which would be 'poor comfort to the Irish'), he did not carry through the full-scale changes suggested. The commission discovered that there was widespread dislike of the powers exercised by SRMs as 'calculated to harrass and disorganise the force'. In the nature of things, however, precise definition was difficult.

It is difficult for an official to discharge important duties for the detection of crime without guiding to some extent the action of the constabulary on whose assistance he relies. Indeed, his business is rather the work of a police officer than that of a magistrate.[3]

The position of SRMs was regularized in September 1883 when they were replaced by four divisional magistrates, three of whom were ex-SRMs; and a fifth was added in 1885 so that the whole country, not just the exceptionally disturbed part, was subsumed within 'divisions'.[4]

---

[1] 'As a class' he thought the RMs 'competent and reliable' in spite of his earlier criticisms: to Gladstone, 8, 11 May, to Harcourt, 18 May; Harcourt to Spencer 17 May 1882 (BL Add. MS 44308; Harcourt MSS 39).

[2] To Spencer, 25 May 1882 (loc. cit.),

[3] Report of Committee of Inquiry for Ld.-Lieutenant, 17 Aug. 1882 (HC 1883 (c. 3577), xxxii).

[4] The DMs were to 'have the general supervision of all matters connected with patrolling, and the establishment of military and constabulary posts' (RIC Circular, 1 Oct. 1883, PRO HO 184 116). Clifford Lloyd was predictably 'lost' in this reconstruction, Spencer making unsuccessful efforts to secure him a colonial governorship to reduce the political effect of his removal: to Gladstone, 1 Aug. 1884 (BL Add. MS 44311, f. 143).

The police continued to trouble Spencer. He found, for instance, in August 1882 that they were tearing down all placards in any way connected with the name 'Land League' regardless of whether the notices were loyal or not—they had torn down the manifesto of Parnell, Davitt, and Dillon denouncing the Phoenix Park murders. In the same month, discontent over pay and conditions, built up over years of grinding Treasury meanness, erupted into a police strike, a terrifying phenomenon for the government.[1] Spencer kept a cool head, increasing Harcourt's admiration for him. But his request for 1,000 English police was rejected: Harcourt sensibly maintained that (i) few would go, even if offered large bonuses; (ii) the effect on the RIC would be 'very disastrous'; (iii) the people would not accept them, and the policemen would not know how to deal with the people. 'The English constables would almost certainly be shot as are the occupants of evicted farms and from the same spirit.'[2] Spencer enrolled some 8,000 loyal men as special constables: this was almost the only time that 'some show of public spirit appeared'.[3] Detachments totalling 300 Royal Marines were brought into Dublin, where they operated with great efficiency.[4] Otherwise the strike was coped with by the dismissal of 208 policemen. Thereafter the situation improved considerably.[5] The committee of inquiry recommended pay increases, pointing out that men had had to spend their savings to meet the extra expenditure forced on them by the intense activity of 1880-2.[6]

The police began to perfect the system of intensive surveillance known as 'shadowing', which they disliked because it reduced the chance of an arrest, but which was effective in hampering the actions of suspected secret-society

[1] Spencer to Harcourt, 7 Aug., 1 Sep. 1882 (Harcourt MSS 40). Cf. Turner, *Sixty Years*, pp. 64–5.

[2] Harcourt to Spencer, 8 Aug. 1882 (Harcourt MSS 40).

[3] Harcourt to Gladstone, 27 Nov. 1882 (loc. cit.).

[4] Marines began to be deployed in Dublin on 3 Dec.; they were posted at various points connected to the castle by telephone, and were used in patrolling and close support of the DMP. They were finally withdrawn in July 1883: *Irish Times*, 26 July 1883.

[5] Cf. Deputy IG, RIC, memo., 'How the Civil Force in Ireland ought to be organised', 6 Sep. 1882 (BL Add. MS 44309, ff. 144-7).

[6] HC 1883 (c. 3577), xxxii.

men.[1] One of Spencer's main ambitions was realized as the police closed in on the Invincibles. In spite of continuing confusion, including a major gunfight between two rival Fenian gangs in Abbey street, in which one of the police 'shadowers' was killed, a system of investigation based on Spencer's old nostrum, the magisterial power of interrogation, bore fruit. On 13 January 1883 dramatic arrests were made by detectives accompanied by marines in plain clothes, and within weeks the conspiracy was smashed open.[2] Throughout 1883, while fears of secret-society activity continued, and Harcourt expressed severe lack of confidence in intelligence chiefs like Anderson,[3] the crime figures steadily improved.

TABLE IV

RIC Outrage Statistics 1881–3: agrarian crime*

	1881	1882	1883
January	448	495	90
February	170	410	54
March	151	542	93
April	308	465	73
May	351	401	93
June	332	284	67
July	271	231	61
August	373	176	70
September	416	139	79
October	511	112	53
November	534	93	55
December	574	85	46

* *Source*: Memo by Lord-Lieutenant, Gladstone MSS, BL Add. MS 44311.

The fall in the overall total of outrages from 3,433 to 834 was caused mainly by a dramatic fall in threatening letter cases from 2,010 to 408, though murders also dropped from

---

[1] Harcourt to Spencer, 28 Nov. 1882 (Harcourt MSS 40).

[2] Corfe, op. cit. 236 ff.

[3] Who 'bottles up what little information he possesses—and it is mighty little—and fiddles about with the Irish police in London' (to Spencer, 16 Mar. 1883, Harcourt MSS 42).

26 to 2. On the face of it, this was strong evidence that the 'intimidation' clause of the Crimes Act was effective. It is not easy, however, to distinguish the specific effects of coercive measures from the effects of reforms such as the Arrears Act—and indeed, the Land Act itself, whose long-term consequences were now being felt.[1] The general impression was that, whatever the cause, violence was in decline, and social life was moving back towards normality. In May 1883 Jenkinson reported the 'blowing up' of four secret societies in the west in three months, and estimated that 500 secret-society members had left the country.[2] Spencer suspected, though, that there remained a great deal of 'secret intimidation' even if written threats had declined, and it occasionally broke through into open boycotting as late as August 1884. Secret societies were 'quiet but determined'.[3]

At the beginning of 1885 Spencer occupied a position not unlike Forster's in early 1882. He had defended his position as the real head of the Irish executive in face of Trevelyan's request to be made a member of the Cabinet, arguing that executive authority would be harmed by 'coequal' authority with the Chief Secretary, or by parliamentary watering-down of the Lord-Lieutenant's decisions.[4] And though a 'hawk' like Harcourt was still in full coercive spate, he faced a revived challenge from the doves who now stepped up pressure for a new political initiative. Chamberlain's ill-fated 'central board' scheme for reconstructing Irish local government was launched at the end of 1884 in the hope of heading off the demand for Home Rule.[5] It foundered not only on Parnell's repudiation of it, but also on Spencer's insistence that repression must be continued. Early in 1885 Gladstone received from Spencer a comprehensive set of proposals for reform reviving his favourite proposal (dating

---

[1] Cf. Leadam, *Coercive Measures*, p. 29. It should be remembered that the tightening-up of reporting procedure may have led to some reduction in the apparent incidence of intimidation cases.

[2] Memo. 'The Growth and Prevention of Crime in the District of Castleisland, County Kerry', Nov. 1883 (Harcourt MSS 42); Jenkinson to Harcourt, 7, 10, 24 May 1883 (Harcourt MSS 103). Cf. Crime Special Branch reports 1883-4 (PRO CO 904 10).

[3] Spencer to Gladstone, 26 Aug. 1884 (BL Add. MS 44311, ff. 179-86).

[4] Ibid.

[5] Garvin, *Chamberlain*, i, 576-84.

back to 1870) of creating a royal residence in Ireland to make possible a closer attachment to the Crown, while at the same time removing the Crown from the direct arena of executive policy by abolishing the Lord-Lieutenancy and replacing it with a Secretaryship of State.[1] In March a dispirited Cabinet was presented with a grim set of memoranda which endeavoured to assess the operation of the Crimes Act since 1882. Spencer pointed to the sections of the Act which had either never been used (such as Part I, providing for the special commission of judges), or had proved of limited use (such as section 11, the curfew clause) or actually unworkable (such as section 15, on aliens), but maintained that the remainder must be kept in force—that is to say, re-enacted in the summer. Fenianism remained 'completely organized', and its membership was estimated at 36,000 in Ireland and 11,500 in Britain; the National League was a formidable organization.

In such a state of things I feel that without certain provisions of the Crimes Act, crime would again go unpunished, intimidation would spread, agitation would exceed the bounds of constitutional discussion, and good government would again become impossible.

Ideally (and here Spencer anticipated Dicey's argument) the necessary clauses should be made a permanent part of the criminal law of the United Kingdom: this would remove the reproach of 'exceptional legislation'. It would present political difficulties, of course, and Spencer was aware that 'it would be a great misfortune if the Govt. had to meet the new constituencies as having just passed a Coercion Act and nothing else': he recommended, amongst other things, a land purchase scheme.[2]

The government was already demoralized before it turned from the Sudan and Afghanistan to the less congenial issue of Ireland, but disagreements over coercion catalysed its final collapse. By 9 May it had reached the point where 'Eventually Spencer and Chamberlain both pinned them-selves down—S not to swallow C's bill, C not to swallow

---

[1] Hamilton's diary, 28 Jan. 1885.
[2] Memos. by Ld.-Lieutenant, 23, 25 Mar.; by Chief Secretary (Campbell-Bannerman), 25 Mar.; and by Ld. Chancellor Ire., 31 Mar. 1885 (PRO CAB. 37/14).

S's crimes bill'.[1] In early June attempts to manœuvre out of the impasse via a proposal of Shaw-Lefevre's that the Crimes Bill operate only at the discretion of the executive, not automatically, failed.[2] After a final disagreement over coercion on 9 June the Cabinet agreed, with relief, to resign. Consequent animosities were evident in 1886: in January Loulou Harcourt recorded that Chamberlain refused to meet Spencer, saying 'I attribute the present difficulties in Ireland entirely to his opposition and rejection of my National Council scheme last summer'. And when Spencer said '(as if he had always thought so) that all the misfortunes of Ireland have come since and in consequence of the Union', Harcourt

jumped down his throat & said 'why for God's sake did you not say this last June when you broke up the Govt. by refusing to accept any part of Chamberlain's scheme and insisting on the renewal of most of the Crimes Act?'[3]

---

[1] Lord Rosebery's diary: A. B. Cooke and J. R. Vincent, *The Governing Passion* (Brighton, 1974), p. 231.

[2] Ibid. pp. 246–53. For a last-minute Liberal defence of coercion see Lord Monteagle, 'The Crimes Act', *Nineteenth Century*, c. (June 1885), 1072–6.

[3] L. Harcourt's diary, 12 Jan. 1886 (Harcourt MSS 376).

4

Pacification

The only course is to go on 'pegging away'. You will soon by experience learn the precise limit of your powers, and then within those limits you will be able without ever, or often, incurring a defeat, to inflict an intolerable amount of annoyance.

Lord Salisbury[1]

(i) *Fights in Ulster; 'Ulster will fight'*

The Tory party here will sacrifice you by and by without the smallest compunction, that is when an enlarged franchise renders you incapable of rendering further service to the 'cause'. Things are moving so fast in England itself, Ulster will be left to shift for herself as best she may.

J. A. Fox[2]

The Ulster labyrinth, doomed to become the vortex of political violence in Ireland, reached its final form during the last decade of Gladstone's career. It has recently been asserted, with lofty aplomb but without evidence, by the leading authorities on the period that the 1881 Land Act had as one of its principal objects (the other being 'the breaking of the Land League') the detachment of Ulster from Irish nationalism.[3] The government's extraordinary perfunctoriness towards Ireland—Ulster not excluded—so amply attested elsewhere by these authors may cast some doubt on the deliberateness of this plan. If they are correct, the policy was unusually acute, and uniquely (albeit fatally) successful. In fact, no such legislation was needed. The cultural distinctness of the North, and especially of its capital, came easily to delineate a new arena of political confrontation.

---

[1] Salisbury to A. J. Balfour, October 1887 (Balfour MSS, BL Add. MS 49688, f. 153).

[2] Fox to Hugh de Fellenberg Montgomery, January 1884 (Montgomery MSS, PRONI D. 627/250).

[3] Cooke and Vincent, *Governing Passion*, p. 50.

At the same time traditional forms of communal conflict were sharpened by the politicization that was part of the new democracy. Modernization of method was not accompanied by modernization of myth. There were to be Protestant general strikes in the future, but no image of proletarian revolution. The Protestant revolution remained spiritual; but it was none the less powerful for that. The political figment called 'Ulster', less a geographical expression than a value, was brought into prominence as a pawn in English party manœuvre, but it had an existence outside the insubstantial world of high politics. It became a bearer for the collection of symbols which reciprocally expressed and shaped the identity of Northern Protestant groups.

The concrete mechanism through which these quasi-metaphysical entities could be realized was the enduring tradition of group action previously referred to as 'banding'. The Orange Order, despised though it was by the urban Protestant élite, remained the most important carrier of this tradition. It was certainly not the sole manifestation, much less the cause, of the propensity for collective action and collective violence. It still appears that the persistence of frontier responses underlay the institution of communal self-policing, identifiable in its mechanics with the phenomenon known in nineteenth-century America as vigilantism.[1] Northern self-reliance had produced a judicial infrastructure markedly stronger than elsewhere in Ireland. In 1866, for instance, local magistrates organized patrolling, and some even supplied their 'sound' tenants with 'very superior rifle arms'.[2] Resistance to the Land League was also noticeable well before the Land Act; and while Ulster ranked high in the table of evictions, it was low in agrarian

---

[1] On the relationship between vigilantism and political violence, and the problem of analysing this phenomenon, see J. F. Kirkham *et al., Assassination and Political Violence* (New York, 1970), pp. 293–4. On Protestant vigilantism see also below, p. 386.

[2] Wm. Patterson to Montgomery, 29 Feb. 1866 (Montgomery MSS, loc. cit.). This could be overdone, however, as when D'Arcy Irvine marched into Enniskillen on a fair day in 1870 'accompanied by 100 tenants armed with Snider rifles'. 'Just fancy', as Col. Saunderson commented to his wife (16 May 1870) (Saunderson MSS, PRONI T. 2996/2/13/78).

crime.[1] Although the Orange Order cautiously backed the tenant-right movement (officially in Armagh, though not in Fermanagh), it mobilized rapidly against the League as soon as its hypersensitive antennae identified the latter with the home rule movement.[2] By November 1880 the Order had issued instructions that every League meeting should be matched by a counter-meeting, and not long afterwards the League retaliated with economic sanctions—'blacking' Orangemen's merchandise at markets—foreshadowing the later Belfast boycott.[3]

A collective manifestation particularly alarming to the government was the Roslea or Rossmore incident (named after its location or its principal figure) in October 1883. Lord Rossmore, who in his youth as 'Master Darry' had revelled in terrorizing his patrimony and organizing faction fights, carried his cavalier spirit (in the 9th Lancers he was a boon companion of the young Hubert Gough, later to frighten the Liberals away from imposing home rule on Ulster)[4] into his function as a magistrate. On 16 October he and Lord Crichton led a great Orange posse, recruited under the slogans 'Down with Parnell and rebellion' and 'Emergency and Boycott Men to the front', to counter a National League (or in Rossmore's word 'rebel') meeting which was due to be addressed by T. M. Healy. Crichton, leading the way, was met by the resident magistrate, Captain McTernan, commanding 550 troops and police, and asked to alter his route so as to avoid a clash. Crichton complied, but when Rossmore's column—'a most respectable, determined-looking body of men numbering more than two thousand'—came up, its leader refused to bow to an 'insufferable' (and

[1] Agrarian outrages	1879	1880	1881	1882	1883
Ulster	111	259	414	320	89
Leinster	147	351	833	732	184
Munster	136	1,019	1,957	1,500	446
Connacht	476	961	1,235	881	151

Figures compounded from Parliamentary Reports, in R. W. Kirkpatrick, 'Origins and development of the land war in mid-Ulster, 1879–85', in Lyons and Hawkins (edd.), *Ireland Under the Union*, pp. 224–5.

[2] Ibid. 229.

[3] Ibid. 231.

[4] See below, pp. 270–2.

Catholic) officer of the law. He forced his way through in close proximity to the League meeting, and on a nearby hillside he pledged his men 'to resist in every way in our power any attempt to place Ireland under a government of murderous butchers and socialistic rebels', indicating 'that scum on the hill beyond'.[1] Subsequently he was dismissed from the magistracy for 'deliberately endangering the public peace', but this indignity only served to inflame Orange tempers still further. In December the military had to intervene to control a pro-Rossmore riot at Dromore, and an Orangeman was fatally wounded in a police bayonet charge.[2] Rossmore was later quietly reinstated by the Conservative government.

The year 1883 was an altogether grim one. Healy's victory in the Monaghan election launched the cry 'the invasion of Ulster'.[3] An Orange pamphlet spoke of an open call to arms, a Protestant *levée en masse*.[4] Worse, perhaps, riots in Londonderry forced Lord Spencer back on his unpleasant memories of 1872 and the apparently insoluble problem of policing the northern towns. The riots stemmed from the illegal seizure by the 'Prentice boys' of a hall in which a Nationalist meeting was to be held. The magistrates and police had failed to prevent this; but, as Spencer saw, their failure was more or less rooted in the legal system:

> on a former occasion Colonel Hiller, Deputy Inspector General of Constabulary, when in command of a large force to keep the peace, stopped men entering the Hall. Several actions were brought against him and he lost them.[5]

Such inhibitions would afflict the forces of law into the twentieth century. The question was arising, however,

---

[1] *Dublin Weekly Mail*, 20 Oct. 1883; Rossmore's own account of the affair can be found in his unattractive memoir, *Things I Can Tell* (London, 1912), pp. 240-6; for a map see Harcourt MSS 42. McTernan was once again to protect Healy from an Orange squad, at Dungannon: Healy, *Letters and Leaders of My Day*, i, 197-8.

[2] Kirkpatrick, op. cit. 234. For Rossmore's dismissal see Memo. for Ld.-Lieutenant, 28 Jan. 1884 (BL Add. MS 44311, ff. 13-26).

[3] Miller, *Queen's Rebels*, p. 88.

[4] *The Orange Secret* (Belfast, 1883), quoted in Baker, 'Orange and Green', p. 808.

[5] Spencer to Gladstone, 28 Feb. 1884 (BL Add. MS 44311, f. 72).

whether the police force was adequately adapted to its function. The riots which broke out in Belfast in 1886 over-shadowed anything that had occurred in 1883, perhaps even since 1864 (the riots which had led to the replacement of the city police by the RIC). They were more protracted than any previous outbreak; intensely violent; and, for the first time, overtly political. This political content was seen most startlingly in Protestant hostility to the RIC.

The immediate occasion of the 1886 outbreak, and the microdynamics of its early development, were traditional. An argument and fight between a Catholic and a Protestant amongst the hitherto peaceable mixed workforce at the Alexandra Dock construction site called forth a punitive expedition from the exclusively Protestant 'Island men' (shipbuilders at the Harland and Wolff yard on Queen's Island). The highly developed cohesive sense of these artisans was evident in the way that

at their dinner hour—about one o'clock—on the 4th of June a body of the Queen's Island workmen left the Queen's Island works, armed with sticks and various missiles, and rushed to the Alexandra Dock.[1]

The police, who did not arrive until some time later, estimated the strength of the attacking group at 100, with 1,000 others following. The Catholic workers did not attempt to fight: most of them fled, and those who did not were beaten up or hurled into the Lagan, and there pelted with steel bolts and other debris. One, a youth by the name of Curran, was drowned. The police made no attempt to arrest any of the attackers. That evening they concentrated their efforts on preventing any retaliatory assault on the Island men on their way home after work, which took them across much of Belfast. As the massive report of the commission of inquiry explained,

The extremity to which party and religious feeling has grown in Belfast is shown strikingly by the fact that the people of the artisan and labouring class, disregarding the ordinary considerations of con-venience, dwell to a large extent in separate quarters, each of which

[1] *Report of the Belfast Riots Commission, with Evidence and Appendices* HC 1887 (C. 4925), xviii. 1. The minority report referred to an 'organised body' of Island men.

is almost entirely given up to persons of one particular faith, and the boundaries of which are sharply defined.[1]

The police themselves were approximately 525 strong on 4 June (their strength on paper being 598, of whom 268 were Catholics), under two resident magistrates and over eighty JPs. These were brought out in force on the 6th to control another traditional, inevitable, development: the funeral of the boy Curran. This highly emotional procession took a demonstrative route across the Brickfields, one of the central 'shatter zones' of Belfast conflict.

The great points of danger to the peace of the town are open spaces on the borderland between the two quarters; and two of these spaces— the Brickfields and Springfields—will be found to have been the theatres of some of the worst scenes of the riots.[2]

The police succeeded in keeping the two sides apart, but this success antagonized what the police called the Protestant 'Shankill Road Mob', who manifested a 'very determined spirit of hostility' towards them throughout the night. As a result the magisterial authorities met on the 7th and decided to call for reinforcements.

This was to prove a detonating point. Subsequent criticism of the RIC turned on the fact that its Belfast force was kept too weak in quiet times, as well as being hampered in building community relationships by constant transfers (basic to RIC central policy), so that when a crisis broke it could only be met by drafting in large numbers of outsiders. As the first 400 country police arrived there was mounting popular antagonism. An attempt by Town Inspector Carr to stop the wrecking of a Catholic pub in Percy Street was met by a heavy fusillade of stones, wounding Carr and breaking up his force. In desperation, as the crowd bore down on him, he ordered fourteen of his remaining men to load, and three of them to fire a shot. In fact nine did so. The crowd, stunned, retreated temporarily, but then hurled itself against a group of police defending another Catholic pub, with cries of 'Murder the Fenian whores!' and 'Morley's murderers'. The police broke and ran back down the Shankill Road to Bower's Hill barrack.

[1] *Report of the Belfast Riots Commission.*
[2] Ibid.

This retreat was judged by the commission of inquiry to have been 'disastrous'. After it the rioting became uncontrollable, lasting, with short intermissions, for over three months. The police were reinforced to nearly two thousand, but continued to be attacked with unprecedented violence and persistence. The confrontation, and the lasting hatred for the RIC engendered in Protestant working-class districts, originated in a belief that the force was now in the hands of Home Rulers. The declaration of John Morley, former radical prophet and Gladstone's new Chief Secretary for Ireland, that the constabulary would prevent any open resistance to constitutional change, was perceived by Protestants as a threat to use force to impose home rule—or worse. The commission of inquiry found that 'the wild and unreasoning hostility exhibited by a large section of the Protestants' was

an expression of the extraordinary belief which so largely prevailed . . . that the late Government of the Queen [i.e. Gladstone's third ministry] was packing the town of Belfast with Catholic policemen, carefully selected from certain southern counties, and charged with the duty of shooting down the Protestants.[1]

This extravagant cognitive dissonance, which so fatally determined reactions to the RIC reinforcements, was by now fundamental to Protestant perceptions. The atmosphere of hysteria was heightened by a new political awareness, and a near-revolutionary development in British politics—the adoption of home rule by Gladstone and a majority of the Liberals. For the first time the idea of tampering with the Union had been openly accepted. The continuing arguments over Gladstone's motives, and the question of whether the first Home Rule Bill was a serious legislative proposition, are entirely academic as far as the impact of the matter on Ulster is concerned.[2] Gladstone's apparent belief that home rule would reinforce rather than weaken the Union, his mental ingenuity and verbal complexity, were all lost on a community of instinctive simplifiers. Even Lord Randolph

---

[1] Ibid., quoted in A. C. Hepburn (ed.), *The Conflict of Nationality in Modern Ireland* (London, 1980), p. 37.

[2] The most substantial, and most academic, reassessment is Cooke and Vincent, *Governing Passion*, esp. at pp. 48–56 and 312 ff.

Churchill, who sought (with that Tory superciliousness which often added an edge of hostility to the complaisance of loyal Ulstermen) to manipulate Orangeism like a playing-card, became a victim of its ruthless manner of perceiving only what reinforced its preconceptions. In the simple pattern of Protestant political categories, home rule became immutably fixed as 'Rome Rule'; the power of slogans, as always a substitute for intellectual effort and political maturity, was brought to the standpoint henceforth known as 'loyalism'. Churchill's 'Ulster will fight, Ulster will be right' was rhetoric aberrant even by the standards of that changeful politician.[1] But loyalists seized upon it with alacrity and clung to it with passion, turning it into perhaps the most celebrated utterance of his career, and identifying him forever with Protestant intransigence.

The symbols of Crown and Empire, and the institution of the Union, were enough to cement Protestant political opinion, including that of former Liberals.[2] These abstractions were, however, improbable mobilizers of popular energy. The core of loyalism, the true focus of loyalty, was the Ulster Protestant way of life. Loyalists were principally loyal to themselves, their 'freedom, religion and laws'. The idea of the 'constitution' was a general expression of this, guarantee-ing the status of Protestants amidst a hostile Catholic population. Loyalty to the Crown was conditional upon reciprocity. If the Crown ceased to guarantee the Protestant constitution, it would cease to command loyalty.[3] Aware-ness of this conditionality accounts for the continuing tradition of Protestant self-reliance, the maintenance of an organizational structure for preserving Protestant dominance, in the last resort by force. Unfortunately, British statesmen found it hard to grasp this crucial point. As a result, the

[1] For a contextual account, R. F. Foster, 'To the Northern Counties Station: Lord Randolph Churchill and the prelude to the Orange Card', in Lyons and Hawkins, *Ireland Under the Union*, pp. 237-87. Cooke and Vincent's interpre-tation of Churchill's Irish policy is systematically criticized in R. E. Quinault, 'Lord Randolph Churchill and Home Rule', *IHS* xxi (1979).

[2] Ulster Liberals did not join the Ulster Loyalist Anti-Repeal Union, but on 13 April formed their own Liberal Unionist Committee: P. Buckland, *Irish Unionism 1885-1922* (London, 1973), p. 6.

[3] The loyalist conception of the constitution is analysed lucidly in D. W. Miller, *Queen's Rebels*, pp. 27, 35, 61.

complex excitements of the 1886 political crisis at West-minster have in retrospect an air of irrelevance if not of absurdity.

The significance of the Belfast outbreak was lost on the English. With their impressive capacity to ignore what they disliked or did not comprehend, they worried about other things.[1] Only the Riots Commissioners applied their pro-digious energies to investigating the disaster which had killed 32 people and injured 371; and in the end they took refuge in the expedient which a recent historian has called 'the formula of tinkering with the police'.[2] It was not the last time this formula was to be invoked. They held that notwithstanding public hostility towards it the RIC should continue to be the police of Belfast. A local force such as had existed before 1865 would be still worse.[3] But it should be commanded by a Chief of Police who would be sub-ordinate only to the Inspector-General.

> We thoroughly concur with the military witness . . . who told us that what was wanted at Belfast was some head—some individual chief who would act promptly and decisively, without any communications, and who would be perfectly willing to take all the responsibility of any action which he might think fit to direct.[4]

The persistence of the riots was attributed to 'divided author-ity', but apart from recommending that this be rectified, and that the city's paving-stones be changed so as not to provide rioters with instant ammunition, the commissioners could offer little advice on deeper problems.

Belfast was never entirely reconciled with the police. On several occasions hostility erupted on slight provo-cation, and only the military—who were regarded as fellow British Protestants—could enter the shipyards or the

---

[1] Cooke and Vincent, *Governing Passion*, p. 7 n.

[2] Stewart, *Narrow Ground*, p. 151.

[3] The minority report did recommend the creation of a special force for Belfast. It also attributed the 'condition of derangement into which all the elements of the civil power in Belfast were allowed to drift during the distur-bances in June, July and the first week of August' in some degree to 'careless-ness or indifference engendered by a knowledge of the fact that "happen what might" the military were available to supply all deficiencies and to retrieve all blunders' (Report by One of the Commissioners of Inquiry, 1886, HC 1887 (C. 5029), xviii. 631).

[4] HC 1887 (C. 4925), xviii, p. 20.

Shankill.[1] The deeper problem also persisted, and worsened as it became more overtly political. As one perceptive historian has observed, violence was a characteristic of the early frontier of urbanization elsewhere in Britain too, but the peculiar disorder of Belfast was that it was perpetuated on sectarian lines into the last quarter of the nineteenth century, and that the middle classes—both Protestant and Catholic— came to tolerate it.[2] Although the poverty of the Catholic working class remained both a distinguishing mark and a cause of discontent, such facts are altogether inadequate to explain the mentalities which developed on both sides. The mechanism lay deep in the process of socialization. A vital determinant was the defensive Catholic refusal, stemming from fear of the Protestant 'crusade' and memories of 'souper' proselytism during the famine, to countenance educational integration. Identities were fostered in separation, and were defended, perhaps in an important way experienced, through physical force or quasi-military display.

Of more direct political significance even than the riots in Belfast in 1886 was the less publicized Richhill drilling case, when the right to breach the Statute of Liveries in the cause of defending the 'constitution' (to reach a spectacular culmination in 1912) was established. When the government's prosecution of Armagh loyalists for drilling in Richhill broke down at Armagh petty sessions on 17 June 1886, a demonstration of several hundred people celebrated the triumph. The Richhill band paraded the town amidst cheers for the defendants and groans for Gladstone, Morley, and Parnell. At a meeting in the Temperance Hall the main speaker told his audience they 'had a right to drill', because

They were representatives of a people who came here 200 or 300 years ago, and they had a right to be in this country, and they meant to be in it. (Cheers.) Some parties, however, thought they ought to be out of this country altogether . . . If they did not remain in this country it was their own fault.[3]

---

[1] SPO, CSO RP 1900/15358, 1912/15601; Baker, 'Orange and Green', pp. 805-6.

[2] Ibid. 801-4.

[3] *Ulster Gazette*, 19 June 1886 (PRO CO 904 28/1).

After this habitual reminder of the struggle for survival and the need for self-reliance, a solicitor advised them that 'they were assembled for a loyal and lawful object', and another speaker complained that 'what people formerly looked on as constitutional, right and proper' was now held improper by a government which was under the control of the National League. The Belfast *Morning News* reported that the Richhill drillers were 'members of the Grand Orange Army', and their exercises were publicly declared to be 'preparations for the civil war to be waged against the Queen's forces in resisting Home Rule'.[1]

Altogether the crisis of the 1880s compacted Ulster Unionism and fixed its methods of action. Its parliamentary leader, Saunderson, grimly warned Churchill early in 1887

Very bitter feelings are rising up amongst the Northern Loyalists owing to the fact that the lawless portion of the community are allowed to have everything their own way. If it should continue to be shown that disloyalty and lawlessness means amongst other things immunity from paying just debts I need hardly point out how popular disloyalty and lawlessness are likely to become.[2]

The creation of a parliamentary grouping was followed during the second home rule crisis by the appearance of a quasi-constitutional mass organization with the capacity, if not yet the intention, to act as an alternative government. The Ulster Unionist Convention in June 1892 was primarily a political demonstration, intended to obviate by its effect the necessity for further and more dangerous action. But the possibility of such action was preserved, from 1893 onwards, by the first permanent loyalist organization, the Ulster Defence Union. The signs were there to be read, even if Liberal statesmen insisted on deciphering them as an elaborate joke.[3]

[1] *Morning News*, 18 June 1886. For examples of 'colonist' fears of expulsion from Ireland see Miller, *Queen's Rebels*, pp. 88–9.

[2] Saunderson to Lord R. Churchill, 12 Jan. 1887 (Saunderson MSS, PRONI T. 2996/3 19).

[3] Harcourt in particular treated Saunderson's warning that underestimation of Ulster resistance 'may ultimately lead you fatally astray on the Irish question, a disaster which might be avoided by accurate information' with open derision. 'When your hypothetical insurrection is a little more advanced and war is actually declared', he suggested that he might meet Saunderson's army on its way to London

(ii) *The discreet charm of devolution*

> Just as I have seen in English colonies, across the sea, a
> combination of English, Irish and Scotch settlers bound
> together in loyal obedience to the law and the Crown
> and contributing to the general prosperity of the country,
> so I cannot conceive that there is any irreconcilable bar
> here in their native home and in England to the unity and
> amity of the two nations.

The Earl of Carnarvon[1]

Before the English Tory party stood itself unflinchingly
alongside the 'foul Ulster Tories' (Churchill's phrase), it went
through a phase of curious flexibiltity. During Lord Salisbury's first government, from June 1885 to January 1886,
room for manœuvre seemed to be given to two heterodox
Conservatives, Randolph Churchill and the Earl of Carnarvon.
At the same time, through Lord Ashbourne's Act, a step
was taken towards solving the land problem by removing
the landlords.[2] Coercion was ostentatiously abandoned as
a failed Liberal device. This new departure was felicitously
labelled by Hammond 'the Carnarvon adventure'.[3] Carnarvon
had been Colonial Secretary in 1867–8 when the federal
structure of Canada was finalized, and believed in the possibility of an accommodation with Parnell. In retrospect,
Salisbury's hostility to Carnarvon's ideas and his expressed
belief in the need to strengthen the Union by twenty years
of resolute government make it strange that he appointed
the suspect peer to the Lord-Lieutenancy of Ireland.[4] Salis-

at Derby, where 'the Rebel Army would effect its junction with the ducal contingent from Chatsworth'. Meanwhile, 'I shall watch your strategy with interest
and try to alarm myself as much as I can manage' (Saunderson to Harcourt and
replies, 23, 24, 28, 29 May 1892, Saunderson MSS, loc. cit.). Such attitudes certainly paved the way for the Liberals' later mishandling of the Ulster crisis
after 1911.

[1] House of Lords, 7 July 1885.
[2] By providing public finance to facilitate the buying-out of landlords by
their tenants.
[3] Hammond, *Gladstone and the Irish Nation*, pp. 376–89.
[4] In the view of Peter Marsh the apointment was 'as unnecessary as it was
mistaken', and was based on Salisbury's caste sense rather than assessment of
Carnarvon's ideas. Carnarvon and Salisbury had been contemporaries at Eton
and Christ Church, and in spite of his federalist unorthodoxy Carnarvon was a
sound 'old guard' Conservative. Cf. the analysis of the *ad hoc* formation of

bury's own view was simple: 'Ireland must be kept, like India, at all hazards: by persuasion, if possible; if not, by force.'[1]

The political situation, however, made it expedient to try persuasion at this time. Churchill had indeed bought the Irish vote with a promise that coercion would be abandoned. This did not necessarily imply a policy of kindness rather than kicks, as many Conservatives shared Clifford Lloyd's belief that the ordinary law was quite sufficient to maintain control if properly administered, and that continual exceptional legislation was subversive of the concept of the Union. In July 1885 Carnarvon received from Jenkinson and the Under-Secretary, Sir Robert Hamilton, advice that coercion could be safely dropped, and the Cabinet agreed not to try to renew the Crimes Act.[2] Carnarvon crossed to Dublin, arriving amid 'loud and continuous cheering', which much impressed him (as far as he could see, only five or six individuals expressed 'a solitary opposition'). His surviving papers cast a flood of light on the Irish administration and its problems in the next six months. Most of these problems he laid, unsurprisingly, at the door of the Liberals.

The utter mismanagement of Ireland as of every part of the Empire & country during the late govt. has brought us here to a position from which it is alike difficult to advance or retire—I believe that 'boycotting' though very bad is not so bad as it is represented . . . I am endeavouring to counteract it in every way I can.[3]

Even this cautious optimism was a little rash, at least in the opinion of one divisional magistrate, Captain Slacke of the

Salisbury's ministry and its Irish policy in Cooke and Vincent, *Governing Passion*, pp. 69–74; Marsh, *The Discipline of Popular Government*, p. 76.

[1] L. P. Curtis, jr., *Coercion and Conciliation in Ireland, 1880–92. A Study in Conservative Unionism* (Princeton, 1963), p. 33.

[2] A new reassessment of the working of the 1882 Act, prepared for Carnarvon, departed in several respects from Spencer's views. For instance, the power of the Lord-Lieutenant to order searches for arms, held by Spencer to be a continuing necessity, was thought useful only 'if an armed outbreak was apprehended': otherwise it 'caused considerable exasperation'. (Memos. on Crimes Act, Carnarvon MSS, PRO 30/6 64).

[3] Carnarvon to Sir J. Macdonald, 2 Oct. 1885 (Carnarvon MSS, PRO 30/6 65).

South-Eastern Division.[1] In July Slacke reported that even
with the Crimes Act in force, intimidation was so pervasive
that the Act was becoming useless. Every branch of the
National League was 'in reality constituted as a court of
arbitration and decision with reference not only to land
questions, but to all matters of public interest in each locality',
though he allowed that branches varied in their activity
and daring.[2] He summed up the challenge next month by
declaring that the League 'has practically assumed the
Government of the Country'. One of its most aggressive rules
was now that no member was to deal with or work for anyone who was not also a member.[3] In October he reflected
helplessly,

It is extraordinary the belief which the Irish people invariably entertain of the strength of any illegal combination, which they regard
with much greater awe than they do the established authority of the
country.[4]

The deep-seated power of the associations was still resisting
'authority' in its self-appointed task of establishing acceptance of its own control.

Resistance was noticeably concentrated into the boycott
system, which was becoming increasingly comprehensive.
Traditional rural outrage, though once again on the increase
in 1885 and 1886, was never to return to the levels of
1880-2.[5] While murder returned to the countryside, directed
accurately against land-grabbers, it did not reach half the
1881 total. (See Table V.) Boycotting came to monopolize,
even mesmerize, the attention of government. Carnarvon
told Lord Middleton in September 1885 that during the
previous two years it had 'grown to an immense head'; the
Crimes Act had not prevented it, and 'if that Act were
again enforced, it would not in this particular make any

---

[1] Slacke was, however, one of the less vertebrate of senior law-officers. By
late 1887 the Under-Secretary was complaining that there was 'general apathy'
in Slacke's Division, and that he would 'have to be stirred up soon' (Ridgeway to
Balfour, 27 Nov. 1887, Balfour MSS, BL Add. MS 49808).

[2] Report by DM, SE Div., July 1885 (PRO 30/6 64).

[3] Ibid., Aug. 1885.

[4] Ibid., Oct. 1885.

[5] There is a useful short survey of agrarian outrage in the Carnarvon period
in Curtis, *Coercion and Conciliation*, pp. 54-6.

TABLE V

Agrarian Outrage, 1881–9*

Agrarian Outrage	1881	1884	1885	1886	1887	1888	1889
Total	4,439	762	944	1056	883	660	534
Firing at person	66	7	12	16	19	14	11
Assault on bailiff, process-server	45	1	7	11	11	2	1
Incendiarism	356	110	94	103	125	73	74
Cattle-maiming	155	51	59	73	54	55	50
Intimidation	1,576	413	512	516	385	316	232
Firing into dwellings	144	18	33	43	35	30	29
Murder	17	—	6	7	6	6	1

* *Source*: RIC Outrage Statistics.

material difference'.[1] In fact, reported instances of boy-cotting quadrupled between June and October. Hamilton prepared a statement which warned that

An erroneous idea appears to be prevalent that boycotting was only made a crime by the Prevention of Crimes Act, and that it can now be practised with impunity. It is true that the summary powers of dealing with this class of offence which the Act gave no longer exist, but intimidation is a crime punishable by the statute law . . . and further by a much earlier statute persons offending in this respect can be required to give security for good behaviour, or in default go to prison.[2]

This was correct as far as it went, but without summary powers it was as difficult as ever to obtain the evidence on which any statutory conviction depended. Carnarvon seems to have recognized the problem in issuing a confidential instruction that

While the law is put vigorously in action in all cases in which a breach of it can be proved, there are many incidents in the practice of boy-cotting which can only be successfully met by independent and local action.[3]

[1] Carnarvon to Midleton, 15 Sept. 1885 (PRO 30/6 57).
[2] Note by Under-Secretary, 26 Sept. 1885 (PRO 30/6 57).
[3] Carnarvon to F. Townsend French, 16 Oct. 1885 (loc. cit.).

Such (carefully unspecified) action would have the 'full support of Government'; and the Viceroy, aware of doubtful morale amongst the police and the magistracy, promised that every protection would be afforded to 'any local endeavour' to counteract the tyranny of boycotting groups.

At this time 165 people were being 'wholly' and 714 'partially' boycotted, the great majority in the south-western and south-eastern divisions. The police were developing techniques for dealing with certain manifestations of the problem —for instance, attending forced sales in plain clothes, a policy which the Inspector-General declared somewhat impressionistically to have 'been attended with great good'.[1] But the police themselves had not been cured of the malaise that had affected them in the first phase of the land war. Shortly after his arrival Carnarvon found that they were 'getting rather out of hand, and are not in the condition in which they should be, if an emergency were to arise'.[2] He wanted immediate legislation to resolve what Jenkinson called 'the present dual authority over the RIC and its attendant evils' by empowering the Viceroy to appoint Deputy Inspector-Generals to command the divisions in place of the divisional magistrates. The Cabinet failed to find time to discuss this. Nor, in spite of Carnarvon's support ('I think him a *very* good public servant'), was Jenkinson able to secure a stopgap reorganization abolishing Brackenbury's old post of Assistant Under-Secretary for Crime (since 'there is now hardly any crime in Ireland') and creating an imperial post for Jenkinson himself as intelligence co-ordinator— 'collecting information from all parts and weaving it into a whole'.[3] Carnarvon's colleagues were not impressed by his warning that secret societies were merely scotched and might be 'in full activity' very suddenly, or by the Inspector-General's news that secret-society activity was 'much increased' in November.[4] Jenkinson's pleas for more secret-

---

[1] Report by IG RIC, Nov. 1885 (PRO 30/6 64).
[2] Ld.-Lieutenant to Home Secretary, 25 July 1885 (PRO 30/6, W.2148).
[3] 'Proposals for Reorganising R.I.C.', Memo. by E. G. Jenkinson, 5 Aug. 1885 (loc. cit.). 'Crime' here refers to secret-society crime.
[4] Report of RIC, Dec. 1885 (PRO 30/6 64).

service money likewise fell on deaf ears.[1] In the end, as the Home Office casually dispensed with Jenkinson's services, Carnarvon was left to storm impotently to the Chancellor of the Exchequer about the Home Secretary's supine attitude.

I must presume that (Cross) is aware of the secret organizations in America & in many parts of England as well as in Ireland, of their very grave nature, and the certainty that they will take effect in outrage of all kinds on the failure of the Irish Parliamentary Party to come to terms with the govt. and I must suppose that he knows that Jenkinson holds the threads of these conspiracies, is alone able at present to deal with them, and has repeatedly declared that he can deal best with them in London rather than Ireland. To set all this aside seems to me simple madness & I must distinctly protest against it & wash my hands of all responsibility in regard to it . . . and I must say I am astonished at (the Home Office) treating what may be so serious a matter so lightly.[2]

Carnarvon's grander constitutional notions were also stymied by a Cabinet which was not so much intransigent on the Irish question as 'dull and unimaginative' at this stage.[3] His most prized idea, the endowment of a Catholic university, was deemed too offensive to Protestant English opinion.[4] A critical point in the hardening of Conservative opinion came early in the ministry's life, when Parnell reopened for the third time the grim Maamtrasna case. The renewed attack impeached, as *The Times* observed, not only Lord Spencer but also 'the Irish judiciary, the law officers of the Crown, the public prosecutors, the magistracy and the police'.[5] Salisbury told Beach and Carnarvon 'that we should lose confidence as a Government if we seemed to allow Parliamentary tactics to interfere with the administration of the Criminal Law'.[6] In spite of this, the debate on 17 July became a ministerial shambles, as Beach denounced Spencer

---

[1] Memo. by Jenkinson, 24 July; Carnarvon to Cross, 25 July; Hamilton to Carnarvon, 9, 13 Aug. 1886 (PRO 30/6 62).

[2] Carnarvon to Hicks Beach, 3 Jan. 1886 (loc. cit.).

[3] Cooke and Vincent, *Governing Passion*, p. 73.

[4] Harrowby to Carnarvon, 22 July 1886; Hardinge, *Carnarvon*, iii, 171-2. Ashbourne told Carnarvon that such a policy would cost the Conservatives from thirty to forty seats: Curtis, *Coercion and Conciliation*, p. 45.

[5] *The Times*, 18 July 1886; Hammond, *Gladstone and the Irish Nation*, p. 381.

[6] Hardinge, *Carnarvon*, iii, 169.

whilst avoiding giving any promise that the Maamtrasna case would be reviewed, and Churchill attacked the government itself. The result was a steady groundswell of backwoods Conservatism against the 'supposed Irish alliance'.[1] After this the Carnarvon *démarche* limped along for a few months; but, notwithstanding Parnell's declaration of support at the December general election, it could not survive Gladstone's adoption of home rule.

(iii) *Plan of campaign*

> I tell you, and I wish the Government reporter was here to listen to it, that if our people had the power to meet them, man to man and rifle to rifle, I for one would cut short my speechmaking this very moment and the next speeches that the destroyers of your homes would hear would be the speeches out of the mouths of your guns.
>
> William O'Brien[2]

> Any one who wishes to realise what is before the Irish Government if they are called upon by the landlords to support them in a policy of extortion and eviction, had better read the history of the autumn of 1880 and the spring of 1881, and he will then be able to form an opinion for himself.
>
> John Dillon[3]

Seen from the Irish countryside—say the Marquess of Clanricarde's Galway estates—the political crisis of 1886 was of marginal importance. Even without knowing that, as now appears, the Home Rule Bill was so drafted as to have been inoperable, the excitement over legislative independence had little relevance to western rural life.[4] Even before Gladstone's conversion, under the fear of violence,[5] conditions

[1] e.g. Harrowby to Carnarvon, 22 July 1886; Cooke and Vincent, *Governing Passion*, pp. 276–8. Cf. Quinault, op. cit. 387.

[2] Speech in Clare, *United Ireland*, 5 Feb. 1887.

[3] J. Dillon, 'The Coming Winter in Ireland', *The Nineteenth Century*, cxvii (Nov. 1886).

[4] F. S. L. Lyons, 'John Dillon and the Plan of Campaign, 1886–90', *IHS* xiv (1965), 313.

[5] According to Balfour, Gladstone told him privately, at Eaton Hall in Cheshire in December 1885, that unless concessions were immediately forthcoming a campaign of terror would begin in England: A. J. Balfour, *Chapters of Autobiography* (London, 1930), pp. 211–12.

worsened. The Liberal defeat in July 1886 freed the tongues
of the land movement leaders from temporary enchantment;
the final trigger for renewal of the land war was the blocking
of Parnell's Tenants' Relief Bill (designed to enable the land
courts operating under the 1881 Act to defer eviction if a
tenant had paid half the due rent, and give them power to
reduce the judicial rents already fixed, and also to admit
leaseholders to the benefits of the 1881 Act).[1] In an effort
to salvage the New Departure Davitt went with William
O'Brien, the combative Parnellite editor of *United Ireland*,
to the Irish Race Convention in Chicago to head off a revived
terrorist initiative from the Clan na Gael dynamiters.[2] Parnell
himself became detached from the land agitation, whose
leadership passed into the hands of his more bellicose lieutenants, O'Brien, Dillon, and Harrington.

The basis for a new phase of rural struggle was sketched
out as early as February 1885 in O'Brien's newspaper, which
suggested that 'once the tenants on an estate have come to
a conclusion as to what would be a fair rent', they should
lodge that sum in a joint bank account which could not be
touched 'until an arrangement has been effected with the
estate as a whole', or unless a member of the combination
were evicted.[3] After the bursting of the home rule bubble
a refined version of this advice was produced in an unsigned
article (written by Harrington, and not approved by Parnell)
with the resonant title 'A Plan of Campaign'. At the same
time Dillon launched the plan in a speech on the Clanricarde
estate at Woodford, Co. Galway.[4] Here conditions had
reached a nadir: the agricultural depression was accompanied
by a general failure of rent payment and a mass of eviction
processes initiated by the stony marquess. In August the
resistance of several tenants in traditional land-war style
proved so formidable that bailiffs and emergency men—
quasi-professional hired heavyweights sometimes called the
'crowbar brigade'—had to be escorted by two RMs and over

[1] Lyons, *Parnell*, pp. 359-60.
[2] J. V. O'Brien, *William O'Brien and the Course of Irish Politics 1881-1918*
(Berkeley, 1976), p. 34.
[3] 'A Remedy for Rack Rent', *United Ireland*, 21 Feb. 1885.
[4] *United Ireland*, 23 Oct. 1886; Lyons, 'John Dillon and the Plan of Campaign', pp. 315-16.

500 police. This battle, in which every method of siege warfare short of explosives was employed, cost the government some £3,000.[1] The possibility of lethal violence was evident, and the Plan of Campaign itself may well have been in part an attempt by the political leaders to channel and sublimate rural anger. It was a renewal, in modified form, of Parnell's 'better way'. Thus, on 10 October O'Brien appealed to tenants at Gurteen, County Sligo, to 'stick to honest combinations . . . do not stain your hands with those cowardly and disgusting crimes that revolt the conscience of every civilized human being'.[2]

Harrington's plan involved handing over the proposed 'fair' rents to two or three trustees, whose probity would be guaranteed by the National League. On no account were the funds to be frittered away in legal costs. The plan relied fundamentally on social policing to defend its participants: 'public sympathy' would be brought to bear against evictions, as before. And although professedly non-violent, organizers like O'Brien were fully conscious of the dimension added to the struggle by the vague and unspecified threat of violence. The plan went ahead at Portumna on 18 November, with Dillon and O'Brien heading the trustees. The language employed was significant. When the land-agent refused to accept the offer of sixty per cent of the rental, and the demand that evicted tenants be reinstated, the tenant representatives turned away saying 'This means war'. They marched off with a band playing 'The minstrel boy'.[3] Several other estates took up the Plan in November, and more followed next month; but resistance was never to become as widespread as five years before. After Parnell expressed strong reservations about the scheme in December, its national organizers restricted its operation to selected estates. O'Brien bowed reluctantly to Parnell in this, though he may not have been altogether confident that much wider resistance could in any case have been sustained.[4]

---

[1] Curtis, *Coercion and Conciliation*, p. 139.

[2] *United Ireland*, 16 Oct. 1886.

[3] *Freemans Journal*, 19 Nov. 1886; Lyons, 'John Dillon and the Plan of Campaign', p. 317.

[4] O'Brien, *William O'Brien*, p. 40. For an interesting discussion of Parnell's

For the authorities, in spite of their own reservations, were backing the landlords in the most forceful attempt so far made to enforce the law. Some groups of landlords, most notably the Cork Defence Union organized by Arthur Smith-Barry, were starting to combine to counter their tenants' combinations: boycotting was to be defeated by pooling machinery and supplies.[1] The Chief Secretaryship in the new government was given to the most able Conservative minister in the Commons, Sir Michael Hicks Beach. A note of alarm was sounded by Dillon on his reaction to Beach's attitude in the debate on the Tenants' Relief Bill. His speech, Dillon alleged, was 'the first, coming from any one of importance, which contained a note of hatred, contention, and strife'. Its whole tone 'was one of insult and of menace',

calculated to blood on the Irish landlords to deeds of oppression during the coming winter, and to fix more firmly than ever in the mind of the Irish tenant the old conviction that his sufferings and persecutions are matters of contemptuous indifference to the English government.[2]

This inflammatory allegation was a serious misreading of Beach's mind, however. The ex-Chancellor had few conventional Tory views on Irish matters, and especially not on Irish landlords. The drift of his administration was to reduce the appeal of nationalist combativeness like Dillon's by eliminating agrarian conflict and the resulting disaffection. Beach saw Irish disorder as unpolitical in itself—in this he was unusual amongst English statesmen—and came to blame it largely on bad landlordism. His efforts were directed towards inducing landlords to reduce rents and, still more importantly, to participate in the reinvestment of wealth to improve Irish agriculture and industry.[3] Here was the germ of a real response to Disraeli's diagnosis of Irish disorders:

reasoning see Lyons, *Parnell*, pp. 440-2. An indication of tenant backsliding may be given by the fact that of thirty-six people receiving police protection in the Western Division in January 1888 only two were 'of the landlord class': SPO, Report of Div. Comm., W. Div.

[1] The CDU was a subsidiary of the Irish Defence Union, formed by the Earl of Bandon in 1885. For other instances see Curtis, *Coercion and Conciliation*, pp. 56-7.

[2] Dillon, 'The Coming Winter in Ireland', p. 613.

[3] Curtis, op. cit. 127 ff.

if the state was blocking political revolution, it must foster a social revolution. The Conservatives were to move further along this path during the next twenty years.

Yet the government could not actually refuse to back up, by force if necessary, the legal processes used by unprogressive landlords to secure their rents or evict their tenants. It was as always concerned 'to administer the law without fear or favour', and though Beach had no faith in repressive legislation, believing that if anything it provoked greater lawlessness, he was confronted with circumstances in which the 'ordinary law' had for a long time been an almost meaningless term. In the words of one Irish judge, the situation in Co. Mayo in the summer of 1886 'approached as near to rebellion against the authority of the country as anything short of civil war could be'.[1] When Beach arrived in Ireland on 5 August he was immediately confronted with a renewed outburst of the Belfast riots, so serious as to have led to a desperate invocation of martial law in the last days of Morley's administration. Beach sent 1,200 troops there, and this action was at last followed by (and appeared to cause) the cessation of rioting. The intractable rural disorder in the south-west was in turn tackled, in the absence of special legislation, by the administrative device of a special officer. In fact the title 'commissioner' was now used.[2] To the alarm and outrage of radicals Beach appointed to this position a serving soldier—Major-General Sir Redvers Buller, pacifier of the African bush.[3]

[1] Charge to Grand Jury, quoted in Cabinet Memo. on Irish Crime, 26 July 1901 (Salisbury MSS, quoted in Curtis, op. cit. 128). As Curtis points out, however, disorder formed by this time an odd patchwork pattern, with quiet areas next to intensely disturbed ones. In his view the condition of each parish varied 'with the poverty and landlord–tenant relations prevalent there'—perhaps too mechanistic an explanation.

[2] The Secretary of State for War, W. H. Smith, noted of the appointment that 'the officer sent should be made as "special" as possible, to safeguard his rank', and would need full executive powers (not possessed by DMs) over the police. His primary duty was airily described as 'so overhauling and reorganising existing police arrangements as to cope with "moonlighting" and such crimes'. The hope was that 'if he succeeds, a couple of months should suffice': 'the example · will tell all over Ireland', showing how to use the ordinary law 'with energy and fearlessness' before asking to have it changed, Note by Secretary of State for War (Buller MSS, PRO WO 132/4A).

[3] Maj. Gen. Sir A. E. Turner, *Sixty Years of a Soldier's Life* (London, 1912), p. 190.

The creation of a 'generalissimo' with command of both civil and military forces was a remarkable development in the administration of British law. It was a device that was to be used with success overseas, and very occasionally within the United Kingdom. It carried undertones of martial law, and its admissibility depended in part on the peculiar qualities of the person appointed. In this case, Buller proved to combine firmness with good humour and tact. He refused to become a mere protector of the 'crowbar brigade'; in fact he returned from his first tour of inspection in Kerry and Clare sharing Beach's belief that if only landlords could be induced to help solve the land problem, the political problem would disappear.[1] As a soldier he approached this in a way as yet unfamiliar even to a Conservative of Churchillian stripe: 'You must combine a species of coercive land settlement with a coercive crime settlement.'[2] Beach responded to his subordinate's enthusiasm with instructions as innovatory as Buller's post itself—to try to eliminate evictions by private pressure on landlords, and to approve only the eviction of the most unreasonable tenants. Beach even envisaged the possibility of making landlords pay for police assistance, or of refusing assistance altogether where landlords were unreasonable.[3]

Buller went some way towards this by drawing up a new form of requisition for protection parties, and trying to use administrative obfuscation as a way of reducing landlord demands for protection. But as he told Beach,

You are asking the District [*sic*] Magistrates and County Inspectors to take a small risk and a good deal of obloquy by refusing protection, and you are further asking them to take a good deal of responsibility by squeezing the landlords about evictions. I believe they are doing this but I know privately from all of them that they none of them think they have the sort of authority they would like for it.[4]

In practice, fortunately, the combination of intensified tenant resistance under the Plan and discreet governmental

---

[1] There is a good account of Buller's commissionership by his assistant and successor in Turner, op. cit., pp.197-9.

[2] Buller to Beach, 5 Sept. 1886 (St. Aldwyn MSS, quoted in Curtis, op. cit. p. 141).

[3] Lady V. Hicks Beach, *The Life of Sir Michael Hicks Beach, First Earl St. Aldwyn* (London, 1932), i, 289-90.

[4] Buller to Beach, 26 Oct. 1886 (Curtis, op. cit. p. 149).

hints proved sufficient to induce many landlords to grant voluntary abatements, defusing the tension on their estates. These good intentions did not, of course, prevent 'Black Michael' and his henchmen from being portrayed as oppressors of the Irish, while landlords recoiled from them in horror as virtual Jacobins.[1] The constant barrage of vituperation was to have severe effects on Beach's health. In November he instituted proceedings against Dillon for the use of violent language, and his move was branded by the nationalist press as 'a declaration of war'. The Prime Minister remained insistent that the government should be seen to vindicate the law. His St. James's Hall speech earlier in the year, whilst rejecting exceptional coercive legislation, proposed government 'honestly, consistently and resolutely applied for twenty years'.[2] This would include permanent reform of the criminal law to 'protect the liberty of innocent people against the encroachments of criminally inspired organizations'. In October 1887 he told a confidant, Alfred Austin, that 'the cumbrous processes and precautions of English law are an unwieldy armoury against modern forms of lawlessness'; if the Russian or German governments were faced with the Parnellites, they would make short work of them.[3] In 1886, while the Dublin Castle officials hesitated, Salisbury led the way in declaring the Plan of Campaign illegal. He was followed by the judge at Dillon's trial, who called the Plan 'an absolutely illegal organization';[4] at last, on 18 December, the Irish executive declared it 'an unlawful and criminal conspiracy'.[5]

With a sudden access of boldness the government now decided to bring Dillon—who while on bail had acted as

[1] Curtis, op. cit. 142, 155-6; Turner, *Sixty Years*, pp. 195-6. Evictions of course continued, and Turner participated (pp. 198-200) in grim scenes at Glenbeigh and Ballyferriter on the Kerry coast.

[2] This became in nationalist language 'twenty years of manacles and Manitoba'.

[3] Salisbury to Austin, 27 Oct. 1887. The American journalist W. H. Hurlbert suggested that the US would also be less legalistic, quoting a fighting member of Lincoln's Cabinet: 'to await the results of slow judicial prosecution is to allow crime to be consummated, with the expectation of subsequent punishment, instead of preventing its accomplishment by prompt and direct interference' (*Ireland Under Coercion. The Diary of an American* (Edinburgh, 1888), i, 8-9).

[4] *The Times*, 9 Dec. 1886.

[5] Lyons, 'John Dillon and the Plan of Campaign', p. 318.

rent-receiver for the Plan—and O'Brien to trial for conspiracy. This notoriously difficult charge was a perilous proceeding for an administration acting under the 'ordinary law'. Possibly it was encouraged by a timely article published by the noted jurist Sir James Stephen in November. Stephen held that boycotting amounted to usurpation of the functions of government. The acts by which so-called rent strikes were controlled, he said, 'should be recognized in their true light as acts of social war, as the modern representatives of the old conception of high treason'.[1] Boycotting in Ireland had 'enabled a small number of ruffians, by the help of a moderate number of outrages, to paralyse the law of the land and to erect a government which confronts and defies the lawful government'.[2]

Stephen's lengthy analysis was a major exemplar of the 'murder gang' theory, the belief (shown by Forster earlier) that the mass of the Irish people were simply terrorized by a small group into actions they did not wish. But it made clear the difficulty of identifying the point at which popular sanction thus enforced amounted to lawlessness or 'social war'.

To resent what you regard as harsh conduct in a landlord in evicting a tenant, or as meanness in a tenant who plays into his hand by taking the farm from which the tenant has been evicted, by refusing to have any dealings with either, may be wise or foolish . . . if it is a mere individual act, the *bona fide* result of the natural feelings of the person who does it. The transition from this to concerted action is not one which shocks the common and uninstructed mind, and the further and final step which leads you to help to compel others by fear to do that which you rather like to do yourself is little less natural and easy.[3]

The legal strength of boycotting lay in its diffuse character. It was the repetition of a number of 'disobliging acts' so concerted and repeated as to make life wretched, though, as Stephen admitted, each individual act was unimportant and usually well within the rights of anyone who did it. 'To refuse to sell a man a loaf of bread is in itself nothing.

[1] J. F. Stephen, 'On the Suppression of Boycotting', *The Nineteenth Century*, cxviii (Nov. 1886), 769.
[2] Ibid. 774.
[3] Ibid. 775.

In connection with other things it may be a step in the execution of a sentence of death.'[1] He insisted that the whole process must be seen as one of intimidation:

It is impossible to intimidate a man—to make him afraid—in a more definite emphatic way, in order to compel him to abstain from paying his rent or evicting a tenant for not paying it, than by threatening him with all the penalities of social excommunication.[2]

But how to pin this charge on a whole community if indeed it did regard these objects as reasonable, his article did not say.

In fact the Dublin conspiracy trial collapsed in February 1887, and the whole position suddenly appeared markedly worse. Certain administrative improvements had been made, but were not showing any result. Buller, promoted from special commissioner to Under-Secretary, made some important changes in the secret-service system which put it on a sounder long-term footing. Now, however, he advocated new legal powers as the only way of avoiding a descent into internal war. 'I am coming to the conclusion', he wrote at the beginning of February, 'that Ireland never was in a worse state.'

There is not much outrage because the League is so firmly established, but the people are rapidly losing any regard for the law . . . . My deliberate opinion is that unless you can introduce *very shortly* a summary method of procedure for the prosecution of crime and also take some powers which will enable you to coerce bad landlords such as Colonel O'Callaghan, so far as governing Ireland is concerned, you may as well chuck up the sponge.[3]

Once again the overwhelming challenge was seen as 'to show people that the law is the strongest': otherwise the whole existence of government was imperilled. Ireland had defeated the efforts and broken the health of a first-rate minister. Beach's administration had failed, and a new team was brought in to administer a new coercion act. Salisbury decided that the Irish must 'take a licking' before concessions would do them any good.[4] Beach anxiously pointed out that his successor must be physically as well as mentally strong:

---

[1] Stephen, *The Nineteenth Century*.
[2] Ibid.
[3] Buller to Beach, 2 Feb. 1887 (Curtis, op. cit. pp. 167-3).
[4] Salisbury to Beach, 28 Feb. 1887 (Curtis, op. cit. pp. 168-9).

If he breaks down, after me, how much does that strengthen the Home Rule argument. Forster and Trevelyan suffered very heavily in health: I have failed altogether: a fourth failure would almost prove that no man can do the work.[1]

(iv) *Bloody Balfour*

> The Irish populace will lean to whichever side proves itself strongest. They are sick and tired of land league tyranny but they will not cut themselves away from it until they are convinced that the Government is stronger and more certain in its action than the league.
>
> Lord Castletown[2]

Beach's unease was increased by Salisbury's choice as his successor, Arthur Balfour. Apart from a few months at the Scottish Office, the Prime Minister's nephew had been noted mainly as an effete hanger-on of Churchill's 'fourth party'. In the event he became one of the toughest and most successful of all Chief Secretaries. The rapidity with which he restored confidence in Dublin and instilled new energy into the creaking executive machine stands out as a major ministerial achievement. As a minister, Balfour had unexpected weight. His period at the Scottish Office proved to be a vital preparation; there he had to deal with the crofters' land struggle in the Highlands and islands, a struggle which imposed tests on government comparable to those in Ireland.

The origins of the conflict were to some extent the same: evictions (albeit much less extensive than in the earlier clearances) and economic depression.[3] Certainly the Scots showed an awareness of the Irish land war from 1880 onwards.[4] Their own war was less violent, perhaps: serious violence was confined to the very poorest areas. The major forms of disorder recorded by the police were 'mobbing', 'rioting', 'deforcing officers of the law in the execution of

[1] Beach to Salisbury, 1 Mar. 1887 (Curtis, op. cit. p. 170).

[2] Castletown to Balfour, 17 July 1887 (Balfour MSS, BL Add. MS 49826).

[3] H. J. Hanham, 'The problem of Highland discontent, 1880-5', *Tr. R. Hist. S.*, 5th ser., xix (1969). The most substantial study of the struggle is J. Hunter, *The Making of the Crofting Community* (Edinburgh, 1976), esp. pp. 131-83.

[4] J. P. D. Dunbabin, 'The Crofters' "Land War" ', *Rural Discontent in Nineteenth Century Britain* (London, 1974), pp. 183-7.

their duty', and 'malicious mischief';[1] but through the different police terminology one can perceive activity similar
to that in Ireland. 'Deforcement' (a criminal offence in itself
in Scotland) meant in effect the burning of writs or the exercise of crowd pressure against sheriffs and police. It was
sufficiently formidable to make the law unenforceable in
Skye in 1882, and order was messily restored by mainland
police in the so-called 'Battle of the Braes'. Thereafter the
agitation became more systematic (possibly in imitation of
Ireland), involving the occupation of grazing land and the use
of threats of violence against landlords' agents. In the end an
expeditionary force of 300 marines was dispatched reluctantly by Harcourt—himself accustomed to more urbane
amphibious operations against wildlife in the isles—who
forbade their use to protect the service of writs for the
recovery of rent. The situation was still confused when
Balfour arrived at the Scottish Office. Within three months
a new expedition was sent, which overpowered all resistance
with vigour bordering on brutality—but without bloodshed.[2] The chief law-officer involved, Sheriff Ivory, pre-
echoed the enthusiasm of Irish officials when he wrote that
the speedy collapse of the agitation was entirely due to Balfour's 'sagacity . . . courage and firmness'.[3]

Balfour himself was soon pressing, interestingly, for
powers like those of the Irish Chief Secretary, arguing that

While the condition of the lawlessness [in Scotland] exceeds that
of any part of Ireland, the machinery which necessity has given
rise to in Ireland (in the shape of a strong central authority having
direct control over practically unlimited forces of police, and having at
its command constant and accurate information with respect to all
parts of the country) does not exist even in its most rudimentary
form in the Highlands.[4]

He was now given the chance to test this somewhat rosy
estimate of the Castle system. He began, as he had begun
with Scotland, by turning a deaf ear to public outcry against

[1] *Return of Offences committed in Crofting Parishes of the Highlands and
Islands of Scotland*, HC 1888 (383), lxxxii. 1.

[2] Dunbabin, op. cit. p. 204; Hunter, op. cit. pp. 165–70.

[3] Ivory to Balfour, 30 Dec. 1886; M. Egremont, *Balfour: a life of Arthur
James Balfour* (London, 1980), p. 80.

[4] Ibid. p. 78.

forcible imposition of the law (in this case Captain Plunkett's decision to fire on a rioting crowd in Youghal). Buller immediately responded, 'You have earned the gratitude of every Irishman I have spoken to by your reply about Plunkett; it is that sort of support Irish officials have so long needed.'[1] Balfour's attitude had indeed a galvanic effect. One landlord who had nearly come to accept the Plan terms, as Harrington told Dillon, 'went over to London and had an interview with Balfour and when he came back he would hear of nothing but war'.[2]

The instrument of 'war' was the new, permanent, Criminal Law Amendment Act carried through the Commons by Balfour in face of fierce nationalist opposition between March and July 1887.[3] The Act restored the magisterial power of investigation (section 1)—branded as the 'Star Chamber' procedure—and extended summary jurisdiction for offences of conspiracy and intimidation. Its definition of conspiracy,

to compel or induce any person or persons not to fulfil his or their legal obligations, or not to let, hire, use or occupy any land, or not to deal with, work for, or hire any person or persons in the ordinary course of trade, business or occupation; or to interfere with the administration of the law,[4]

was wider than that of the 1822 Act, but fell far short of the comprehensive provisions suggested by Sir James Stephen.[5] The major provisions of the new law were to be brought into force by the proclamation of districts, at the discretion of

[1] Buller to Balfour, 16 Mar. 1887 (BL Add. MS 49807, ff. 35-7). This verdict was echoed two years later by Col. Turner: 'Your constant and perfect support has alone enabled us to do what has been done, as it has supplied what did not exist before your time, pluck & backbone' (Turner to Balfour, 19 Mar. 1889, BL Add. MS 49820). (Turner had served for three years under the Spencer regime, and had expressed a high opinion of Spencer.)

[2] T. C. Harrington to Dillon, 23 Mar. 1887 (Dillon MSS, quoted in Lyons, 'John Dillon and the Plan of Campaign', p. 321).

[3] Opposition continued, of course, after its enactment: 'Resistance to the Crimes Act', File No. 1, Balfour MSS (Whittingehame) 36.

[4] Criminal Law and Procedure (Ireland) Act, 19 July 1887. 50 & 51 Vict. c. 20, s. 2.

[5] These included the inflicting of 'any kind of inconvenience or loss or damage whatever' on any individual, the publishing of names, and refusal to deal 'in the ordinary way of business': Stephen, 'Boycotting', pp. 777-8.

the Lord-Lieutenant and Privy Council.[1] An association might be proclaimed dangerous under the Act if the Lord-Lieutenant was satisfied that it was

(a) formed for the commision of crimes
(b) carrying on operations for or by the commission of crimes
(c) encouraging or aiding persons to commit crimes
(d) promoting or inciting to acts of violence or intimidation
(e) interfering with the administration of the law or disturbing the maintenance of law and order.[2]

Balfour proceeded on 19 August to proclaim the Irish National League as a dangerous association. This did not amount to suppression, but a number of branches were closed, particularly in Kerry and Clare, while others collapsed.[3]

The essence of Balfour's technique was well expressed in his uncle's pragmatic advice to 'go on pegging away', learning the limit of executive powers and within that limit inflicting 'an intolerable amount of annoyance'.[4] Between 19 July and 31 December 1887, 373 people were imprisoned under the Crimes Act.[5] The main line of Balfour's offensive was directed against the leaders, or 'pseudo-leaders' as they were called by the new Under-Secretary, West Ridgeway. (Ridgeway expected that after their arrest a 'no rent' strike would be tried by 'leaders who remain at present in the background'.)[6] A prosecution was directed against O'Brien for incitement to resist the law, though the opening of the

[1] It may be pointed out that in a sense the Act restricted the power of the executive, in that it forced the proclamation of an organization as illegal before action could be taken, and restricted punishments to proclaimed areas. But its provision of a basis on which the status of the National League could be tested was vital: Notes, CO 903 2, Part VI.

[2] 50 & 51 Vict., c. 20, s. 6.

[3] In mid 1887 there were over 1,200 League branches, and though new branches continued to be set up, the total dropped to 1,000 by the end of the year. 141 branches were suppressed and 71 collapsed: SPO Fenian MSS.

[4] Salisbury to Balfour, Oct. 1887 (BL Add. MS 49688, f. 153).

[5] As against 418 in the equivalent period (July–Dec. 1882) of the earlier Crimes Act. Only 35 persons in 1887, as against 199 in 1882, were imprisoned for intimidation, though 293 as against 113 were imprisoned for violent offences: Notes, CO 903 2, Part VI.

[6] Note on Report of DI Crime Special, W. Div., Oct. 1887 (SPO CBS MSS). (This appears to have paralleled Gladstone's belief in 'a power behind Mr Parnell': Balfour, op. cit. p. 211.)

trial at Mitchelstown, Co. Cork, on 9 September had unlooked-for consequences. The RIC forced a passage for the government reporter through a big demonstration meeting that was being addressed by Dillon. A violent scuffle developed, in which the police retreated to their barrack. There, in what seems to have been a collapse of discipline, they opened fire, killing three people.[1] 'Remember Mitchelstown' became a constant refrain in nationalist and Liberal denunciations of Balfour (who gained from the incident the epithet 'bloody'). Political pressure intensified, as during the autumn and winter Ireland 'swarmed with radicals'—no fewer than forty MPs in ten separate delegations (or what would now be called 'fact-finding missions').[2] The Chief Secretary none the less held to the policy of backing up the police, despite a private conviction that they had panicked, and pressed on with the prosecution of O'Brien, who was at length committed to Tullamore gaol on 2 November.

The struggle that was then fought out within the gaol, where O'Brien refused to wear prison clothing, became the dominant political clash of the following year. In a conscious reversal of the implicitly 'political' treatment of prisoners under the 1881 Act, the harshest rigours of prison discipline, including the 'plank bed', were imposed on those now incarcerated. Balfour had told Buller before the passage of the Crimes Act that the government would not suspend Habeas Corpus 'because it is understood that anybody imprisoned under such a suspension would have all the privileges of a man sent to jail for a first-class misdemeanour; and experience under Forster's Act appears to show that they rather like this than otherwise'.[3] Such cool Machiavellianism was what turned Balfour into the Tory cynosure. One of his victims, Wilfrid Scawen Blunt, was a member of Balfour's own social circle and had heard the iron Chief Secretary relish over dinner the torments of his opponents. Blunt's disclosure of this made Balfour look, to some, like a monster;

[1] Turner, who sat on the inquiry, gives an account in *Sixty Years*, pp. 227-9.

[2] T. W. Heyck, *The Dimensions of British Radicalism. The Case of Ireland 1874–95* (Illinois, 1974), p. 191. Cf. A. L. Thorold, *The Life of Henry Labouchere*, pp. 331-4.

[3] Balfour to Buller, 13 Mar. 1887 (Buller MSS, WO 132 4A).

but his exaggerated cynicism was rather, as a recent biographer says, a mannerism encouraged by the 'fawning delight' with which his remarks were received. This delight was mirrored by the extravagant denunciations heaped on him by the hostile press—such, for instance, as the *Connaught Telegraph*'s description of 'that black-livered, cold-blooded, ruffianly liar of a Chief Secretary—in whose composition there is not room for a particle of truth, honour, or common decency', and of 'the degraded mind . . . suited to the bloody-souled nephew of the tyrannical, knave-like Salisbury'.[1]

He believed that he was fighting for universal principles, conducting a civilizing mission in restoring order and cementing the Union. To allow the Parnellites or the Land League (as he always called the National League) to win would be 'simply to give up civilization'. In this crusade he was ready to envisage widespread suppression of newspapers which fomented hostility (such as the *Connaught Telegraph*), and even prosecution of news-vendors. Only Salisbury's uneasy awareness of 'the general [English] prejudice about the press' caused a modification of this policy.[2] On the question of preferential 'political' treatment for certain prisoners, his response was sharp: a crime did not become political simply because it was committed by a politician.[3]

But what sort of crime confronted Balfour's civilization? It must be said that, as before, much of it had been created by the government, which had defined new offences because it had detected a wider threat in the otherwise minor crimes attached to boycotting. Although Mayo and Galway were held by the Western Divisional Commissioner to be 'in a state closely bordering on rebellion' in which 'on the slightest excuse police are attacked and savagely assaulted', the RIC's own statistics cast doubt on this.[4] The threat seems to have been impressionistic rather than measurable. There was

---

[1] Egremont, *Balfour*, p. 87; CO 903 2, Part V.

[2] Salisbury to Balfour, 24 Dec. 1887 (Balfour MSS (Whittingehame) 33).

[3] Letter to *The Times*, 26 Nov. 1887; Curtis, op. cit. p. 222.

[4] SPO, DM Reports, W. Div., Mar. 1887. Agrarian assaults on police, which totalled 12 in 1880 and 24 in 1881, thereafter fell to zero until 1885 (7), 1886 (4), 1887 (11), 1888 (1), 1889 (3), 1890 (1). Total assaults on police were between 12 (1884) and 89 (1881).

perhaps something alarming in a declaration like that of Father M'Fadden, 'I am the law in Gweedore':[1] and Lord Midleton remained convinced in March 1888 that it was the League and not the government who ruled the country: 'They fix rents, impose and levy fines, settle disputes, and prescribe courses of action to all who are not strong enough to defy them—about 1 in 100.' He added

the National League and the Govt. *cannot coexist*. One must destroy the other. The people—and of all other people—the Irish people cannot serve two masters, and they will not try to do so.[2]

Similarly, the Attorney-General held in June that intimidation was still effectively paralysing the judicial process in many areas.[3] This was hardly a novel phenomenon, however, and did not require the work of the League as an explanation. And, as has been pointed out, the foremost Plan leaders, Dillon and O'Brien, constantly harped on the need to curb violence in 1887, with considerable apparent success. In F. S. L. Lyons's words, there was 'little of that elemental savagery which had flared up time and again in the earlier land war'.[4] W. H. Hurlbert's impression was that much of the violence was bogus—certainly in Ulster. According to landlords he met in the Kildare Street Club, hunting still went on happily with never a dog harmed.

They were poisoned, whole packs of them, in the papers, but not a dog really. The stories were printed just to keep up the agitation, and the farmers winked at it so as not to be 'bothered'.[5]

This perhaps underlines the fact that the Plan of Campaign was primarily one of well-organized political publicity, rather than of concrete resistance.

Intimidatory violence did persist, but was increasingly directed against animals rather than people. (Cattle-maiming reached nearly half the 1881 level, while firing at the person or into houses did not reach one-third. See Table V, p. 195

---

[1] Hurlbert, *Ireland Under Coercion*, i, 17–18.

[2] Midleton to Capt. Jekyll, 20 Mar. 1888 (Carnarvon MSS, PRO 30/6 57).

[3] Att.-Gen. to Chief Secretary, 26 June 1888 (Balfour MSS (Whittingehame) 36).

[4] Lyons, 'John Dillon and the Plan of Campaign', p. 323. On O'Brien's call for 'no crime and no surrender' cf. O'Brien, *William O'Brien*, pp. 53–4.

[5] Hurlbert, op. cit. i, 50.

above.) Wells were poisoned, and poisoned meal was scattered in fields. When animals were injured it was sometimes only by the stripping of their tails; sometimes they were simply marked to prevent sale. Traditional demonstrative gestures continued. Farm walls were knocked down; hay burned; iron pins were driven into meadows. Occasionally more prophetic forms of sabotage appeared, as when Achill islanders trenched and barricaded roads and broke bridges to prevent the government reporter and his police escort from reaching meetings in January 1888.[1] The bulk of the intimidation which the government deplored was non-violent: at least, threats proved efficient by themselves. Boycotting declined in incidence as it became more tightly organized. Although, by one computation, the number of people 'affected' in the Western Division alone totalled 320,389 in July 1887, in the South-Western Division 895 people were more realistically reported as being boycotted in June. By January 1888 this total had fallen to 250.[2] Six months later it was down to a mere 87, of whom only 21 were 'wholly' boycotted; and by the end of the year only 13 were wholly boycotted despite a slight rise in the total to 100.[3]

This trend was naturally regarded by the executive as proof of the Crimes Act's efficacy. But there were, also, obvious structural causes. The Plan of Campaign was never as extensive as the earlier land war: at most 84 estates were involved. Within months this number was reduced to 24 estates where no settlement had been reached, and only on 17 of these did the dispute—now centring above all on the reinstatement of tenants evicted during the campaign—prove so intractable as to drag on into the 1890s. In the view of the radical MP G. J. Shaw-Lefevre, who had held

[1] SPO, DC Reports, W. Div., 4 Feb. 1888.

[2] The figures by counties were Clare, 490/115; Kerry, 405/135: SPO, DC Reports, SW Div.; Memoranda relative to Counties proclaimed under secs. 1, 2, 3 & 4 of Criminal Law and Procedure (Ireland) Act 1887, Reports by DMs (Balfour MSS, BL Add. MS 49822).

[3] PRO 30/6 57 gives figures for boycotting in Oct. 1885 as

	wholly/partially boycotted	
W. Div.	15	99
SW. Div.	35	223
SE Div.	82	269

Cabinet office briefly in 1885 and had a long-standing interest in Ireland, the government could have got these cases settled if it had held to the policy begun by Hicks Beach. Balfour's readiness to back up recalcitrant landlords, even the stage-absentee Marquess of Clanricarde, was in his view wrong on all counts. Repeated harassing prosecutions and imprisonments under the 1887 Act, so central to Balfour's method, by Lefevre's observation 'far from frightening or deterring others . . . stimulated them to follow the example' and 'intensified public opinion against the authorities and the government'. Altogether,

The impression left on my mind, by [my] visits to the Campaign estates, was that a graver misconception of its duties by the Government had never occurred, even in Ireland.[1]

This indictment was rejected with contempt by the authorities. Colonel Turner, Buller's successor as commissioner for Clare and Kerry, had direct experience of Lefevre's visits. A Home Ruler of sorts himself, he became angry at 'English perambulatory adventurers of a very low and questionable character'; systematic distortion of his efforts to maintain the law infuriated him further. 'What a lying crew these Gladstonians are', he fumed in June 1889. 'Shaw-Lefevre is no gentleman and cannot be treated as such'.[2] In his later reflections, however, Turner conceded that the suppression of the League might have done more harm than good, demanding an effort beyond the powers of the police —thus revealing their weakness—and provoking 'indignation meetings' which could have serious consequences.[3] For the time being, though, the government claimed that rough justice was working. It found that after the alarming Mitchelstown 'massacre', boycotting in that area practically ceased.[4] Balfour noted that in Kerry, early in 1888, 'the attitude of

---

[1] Lord Eversley, *Gladstone and Ireland*, pp. 341, 345. Shaw-Lefevre's journals published as *Incidents of Coercion* and *Combination and Coercion* contain a comprehensive critical analysis of executive policy.

[2] Turner to Balfour, 9 Sept. 1887; to Seymour, 16 June 1888; to Browning, 9 June 1889 (Balfour MSS, BL. Add. MS 49820; SPO, DC Reports, SW Div., Sept. 1887).

[3] Turner, *Sixty Years*, pp. 226-7.

[4] SPO, CBS MSS, Report of DI CS, SW Div.

the people has improved, curiously, in spite of the vigorous measures of suppression'.[1] All the same, he was concerned to reduce the unnecessary violence that had periodically broken out. After Mitchelstown he wrote a long and thoughtful letter to Salisbury, reflecting that

The proper method of handling the Police in the face of a mob appears to be this.—They should be divided into two parties of unequal size. The larger one (probably the much larger one) should be armed only with batons and to them should be entrusted the duty of dispersing the mob or otherwise enforcing the law. The smaller party should act as a reserve; and if through the defeat of the baton party they are called upon to support it, they should not do so (as they did at Mitchelstown) by clubbing their rifles and acting as baton men armed with an inferior kind of baton, but they should either fire or charge with fixed bayonets as the exigencies of the particular case may seem to require.[2]

Still, uncertainty on this point seems to have persisted. Some weeks later he commented in the margin of a Divisional report,

I have long been of opinion that at least a *proportion* of the police should be armed with shot guns: and I should have thought it might be desirable to distribute a certain number among any force called out for active duty, and that these should fire in the first instance should firing unhappily prove necessary.[3]

A further line of discussion was started by Turner's idea that the police in his Division should be armed with revolvers. Ridgeway agreed to issue them, but found that only 80 out of 400 revolvers available to the Division were serviceable.[4] While the Treasury was being persuaded of the need to buy 500 new guns at 35s. each, the whole idea was questioned by the Inspector-General.

---

[1] Memo., Balfour MSS, BL Add. MS 49822, ff. 142-9.

[2] Curtis, op. cit. p. 437. This was in response to Salisbury's suggestion that the problem was not 'Irish blundering which is of course perennial, but a want of definite rules' (15 Sept. 1887, Balfour MSS (Whittingehame) 33).

[3] Note, 18 Nov., on DM Report, SW Div., Oct. 1887 (SPO). Turner had called for shotguns rather than buckshot in rifles as the only effective firearm for use at night—anticipating night attacks on patrols and barracks during the winter.

[4] Notes by Under-Secretary, Deputy IG, 9 Nov.: Under-Secretary, 17 Nov. 1887 (loc. cit.).

I am of opinion that it would not be advisable to arm the entire constabulary force with revolvers. From experience I consider it would
not be safe to do so, as the possession of a loaded revolver is in this
country too great a temptation to a policeman to use it freely under
provocation.[1]

Thus, the problem came back to the discipline and efficiency of the RIC. Balfour told Salisbury after Mitchelstown that 'the Police Officers do not appear to have behaved
with judgment or presence of mind'. A departmental inquiry
indicated to Ridgeway 'a very bad state of discipline and
morale among the officers of the RIC'. This confirmed a fear
he had expressed a month earlier, when the Inspector-General
refused to issue an order 'reminding the Constabulary that it
was their duty (which they have entirely abrogated) to
nominate the jury in a Coroner's inquest' on the ground that
it would not be 'safe' for him to do so.[2] Equally bad was
the attitude of the divisional and resident magistrates. 'The
fact is', Ridgeway said of one of them, 'I believe Slacke
to be afraid of "United Ireland"—like a great many others.'[3]
Even the rough-tongued Ridgeway himself came to be
infected by what he called atmospherically 'Ship Street rot'
—a general state of being run-down common to the Castle's
inhabitants, and contributing to its enervated bureaucratism.
As Buller had said to Balfour, '*You* can take a decision, and *I*
can take a decision, nobody else in Ireland can'.[4]

It was in an attempt to overcome this general paralysis
that Balfour followed the policy of 'backing up' the actions
of law-officers in the field, however dubious. The mettlesome
Colonel Turner was a case in point. His correspondence and his
less reliable memoirs display the real pleasure he obtained from

[1] Note by IG, 21 Nov. 1887 (loc. cit.).

[2] Ridgeway to Balfour, 20 Feb., 23 Mar. 1888 (BL Add. MS 49808).

[3] Ridgeway to Balfour, 16 Mar. 1888 (loc. cit.). Ridgeway had been dismayed when Slacke refused to proclaim a Fenian demonstration at Waterford
in November 1887 (R. to B., 27 Nov. 1887).

[4] Balfour to Salisbury, 21 Sept. 1887, quoted in Curtis, *Coercion and Conciliation*, p. 437. On bureaucracy and the shirking of responsibility see ibid.,
pp. 188–92. The Castle remained obdurately inefficient: in 1891 Ridgeway was
still complaining that a 'catastrophe' could easily occur—'the whole system is
rotten, and if you did not happen to be an all powerful member of the Cabinet,
the catastrophe would have happened long ago' (Ridgeway to Balfour, 28 Mar.
1891, BL Add. MS 49812).

the skilful breaking up and 'moving on' of demonstrations, and his equal distaste for evictions. One of his reports, defending his actions during the suppression of meetings near Ennis in 1888, for which he was violently attacked by the press (one of whose representatives was injured by a hussar who ran amok), may convey some of the problems of upholding the law on the ground.

I had very few police & I sent those in, while I posted a few hussars in the lane across the archway. I gave no orders to draw swords, but as sentries the men had of course their swords drawn. I had given special orders that no batons were to be used or any violence exercised unless in case of resistance or stone throwing.
. . . One hussar as you know broke away from the ranks and did some damage before his officer could get to him & force him back.
. . . I sent in a few infantry to help the police & as stones were still coming from the windows on us in the lane, I posted some infantry to point their [unloaded *inserted*] rifles at the windows. The stone throwing then ceased . . . . No one in their senses would send cavalry into a yard, as I am asserted by the Nationalists to have done, much less an experienced soldier.
. . . I really do not see how I could have acted otherwise in any respect.[1]

Turner assuredly went over the top at times, but, as Ridge-way wrote with uncharacteristic indulgence on another occasion,

I am inclined to think that Turner was a little too impetuous at Ennis last Sunday but his position was very difficult. It is inevitable that our people should now & then lose their patience under such conditions.[2]

The morale-raising effect of 'backing-up' was easy to see, yet hard to measure. It helped to restore the active capacity of law-officers, and hence, as Clifford Lloyd had suggested, of the law itself. It created a new atmosphere in Ireland, in which the old expectation that the 'associations' would prove stronger than the government was for the first time

---

[1] Turner to Seymour, 16 June 1888 (BL Add. MS 49820). Cf. *Sixty Years*, pp. 239–42, 248; Turner admitted to suppressing the fact that the police went into the yard and 'used their batons freely', holding that a commander who did not cover the minor faults of his subordinates would 'never, melancholy to relate, be well served when it comes to the pitch'.
[2] Ridgeway to Balfour, 14 Apr. 1888 (BL Add. MS 49808).

questioned.[1] But it could not altogether uproot the tradition of local resistance.

In part, as Turner later conceded, this was due to the weakness and imperfect adaptation of the police, whose deficiencies could only be compounded by the employment of troops. Balfour's revised instructions on the use of fire-arms may have helped to prevent another Mitchelstown, but they left the RIC with weapons and methods that were increasingly anachronistic and provocative. It continued to patrol in military style, with at best equivocal results.[2] It showed no sign of purging itself of either militarism or bureaucratism. Turner remarked in 1891 that the 'red tape' mentality was 'I am sorry to say rather a salient feature in the RIC administration', and that police-officers' 'inspections and efforts to make soldiers instead of policemen of their men are to my mind utterly wasted—the force is altogether too military'.[3] Calls for actual military assistance declined, which was some compensation. Still, the employment of serving military officers like Buller and Turner in ambiguous civil–military commissionerships showed the extent to which the normal legal adminsitration had been overstrained. Surviving police reports provide little hard evidence that the restoration of order was achieved through the perfection of police techniques, though, as will be seen, a measure of success was enjoyed by the secret intelligence service, building on the work begun by Jenkinson. The most striking development in day-to-day technique was 'shadowing':

The constant watch which is being kept by the Police upon the movements of dangerous persons prevents those constant meetings together which are necessary to form conspiracies, for under the Crimes Act this supervision . . . may become, or lead to, important evidence.[4]

---

[1] This was approvingly noted by W. H. Hurlbert, op. cit. i, 22, who thought that Balfour was at last 'teaching' Ireland 'that the duty of executive officers to execute the laws is not a thing debatable, like the laws themselves, nor yet determinable, like the enactment of laws, by taking the yeas and the nays'.

[2] W. Div. admitted in July 1887 that patrolling had remained slack in some areas, though Turner reported that patrolling had been 'very energetically & well carried out by the police'. But the two instances he gave of its operation were not impressive. He later told Balfour (8 Apr. 1891, BL Add. MS 49820) that police patrolling was 'far too perfunctory'.

[3] Turner to Balfour, 9 Apr. 1891 (loc. cit.).

[4] SPO, DC Reports, W. Div., 4 Feb. 1888.

It was brought to a high degree of effectiveness—the flight of Dillon and O'Brien from intensive shadowing in October 1890 really marked the end of the Plan of Campaign—though it was regarded with some aversion as an un-English form of surveillance.[1]

The general land agitation died away after 1889 mainly under the influence of reforms (Balfour's own included) and improving conditions. By mid 1889 Balfour was able to concentrate all his forces on half a dozen 'test estates'.[2] Constant harassment, imprisonment, release and rearrest of leaders effectively crippled the political apparatus of the National League, giving some apparent colour to Forster's idea that a small number of arrests would produce wide demoralization. By August 1888, thanks in part to the success of Edward Carson as prosecutor, twenty-one members of the Irish Parliamentary Party had received prison sentences (some of six months' hard labour), and eleven more were facing trial by the end of the year. The crucial element in Balfour's strategy was the severe treatment of these unusual prisoners, and this was not achieved without difficulty. When O'Brien's strike against prison dress produced concessions, Balfour complained to Ridgeway that

Tullamore [gaol] was originally selected on the grounds that both the Doctor and the Governor were especially to be relied on. It is characteristic of Irish administration that the best Governor to be found should be, to all appearances, so exceedingly weak.[3]

Gradually the deference of prison officials was eroded, and the results seem at least to have justified the political risks. Exotic publicists like Scawen Blunt were soon disenchanted; Dillon's health was threatened; and few had the resilience of O'Brien, whose lengthy refusal to move his bowels constituted the most remarkable of prison protests.[4] Even the

---

[1] Lyons, 'John Dillon and the Plan of Campaign', pp. 343-4; for a note on shadowing see Curtis, op. cit. pp. 438-9; also 'Some Notes on Boycotting and the Practice of "Shadowing" in Ireland by the Police, and by Vigilance Men and Others', PRO CO 903 2.

[2] Curtis, op. cit. pp. 239-52.

[3] Balfour to Ridgeway, 8 Nov. 1887 (BL Add. MS 49808).

[4] And the one which caused the most perplexed revulsion among the gentlefolk of the administration. For Ridgeway's reaction see Curtis, op. cit. pp. 228-9; cf. also O'Brien, *William O'Brien*, pp. 69-70.

public outcry following the death of John Mandeville in Tullamore gaol in July 1888 failed to deflect Balfour's policy, though some details of prison discipline were discreetly altered.

There might be some political impact in Herbert Gladstone's assertion that 'Mr Mandeville had died for his political convictions, and that would be the opinion of the majority of the English people, whatever sophistries Mr Balfour might use';[1] but local officers had no doubts about the effect of imprisonments at grass-roots level. A South-Western Division report of February 1889 is typical:

> Edw.d Kennedy a rioter who got a month on the plank bed, after coming out privately told Sergt. Brady he would not put in another month under similar conditions for £100. . . . The police towards the end of 1887 were frequently stoned, boycotting notices were posted & the District generally about that time was disturbed. The police under Mr Royse DI had several very prompt & successful prosecutions under the Act, & completely curbed the lawless tendency of the people.[2]

Not long afterwards men were even agreeing to give bail for good behaviour, 'a significant sign of the returning supremacy of the law'.[3] In 1890, Balfour was able to inform the House of Commons that out of 1,614 persons imprisoned so far under the Crimes Act, only eighty had gone to gaol for a second time.

(v) *Revolutionaries underground*

> We have reliable information from several quarters that the Gaelic Athletic Association is the principal nursery now of disloyalty . . . several of the G.A.A. clubs now in the Division are in reality I.R.B. circles.
>
> District Inspector, Crime Special
> South-Western Division, 1888[4]

However successful the prosecutions—and Balfour's administration survived even the error of conniving at *The Times* newspaper's indictment of Parnell as an organizer of violence

---

[1] *Standard*, 1 Aug. 1888.
[2] DICS Report, SW Div. 22 Feb. 1889 (SPO Crime Branch Special MSS).
[3] DC Reports, W. Div., Oct. 1889 (loc. cit.).
[4] SPO, CBS MSS, DICS Report, SW Div., Mar. 1888.

—together with the admixture of constructive reforms (the combination mocked by nationalists as 'heavy punishments and light railways'), the deepest-set roots of violent groups lived on. The limited success of the *Times* Commission's extensive investigations in establishing direct links between the Land League and rural violence point up the latter's diffuse, amorphous nature.[1] Throughout the 1880s steady efforts, hampered only by the miserliness of the Treasury and the complacency of the Home Office, had been made to penetrate the shadowy 'secret societies' which proliferated in disturbed areas. Some success had been claimed by E. G. Jenkinson in this frustrating process; but as the decade progressed, the ramifications of the underground skein became still more complex and mystifying.

Intelligence officers hesitated over the major question, whether the microscopic local groups were part of a co-ordinated organization with political objectives. On balance they decided that they were not. Thus, while the Western Division reported in May 1887 'very great dissatisfaction and a dangerous spirit everywhere', with secret societies 'now very strong'; and repeated this warning next year—'secret societies are at work over the whole of Mayo and private information tells me that they are gaining strength every day', it was confident that this recrudescence (fuelled by the turning-away of 'hard men' from the League after the Papal rescript) could 'hardly ever become a danger to the state'. The societies were riddled with local jealousies and mutual mistrust, and information would 'always be procurable as to their designs'. In the view of the Division's special crime officer,

Further investigation leads me to doubt that these 'Rings' are directed, as has often been stated, by any central authority. They differ very much in character in different localities.[2]

---

[1] The political disaster of the Pigott affair concealed the extent to which the general prosecution case against the League had been made out, though the prejudice of the Commission's testimony makes the whole inquiry difficult to evaluate. The origins and consequences of the Commission are analysed in F. S. L. Lyons, ' "Parnellism and Crime", 1887–90', *Tr. R. Hist. S.* (1973), pp. 123–40.

[2] SPO, DC Reports, W. Div., May 1887, Mar., May 1888 (DICS Report, W. Div., June 1888).

Though this was perhaps to confuse direction and co-ordination, the same view was taken in the South-Western Division.

There is no widely spread well-organised society in existence; but all through the District there are small murder rings or gangs of bravos, who are ready to commit any crime from murder down, for hire. These ruffians keep the people ... in terror, they live in idleness on blackmail, and in some instances on outdoor relief granted by the worthless and corrupt Boards of Guardians.[1]

This was describing Castleisland, Co. Kerry, one of the 'worst' of all districts.

The general opinion of the police was that the most violent groups were the smallest, most ill-organized and unpolitical. At the same time they were aware of a new and potentially more alarming growth in the political sphere. The IRB was enjoying a renewal, partly through attaching itself to a movement which was to form the most successful (and enduring) of its front organizations, the Gaelic Athletic Association. Its apparently harmless devotion to the revival of Irish games had unmistakable nationalist implications. At the GAA elections of November 1886 many names familiar to the police appeared in new, sporting guises.[2] Henceforth the cross-fertilization of these varied groupings blurred the authorities' view of their adversary. In 1888 the Deputy Inspector-General noted that 'the GAA is fast developing into Fenianism', and local officers reported that many GAA branches were in effect IRB circles.[3] GAA meetings provided perfect cover for the organizers of conspiracies, and at the GAA Convention in January 1889 'the organizing power of the IRB leaders, and their wonderful perseverance' gave them control of the executive.[4] Yet, as another officer reported, it was 'remarkable' that

while on the one hand we find the GAA and the IRB becoming more closely united, on the other hand a resolution was passed at the GAA County Convention at Boyle on 20th Oct. that no person be admitted who was not himself (or had not some near member of his family) a member of the I[rish] N[ational] L[eague].[5]

[1] DICS Report, SW Div., Oct. 1888.
[2] W. F. Mandle, 'The IRB and the beginnings of the Gaelic Athletic Association', *IHS* (Sept. 1977), p. 431.
[3] SPO, DICS Reports, SW Div., Mar. 1888, and note by Thynne, Apr. 1888.
[4] DICS Report, SW Div., Jan. 1889.
[5] DICS Report, W. Div. (Gibbons), Nov. 1889.

The signs of a genuinely revolutionary association were clearly appearing, but it was no longer a grouping focused primarily on the use of physical force. It was true that the IRB itself had been 'not as a rule in favour of outrage', as a DICS reported in 1889.[1] John Devoy's denunciation of his rival Sullivan turned mainly on the fact that Sullivan had substituted a policy of terrorism, designed merely to force concessions from the English government, for the winning of national independence by driving the English out of Ireland.[2] By the 1890s frustration, caused by interminable preparation, split forth into schism.

At the same time the great alternative policy, the 'new departure' and the parliamentary strategy, suddenly plunged from apparent triumph to appalling ruin. The breakdown of the *Times*'s case against Parnell seemed to leave the parliamentarians in an impregnable position; yet, as the land agitation died away after the departure of Dillon and O'Brien, the O'Shea divorce crushed Parnell's career with shocking speed. Ground between the millstones of English nonconformity and Irish Catholicism, Parnell fought an increasingly hopeless struggle from late 1890 to his death in October 1891.[3] During this distressing period, opening a split that was to last ten years, and exhaust the catalogue of internecine malediction, Parnell turned to a violent rhetoric which was to prove one of his most damaging legacies. (The other, as will be suggested in the last part of this chapter, being a domineering and over-centralized party structure.) Although he repudiated the 'appeal to the hillside men' published by Fenians who rallied to him in the final crisis, its spirit clung to him. On one occasion, addressing a meeting in Navan as 'men of Royal Meath', he added that in the future someone might 'have the privilege of addressing you as men of republican Meath'.[4] And his earlier verbal device of reference to the 1782 Volunteers reappeared with greater impact now as he urged resistance until Ireland received legislative independence.

The vituperation of the Parnell split damaged the credibility

[1] DICS Report, SW Div. (Gambell), Apr. 1889.
[2] Ó Broin, *Revolutionary Underground*, p. 62.
[3] F. S. L. Lyons, *The Fall of Parnell, 1890–91* (London, 1960).
[4] Lyons, *Charles Stewart Parnell*, pp. 539, 578.

of the whole parliamentary movement. Parnell ended up denouncing the very dependence on the Liberals which had been the corner-stone of his policy since 1886 and the ground for his hindrance of the Plan of Campaign. After the final failure of Gladstone's home rule efforts in 1893, the old Fenian belief that parliamentarism would pervert Irish nationalists was widely readopted, with a new refinement derived from the ideas that had inspired the Gaelic Athletic Association. A new cultural radicalism solidified in answer to Douglas Hyde's call for 'de-Anglicization '. The foundation of the Gaelic League in 1893 heralded a passionate effort to salvage what was regarded as the concrete basis of Irish national identity, the Irish language. Irish-Irelandism brought into public life the cultural awareness which had been marginal to Fenianism, and the fusion of cultural and political nationalism produced a programme almost substantial enough to be called an ideology.[1] In spite of deep differences, the racialism of D. P. Moran, editor of the *Leader*, and the autarchism of Arthur Griffith, founder of Sinn Féin, alike dealt out a barrage of blows against compromise with English values—whether religious, economic, social, or educational.[2] And though Hyde himself always maintained that de-Anglicization was a non-political idea, its political implications were finally unmistakable.[3] The leading mind of the Gaelic League, Eoin MacNeill, was to progress from the blackboard, teaching Irish to enthusiastic evening classes, through the League's campaign for compulsory schooling in Irish, to the map-boards of the General Staff of the Irish

[1] *Pace* attempts to label earlier nationalist ideas as such, e.g. S. Cronin, *Irish Nationalism. A History of its Roots and Ideology* (Dublin, 1980). Compare the judicious account in D. G. Boyce, *Nationalism in Ireland* (London, 1982).

[2] On Irish-Ireland racialism cf. Alf MacLochlainn, 'Thomas Davis and Irish Racialism', *Irish Times*, 20 Nov. 1973. The counter-argument of Boyce, e.g. p. 243, is incomplete.

[3] The growth of the League accelerated dramatically in 1900–2; having reached only 107 by 1899, the number of branches rose to nearly 400 by 1902. It has been suggested with some plausibility that the Boer War was the 'crucial catalyst to development of Irish cultural nationalism because it raised directly the question of whether it was possible to be simultaneously an Irish nationalist and a British imperialist' (M. J. Waters, 'Peasants and Emigrants: Considerations of the Gaelic League as a Social Movement', in D. J. Casey and R. E. Rhodes, *Views of the Irish Peasantry 1800–1916*, p. 164).

Volunteers.[1] The League also acted, somewhat paradoxically, as an agent of modernization. Many of its leaders were ex-peasant emigrants who had absorbed secular ideas abroad.[2]

For some time, however, the significance of the new cultural movement eluded the baffled, directionless, schismatic remnant of the Fenian organization, whose internal feuding and outward ineffectiveness reached a new extreme in the later 1890s.[3] Until the revival of the IRB commenced with the clubs organized by Bulmer Hobson and partially inspired by Sinn Féin, the political alternative to parliamentarism remained unclear. The centenary of 1798 passed without an insurrectionary gesture. However, the year 1898 produced a new popular movement which opened up rather different revolutionary possibilities, though unexpectedly this tremendous popular impulse was to be channelled by its creator towards assimilation, and was to be steadily opposed and undermined by Irish-Ireland intellectuals.

(vi) *United Irish*

> Mr Balfour has been thrashed clean out of his coercive mood. He began by bludgeoning a peaceful crowd, sending young men to jail for booing a land grabber, suppressing the right of public meetings and threatening the leaders with fire and

[1] M. Tierney, *Eoin MacNeill. Scholar and Man of Action 1867–1945* (Oxford 1980), p. 67, argues—more convincingly for MacNeill than for Moran—that neither was a 'racialist'. He presents an interesting analysis of MacNeill's conception of national identity, observing that the 'real cleavage in the Irish approach to politics' was between 'the revolutionary nationalists with their perpetual emphasis on the achievement of statehood, and the (traditional) nationalists who did not acknowledge any revolutionary ancestry and who put the state last rather than first in their order of priorities' (p. 64). This may have been because there was no traditional basis for the modern concept of the state in Irish culture.

[2] Waters, 'Peasants and Emigrants', *passim*.

[3] Though the same might be said of the government's anti-Fenian organization. Major Gosselin was still warning of dynamite threats in 1896, and complaining that his own lack of authority would oblige him to resign 'having given 14 years nearly of my life for nothing'. The cause of the problem, unsurprisingly, was Anderson: 'I hope Robert Anderson will live long and die happily but if he should die from some uncanny cause and I am alive I will certainly be present at the autopsy that I may see what size his heart is—he has me nearly demented' (Gosselin to Sandars, 16 Sept. 1896, Balfour MSS (Whittingehame) 32).

sword. Coercion, as usual, only spread the flames of popular spirit.

William O'Brien[1]

The West Mayo United Irish League, inspired by William
O'Brien, was a demonstration of the steam-pressure still
left in Lalor's agrarian 'locomotive'. The stultification of
nationalist activity during the split, which had led O'Brien
into despairing political retirement, was reversed with revolutionary speed. This happened from the base upwards. As its
original title indicates, the new League had its source in
immediate local problems. It derived its dynamism from the
persistence of hardship in the marginal farmlands ('Congested Districts' in official tongue) of Mayo, and from
resentment against land-grabbers and big graziers or ranchers.
Yet it was undoubtedly a political organization from the
start. More than that, it had—inevitably, in view of its
leaders' background—a national, and nationalist, outlook.
It was a specifically political mechanism designed to improve
on the sporadic and ineffective agrarian agitation of the mid
1890s.[2] Its purpose, announced in the advertisement for its
inaugural meeting at Westport in January 1898, was to
organize public opinion so that the pressure on the government for action would be irresistible. While this formulation
was no doubt designed to broaden the League's attraction,
it showed that in spite of its political consciousness the new
movement was reformist rather than revolutionary in spirit.
The revolution it looked to was, indeed, one blessed by the
Conservative government. Its most straightforward aim was
to hasten the Congested Districts Board's own scheme for
land purchase and redistribution.

The Westport meeting nevertheless gave the government a nasty surprise. It was an organizational triumph,
intended by O'Brien as 'a *really* big '98 celebration' to
attract Irish American attention, and was attended by some
4,000 people. Local grievances dominated the speeches,

---

[1] O'Brien to Patrick Ford, *Mayo News*, 23 July 1898.

[2] This section draws heavily on the analysis of the UIL in P. J. Bull, 'The
Reconstruction of the Irish Parliamentary Movement, 1895-1903' (Cambridge
University Ph.D. thesis, 1973), pp. 140 ff. though its interpretation of the League's
quasi-governmental role is somewhat different.

but the local Nationalist MP predicted that the League would spread through Ireland until they achieved 'the right to make and administer their own laws in their own country'. More concretely, a priest advocated the boycotting of all land-grabbers, ranch-holders, and their allies: while O'Brien's former comrade-in-arms, John Dillon, though now so obsessed with parliamentary problems as to see agrarian agitation as a tiresome distraction, urged the formation in each parish of an organized force of young men under a 'captain', to be ready to 'mobilize the people . . . by day or by night' to act against land-grabbers and 'enemies of the people'.[1] Such a proposal, more openly aggressive than anything advocated during the Plan of Campaign, triggered the government's repressive response.

As often before, it proved relatively simple for the League leaders to out-manoeuvre the inelastic Irish administration. The first confrontation occurred in Westport on 3 February, when a number of agrarian prosecutions came to trial. The authorities, surprised by the inauguration of the League barely a week earlier, had made no preparations. The police were disinclined to take it seriously, and remained so for some time to come. As a result local officers were over-whelmed by an impressive demonstration which paraded around the town, accompanied by a band, hooting and 'groaning' the estate office of Lord Sligo and the homes of local magistrates. During the next fortnight the League assembled demonstrations against several graziers, threaten-ing them with 'war to the knife', and appeared to be success-ful in inducing herds and other employees to abandon work.

The authorities decided, in consequence, to use the next major trial on 17 February to crush open opposition.[2] Extra police were drafted into the disturbed area, and the resulting peace-keeping operation was described by all observers (except the RIC themselves) as provocatively violent.[3] It was

---

[1] Bull, 'Reconstruction', p. 148; Lyons, *John Dillon*, p. 185.

[2] The Attorney-General had ruled that intimidatory deputations and assem-blies such as had taken place on 8, 11, and 15 February were unlawful and that the police were bound to disperse them. The police had been expanded by 30 extra force, and a temporary reinforcement of 100: PRO CO 903 8/1.

[3] *Freeman's Journal*, 18 Feb., *Mayo News*, 19 Feb. 1898, quoted in Bull, 'Reconstruction', p. 162.

accompanied by a belligerent warning from the Crown Prosecutor that 'lawlessness would not be tolerated by the authorities'. Replying to Nationalist parliamentary protests, the Chief Secretary, Gerald Balfour, confirmed the Crown Prosecutor's declaration that the government would not shrink from prosecuting the leaders of the agitation. This gauntlet-hurling must be seen as an over-reaction, since police reports continued until late in the year to be confident that outside Co. Mayo the country was undisturbed.[1] Its main effect was to stiffen and focus resistance.[2]

Ironically, it helped to turn the League into the very thing the government feared, a 'rival government'. Not only did the threat of prosecutions create publicity, as always to the government's disadvantage, but O'Brien's successful bluff—by which he induced ministers to think that he wanted to be arrested and that they should at all costs avoid playing into his hands—severely reduced the prestige and credibility of the authorities. Crude police responses assisted the League in building up its central power and its control over spontaneous violence.[3] In turn, police impotence in face of O'Brien's challenge heightened the quasi-governmental attributes of the new association. In May 1898 O'Brien suggested that anyone with a grievance should lay it before the UIL Executive, 'this tribunal of the delegates of the people'. In October, the Glenisland branch summoned before it several people charged with breaches of League 'laws', and this tendency became still more marked later. Between October 1899 and October 1900 over 120 'cases', including some for 'contempt of court', were brought before UIL branches.[4]

After building a secure base in Mayo during its first nine months, the organization expanded across Ireland. It failed to establish itself only in Ulster and—crucially for its

---

[1] IG Report, Sept. 1898 (CO 904 69),. Even in Mayo 'a new and disquieting' tendency had only just been noticed—'to originate and foster a bad feeling towards the police'.

[2] Bull, 'Reconstruction', pp. 164–5.

[3] Such as the brutal attack on John Mooney on 8 Feb. CO 903/8/1.

[4] Irish Office Confidential Prints, CO 903 8/2. For the substantial discussion of what he calls the 'pseudo-governmental' role of the UIL see Bull, 'Reconstruction', pp. 205–20.

eventual aspirations—Dublin.[1] It is not altogether obvious why a movement with such local concerns should have found such wide acceptance. Its most competent analyst has been unable to improve on the contemporary metaphor of spreading fire.[2] In these terms Ireland was clearly in an inflammable state, but its combustible nature is not to be explained so much by absolute hardship—though a few cases of real hardship were sufficient to revive the memory of general crises—as by the habit of rural combination. There was a marked mimetic propensity for localities to be spurred or shamed into activity by the example of their neighbours. This was a result of historically conditioned expectations, which formed part of the 'organizational density' of the Irish countryside. The League stepped naturally into the role played by earlier agrarian associations, and used the same methods. The high level of popular acceptance is indicated by the relative infrequency of outrage attributed to the League.[3] The rhetoric of violence was more freely employed. At Aughagower, Co. Mayo, on 30 April 1899, for instance, one speaker referred to old secret societies such as the 'Slashers' and 'Houghers', and said that they could now 'make it hot' for the grazier and the grabber without making themselves liable for malicious injury; another advocated a 'good lively constitutional agitation with a little bit of the slashing, houghing and levelling thrown in'.[4] (In effect, Parnell's own recipe.)

Boycotting never reached the proportions of the 1880s. In August 1900 a new Inspector-General of the RIC divided

---

[1] By 30 Nov. 1901 there were, according to police calculations, 1,098 League branches with a total of 114,709 members. The largest number of branches in any county was 73 in Limerick (Mayo, with 84, was divided into two ridings): the smallest was 2—with only 12 members—in Co. Dublin: return of Branches of UIL, CO 903 8.

[2] Bull, 'Reconstruction', p. 206.

[3] The extensive RIC statistics in CO 903 attribute to the UIL 149 out of 716 agrarian offences between 1 Feb. 1898 and 31 Oct. 1899; in the following year they added 41 out of 234. Thus, the proportional contribution of the UIL appears to have been small. Moreover, the overall total of outrage in the forty-five-month period 1 Feb. 1898—31 Oct. 1901 (950) was actually less than in the preceding forty-five months (956): CO 903 8, pp. 183, 247. Cf. also Return of Outrages and Minor Offences, CO 904 20/3.

[4] Police notes on UIL meetings, CO 904 20/3.

UIL intimidation into four types: first, by 'courts' held
to decide on agrarian cases; second, by resolutions against
individuals published in sympathetic newspapers; third, by
public meetings at or near the residence of the threatened
person; and fourth, 'as a last resource', by actual outrage.
He was surprised to find that when this resource was applied,
the injured parties were reluctant to give the police any
information or assistance. They submitted to outrage 'rather
than do anything to bring themselves into antagonism to
the general feeling'.[1] The new Inspector-General was Neville
Chamberlain, a regular army colonel, former commandant
of the Khyber Pass and military adviser to the Kashmir
Government: 'good looking, fine presence, charming manners, plenty of self-reliance, an unusual amount of common
sense, and that unusual quality, tact' in the opinion of Lord
Roberts, who added reassuringly that Chamberlain also 'had
experience of dealing with Europeans'.[2] Notwithstanding
all these qualities he was as baffled as any of his predecessors
by the nature of the organization, semi-visible as it was,
that he confronted. But he put his finger on an interesting
aspect of the League's ubiquity in rural areas.

While it remains true that the recognised leaders of the extreme revolutionary section in the large cities and towns are opposed to the League
as contrary to their policy of physical force, it is yet a fact that in
many districts, and in most cases the places where trouble is likely to
arise, the local IRB and secret society suspects are ardent Leaguers.[3]

In the countryside it was not profitable or popular to be
anything else.

The habitual, sometimes rather desperate, optimism of
the constabulary reports for this period does not conceal
the fact that the police were able to do little to inhibit
the power and progress of the League. Demoralization
started with the early failure to prosecute O'Brien, and
paralysis extended alongside the steadily growing resistance
to the Queen's writ. Reports constantly showed the police

[1] IG Report; County Inspector's Monthly Report, E. Galway, Aug. 1900
(CO 904 71).
[2] Roberts to Lord Cadogan, 5 Dec. 1899, in Cadogan to G. Balfour, 6 Dec.
(Balfour MSS (Whittingehame) 111).
[3] IG Monthly Report, Oct. 1900 (CO 904 71).

'restoring order successfully' in one townland only to have disorder break out in another. Opposition was doggedly ascribed to marginal minority groups; the 'general feeling' referred to by Chamberlain was put down to intimidation rather than genuine public sentiment. Before the Queen's visit to Ireland, the Inspector-General stoutly maintained that the whole country was looking forward to the event—except only Limerick city, where

the scandalous action of John Daly, a licensed Convict who owes his freedom to the clemency of the Crown, has stirred up and keeps inflamed the worst possible spirit of disloyalty and sedition amongst the low class of extremists who are unfortunately numerous in Limerick.[1]

In September 1900 he claimed that two particularly turbulent League branches, at Knocknagree in Co. Cork and Craughwell in East Galway, had been 'handicapped' by a new system of surprise police patrols, and five months later that the 'excellent effect of police supervision over the turbulent branches' had been 'most marked'.[2] A year after this, however, he had to admit that in the worst districts—parts of Clare, East Cork, Fermanagh, Galway, Roscommon, Sligo, and Tipperary—the level of interference with individual liberty was 'unparalleled in any civilised country at the present time'.[3] Extra forces had been sent to several areas and were (surely not before time) developing skill in dealing with 'both open and covert intimidation'. None the less,

the League, as an intimidatory power, is, in my judgement, at the present moment stronger than it has ever been, and is steadily increasing its influence for evil over portions of the country originally unaffected.[4]

In the view of experienced RIC officers the general peace of the country was endangered, and the ordinary law was inoperative in face of such methods.

Once again, therefore, an organization had emerged which successfully resisted the authority of the state. But although

---

[1] IG Monthly Report, Mar. 1900 (CO 904 70).
[2] IG Reports, Sept. 1900, Feb. 1901 (CO 904 71, 72).
[3] Ibid., Feb., Mar. 1902 (CO 904 74).
[4] Ibid., Jan. 1902 (CO 904 74).

the UIL possessed the capacity to become an alternative government, it did so only to a limited extent. It was not part of its function to be a counter-state. Its diffuse localism kept it within the anarchic tradition of the associations, and, in spite of the widespread paralysis of law, there was never any apprehension of outright rebellion. O'Brien's own purpose in forming the League had not only been to pursue the agrarian struggle, but to use those energies to rebuild a unified nationalist movement, with a wider base than the old parliamentary party. The most substantial political success of the UIL, its sweeping victory in the elections under the Irish Local Government Act of 1898, showed its preparedness to participate in the British state-structure (and reflected a broader tendency towards Anglicization even among those whose intellectual hostility to Saxondom was greatest). The rout of the landlords certainly represented a revolution in rural society, but, like the land reform, it was a revolution that paved the way for assimilation.

The League could, perhaps, scarcely hope to mobilize all national energy for what Arthur Griffith branded with classical Fenian contempt as 'a squalid class movement'. As the movement grew it shifted from its lowly but secure origins towards the treacherous sphere of high politics. In the end, after a fierce struggle between O'Brien and the party leadership, it sank into the constituency organization of the born-again INP. In spite of its awesome vitality it fell victim to what David Fitzpatrick has called the 'vampirism' of the parliamentary party—its urge to suck into itself all manifestations of national energy which might diverge from or threaten its programme. This imperative might equally be labelled Parnellism, a term which also conveys its authoritarian character. It is true that although it merged into the party, the League retained greater weight than the old National League had possessed: it restricted the party central executive to controlling only 25 per cent of the funds, as against 75 per cent under Parnell. But the authentic energy of a popular movement was gradually eroded, perhaps in part by its most significant result, the Wyndham Land Act of 1903, the summit of the Conservative endeavour to kill home rule with kindness. The reunited party had a difficult task to repair the damage done to the credit of representative institutions by the faction fighting of the 1890s. The mass-parliamentary composite movement on the Parnellite model 'depended ultimately on the achievement of results'.[1] Without them it had no real base, and would be vulnerable to those who believed that a rejection of political compromise was the only way in which Ireland could free itself from the ever more complex web of English control.

[1] Bull, 'Reconstruction', p. 28.

5
Political Armies

(i) Constitutionalism and Nationalism

> The forces of nature seem to me to be working for Home
> Rule; and it will come about under one English party
> just as much as another *if*, an important *if*, the Irish con-
> tinue to press as strongly for it. That is perhaps not so
> certain. When they have the land, much of the steam will
> be out of the boiler.
>
> James Bryce[1]

Politically, the decade after Balfour's resignation in December
1905 was dominated by the Liberal party. The massive
Conservative defeat in January 1906 gave the Liberals greater
effective power than at any time since the beginning of
Gladstone's second government. Even the immovably hostile
power of the House of Lords was finally to be challenged and
crushed during this crisis-rich period. From the Irish point of
view, the Nationalist party's policy of adhesion to the Liberals,
which had been a matter of angry debate during the Parnell
split, and which had produced nothing but the defeat of
1893, appeared to be triumphantly vindicated. Although
the Liberal leadership had steered suspiciously clear of any
substantial reference to Irish home rule in the 1905 election
campaign, it seemed impossible that a party with so overwhelming a majority could fail to put through a policy which
had been the *idée fixe* of Gladstone and of the weightiest
surviving Liberal ideologue, Morley. Unfortunately, the
party, much of which had never shared Morley's attachment
to the 'one idea', took a different view. It had too many
experiences of sacrificing power on the altar of Irish aspirations. It saw home rule as imperilling its programme of social
reforms; home rule simply did not command support from
British opinion.[2] As a result, five years passed with no more

---

[1] Bryce to Dicey, 3 Feb. 1905 (Bryce MSS, NLI MS 11011).
[2] P. Jalland, *The Liberals and Ireland. The Ulster Question in British Politics*

than a gesture in the direction of Irish self-government. For 'advanced' Irish nationalists, not only those of the physical-force tradition, this inaction was a conclusive demonstration of the futility of constitutional politics.

The gesture produced by the Liberal government in its early months was consigned to the dust-heap of history so rapidly that its potential significance has often been missed. The proposed Irish Councils Bill of 1906, initiated by the new Chief Secretary James Bryce (the prime intellectual antagonist, on Irish matters, of his friend A. V. Dicey), was calculated to exploit the slight potential consensus revealed by the so-called 'Devolution Crisis', which had wrecked Wyndham's political career. Although the Conservative party had violently repudiated the hesitant move of Dublin Castle towards a federal solution to the Irish government problem, federalism remained in the air. There was, at least, more of a chance that the opposition would accept an Irish council than an Irish parliament. In the event, the proposal was rejected by the Irish Nationalists before the Tories had a chance to do the same.[1]

The UIL's repudiation of the proposal showed the dangerously narrow obsession of parliamentary Nationalists with the principle of legislative independence. Outsiders who would later take over from the party, such as Terence MacSwiney and Patrick Pearse, the latter a Gaelic leaguer and educationalist, were more concerned to obtain a real measure of power over Irish life, and advocated acceptance of the bill. Eoin MacNeill put what he called the 'opportunist' position clearly: 'In theory I suppose I am a separatist,

to 1914 (Brighton, 1980) p. 24. Jalland holds that the party retained 'a genuine commitment to Home Rule'. The men of the Relugas Compact, however, were very lukewarm. Cf. S. Koss, *Asquith* (London, 1976) pp. 64 ff; A. O'Day, 'Irish Home Rule and Liberalism', in *The Edwardian Age: Conflict and Stability 1900--1914* (London, 1979), pp. 123-4.

[1] MacDonnell, originator of the devolution scheme, remained in office as Under-Secretary until 1908, serving under both Bryce and Birrell. Devolution increased in importance as a political idea before 1914, and continued to have appeal (albeit amongst peripheral intellectuals rather than leading politicians) as a dexterous conceptual resolution of the Irish problem: Earl of Dunraven, 'The History of Devolution', in J. H. Morgan (ed.), *The New Irish Constitution. An Exposition and some Arguments* (London, 1912), pp. 337-60. On Councils Bill, see O'Day, 'Irish Home Rule', pp. 125-9.

in practice I would accept any settlement that would enable Irishmen to freely control their own affairs.'[1]

Rebuffed on the constitutional question, the Liberals confined their attention to the important but less contentious question of Irish university education. This long-standing issue was substantially settled by the creation of the National University in 1908, but not until the crisis over the Lloyd George budget did the government turn— with little show of enthusiasm—back to the great question of home rule. In so doing it opened up fearful political rifts which threatened the foundations of the state itself, and seemed to demonstrate that Irish conflicts could not be resolved by British methods.

At the commencement of the third Ulster crisis in 1912, Irish public opinion was remarkably inert and unconcerned. In retrospect 'advanced' nationalists remembered this time as one of 'de-nationalization'. Irish farmers were interested (as they had always been, it may be suggested) above all in the transfer of land and increasing agricultural prosperity. At this level the 'knife and fork' philosophy of constructive unionism seemed to have worked. Materialism had sapped enthusiasm for theoretical postulates like national freedom. Voters abstained from rejecting, rather than actively supported, the Nationalist party. Yet events were to demonstrate that no great stimulus was needed for the recrudescence of national organization and activism. The economic analysis of Irish discontent was, rather suddenly, discredited. Why did nationalism re-emerge so dramatically? It may be that to express the change in these terms is to perpetuate a false dichotomy between the 'ideal' national object and the 'material' economic object. Philip Bull's approach to the national dimension of the UIL suggests that the nationalists were not merely capitalizing on the apolitical material desires of the rural population, but that they served a functional purpose in focusing those desires. Their symbolic struggle led emotions at the lower levels of the movement to be diverted from finding expression through petty violence

---

[1] MacNeill to Fr. Convery, 2 July 1904, quoted in Tierney, *Eoin MacNeill*, p. 104. He added, surely correctly, 'If the truth were known, I think that this represents the political views of 99 out of every hundred nationalists'.

into a vicarious participation in the formalized conflict between League and government.[1] National issues were not merely icing on the cake. Experience of the Land League and the UIL had demonstrated that national organizations —which were almost invariably created or staffed by national*ist* leaders—really worked. Even if the intellectual trappings of nationalism were uninteresting or incomprehensible, and even the Irish language itself almost universally rejected, the tradition of adhesion to communally based associations 'agin the governments' sustained the sense of identity prized by nationalist theoreticians. Above all, perhaps, the sense of common action, the pure carnival quality of music-accompanied demonstrations and marches, still provided vital recreation for a rural society.

(ii) *Sinn Féin and Republicanism*

> If Ireland is governed it is because the people obey. They need not obey, and they need not be governed a day longer than they wish.
>
> Bulmer Hobson[2]

There was no reason why the capacity for anti-government combination which lay so close to the surface of rural life should necessarily have found expression in open violence. The nicely balanced mixture of mass agitation and selective violence was by now a traditional technique, brought to a high pitch of perfection by the UIL. Disorder, in particular cattle-driving, remained rife in the countryside. Indeed, an upsurge in agrarian agitation in 1907 created 'very serious difficulties in the maintenance of order' in five (mainly central) counties.[3] But the advocates of open violence and insurrection had less of an audience in the first decade of the twentieth century than ever before. The IRB was a decayed husk of its former self, and its revitalization during

---

[1] Bull, 'Reconstruction of the Irish Parliamentary Movement', p. 166; cf. also p. 220.

[2] B. Hobson, *Defensive Warfare* (Belfast, 1909).

[3] Leitrim, Roscommon, King's Co., East Galway, and Clare. There was also 'much unrest' in Queen's Co., Sligo, West Galway, and West Cork. See also map of disturbed area in CO 904 121/1. An RIC additional force of 400 was supplied in August 1907, followed by a further 350 in June 1908.

this decade was begun by men with ideas very different from those of the old organization. Throughout the period before the constitutional crisis there was a marked impulse amongst advanced nationalists towards less violent methods, a synthesis vividly expressed in the phrase 'moral insurrection', coined by a prominent organizer of the 'new' IRB, P. S. O'Hegarty.

The return to 'Moral Force' did not (as time was to show) mean a complete abandonment of 'physical force'. This would have been unthinkable, even to Arthur Griffith, a fact which itself makes an important comment on the Irish approach to politics. But it did permit a reordering of priorities, and an escape from the paralysed sterility of old Fenian doctrine. This doctrine, enshrined in the third clause of the 1873 constitution, held that

The IRB shall await the decision of the Irish Nation as expressed by a majority of the Irish people as to the fit hour of inaugurating a war against England and shall pending such an emergency lend its support to every movement calculated to advance the cause of Irish independence, consistently with the preservation of its own integrity.[1]

Thus, the IRB had escaped from the pure Blanquism of the secret-society insurrection, which had served so poorly in the 1860s. Unfortunately it had not been able to define the way in which the mass support indicated by the 'decision of the Irish nation' was to be measured or created. For the latter, the 'exercise of moral influences' referred to in clause 2 of the constitution seemed to be the only course, and the Gaelic revival fortuitously provided the *deus ex machina* (or the *machina ex deo*, in the form of the Gaelic League and GAA). Still, the concept of 'war' in all its assumed forms remained distinctly unpromising.

A solution was offered by a return to the diffused form of struggle advocated half a century earlier by Lalor. Lalor had indicated the futility of assaults by Irish rebels, necessarily ill-trained and ill-armed, on the 'entrenched power' of England. What had to be done was to force the English garrison into an aggressive posture, whereupon the military as well as moral advantage would pass to the Irish. Lalor's

---

[1] Amended IRB constitution, 17 Mar. 1873 (Hobson MSS, NLI MS 13163).

trumpet blast had died away after 1848, but in 1909 a work directly echoing his ideas, Bulmer Hobson's *Defensive Warfare: A Handbook for Irish Nationalists*, was published by the West Belfast Branch of Sinn Féin.

Sinn Féin, the concept of self-reliance, was in currency amongst advanced nationalists before it was given the powerful personal imprint of Arthur Griffith. It expressed a tendency which gradually, after 1900, came to provide the basis of a political movement. Its core was the rejection of parliamentary participation at Westminster, and the unilateral establishment of an Irish government backed by what would later be called 'passive resistance' on the part of the people as a whole. Even the parliamentarians (Dillon in the 1880s, O'Brien in the 1890s) had toyed with the idea of withdrawal from Westminster, but in the spirit rather of tactical manoeuvre than of grand strategy. The new approach was clearly a radical departure from the old, though around the core idea there were several possible variations. The most substantial divergence was in the end to be between those who held that the only political form appropriate to 'ourselves alone' was an independent republic, and those who thought it possible to achieve the reality of autonomous development without insisting on the symbolic step of total separation from Britain.

Inevitably, the process by which the new Sinn Féin grouping emerged was halting and confused.[1] Griffith's own position, whilst always one of pre-eminence, never amounted to leadership in a party-political sense. The intellectual propositions on which the Sinn Féin movement was based were more sophisticated than those of earlier nationalists, whether Fenians or Home Rulers. Intellectual disagreements were unavoidable, and Griffith's highly idiosyncratic approach could not command unreserved support. Amongst Irish-Irelanders a somewhat bizarre and jarring note was struck from the start by the historical case-study on which Griffith based his programme of national self-regeneration. Hungary was certainly not an unknown country (to a culture where Kossuth had been lionized a generation

---

[1] The confusion is evident in the recent account by R. P. Davis, *Arthur Griffith and Non-Violent Sinn Féin* (Dublin, 1974), pp. 17–37.

previously) but flaws could be detected in any close analogy between the Hungarian experience and that of Ireland. Even Griffith's economic ideas were modelled on the (admittedly less exotic) German example of Friedrich List.[1] D. P. Moran's xenophobic mockery concealed a deeper critique. Even when Sinn Féin had shaken off his epithet 'the green Hungarian band', a degree of uncertainty remained about the extent to which the strategy of 1867 could be taken as any sort of blueprint for action. Griffith himself originally preferred the physical-force republican approach of Kossuth to that of the monarchist Deák, and had a shifting and shrouded relationship with the IRB, of which he was for a time a member.[2]

Griffith was a brilliant and perhaps unrivalled publicist. His natural medium was the newspaper, and the *United Irishman* and *Sinn Féin* (which succeeded it in 1906) were major intellectual impulses. He was less successful in the heavy spadework of organization-building, and it was here that the new generation of republicans excelled. The young Belfast IRB man, Bulmer Hobson, was an instinctive political engineer. He had already started a boys' club[3] and attempted to establish a Protestant nationalist society, as well as occupying important positions in the Gaelic League and Griffith's Cumann na nGaedheal, when together with Denis McCullough he set up the first Dungannon Club and issued the 'Dungannon Club Manifesto to the Whole People of Ireland' in 1905. The new organization was immediately successful, partly perhaps because of its local, non-Dublin origin.[4] Dungannon clubs spread across Ulster, tackling Orange hostility head-on, and also meeting with violence

[1] R. M. Henry, *The Evolution of Sinn Féin* (Dublin, 1920), pp. 71–6.

[2] Davis, *Arthur Griffith*, p. 21; Ó Broin, *Revolutionary Underground* pp. 108–20.

[3] Which later inspired Countess Markievicz to form the celebrated organization Na Fianna Éireann: Hobson, in F. X. Martin (ed.), *The Irish Volunteers 1913–1915. Recollections and Documents* (Dublin, 1963), pp. 19–20.

[4] McCullough later recalled that the Cumann na nGaedheal branches in Belfast 'were mostly composed of irresponsible young publicans' and grocers' assistants, with little or no national tradition behind them . . . Hobson and myself decided to close down the whole lot and start a new organisation, which would do some serious national work and which we could control in Belfast' (Interview with R. Davis, quoted in *Arthur Griffith*, pp. 25–6).

from the Hibernians, the Nationalist party's strong-arm organization.[1] The fourth Club was formed in London by P. S. O'Hegarty in October 1905, and the growing movement acquired a full-time organizing officer, Seán MacDermott. It remained a loose confederation, but took its lead from Hobson's Belfast Club, and was deeply imprinted with his ideas. In particular, his advocacy of temperance, so little akin to the hard-drinking image of former Irish rebels, became a hallmark of Sinn Féin.

Hobson's pamphlet *Defensive Warfare* sketched out the new, non-violent, framework for struggle which formed the Sinn Féin ideology. Deliberately ditching the Hungarian parallel, he returned to the ideas of Lalor. The Fenian premise remained: 'the primary cause of all Ireland's disease is the existing connection with England'. However, behind a declamatory mode of expression ('As a plant grows in accordance with the great and unalterable laws, and out of many trees is made the forest, so men live and evolve, and out of many men the nation governed by the laws of nature even as the blade of grass') lay a new realism of method. Ireland was too weak to resist the inexorable English campaign of 'extermination' in an open way, so what could it do? The failure of military insurrection had led people to think that there was no alternative to 'constitutional agitation', but this was a delusion. Such so-called 'moral force' was 'not force, neither is it moral': in fact it amounted to submission. The Irish people *could* do something to help themselves. First, they could 'cease actively helping England to destroy them'. Second, Ireland could build 'that position of national self-dependence which must *precede* any real movement for independence'.[2] Here was the kernel of the Sinn Féin argument.

The fundamental proposition, Clausewitzian in essence, if rhetorically emotional in expression, was that

To recognise an aggressive government is national suicide, it is a crime committed against one's own nation; a thing as immoral and indefensible as any crime in the calendar.[3]

---

[1] On AOH violence see A. C. Hepburn, 'The Ancient Order of Hibernians in Irish Politics, 1905–14', *Cithara*, x (1971), 5–18.

[2] Hobson, *Defensive Warfare*, pp. 8, 12–13, 14, 16, 17 (emphasis added).

[3] Ibid. 23.

This was accompanied by a reassuring (and more openly Clausewitzian) assertion of the military superiority of the defensive position. Hobson argued for a 'negative' war, designed not to overthrow the enemy, but to make enemy government impossible. It would be 'easy to create and difficult to destroy' a position from which Ireland could 'offer an even, steady, invulnerable resistance to all government'.

The distinctively modern dimension to Hobson's analysis was the realization (albeit unstated in this form) that the ever-multiplying ramifications of twentieth-century state activity, whilst apparently increasing the power of the government, also exposed it to a much wider range of resistance if popular consent were to be withdrawn. The modern state relies on the habit of acquiescence amongst its members. If that habit were broken, the administrative machine would rapidly be paralysed. Resistance could take practically any form, from hampering the collection of taxes, through 'destruction of the means of communication and transit', to the 'more ambitious wholesale destruction of government property'. The Local Government Board and the legal system were particularly exposed to paralysis through non-co-operation.[1]

Faced with this challenge, the state would be thrown back on relatively primitive methods of asserting its power. Coercion, whether in the form of imprisonment or 'plunder' (seizure of goods or imposition of fines), could be effectively neutralized by modern methods of collective reinsurance.

You cannot prevent the oppressing nation from imprisoning men and women, and such imprisonment often financially hits them harder than plunder, but you can so distribute the loss over the whole, that it will never be a serious loss to any individual.

This highly materialistic prognosis of Irish reactions was linked with an unconscious spiritual tribute to Liberal England. The whole policy of defiance rested on the assumption that England would be bound by codes of civilized

[1] Hobson, *Defensive Warfare*, p. 35-7, 41-6.

behaviour, largely of its own making, notwithstanding nationalist denunciations of its brutality.[1]

A curious mixture of realism and Utopianism pervaded Hobson's economic proposals, which formed an integral part of the defensive programme. Whilst avoiding any mention of List, these were rooted in Griffith's master idea of protection.

If the people of Ireland will build a brazen wall around their coasts, past which no English product will make its way, the industries of Ireland will spring forward at a bound, and the domination of England will be shaken to its foundations.

The first step was to desist from buying goods on which substantial indirect tax was levied; this would also directly affect the government's financial resources. It was obvious enough that this concept was merely an amplification of the traditional boycott, and it would be incumbent on the new nationalist organization, like the Leagues in the past, to impose this by all means in its power.[2] Of perhaps greater value in bolstering psychological cohesion than in inflicting real economic damage, economic boycott was to become increasingly prevalent after 1916, and, sadly, to be most bitterly directed against Ireland's only industrial city, Belfast.

In the end, the crucial sentence in Hobson's tract was his argument that 'if Ireland is governed it is because the people obey. They need not obey, and they need not be governed a day longer than they wish'. To him, as to other advanced nationalists, it was inexplicable that the Irish people did not seem to want to take the easy step which would make them masters of their own country. In fact this was, surely, the proof that the national issue was still, on its own, unable to mobilize popular energy. As in the past, only an organization with a sense of momentum and a prospect of concrete success could articulate a mass mobilization. Sinn Féin, even after its rickety unification in 1906, was unable to transform itself into such an organization. But other, deep-rooted,

---

[1] Hobson, *Defensive Warfare*, p. 25: 'the day is past when artillery can be trained on an unresisting population, wholesale massacre of non-combatant people is obsolete in Europe.'

[2] In fact Hobson held out the fascinating prospect of a boycott organized jointly by Ireland, India, and Egypt.

organizations remained in Ireland, whose activity was cyclicly triggered by critical political circumstances. The constitutional crisis which dominated the last years of the last Liberal government rapidly revealed the limits of consensual politics in Ireland, and called forth a popular reaction in which the threat of violence became once again the dominant form of political dialogue. By the beginning of 1911 the rhetoric to be heard, for instance, at meetings of the Gaelic Athletic Association was less equivocal than for many years. The GAA was proclaimed as

an organization to keep the bone and muscle of our country from donning the red coat or the black coat of England . . . We want our men to be physically strong, and when the time comes the hurlers will cast away the *caman* for the sharp, bright steel that will drive the Saxon from our land.[1]

(iii) *Volunteerism: the North*

. . . if the time came for organised defence against invasion of their constitutional rights as citizens of the United Kingdom, no one was going to have time to ask for gun licences then.

The Rt. Hon. J. H. Campbell, MP[2]

The history of the Ulster Volunteers, amply and brilliantly recounted elsewhere, can be at best briefly and inadequately referred to here.[3] It is possible, from one standpoint, to look at the development of the Ulster crisis after 1910 and to conclude that the unionist groups were surprisingly slow to resort to organized force in face of the threat (as they believed) to their existence. From the English point of view, however, it is surely the case that the call to arms and the creation of formal military forces went ahead with shocking and disorienting speed. The shortness of English political memories and the ill-informed optimism of Asquith's Cabinet helped to guarantee disconcertment, and the Liberals, despite their professions of horror at the violent Conservative reaction

---

[1] *Wicklow People*, 21 Jan. 1911, quoted in W. Alison Phillips, *The Revolution In Ireland 1906-1923* (London, 1923), pp. 59-60.

[2] Speech of Mr Campbell, MP, at Coleraine, Co. Londonderry: *Northern Whig*, 9 Jan. 1912.

[3] In particular A. T. Q. Stewart, *The Ulster Crisis* (London, 1967).

can scarcely have been unaware that the twin blows of the Parliament Act and the Home Rule Bill would strain to its limits the system of politics founded on gradualism and compromise.

Unfortunately, it was easy for optimists to discover signs of disintegration amongst Unionists, even in Ulster. Although a new organizational cadre, the Ulster Unionist Council, had been formed in 1905 in reaction to the 'devolution crisis', the UUC appeared to decline into ineffectiveness thereafter. At the same time the Orange Order, regarded by many, including the government, as the principal mass-based anti-nationalist organization, was undergoing a severe and unique schism. The victory of an independent Orange candidate, T. H. Sloan, in a by-election in South Belfast, and Sloan's expulsion from the Orange Order in 1903, led to the creation of the Independent Orange Order. Under its strikingly untypical leader, Robert Lindsay Crawford, elected Imperial Grand Master in February 1904, the new organization moved away from the sacrosanct rigidity of traditional Orange attitudes. In 1905 Crawford published a manifesto declaring that the new order 'stood on the banks of the Boyne, not as victors', but to 'hold out the right hand of fellowship to those who, while worshipping at other shrines, are yet our countrymen', attacking the recently formed UUC and calling amongst other things for compulsory land purchase, and a national university.[1] At the general election a working alliance was formed between Labour, Nationalist, and Independent Unionist candidates in Belfast, and the official Unionists were reduced to 15 out of 33 Ulster seats.

The singular course of the Independents was pursued until Lindsay Crawford's open espousal of home rule, and his equally open hostility to exploitation in the linen industry, led to his expulsion from the order in 1908. The threat to monolithic Protestant Unionism finally dissolved with Sloan's double defeat in the 1910 elections.[2] In retrospect it may be the case that, as F. S. L. Lyons suggests, Independent

---

[1] A. McClelland, 'The Later Orange Order', in T. D. Williams (ed.), *Secret Societies in Ireland*, pp. 133-4.

[2] J. W. Boyle, 'The Belfast Protestant Association and the Independent Orange Order, 1901-10', *IHS* xii (1962-3), 117-52.

Orangeism was merely a manifestation of a constantly recurring element in Ulster history, 'the tendency of tough-minded, argumentative people to go their own way'.[1] At the time, many Unionists were deeply alarmed—and their opponents excited—by the schism, and above all by the challenge of Larkinite organized labour. Major F. H. Crawford, the impeccable (if ungrammatical) voice of ruling Unionism, saw the 1907 strike as

a big political plot to ruin Belfast trade. The Nationalists are sick of people pointing out to them the Prosperity of Belfast and protestant Ulster, they want to ruin us & this is one move in that direction. The serious part of the business is that they have duped a lot of protestants, who call themselves Independent orangemen, & a few demagogues who love to hear their own voice.[2]

The strike precipitated the most severe violence in Belfast since 1886, and the unreliability of the police (who, as will be seen later in the chapter, were seriously discontented with their own pay and conditions) led to the reinforcement of the military garrison by some 6,000 troops.[3] In the end a gruesome clash occurred in the Cullingtree–Falls Road area, when cavalry swept the streets clear of rioters.[4]

It may indeed be suggested that it was the fear of renewed disruptive sectarian violence which spurred the Unionist leadership to create a new focus of resistance to home rule. In 1911, faced at last with the long-delayed parliamentary compact between Liberals and Irish Nationalists, and the attack on the House of Lords, the UUC underwent a renascence. On 25 September 400 delegates unanimously agreed to resist home rule and, more dramatically, to appoint a committee to prepare a constitution for a provisional government.

In the same year the Unionist Clubs movement was successfully revived as a grass-roots organization, politically more attractive to the UUC than was the tainted Orange Order. Over the next two years 381 Clubs were formed, and

[1] Lyons, *Ireland Since the Famine*, p. 295.

[2] Crawford to R. W. Doyne, 20 Aug. 1907 (PRONI D. 1700/10); Buckland, *Irish Unionism*, p. 215.

[3] J. McHugh, 'The Belfast Labour Dispute and Riots of 1907', *International Review of Social History*, xxii (1977), 9–10.

[4] The military action was supported by *The Times*, 14 Aug. 1907.

served important community functions.[1] During 1911 and 1912 the technique of mass demonstration was developed to help channel and reinforce Unionist energy. Following the Craigavon rally on 23 September 1911, a great meeting held on 9 April 1912 at the agricultural showground in the Belfast surburb of Balmoral was opened by the Primate of All Ireland, addressed by Bonar Law, the Conservative leader, passed a resolution against home rule, and witnessed the breaking out of the largest Union flag ever woven, 48 by 25 feet. The meeting was a display of thoroughly professional staff work, and its military atmosphere was underlined by a march-past of 100,000 men. Still more imposing as an instrument for asserting order and control was the Solemn League and Covenant, inspired by the seventeenth-century Scots covenant, and signed by nearly a quarter of a million men in a huge ceremony on 28 September.[2]

It is difficult to find a precise parallel for the situation of the 'Ulstermen'; but certainly it would be wrong to accept Carson's characterization of the proposed law as the 'unprecedented driving out by force' of 'loyal and contented citizens from a community to which by birth they belong'. No 'community' was driving forth any of its members. The constitution of the United Kingdom was being changed, as it had been changed in 1832, 1864, and 1884, as well as in a host of less spectacular reforms throughout the previous century. The opponents of change were, as on other occasions, a minority who feared—reasonably or otherwise—for their position under a new political system. They had not, under the constitution, any more right to threaten or use force to uphold the status quo than had the die-hard opponents of the Reform Bill or the opponents of vaccination. Yet the curious set of attitudes surrounding 'the Union'

[1] Buckland, *Irish Unionism*, pp. 207-12.

[2] The distilled argument of the Covenant was that 'Being convinced in our consciences that Home Rule would be disastrous to material well-being of Ulster as well as the whole of Ireland, subversive of our civil and religious freedom, destructive of our citizenship, and perilous to the unity of the Empire [we] do hereby pledge ourselves . . . to stand by one another in defending for ourselves and our children our cherished position of equal citizenship in the United Kingdom and in using all means which may be found necessary to defeat the present conspiracy to set up a Home Rule Parliament'.

gave scope for portraying its rupture as a national catastrophe.

Chief among the devices employed by the Unionist leadership to channel Protestant activity away from spontaneous and counter-productive violence was the creation of the Ulster Volunteer Force. Characteristically, the impulse towards this came from a local rather than a central source. An Orange contingent from Co. Tyrone caused a stir at the Craigavon meeting in September 1911 by their smartness and precise marching. They had, on their own initiative, been practising military drill.[1] In effect they were once more giving natural expression to the ancient tradition of public banding. During 1912 the volunteering craze spread across Ulster as it spread in 1859 in England; it became a dominant social activity. To the apparent surprise of everyone, drilling was discovered to be perfectly legal provided it was used by people 'to make them more efficient citizens for the purpose of maintaining and protecting their rights and liberties', and provided that it was authorized by two Justices of the Peace. In Ulster, few except stipendiary magistrates were likely to withhold their consent.[2]

Nobody in government thought to challenge this interpretation of the law until the end of 1913, when the Attorney-General pointed out to the Cabinet that drilling, 'without lawful authority', whether armed or unarmed, was illegal under the Unlawful Drilling Act of 1819. In Simon's cogent view,

Even if those who are drilling Ulster Volunteers have secured documentary 'authority' from two Justices of the Peace, I do not think this would amount to 'lawful authority' in a case where the whole proceeding is a seditious conspiracy. Indeed, I think the Justices of the Peace who gave such authority would be accessories to the crime.[3]

As will be seen, however, no direct measures were ever to be taken against these forces.

[1] Stewart, *Ulster Crisis*, p. 69.
[2] Section 1 of 60 Geo. III & 1 Geo. IV, c. 1. By 1913 these authorizations were supplied in pro forma style: see the example in Buckland, *Irish Unionism*, doc. 131. It is interesting to note, however, that later application forms (in 1914) omitted the second paragraph, after 'evolutions'.
[3] Sir J. Simon, Cabinet Memo., 'Illegalities in Ulster', 29 Nov. 1913 (PRO CAB.37 117, f. 81).

The inevitable incorporation of these local groups in a single body occurred in January 1913 when the UUC announced the formation of the Ulster Volunteer Force, to consist of up to 100,000 men who had signed the Covenant and were aged between 17 and 65. Within six months a full command and staff structure had been created, and a Commander-in-Chief appointed (Lieutenant-General Sir George Richardson, a retired Indian army officer, personally recommended to the post by Lord Roberts). The purpose of the new force, however, remained ambiguous. Was it designed primarily to frighten the government, or to act as the military arm of the putative Provisional Government of the 'Protestant province of Ulster'? If its bluff were called, how would it operate?—could it hope to seize control or would it take up the defensive, and, if so, where? Would it fight openly or by guerilla methods?

The last question was apparently answered in favour of regular warfare. In spite of its inescapably territorial basis, the organization of the UVF into county divisions (supervised by county committees), subdivided into regiments and battalions, directly imitated British military practice. An opinion delivered in July 1913 to the staff section which was weighing up military possibilities advocated the style of combat which followed upon this structure.

You and your men are suited to a stubborn stand up fight—Neither this country nor your men are suited to 'Guerrilla Warfare', 'Boer Tactics' and so on. If you stake all on a big fight there will be no doubts or hesitations.[1]

Six months later, however, real uncertainty remained about the function of the UVF—both in general terms and in precise operational particulars. At a tough conference in London on 17 December the political leaders were confronted with the UVF's demands for a clear statement of plans and priorities. The politicians fenced somewhat: their reply to the question 'What early developments should the military leaders be prepared to meet?' in regard to the contingency of large-scale seizure of UVF arms by the

[1] UVF Confidential Circulars: Intelligence. Notes on Military Possibilities (PRONI D.1327/4/21).

government was recorded as 'Resistance, organized if possible. No shooting'. What if the government began to draft into Ulster (or the borders of Ulster) large numbers of extra troops or police? They replied, 'Must hear of beforehand. Action then considered'. On the question of arms importation previously uncontrolled because of the lapsing of the last Peace Preservation Act, but now threatened by new proclamations, the leaders declared that 'officially' imports were to stop. They agreed, however, that plans should be made 'for their future importation on a large scale in view of possible emergencies'.[1] The only concrete outcome of the conference was the decision to establish and equip a 'Special Service Force' of 3,000 men, to be drawn from the 20 Belfast battalions (each having an SS company of 150), and evidently to act as a quasi-regular formation.

By March 1914 the military correspondent of *The Times*, in an article fortuitously published at the height of the Curragh crisis, held that

It is probable that the whole of the operating strength of the Volunteers could be not only mobilized but concentrated at any point in Ulster in a much shorter time than that required by the British Army at home to complete its mobilization in its garrisons.[2]

But this opinion, based on a trial mobilization of the 3rd battalion of the Tyrone Regiment, looks to have been somewhat optimistic. It is obvious that some senior UVF officers remained dissatisfied with the vagueness of their role. Others, at least in the view of Captain F. P. Crozier, hoped to have none at all: 'they lived in daily dread of arrest, forfeiture of pensions or assassination.'[3] The main exception, in Crozier's opinion, was the brilliant staff officer, Captain Wilfred Spender. He was probably responsible for the extremely

---

[1] Notes of conference, 17 Dec. 1913 (loc. cit.); Stewart, *Ulster Crisis*, pp. 112-13.

[2] 'The Volunteers of Ulster. Training and Spirit. II. Mobilization', *The Times*, 19 Mar. 1914. Lord Riddell, *More Pages from My Diary 1908-1914*, p. 210, said that 'L. G. Masterman and Sir J. French all admit' that a private letter from Repington to Asquith precipitated the government's 'action in Ulster'.

[3] F. P. Crozier, *Ireland for Ever* (London, 1932), p. 42. Crozier led the most 'professional' UVF unit, the Special Service Section of the West Belfast Regiment.

interesting document, labelled 'No. 1 "scheme" ' (but unfortunately undated), whose concluding section came closer than anything else to a specific operational plan. Candidly headed 'The Coup', it recommended that a 'sudden, complete, and paralizing [*sic*] blow should be struck at the right moment'. Simultaneously

1. All railway lines should be severed whereby forces of Police and Soldiers can be sent to ULSTER.
2. All telegraph, telephone, and cable lines to be cut.
3. All depots of arms, ammunition, and military equipment should be captured.
4. All avenues of approach by road for Troops or Police into ULSTER should be closed by isolated detachments of men occupying defensive positions commanding such roads.
5. Wherever possible the guns of any Field Artillery should be captured either by direct attack or else by previous arrangement with the gunners concerned.
6. All depots of supply for Troops or Police should be captured.[1]

This document is fairly unambiguous, and if, as Stewart suggests, it was drawn up 'early' in 1914, it may have been kept very secret. According to Crozier, another steamy UVF conference held at Craigavon at the time of the Curragh crisis produced strong criticism of the political leadership for 'letting down' the UVF by giving the impression that they were armed and would fight to the bitter end, but not making realistic preparations—above all, not supplying large quantities of arms. This indictment 'burst as would a bombshell in the midst of a mothers' meeting'.[2] Clearly the extensive preparations for the great gun-running under the command of Major Crawford had not been revealed to the middle-ranking UVF officers, even those who were Unionist MPs. Finally, on 21 March, Carson issued verbal instructions specifying that

1. On mobilization being ordered the RIC are to be arrested and their arms seized. This should be done by surprise, such as when the constables are patrolling &c.
2. Under no circumstances are Ulster Volunteers to use fire arms of any description until they have been fired on.
3. On the arrest of any commander U.V.F. his next in command

[1] UVF Confidential Circulars (PRONI D.1327/4/21).
[2] F. P. Crozier, *Impressions and Recollections* (London, 1930), p. 148.

should take the best action that he can, following out the instructions for mobilising and for arresting the police.

4. In the case of attempted arrest of U.V. Commanders, or of seizure of arms &c, if the senior U.V. present thinks he has sufficient force such arrest is to be forcibly prevented, taking care that the U.V.F. are not the first to fire. If sufficient force is not at hand resistance is to be made as forcible as possible without needless sacrifice of life.[1]

The supply of arms was an extremely vexed question.[2] The political leadership displayed, throughout, considerable reluctance (supposing sufficient weapons to be available) to place them in the hands of the mass of the UVF. This was the reason for establishing the fully armed Special Service companies of selected men. It seems that the leaders both feared to push their bluff too provocatively in the face of the government, and distrusted the discipline of their stage army.[3] Only the strong suspicion that a Cabinet 'plot' existed to call the Ulster bluff and force a military showdown impelled them to sanction Crawford's ambitious scheme of running in 20,000–30,000 rifles and several million rounds of ammunition at a stroke. The mutual suspicion of Unionists and government fostered the murky Curragh 'incident' in March 1914, which in turn reinforced the determination of the UVF. The gun-running was accomplished on the night of 24–5 April, and was equally imposing as a piece of staff-work on Spender's part as it was as a crude amplification of the UVF's fire-power. The army, which had so far existed primarily as a political threat, and also as an absorber of local tension, could no longer be seen as anything but a formidable military force.[4]

---

[1] UVF Records, N. Antrim Regt. (PRONI D.1327/4/21).

[2] On 20 Jan. 1914 the Antrim UVF complained of having only 150 .303 rifles and carbines, together with 50 Italian Vetterli rifles (with no ammunition) for a force of 10,700 men. Such local forces believed that they were being discriminated against: PRONI D.1238/108, quoted in Buckland, *Irish Unionism*, p. 243.

[3] See, e.g., the mixture of control and indiscipline shown in a S. Down Regt. report, 8 Oct. 1913 (PRONI D.1540/3/14); Buckland, *Irish Unionism*, pp. 233–4.

[4] There remains some uncertainty about the number of weapons run in: see Stewart, *Ulster Crisis*, Appendix, pp. 244–9. The most likely total is 20,000 Mannlichers and Mausers (the proportion uncertain, probably 11,000 : 9,000) with 2 million rounds of ammunition and 4,600 Vetterli–Vitalis with 1 million rounds.

Its style became increasingly aggressive. Although the long-standing injunction that 'the UVF should not be responsible for any violence which can be avoided' remained, and strict orders were issued that the force should not fire first, the gun-running permitted a further shift towards regular military methods. On 7 May the Chief of Staff, Col. Hacket Pain, issued instructions that

the time has come when the main body of the armed men in each area, according to local conditions, should be prepared to move in any direction in the service of the Cause. It appears that the formation in each Regiment of 'marching Battalions' (bataillon de Marche) should now be undertaken.[1]

This mistaken use of fashionable French military terminology indicated a Foch-like belief in *élan*. On 14 May, instructions on 'Protective measures' supplemented earlier instructions that

in the event of the Police unduly interfering with any movements of the UVF, on duty, or going and coming from . . . camps or exercises, the police are to be warned that if they persist in such interference force will be used to prevent the same.[2]

With a variation on the old governmental doctrine of 'over-awing force', if the police were to attempt any seizure of arms,

the UVF should be present in such strength as by sheer weight of numbers to overpower the attacking force, and to render its success manifestly hopeless.

If the police used 'ordinary force', this was to be met by 'superior force used in the same form as that employed by the Constabulary'. If the police produced weapons, a greater number of armed Volunteers would come forward.

Every means will be used to point out to the Constabulary Officers in charge that responsibility for any action they may take and its consequences will rest with them. Only if and when the Constabulary commit the first act of aggression by firing will the Volunteers fire in reply.[3]

[1] Circular Memo. to Div., Regt., and Battn. Commanders, 7 May 1914 (PRONI D.1238/88).

[2] N. Antrim Regt. UVF Records, Orders 5 Mar. 1914 (PRONI D.1238/7).

[3] UVF Confidential Circulars, 'Protective Measures', 14 May 1914 (PRONI D.1327/4/8).

In the circumstances of the RIC in 1914, this 'pointing out' was likely to prove highly effective.

Two days later the continuing problem of the UVF's armament was again addressed. For all its brilliance the Larne gun-running had left the force with its split armoury of British, German (Mauser and Mannlicher), and Italian (Vetterli) rifles. (Revolvers were never officially acquired or issued).[1] The limited powers of the central staff were displayed in its suggestion that, 'failing an inter-county agreement' on the rationalization of rifle-types, individual counties should equip each of their regiments with one of their two main types, or, if this did not work, equip their 'marching battalion' with the best type and distribute the remainder as sensibly as possible. In a full-scale military clash the UVF's weaponry would have created a logistical nightmare.

Eventually, on 27 June, Hacket Pain drew up an uncompromising instruction that

the time has come when arms may be carried openly by members of the Ulster Volunteer Force (whether they have or have not Gun Licences in their possession), and that any attempt by the Police, or other persons, to seize arms from individuals who may be carrying them in accordance with these instructions, is to be resisted in accordance with former instructions issued on this subject in Circular Memorandum dated 14th May 1914.[2]

Already, however, the dimensions of the confrontation were shifting and expanding. In 1914 a new and unwelcome element entered into the UVF's calculations. The Nationalist Volunteer movement meant that the force was now threatened from two directions, and a reappraisal of its plans was necessitated. For instance,

Possibly parts of Co. Antrim which have hitherto been considered probable areas of trouble can now be classed either as containing a determinable force of I.N.V. of a determinable military value, requiring a determinable force of UVF to keep it in check, or as a negligible area.[3]

[1] Memo. by R. Hall, OC 2nd Battn., S. Down Regt., 14 June 1914 (PRONI D.1540/3/74B); Buckland, *Irish Unionism*, doc. 143.

[2] UVF Confidential Circulars (PRONI D.1327/4/8).

[3] N. Antrim Regt. UVF Records, 22 June 1914 (PRONI D.1238/164, 166). Cf. also Hacket Pain's 'Circular on County Defence Schemes', 4 July 1914 (loc. cit.).

(iv) *Volunteerism: mimesis*

> The Carsonite movement in Ulster shattered this futile
> reliance on legal arbitration . . . it broke up the political
> make-believe on which the majority of the Irish people had
> subsisted for years and compelled them to face realities.
>
> Bulmer Hobson[1]

If the channelling of violent tendencies in the North into the
Volunteer movement occasioned the Unionist leaders some
unease, it seemed to work on the Liberal Cabinet like a
charm. Through 1912 and especially 1913 the government
tried every shift of policy to neutralize the fierce resistance
of Ulster to the Home Rule Bill. Gradually the bases of a
modus vivendi emerged: Unionists accepted that home rule
would go ahead, and the government accepted that Ulster
would be excluded from it. This inevitable compromise was,
equally inevitably, rejected by Irish Nationalists, whose
perceptions had long been conditioned by their own rhetoric
about the essential unity of Ireland. 'We cannot give up a
single Irishman', as Parnell had said. He, at least, like Davis,
believed that all inhabitants of Ireland were equally Irishmen.
D. P. Moran did not. Yet, oddly, the Irish-Ireland movement,
which should have made it easier to accept that Ulster
Protestants were vitally different from 'the Gael', did nothing
of the kind. Gaelic Leaguers in the last analysis became the
most radical islandists on this issue. Eoin MacNeill, not
unaffected by his own origins in Antrim, and P. H. Pearse,
from a very different ethnic background, personified the
opinion which put pressure on Redmond to reject all
compromise.

   The apparent success of Unionist extra-parliamentary combination unavoidably stimulated a reactive imitation on the
other side. Once again, as in Ulster, the spontaneity of this
process must be stressed. Partisans of MacNeill and Pearse
have asserted their respective claims as originators of the
Irish Volunteers. Even The O'Rahilly, editor of *An Claidheamh Soluis*, has been put forward as inspirer of MacNeill's
famous article 'The North Began'. The article itself was

---

[1] Holograph article, 'Origins of Irish Volunteers', Hobson MSS, NLI MS
13169.

clearly an important stimulus to the new movement, though a modern reader, aware of its reputation, may be surprised by its shallow casuistry and its lack of precise proposals. What public result was produced by MacNeill's brilliantly paradoxical statement that 'The Ulster Volunteer movement is essentially and obviously a Home Rule movement'?[1] The most effective phrase in the article was no doubt the sardonic observation that if Carson were to march to Cork at the head of his Volunteers,

their progress will probably be accompanied by the greetings of ten time their number of National Volunteers, and Cork will give them a hospitable and memorable reception.

In fact, behind its stress on unity, MacNeill's piece bristled with hostility to those who claimed separate treatment for a 'homogeneous Ulster'. He could not resist mocking the UVF's million-pound insurance scheme as 'the crowning sham'—something to which those who were 'in earnest about war' would not devote a penny—yet this was precisely the scheme advocated by Hobson as the basis of Sinn Féin's 'defensive warfare'.

Such political point-scoring was much less evident in the article by Pearse, who followed MacNeill a week later with a direct call to arms. He asserted that 'nationhood is not achieved otherwise than in arms'; 'Ireland armed will attain ultimately just as much freedom as she wants'. His oft-quoted final paragraph announced a vital new orientation in intellectual nationalism. He was, he wrote,

glad then that the North has 'begun'. I am glad that the Orangemen have armed, for it is a goodly thing to see arms in Irish hands.

He would like to see the Hibernians, the Transport Workers, indeed 'any and every body of Irish citizens' armed.

We must accustom ourselves to the thought of arms, to the sight of arms, to the use of arms. We may make mistakes in the beginning and

---

[1] E. MacNeill, 'The North Began', *An Claidheamh Soluis*, 1 Nov. 1913; F. X. Martin (ed.) *Irish Volunteers*, p. 58. More specifically, MacNeill suggested that 'the Orange democracy and the Presbyterian rural party are home rulers in principle and essence'; it did not matter *for* whom Ireland was held, but *by* whom. But MacNeill's inference that it did not matter *against* whom Ireland was being held by the Protestants was surely less than honest.

shoot the wrong people; but bloodshed is a cleansing and a sanctifying thing, and the nation which regards it as the final horror has lost its manhood. There are many things more horrible than bloodshed; and slavery is one of them.[1]

This chilling romantic conception was to form most of the bare mental furniture of Irish republicans for generations to come. The remainder was to be put together by Pearse during his brief, intense career as a physical-force ideologue over the next two and a half years.

Neither Pearse's nor MacNeill's article, however, in spite of prophetic phrases, could create the popular impulse for a new organization. It is evident that such an impulse pre-dated MacNeill's piece and the formation of the Provisional Committee of the Irish Volunteers. A number of surviving records show spontaneous organizational activities in the provinces a month earlier, and it is reasonable to assume that there were more.[2] On 11 October there had even been a full parade of the newly formed Midland Volunteers in Athlone. The *Westmeath Independent* reported that

The efforts being made to terrorize the country when Home Rule becomes law next year, though looked upon more with contempt than apprehension, nevertheless suggested retaliatory preparations, and these have been going on for some time about the midlands where the nucleus of a formidable Volunteer Force has now been called together.[3]

Many of the volunteers were ex-soldiers with considerable service experience, and the force was 'in a state of prepared-ness that is being made to meet force with force'. On 25 October the Dublin *Leader* put the practical suggestion 'Why should not every Gaelic Athletic Club, for instance, turn out as Volunteers?', adding that 'Historic Athlone has given Nationalist Ireland a lead, and has held its first parade'. This vital practical proposal was repeated by Moran's journal on 8 November: 'The important thing is to get Volunteer companies started. Athlone has led the way, who will follow

---

[1] P. H. Pearse, 'The Coming Revolution', *An Claidheamh Soluis*, 8 Nov. 1913; Martin, op. cit. p. 65.

[2] e.g. statement by C. M. Byrne of Ballykillivane, Glenealy, Co. Wicklow (NLI MS 21142).

[3] *Westmeath Independent*, 18 Oct. 1913; O. Snoddy, 'The Midland Volunteer Force 1913', *Journal of the Old Athlone Society* (1968), p. 40.

suit?'[1] If the Midland Force was for the time being a still-born initiative, it showed a popular readiness to participate. The idea of citizen forces was in the air; and it was on 23 November that the Irish Citizen Army—albeit intended primarily for class rather than national struggle—was inaugurated by Labour leaders at Liberty Hall, Dublin.[2]

The centrally organized Irish Volunteer movement was launched at the Rotunda Rink in Dublin on 25 November, accompanied by a long manifesto whose central and most emphatic phrase was 'They have rights who dare maintain them'. It accused the Unionists of adopting a plan to make 'the display of military force and the menace of armed violence the determining factor in the future relations between this country and Great Britain', and held that if the political franchise were not to be effectively annihilated there must be, now and for the future, a Volunteer organisation as a guarantee of the Irish people's liberties. Its duties would be purely 'defensive and protective'. Its framework was territorial and, to begin with, extremely loose. When instructions on the forming of companies were issued in 1914 they followed with almost absurd closeness the British regular model, with sections and Left and Right Half Companies commanded by corporals, sergeants, lieutenants, and captains, and battalions commanded by colonels. Prescribed drill was to follow that in the British Infantry Manual of 1911, available at 1s. per copy.[3] The force was self-financing, though it issued an appeal in December 1913 for funds to buy 'material equipment'.[4]

The early growth of the movement was unspectacular by Ulster standards, with some ten thousand enrolments by the end of 1913. Its significance was recognized, if not indeed

---

[1] *The Leader*, 25 Oct., 8 Nov. 1913, Snoddy, 'Midland Volunteer Force', p. 41.

[2] Larkin argued that 'Labour in its own defence must begin to train itself to act with disciplined courage and with organized and concentrated force. How could they accomplish this? By taking a leaf out of the book of Carson' (S. O'Casey, *The Story of the Irish Citizen Army* (Dublin, 1919), p. 4).

[3] General Instructions for forming Companies, 1914; Military Instructions for Units, 1914 (Hobson MSS, NLI MS 13174). Cf. the later scheme of military organization, Dec. 1914, in F. X. Martin (ed.), *Irish Volunteers*, pp. 170–83.

[4] 'We Have the Men!', Address by Provisional Committee, Dec. 1913 (Hobson MSS 13174).

exaggerated, in an editorial in the *National Student*, which
held that 'the dominant import of the Irish Volunteer movement is that it makes for a definitive political philosophy'.[1]
Some doubt may be cast on this idea of definition by the fact
that many passed, apparently without much thought, from
non-violent Sinn Féin to the threat of arms (or at least
'armed neutrality').[2] Even Sinn Féin itself retained in rural
eyes some attributes of more traditional associations: one
member of the later IRA recalled that he and his friends
found that there was an organization called Sinn Féin, but
were refused 'initiation' on several occasions 'due to the
fact of our being to [*sic*] young was the answer'.[3]

The primary problem of the Volunteers was to obtain
arms. The UVF, for all its grumbling, had a long head start
in this. Even by the time of the March 1914 crisis, when IV
membership shot up to the 100,000 mark, the Nationalist
armament was trivial. The Volunteer Executive, dominated
by Hobson and his IRB siblings, turned to dramatic action
both to solve this problem and, through its public impact, to
improve in turn the movement's financial position.[4] A loan
of £1,500 was used to purchase 1,500 obsolete Mauser
rifles and 45,000 rounds of 9 mm ammunition, and most of
this consignment was run into Howth harbour on 26 July
1914 in Erskine Childers' small yacht.

It has often been said that the government, having turned
a blind eye towards, or in any event failed to cope with, the
huge UVF gun-running at Larne, proceeded inequitably to
interfere with the Nationalist imitation. This inference of
partiality is seriously misleading. Not only does it ignore
the manifest Nationalist sympathy of the Dublin administration under Birrell, but it fails to grasp the vital point
that whereas the UVF leaders had consciously (if reluctantly)
played safe in running their arms to Larne rather than
Belfast,[5] Hobson chose with equal deliberation the most

---

[1] *The National Student*, iv, 2, Dec. 1913.
[2] Cf. Robert Brennan on the Wexford 'Sinn Féin Volunteers', *Allegiance*
(Dublin, 1950), pp. 20–36.
[3] Narrative of Edward O'Connor (McGarrity MSS, NLI MS 17506).
[4] B. Hobson, 'Foundation and growth of the Irish Volunteers, 1913–14', in
Martin (ed.), *Irish Volunteers*, pp. 32–3.
[5] Stewart, *Ulster Crisis*, pp. 121, 196–7.

provocative method, a daylight landing, to compensate for the relative smallness of his shipment. The government was confronted with a challenge it could scarcely ignore. None the less, it succeeded to a remarkable extent in doing so. As will be seen in the final section of this chapter, the affray which occurred as the rifles were being marched into Dublin was unplanned, and was hastily repudiated by the government. So unnerved, indeed, were the Castle authorities that even the nineteen rifles damaged and captured in the mêlée were handed back to a Volunteer officer the next day.[1]

(v) *Policing the crises*

> Obedience to law has never been a prominent characteristic of the people. In times of passion or excitement the law has only been maintained by force, and this has been rendered practicable owing to the want of cohesion among the crowds hostile to the police. If the people became armed and drilled, effective police control would vanish. Events are moving. Each county will soon have a trained army far outnumbering the police, and those who control the volunteers will be in a position to dictate to what extent the law of the land may be carried into effect.
>
> Inspector-General, RIC, June 1914[2]

By early 1914 there were four armies in Ireland—five, if one were to follow Nationalist terminology and label the RIC an 'army of occupation'. This was certainly too many for comfort or safety, and it may be thought extraordinary that the government had permitted, or failed to prevent, such a situation. Three of the armies were overtly political; the fourth, the British army, was believed to be altogether outside politics in the day-to-day sense, but was now—through the agency of a small group of officers—on the brink of a political *démarche* unique in recent times. Throughout the last year of the Ulster crisis the government was in the hitherto unknown position of having to think, even to ask questions, about the obedience of the army.

---

[1] Hobson, op. cit. p. 39; the officer was Col. Moore.
[2] Report of IG RIC, 15 June 1914 (*Royal Commission on the Rebellion in Ireland*, Cd. 8279, p. 7).

Only the last of the five forces, the RIC, seemed to have no dangerous political proclivities. Even this hard-tried body, however, gave cause for uncertainty during the critical decade. The disaffection of the police amidst the 1907 Belfast disturbances, mentioned earlier, was not an isolated instance. The morale of the force had been a matter for concern to its commanders and the government since the 1880s. The problem was exacerbated by inadequate pay and irksome conditions of service: the persistently and depressingly parsimonious attitude of the Treasury went far to undermine the attractions of a secure career with pension rights, while constables (especially junior ones) laboured under burdensome duties and a mass of regulations governing every hour of their lives.[1] Conditions for married policemen and their wives, obliged to live in barracks, were particularly unattractive. The fundamental requirement that constables serve at a distance from their native counties, too, whilst ostensibly designed for their own protection, was not always easy to accept.[2]

Pay and conditions, however, were at bottom less disturbing than the long-term threat to the RIC existence posed by the home rule concept. The force which had shadowed and prosecuted Nationalist MPs, dispersed meetings, and presided over evictions, naturally feared that the worst would befall when Nationalists finally entered into their inheritance. From the 1880s, the RIC was worried about the future.[3] It was sometimes worried, too, about its nature as a semi-military force, which gave such an edge to Nationalist denunciations of the 'army of occupation'. In spite of the quotidian deference accorded to the constabulary, and indeed of the force's entry in its own right into rural folklore, a sense of distance remained. Perhaps this was simply due to the

---

[1] Evidence and Appendices, Committee of Inquiry into Royal Irish Constabulary and Dublin Metropolitan Police, 1914. As D. Fitzpatrick has pointed out, however, it was less absolute need than the need to sustain their social position, of which they were intensely jealous, that led constables to demand increased pay.

[2] The purpose of this system continued to be misunderstood, wilfully or not. George Birmingham suggested that it was designed to prevent the law coming to be regarded, through the familiarity of its agents, as a common thing.

[3] Jenkinson to Buller, 27 Nov. 1886 (Buller MSS, PRO WO 132 4A).

rooted public suspicion of the state and its law; perhaps it was due to faulty police technique. Certainly, the contrast between the centralized, barracked and armed Irish police and the diffuse local police in rural England was more marked than ever by the end of the nineteenth century. Was the lone English 'bobby' the cause of social peace, or was it that social peace had permitted so light-touched a system to work?

Irish 'Peelers', especially in the lower ranks, often felt that their rifles were an insurmountable barrier to 'normal' relations with the people. Their superiors, however, were not prepared to consider the idea of disarmament. On the contrary, at the height of the UIL's activities they rearmed the force with more modern weapons.[1] Senior RIC officers still appeared to regard the suppression of insurrection, or at least mass rioting, as the RIC's primary duty. The military ethos of the force was assiduously preserved. With it went a loftily pragmatic approach to law enforcement. Canon Hannay (the novelist 'George Birmingham') observed sardonically that the RIC took the view that many laws

ought to be considered with due regard to the spirit which underlies all laws, the securing of the greatest good for the greatest number. The mere hide-bound official treats a law as a kind of divine thing to be enforced just because it is a law, against a whole community. The Irish policeman is a much more philosophic man.[2]

In plain words, he often left well alone. Hannay's delightful anecdote of the constabulary who doggedly persist in drill and target practice whilst ignoring complaints of apple-stealing from the next-door orchard well illustrates popular views of the police.[3] General Sir Nevil Macready, nominated to take over control of Belfast in 1914, was blunt in retrospect: this 'once magnificent body of men had undoubtedly deteriorated into what was almost a state of supine lethargy.'

---

[1] On 9 Jan. 1900 the Snider carbine was replaced by the Martini–Henry; henceforth each constable carried 8 rounds of ball and 2 of buckshot ammunition in his pouch, with a further 12 ball and 10 buckshot rounds in his barrack box: RIC Circular Orders (PRO HO 184 118).

[2] George A. Birmingham, 'The Policeman', in *Irishmen All* (London, 1913), p. 40.   [3] Ibid. pp. 42–6.

When I first discussed the state of affairs in Belfast with Mr T. Smith, the then Assistant Commissioner of the RIC in that city, I was struck with, I will not say his reluctance, but a certain hesitation on his part to enforce drastic measures, should such become necessary.[1]

The semi-official *Irish Constable's Guide*, written by the former Inspector-General, Sir Andrew Reed, did not carry sections on rebellion or insurrection as such (these were, of course, scarcely within the day-to-day competence of local constables). But its section on 'Riots', nine pages long, was the third longest in the book, exceeded only by those on fishery and licensing laws (the latter, at thirty-one pages, was twice as long as any other section). 'Murder and manslaughter' received only three pages, 'burglary' two and a half, and 'robbery' a mere half page.[2]

Reed's *Guide* devoted four pages to gun licences or, more strictly, the 1870 Gun Licence Act. The enforcement of this Act—basically an excise matter—represented the limits of its control over the weapons which might be used in the still-apprehended insurrection. The *Guide* added, not very helpfully, in its section on the 1881 Peace Preservation Act, that no arms or ammunition were to be imported into Ireland 'except at the following ports; Dublin, Belfast, Cork, Limerick, Londonderry, Waterford, Galway, Sligo, Drogheda, Dundalk, Greenore, Newry, Wexford, Larne, Carrickfergus, Glenarm, and the Quay of Westport'.[3] Even this restriction disappeared in 1906 when the 1881 Act, having been kept alive since 1887 under the Expiring Laws Continuance Act, was at last abandoned.

Thus, when the Ulster Volunteers made their vital discovery that military drilling was legal they were also in a remarkable position of freedom to acquire whatever weapons they could find and pay for. As early as November 1911 the Irish law-officers addressed themselves to the problem of arms control.

The quantity and quality of the arms would be important elements in the determination of the question whether the purpose was seditious.

---

[1] Gen. Sir C. F. N. Macready, *Annals of An Active Life*, i (London, 1924), 178-9.

[2] Sir A. Reed, *The Irish Constable's Guide* (4th edn., Dublin, 1901).

[3] Ibid. p. 280.

Forty-five rifles might be satisfactorily accounted for, while 100,000 could bear no innocent explanation.

On the other hand, a supply of 45 military rifles obtained by the master of an Orange Lodge whose members had proclaimed their intention to resist by force of arms the execution of an Act of Legislature if passed, would be very strong evidence of sedition.[1]

This hint was ignored by the executive, though the Irish Director of Prosecutions went on to argue early in 1913 that

Drilling with arms under the circumstances existing in the North of Ireland would hardly be regarded as drilling for a lawful purpose even though a licence was given by the Lord Lieutenant of the County or Justices of the Peace.[2]

The claim that the Volunteers used no 'party colours', only the Union flag, conveniently forgot the 'matter of common knowledge that the National Flag is used in the North of Ireland merely as a party emblem'.[3] By July 1912 the RIC was evincing considerable unease on the problem of arms.

It is repeatedly asserted by Unionist leaders that Home Rule will be actively resisted, and rumour is current that arms have been purchased for this purpose. So far, however, the police have not been able to obtain corroborative evidence, except in the case of a consignment of 200 rifles and sword bayonets shipped from Hamburg to Belfast via Leith in April last . . . Since the repeal [*sic*] of the Peace Preservation Act, there is practically no restriction upon the importation of arms.[4]

The only course which the police could think of taking was the hopeless one (as time was to prove) of asking the customs service to be on the alert for suspicious cases.[5]

A year later the bleakness of the outlook was unaltered: the Attorney-General, Sir John Simon, confirmed that 'as regards legislation confined exclusively to Ireland, there is

---

[1] Note by Law Officers, *c.* 20 Nov. 1911 (SPO, Crime Branch Special MSS 23).

[2] Note by I. O'Brien, 7 Feb. 1913 (loc. cit.).

[3] Ibid.

[4] RIC Crime Special Branch Memo., Dep. IG to Under-Secretary, 13 July 1912 (PRO CO 904 28/2). However, the Irish Attorney-General held that in addition to the 200 Leith guns, the police were aware of another 891 rifles imported (12 cases on 8 June, 11 on 11 June 1912, and 10 on 14 March 1913): Note by Moriarty, 9 Apr. 1913 (SPO Crime Branch Special MSS 23).

[5] Under the Customs Laws Consolidation Act 1876 and the Customs and Inland Revenue Act 1879.

no statutory power to prohibit the importation and use of
firearms in Ireland'.[1] The 1870 Gun Licence Act was the
only Act in force which in any way interfered with the use
or carrying of firearms, but anyone who was prepared to pay
for a licence could obtain one. The judgment in *R.* v. *Meade*
(1903) might possibly be used in connection with armed
processions—but there, as usual,

> we have always to contend with the difficulty of finding Grand Juries
> who will be willing to act and find true Bills, and of finding Petty
> Juries who will do their duty.[2]

The same, as Simon later reiterated to his colleagues, applied
to the prosecutions which might (indeed should) in principle
be brought against the Ulster Volunteers for treason-felony
and illegal drilling. As for seizure of those arms already
in Ireland, he doubted if any power to search for arms as
such existed, though he believed that the government might
take action and wait to be prosecuted. Its defence would
then be that the arms were for the purposes of a criminal
conspiracy to which the plaintiffs were party.[3]

Not until the beginning of December 1913 did the Cabinet
decide to issue Royal Proclamations forbidding the importation of arms, in view of evidence that two armies were being
assembled.[4] These proclamations appear to have been
effective: at least they infuriated the newly formed Irish
Volunteers, who saw them as blatant discrimination in favour
of the already (as they imagined) armed Ulster Volunteers.[5]
The latter also, being well short of their own arms target,
believed that their leaders had let them down by not informing
them that the proclamations were forthcoming. Yet the
Cabinet remained undecided about the seriousness of the

---

[1] Memo. by Attorney-General, 23 Aug. 1913 (PRO CO 904 28/2). See also
the file on importation of arms, SPO Crime Branch Special MSS 23.

[2] Ibid.

[3] Simon, 'Illegalities in Ulster', PRO CAB.37 117, f. 82.

[4] Proclamations or Orders in Council could be issued under the Customs
Laws Consolidation Act to prohibit importation of arms. For the legal reasoning
behind the Cabinet decision see Sir J. Simon, 'Power to Prevent Importation of
Arms, &c, into Ulster', Cabinet Memo., 27 Nov. 1913 (PRO CAB.37 117, f. 81).

[5] In fact, as the title of Simon's memorandum shows, nothing could have
been further from the government's intentions.

threat posed by the UVF, and the measures which would be necessary to cope with it. Birrell, in a remakable bout of realism, argued as early as August 1913 that 'the *serious* character of Ulster resistance' would involve, since the police were a doubtful quantity, '*military operation*, which must be on such a scale as to *overawe* the rebels, or to dispose of a considerable number of them'.[1] Six months later, however, he suggested that

The whole question of the reality of the movement regarded from a civil war point of view is overshadowed by the general conviction amongst the rank and file of the Volunteers that the occasion will never arise.[2]

In the period before this hopeful return to the idea that the Ulstermen were bluffing, very little had been done to make the first proposition a possibility. In answer to the King's fear that civil war might involve the army Asquith said that illegal resistance to home rule would have to be crushed, but that the army would only be used as a last resort.[3] Morley, under whom some military plans had actually been drawn up in face of the less formidable 1893 Ulster threat, swerved excitably between confidence that the bluff would collapse and stern determination to repress illegality.[4] Haldane had told Lord Esher that he was

urging upon the Prime Minister and the Cabinet that precisely similar precautions to those taken to guard against the strike in Wales, and the coal strike, should be taken in Ulster. He suggests sending at once for Sir Arthur Paget, and discussing with him the necessary measures: giving him General Macready (who exhibited useful qualities of judgment

[1] This analysis is related to the discussion between Asquith and King George V in September 1913 of whether 'civil war' was a likely contingency in Ulster. Asquith contended that such language was 'a misuse of terms'; the King, however, asked 'will not the armed struggle between those sections of the people constitute Civil War, more especially if the forces of Ulster are reinforced from England, Scotland, and even the Colonies, which contingency I am assured is highly probable' (Asquith MSS, King to Asquith, 22 Sept. 1913).

[2] A. Birrell, Cabinet Memo., 5 Mar. 1914 (PRO CAB.37 119/36).

[3] King to Asquith, 22 Sept.; Asquith to King, 1 Oct. 1913 (MS Asquith 38, ff. 216-7).

[4] On 17 March he reminded Asquith that in 1893 General Wolseley had 'counselled a swift descent on and coercion of Ulster' (Jalland, *Liberals and Ireland*, p. 209). Whilst no doubt horrific to Wolseley's rival Roberts, this advice was as imprecise as any ideas that emerged in 1914.

and tact in Wales) as a Special Staff Officer, and forming a 'Composite Force', comprising battalions of southern regiments and free from Irish influences, to be sent immediately into Ulster.[1]

Unfortunately for the government, Haldane had recently achieved his final ambition by becoming Lord Chancellor, leaving the post as Secretary for War which he had taken up reluctantly in 1905 but had occupied with conspicuous success. The post remained unattractive in a Liberal Cabinet, and its status as a backwater was reflected in the appointment of Yeomanry Colonel Seely: an appointment which was in itself symptomatic of the government's lack of alertness to the impending clash. Henry Wilson (for whom politicians could never do anything right) found it alarming that no plan of any kind existed for utilizing the troops in the event of a crisis in Ulster—alarming not because it might allow the Unionists to succeed but because it would cause a chaotic collision in which the army might be torn apart.[2]

The crisis was dominated throughout by the Unionists and their adherents within the army. It could scarcely have developed, however, if the government had made the effort to formulate the issues involved. The nub of the quarrel which culminated in the 'Curragh incident' was the reluctance of army officers to play any part in the home rule struggle.[3] In the end, of course, ostensible refusal to play a part created a dramatic role. Most officers saw themselves as non-political, but this standpoint habitually found expression in hostility to politicians—especially Liberal politicians —for whom Henry Wilson's contemptuous epithet 'frocks' was amongst their politer terms.[4] When Sir Arthur Paget,

[1] M. V. Brett, *Letters and Journals of Reginald Viscount Esher* (London 1834), iii, 139–41 (cf. also pp. 151–2).

[2] C. E. Callwell, *Field-Marshall Sir Henry Wilson. His Life and Diaries* (London, 1927), i, 137.

[3] In addition to two full studies of the incident, A. P. Ryan, *Mutiny at the Curragh* (London, 1956) (its title unfortunately misleading), and Sir J. Fergusson, *The Curragh Incident* (London, 1964), there are substantial analyses in Stewart, *Ulster Crisis*, pp. 141–75, P. Rowland, *The Last Liberal Governments*, ii, 307–22, Jalland, *Liberals and Ireland*, pp. 207–47, and R. Holmes, *The Little Field-Marshal. Sir John French* (London, 1981), pp. 166–94.

[4] Holmes's study indicates that French was an outstanding exception to this attitude of contempt.

Commander-in-Chief in Ireland, was at last summoned to Whitehall in March 1914 to 'discuss necessary measures', as Haldane put it, he returned to inform his senior officers 'I have just come from London and I believe the swines mean business'.[1]

This 'business' was usually described as the 'coercion' of Ulster. Even within the Cabinet, though Asquith spoke more carefully of preventing illegal resistance, this vague and loaded term was used. Several commentators have since pointed out that there was nothing in the government's proposals as outlined to Paget on 19 March which was not amply justified, and indeed demanded, by its ordinary duty to keep the peace. Even if the worst possible construction, that of the Churchill–Seely 'plot', is put on the orders, the action of reinforcing depots and strategic points in Ulster could not amount to what was commonly understood as 'coercion'.[2] No proscription of the UVF was considered, let alone enacted. The rumours of impending arrest of Unionist leaders had no foundation.[3] No move even to disarm the UVF was contemplated. The worst that the Cabinet can be accused of is attempting to provoke the UVF into an attempted coup which would rob Ulster of English public support. This, in the circumstances of absolute political impasse reached with the Unionist rejection of Lloyd George's scheme of temporary Ulster exclusion, would have been an intelligent plan for the government to follow. There is no evidence that it was doing so, however. More plausible, in view of its past (and future) performance in Irish affairs, is the interpretation which sees the Curragh débâcle as the result of a characteristically hesitant and mismanaged expedient.[4]

[1] Or 'bloody swine' according to Lord Milner's information: 'Diary of Events', Milner MSS 157.

[2] For the charge in extreme form see L. S. Amery, 'The Plot Against Ulster', Union Defence League 1914 (Milner MSS 158).

[3] As Bonar Law himself was sanely (but privately) reminded by Carson, 'it is contrary to Asquith's whole nature to precipitate anything' (Carson to Law, 20 Mar. 1914, Bonar Law MSS 32/1/36).

[4] Jalland, *Liberals and Ireland*, pp. 217–29. Believers in the 'plot'—an article of faith among Unionists—have made much of the fact that the 'evidence' of an impending outbreak, on which Seely based (and French accepted) his instructions to Paget, has never been revealed. Yet, whatever the truth of this evidence, the

The decision of the Cabinet committee (itself belatedly established on 11 March) to improve military security at munitions depots in Armagh, Omagh, Carrickfergus, and Enniskillen, was long overdue. The orders issued verbally to Paget by Seely and Sir John French, the CIGS, at the War Office on 19 March at Downing Street and by Asquith himself on the following day, went further than this. They included the reinforcement of Newry and Dundalk, not amongst the threatened depots, but important points for any future large-scale movement of troops into Ulster. Churchill and Seely, at least, evidently intended to 'overawe' the UVF (the course recommended by Birrell, Morley, and Haldane). But did this amount to 'coercion'? Precisely what actions did the committee envisage following from its instructions? The plan was clearly to throw the onus for violent action upon the UVF by depriving it of the chance of an easy, bloodless 'coup' which would have left it in *de facto* control of the province and pushed the government into the role of aggressor. None of the orders issued to Paget can be interpreted as intending the army to initiate any violent confrontation with the UVF.[1] Indeed, when Paget declared 'I shall lead my army to the Boyne', French told him not to be a 'bloody fool'.

The government had certainly accepted by now that violence was a possibility, and the provision that army officers domiciled in Ulster should be permitted to 'disappear' for a while reflected this acceptance. Carson had, after all, straightforwardly declared that immediately after the passage of home rule the Provisional Government would take over power in Ulster. The orders issued to Paget were designed to ensure that in such an eventuality the government would have the moral advantage of being the defender

extraordinary thing remains that not until well over a year after the creation of the UVF did the government take any steps to improve security.

[1] It is hard to follow Holmes's otherwise judicious analysis when he says that Seely's assertion that the government 'had not the smallest intention of allowing anything like civil war to break out' 'presumably meant that the government intended to use overwhelming military force to crush the Volunteers if they offered armed resistance' (*French*, p. 176). 'Resistance' implies some direct action by the army, such as an attempt to disarm the UVF. No such action was indicated at the War Office or the Downing Street conference.

rather than the aggressor. Unfortunately, as Paget's reaction on the 18th showed, he failed to grasp this intention. The result was his inflammatory address at the Curragh on the 20th, in which he said that the troop movements would create 'intense excitement' and that the country would be in a 'blaze' on the following day. Worse, he gave officers the option of refusing to participate in these vaguely projected operations, whereas his instructions at the War Office had clearly declared that officers were not to be permitted to resign but were simply to be cashiered if they refused to obey orders.[1] Paget's error permitted Brigadier Gough to commit what was, in spirit, mutiny, although since he and his officers never had to disobey a direct order they were not mutineers in a technical sense.[2] Gough exploited the ambiguity of the government's instructions remorselessly, and for political ends.[3] The government for its part traded with doubtful morality on the officers' personal loyalty to the King, whose name was invoked without his consent.

The alarming and unedifying drama reached its denouement with the unprecedented letter concocted by Seely and French to pacify Gough. The Cabinet (in Seely's absence) had drawn up a note reiterating that

It is the duty of all soldiers to obey lawful commands given them through the proper channel by the Army Council, either for the protection of public property and the support of the Civil Power in the event of disturbances or for the protection of the lives and property of the inhabitants,

and saying that the Army Council was 'glad to learn' that there had never been a question of the Cavalry Brigade disobeying lawful orders. Seely realized that this peace-offering would not satisfy Gough, who was transparently out for a political victory over the Liberals. This Seely inexplicably proceeded to give him, by adding, on his own

[1] A. J. Farrar-Hockley, *Goughie* (London, 1975), pp. 92-3, sensibly suggests that Paget's challenge was due to a moral inability to face the uncertainties of the Ulster operation without making absolutely sure of his men.

[2] Farrar-Hockley, *Goughie*, p. 106.

[3] There is something touching in the scene at the War Office on 23 March when the politically innocent French earnestly told the astute Gough 'you don't know how serious all this is' (ibid. p. 109).

authority, two further paragraphs to the note.[1] These, labelled the 'peccant paragraphs' in a late public exercise of Balfour's wit, upheld the government's duty to use Crown forces to maintain law and order in Ireland as anywhere else, but promised that it had 'no intention whatever' of taking advantage of this to 'crush political opposition to the policy or principles of the Home Rule Bill'.

Still, the ambiguity of conception remained. The undertaking might simply mean, as no doubt Seely intended, that the Unionist movement would not be suppressed. It certainly did not say that Ulster would be excluded from home rule. Gough promptly spotted this ambiguity, and insisted on adding his own rider: 'I understand the meaning of the last paragraph to be that the Army will not be used under any circumstances to enforce the present Home Rule Bill on Ulster'. French confirmed in writing, 'That is how I read it'. But what in fact did Gough's own reading mean? He still appears to have been unclear about what sort of actions might be used to 'enforce' home rule in Ulster. As far as the government was concerned, no military operations were envisaged beyond securing the key points in the province in such strength that potential rebels would be deterred from initiating violent action. The day before, Gough had told the Adjutant-General that if he had simply been ordered to take his brigade to Belfast, 'he would have gone without question', and agreed that officers had no right to question when they should or should not go in support of the civil power to maintain law and order.[2] Clearly he believed that the army might be asked to do more than maintain order—or was it rather that in his (political) view the 'law' which they were to be asked to uphold (the Home Rule Act) was a bad law which would justly provoke disorder? Did he distinguish between 'maintaining' an already existing and accepted law, and 'enforcing' a prospective and disputed law? If so, such a distinction was quite untenable, above all for an officer of the Crown.

---

[1] Approved by Morley, who seems not to have grasped their significance.
[2] Farrar-Hockley, op. cit. pp. 105-6; cf. J. Gooch, 'The War Office and the Curragh Incident', *Bull. Inst. Hist. Res.* xlvi (Nov. 1973), 202-7, based on Ewart's diary.

Wilson, who appears to have been partly responsible for Gough's final demand, emerged triumphantly from the meeting declaring that the army had succeeded where the constitutional opposition had failed.[1] The political significance of the negotiations, for all their imprecision, could not be disguised.[2] The resignation of Seely, and the steadying effect of Asquith's own takeover the War Office, secured only a partial recovery of poise. An extraordinary blow had been struck at the power of executive government in Ireland. The sequel was the paralysis of the administration when faced with the gun-runnings of April and July. Its inability to interfere with the Larne shipment was due in part to the efficiency of the operation, in part to the slackness of the RIC, and in part to the blithe detachment of the army. Count Gleichen, GOC Belfast, reacted to his private discovery of weapons in a noble host's croquet-box with nothing more than wry amusement.[3] The only senior officer who showed real signs of wanting to get to grips with the UVF, to 'make them laugh on the other side of their mouths', as Gleichen distastefully put it, was Nevil Macready. His appointment with a dormant commission to take control of both military and police forces in Belfast was the most substantial fulfilment of Haldane's early recommendations, though it is not at all clear what his real status would have been. He himself said that common talk about his becoming Military Governor of Belfast or Ulster was a 'lot of nonsense'.

Such a post could only have been created under Martial Law, and at no time, so far as I am aware, was there any suggestion of such a step, which in the first place would have entailed a very large increase of the garrison, which the Government had no intention of effecting.[4]

Certainly there was no Cabinet discussion of the possibility of martial law. It is, though, hard to see that any effective

---

[1] Callwell, *Wilson*, i, 138–43. Wilson 'wired Hubert (Gough) at midnight (on 23 March) to stand like a rock' against the political backlash.

[2] As was made plain in the Commons debates on 23 and 25 March. Cf. J. A. Spender and C. Asquith, *Life of Lord Oxford and Asquith* (London, 1932), i, 47–8.

[3] Maj.-Gen. Lord Edward Gleichen, *A Guardsman's Memories* (Edinburgh, 1932), p. 387.

[4] Macready, *Annals*, i, 188.

alternative could have been found in event of a serious 'outbreak'. The unusual step was taken of swearing Macready as a magistrate (RM for the nine Ulster counties, and JP for Belfast); this appears to have been done not for judicial reasons but because

the fact of being a magistrate will enable me, should necessity arise, to direct the movements of the R.I. Constabulary as well as any troops that may be, or may have been, called upon to support the constabulary.[1]

From his earlier experience of dealing with the miners' strike in South Wales in 1910, he drew the general principle that

It is no business of a soldier, when called upon to preserve order, to concern himself in any way with the details of a dispute between parties of the community. His business is solely to preserve order, but in doing so he has the right to demand that neither side shall do anything which may aggravate and inflame the opposing party to commit acts of lawlessness.[2]

Such a demand would have been fearfully difficult to make in Belfast. As Macready observed, the government was hamstrung by the paucity of troops in the city and the fact that to bring in reinforcements might 'have precipitated an outbreak'.[3]

Macready, as the army's only senior officer with successful experience in internal security work, was inevitably the repository of somewhat unrealistic political hopes. In Paget's place he would doubtless have avoided the Curragh crisis, but in the end he could not have eradicated a malaise which grew out of the government's own lack of a clear policy. This directional uncertainty was most starkly revealed in July. The Irish Volunteers designed the Howth gun-running as an open challenge to the government, and even the easy-going Dublin Metropolitan Police felt it could not avoid rising to the challenge. The Assistant Commissioner, W. V. Harrel, thought he had obtained the consent of the Under-Secretary for disarming the Volunteers in accordance with

---

[1] Note by Macready, 27 Apr. 1914 (PRO WO 32 5319).
[2] Macready, *Annals*, i, 140.
[3] Ibid. 191.

the proclamation prohibiting importation of arms. He requisitioned military assistance and moved a substantial body of police out to meet the Volunteer column. At the celebrated confrontation on the Malahide Road, Harrel was talked to a standstill by the Volunteer leaders, Hobson, MacDonagh, and Figgis, while the guns were carried around the police block and distributed.[1] Harrel had ordered a forward movement by the police which was disobeyed by a number of constables—who, according to Eoin MacNeill, actually raised a cheer for the Volunteers.[2] Hobson coldly informed Harrel after the first mêlée that the Volunteers

> though they had rifles, had no ammunition, that they were peacefully going to their homes, but that there was ammunition in the column and that if he attacked again I could not prevent the distribution, that a great many of his men and my men would be killed, packed in that narrow road, and that sole responsibility would be his.[3]

Harrel eventually accepted defeat and sent the troops back to Dublin, where the high state of public excitement caused a serious clash. In Bachelors Walk, angry and unnerved soldiers turned on the taunting crowds with bayonets fixed, shot three people dead, and wounded thirty-eight. This grim outcome was all but inevitable. The government, however, laid the responsibility on Harrel for having called for military assistance. That evening Birrell telegraphed to the Under-Secretary:

1. Did the police requisition military entirely on their own responsibility, and, if so, what were the reasons that induced them to take that course?
2. Why did the military fire on the crowd? From the telegrams which have come it would seem that the soldiers were hooted and that there were some stones thrown, but this would not justify firing on the crowd. I should be glad to know why no police accompanied the military on the return journey.[4]

The inference of the Chief Secretary's tone was obvious. Harrel was immediately suspended from duty pending a

[1] Hobson, 'Foundation and growth of the Irish Volunteers', pp. 37–8.

[2] E. MacNeill, 'How the Volunteers Began', in Martin (ed.), *Irish Volunteers*, p. 75.

[3] Hobson, op. cit. p. 38.

[4] Chief Secretary to Under-Secretary, 26 July 1914, copy in Ross file, Balfour MSS (BL Add. MS 49821, ff. 71–86).

full inquiry. In the circumstances this was tantamount to ending his police career, as his superior, Sir John Ross of Bladensburg, angrily pointed out.[1] Ross, who had prepared the 1882 analysis of military operations in aid of the civil power, now resigned his post as Chief Commissioner of the DMP in protest against an 'act of injustice'. He held that, apart from the issue of the arms proclamations,

a body of more than 1000 men armed with rifles marching on Dublin, which is the seat of the Irish Government, is a menace to the King's government and that such a body constitute an unlawful assembly of a peculiarly audacious character.[2]

This was hardly an exaggeration. Birrell, however, was less perturbed by the armed challenge than by the police attempt to neutralize it. It appeared that the government had now come to accept political armies, provided that they marched around 'peacefully' as Hobson put it, as a normal part of the Irish scene and a component of the political system. A contemporary historian wrote of the failure to bring prosecutions after the Larne gun-running that, whether or not it was useful from the standpoint of political manœuvre, for the prestige of government itself it was disastrous.

For the proper function of a government is to govern, and if its authority is defied with impunity it ceases to have any effective existence. Especially is this the case in Ireland, where from time immemorial government has been respected just in so far as it is strong, and no further.[3]

---

[1] Notes on inquiry into Harrel's action, ibid., ff. 83–6; Harrel left the police service and later surfaced in the Admiralty intelligence division: Brennan, *Allegiance*, pp. 41–3.

[2] Ross of Bladensburg to Under-Secretary, 27 July 1914 (Balfour MSS, loc. cit.).

[3] Alison Phillips, *Revolution in Ireland*, p. 75.

6

War, Insurgency, and Emergency

> Did ye think to conquer the people,
> Or that Law is stronger than life and than
> man's desire to be free?
> We will try it out with you, ye that have
> harried and held,
> Ye that have bullied and bribed, tyrants,
> hypocrites, liars!
>
> P. H. Pearse[1]

(i) *War and blood*

> But if we are tricked again, there is a band in Ireland
> who will advise the Irish people never again to consult
> with the Gall, but to answer them with violence and the
> edge of the sword. Let the English understand that if we
> are again betrayed there shall be red war throughout
> Ireland.
>
> P. H. Pearse[2]

The years 1914-18, grimly familiar as an epoch in the history of Europe, are seldom viewed as a distinct period in Irish history. The Easter Rising so dominates the horizon that the overwhelming tendency is to divide that history into 'before' and 'after' 1916.[3] Undoubtedly 1916 was a critical year in Ireland. It would be pointless to deny that something like a 'terrible beauty', new at least in its generation, was 'born'.

---

[1] P. H. Pearse, 'The Rebel'.

[2] P. H. Pearse, in *An Barr Buadh*, 5 Apr. 1912, quoted in R. Dudley Edwards, *Patrick Pearse: The Triumph of Failure* (London, 1977), p. 159.

[3] Even recent attempts to attack—rather than 'revise'—the legacy of 1916 ('the sanctification of violence as a means of achieving a political end, the legitimation of the place of the gun in Irish politics . . . a dead albatross around our necks, dragging us down into a bloody and mindless pit', in the words of T. P. O'Mahony's quirky *The Politics of Dishonour: Ireland 1916-1977* (Dublin, 1977), p. 32), while raising interesting questions about the generation of popular myth, leave the event itself in its central position. See also the significant article of F. Shaw, SJ, 'The Canon of Irish History—A Challenge', *Studies* (Summer 1972) (written August 1966).

It is impossible to quantify the effects of the Rising and above all, of its suppression, to test the unchallenged folk-memory that the execution of its leaders worked a sudden and decisive change in public attitudes. It may, however, be suggested that Ireland was not so far out of line with Europe as can sometimes appear. The year 1916, rather than 1914, was, perhaps, the real point at which the old European order succumbed (to the restructuring and reorientation required by total war, to military dictatorship in Germany, and so on); whilst in Ireland 1914 marks the beginning of processes of which 1916 was rather the symptom than the cause.

It may indeed be argued—and was so argued by those Irish Volunteer leaders opposed to the insurrectionary idea —that the impact of the war as a whole would have produced decisive changes in Ireland, whether or not the Rising had occurred.[1] The threat of conscription was fully capable of mobilizing Irish opinion on a broad front, and by 1915 it was clear that this threat would become ever stronger.

As far as resistance to government was concerned, the crucial effect of the Great War was that it resolved the ambiguity of the Irish Nationalist party's position. The curious situation in which the party had somehow straddled the gap between resistance and government, or opposition and co-operation, ending up defending the British constitution against 'rebels' in Ulster, was ended. Not for Redmond personally: he responded to the war with loyal enthusiasm, pledging Ireland to participation (at least to the extent of defending its shores, releasing British troops to fight in Europe) and encouraging enlistment in the forces.[2] But his performance as recruiting sergeant was crucial: it brought on the split which had been narrowly avoided, or fudged, earlier. His Woodenbridge speech 20 September 1914 was repudiated within a few days by a group headed by MacNeill

---

[1] Such an argument has been implied in F. X. Martin's distinctly revisionist '1916—Myth, Fact and Mystery', e.g. pp. 58-9; it was Griffith's view that 'the change was inevitable . . . the Rising hastened it a little' (R. Brennan, *Allegiance*, p. 209); and Hobson later asserted that the Rising might have wrecked the national movement if the British had not over-reacted to it.

[2] D. Gwynn, *The Life of John Redmond* (London, 1932), pp. 391-2.

and O'Rahilly, and including 'the great majority of the members of the Provisional Committee of the Irish Volunteers, apart from the nominees of Mr. Redmond'.[1] This group declared

That Ireland cannot, with honour or safety, take part in foreign quarrels otherwise than through the free action of a National Government of her own; and [repudiated] the claim of any man to offer up the blood and lives of the sons of Irishmen and Irishwomen to the services of the British Empire while no National Government which could speak and act for the people of Ireland is allowed to exist.

The breakaway group, which retained the title Irish Volunteers, took with it only two or three thousand adherents.[2] Over 150,000 adhered to Redmond's Irish National Volunteers, but this mathematical imbalance was redressed by the higher level of political commitment and determination of the smaller force. Growing by 1915 to ten, and later to fifteen, thousand, its paper strength scarcely exaggerated its real strength.

Resistance to the 'war effort' was not at first universal, nor even perhaps widespread. Recruitment went on well through 1914 and 1915, and Kitchener paid tribute to the response of Ireland, both north and south.[3] However, there was a degree of detachment, or apathy, much greater than in Britain.[4] As a notable Unionist historian disapprovingly remarked, there was 'little appreciation among the masses of the people of the gravity of the issues at stake'.[5] Seen from another point of view, the Irish on the whole failed

[1] Announcement of Provisional Committee, Irish vols., 24 Sept. 1914; Tierney, *MacNeill*, pp. 153–4.
[2] These are the figures suggested by Tierney, loc. cit., and are rather smaller than those commonly given, e.g. in F. X. Martin (ed.) 'Eoin MacNeill on the 1916 Rising', Select documents xx, *IHS* (1961), 227–8, or F. S. L. Lyons, *Ireland Since the Famine*, p. 340.
[3] Though he refused to group Irish recruits into an Irish Division or Corps, a decision which, while explicable in purely military terms, had a dampening political effect: J. J. Horgan, *Parnell to Pearse* (Dublin, 1948), p. 201.
[4] Cf. the waning enthusiasm of the *Clare Champion* outlined in D. Fitzpatrick, *Politics and Irish Life* (Dublin, 1977), p. 109.
[5] W. Alison Phillips, *The Revolution in Ireland*, p. 87. In fact the hysterical over-kill of British war propaganda was double-edged; its obsession with 'atrocity' and 'frightfulness' was in the end to be turned back on Britain itself. See below, p. 320.

to swallow British propaganda. They did not accept that Britain's war of rivalry with Germany was a conflict between civilization and barbarism (as British self-deception at its most intense would hold), or even between democracy and authoritarian militarism. They were too used to seeing Britain itself as the military despot, and talk of the 'rights of small nations', whilst eliciting sympathy for little Catholic Belgium, provoked the obvious response that such respect should begin at home, with Irish rights. As a result there was a widening divergence between Irish public opinion and British governmental ideas. The government once again became the force which brought, not benefits like land transfer, but burdens like the regulations made under the Defence of the Realm Act. DORA in fact gave the executive the sort of powers previously heralded by emergency legislation like the Protection of Person and Property Act or earlier Habeas Corpus Suspension Acts. On 5 December 1914 the controls on arms importation were restored under DORA. (The April Proclamations had been rescinded on 5 August, a gesture that is difficult to explain at the commencement of war.) Until Lord Parmoor's amendment of 18 March 1915, civilians could be tried by courts martial for breaches of Defence of the Realm Regulations, a situation which put the Irish Volunteers at a distinct disadvantage.[1]

As has been indicated, the issue which transcended all others in driving a wedge between government and people was conscription. English liberals found it a bitter enough pill. In 1916 some refused to swallow it, and as a result the Cabinet underwent its second war reconstruction. Conscientious objection, the obverse of total war mobilization, appeared as a phenomenon requiring social adjustment. In Ireland, direct resistance to conscription would undoubtedly have been widespread. It was never called forth, because conscription was never imposed there. The mere threat of it, however, present in 1916 and growing thereafter up to the crisis point of April 1918, produced significant reactions. Even the parliamentary party was forced, after the passage of the Military Service Bill through the Commons on 16 April, to withdraw from Westminster and return to Ireland. This

[1] On DORA, see also below, section (iv), pp. 303–13.

final adoption of a strategy first proposed in the 1880s came too late. It was already the official policy of a growing Sinn Féin party, which gained an incalculable access of strength from its moral leadership of the anti-conscription movement. The Roman Catholic hierarchy completed the revolution in attitudes with its famous declaration that 'conscription forced in this way on Ireland is an oppressive and inhuman law which the Irish have a right to resist by every means that are consonant with the laws of God'.[1] The forces available for potential resistance were enormously greater than any which could have been deployed in 1916. The government was already aware that an attempt to enforce an Order in Council would consume more troops than it would produce: conscription in Ireland was rather a moral sop to British public opinion than a source of useful manpower. In the end, the idea was abandoned—the threat having done its work, and the government as usual getting the worst of both worlds.

For the mass of people, resistance to the war developed gradually. The Irish were perhaps fortunate that patriotism could validate a rejection of the conflict, while it forced the belligerent peoples to support a ruinous struggle which many longed to end. For one group in Ireland, at least, attitudes to the war were clearly defined from the start. The 'Fenian' response was apparently predetermined: the English difficulty must provide the Irish opportunity. In fact, as will be seen, the matter was more complicated. The Fenian commitment to insurrection was limited by the 1873 constitution to circumstances in which a broad measure of public support existed, and Bulmer Hobson was to hold that the striking of a blow in every generation might, in the absence of such circumstances, be unconstitutional. It was Patrick Pearse, a relative latecomer to the IRB, who in effect provided its new theory. His peculiar fusion of pagan and Christian symbolism into a new nationalist religion may not have gained many believers, but his position in the Irish Volunteer organization gave him power to realise his private conceptions.

From the political point of view most of these were as vague and half-baked as any earlier Fenian programmes.

[1] D. W. Miller, *Church, State and Nation in Ireland*, p. 405 n. 19.

A dedicated Gaelic Leaguer, as Pearse had been, naturally laid much greater emphasis on culture as an integral element of the revived Irish nation. Ireland had to be both free *and* Gaelic: either without the other would be empty. Pearse even began, in the short period of his increasing political awareness before the Rising, to develop some definite—if still rather watery—ideas of social and economic revolution. His celebrated dictum of prior collective rights—that no individual right could hold against the right of the nation—was to become enshrined in the Democratic Programme of the first Dáil. But his conception of the nation remained, like Mazzini's, a comprehensive one, innocent of class conflict.[1] He distrusted socialism.[2] Like Mazzini he viewed politics in moral terms. His central idea was that of the blood-sacrifice: insurrection not merely as a tactical device but as an ethical affirmation.[3] Violence came, for him, to represent national political redemption. In his resounding article written at the time of the formation of the Irish Volunteers, he asserted that he was

glad that the Orangemen have armed, for it is a goodly thing to see arms in Irish hands. I should like to see the AOH armed. I should like to see the Transport Workers armed. I should like to see any and every body of Irish citizens armed. We must accustom ourselves to the thought of arms, to the sight of arms, to the use of arms. We may make mistakes in the beginning and shoot the wrong people, but bloodshed is a cleansing and a sanctifying thing, and the nation which regards it as the final horror has lost its manhood.

If there remained in this a trace of hard-headed Fenian pragmatism, Pearse made it clear after the European war had broken out that he saw the effusion of blood as a good in itself. In the wake of the awful 1915 offensives he declared

It is good for the world that such things should be done. The old heart of the earth needed to be warmed with the red wine of the battlefields. Such august homage was never before offered

---

[1] There is a good short survey of Pearse's social ideas in Lyons, *Ireland Since the Famine*, pp. 343-5, and a sparklingly individual analysis in Lee, *Modernization*, pp. 141-8.

[2] R. Dudley Edwards, *Patrick Pearse*, p. 181: the most comprehensive, lucid, and honest approach to his ideas.

[3] F. X. Martin, 'Eoin MacNeill on the 1916 Rising', p. 241 n. 7.

to God as this, the homage of millions of lives given gladly for love of country.[1]

The dogma that 'in every generation must Irish blood be shed', while it stemmed from an aestheticism foreign to the Fenian tradition, fitted the instinctive reaction of the IRB leaders who were determined to use the weapon, the Volunteer organization, which had been placed in their hands. It is clear that the commitment to an insurrection before the end of the war was formed in 1914, and thenceforth for Tom Clarke and Sean MacDermott it was merely a matter of timing.

Another group, much less traditional, was still more impatient to strike a violent blow. Its reasoning was considerably more complex. James Connolly, the dominant theoretician of the Irish Labour movement, explicitly rejected Pearse's romantic—or pathological—blood symbolism. To Pearse's distress, Connolly fumed in the *Workers' Republic* that 'we do not think that the old heart of the earth needs to be warmed with the red wine of millions of lives. We think anyone who does is a blithering idiot. We are sick of such teaching, and the world is sick of such teaching'.[2] Yet, though Connolly viewed the international conflict in completely different terms, he failed to escape from the rhetoric of blood. Indeed, in his doomed attempt to fuse international socialism with Catholic nationalism, he was even drawn at last into giving it a specifically religious inflection. In February 1916 he announced that

deep in the heart of Ireland has sunk the sense of the degradation wrought upon its people—so deep and so humiliating that no agency less powerful then the red tide of war on Irish soil will ever be able to enable the Irish race to recover its self-respect, or establish its national dignity in the face of a world horrified and scandalised by what must seem to them our national apostasy . . . Without the slightest trace of irreverence but in all due humility and awe, we recognize that of us, as of mankind before Calvary, it may truly be said 'without the shedding of Blood there is no Redemption'.[3]

[1] Dudley Edwards, op. cit. p. 179; and *Spark*, Dec. 1915, quoted in Dudley Edwards, op. cit. p. 245.

[2] *Workers' Republic*, 25 Dec. 1915.

[3] Editorial, 'The Ties that Bind', *Workers' Republic*, 5 Feb. 1916: C. D. Greaves, *Life and Times of James Connolly* (2nd edn., London, 1972), p. 396.

By then Connolly, as Sean O'Casey, the secretary of the Irish Citizen Army, ruefully observed, had 'stepped from the narrow byway of Irish Socialism on to the broad and crowded highway of Irish Nationalism'.

The high creed of Irish Nationalism became his daily rosary, while the higher creed of international humanity that had so long bubbled from his eloquent lips was silent for ever, and Irish labour lost a leader.[1]

O'Casey's indictment—which itself was unable to escape from the internal contradiction of 'Irish labour'—has been disputed by those who hold that Connolly was merely following (in fact anticipating) the path charted by Lenin at the Zimmerwald Conference in September 1915.[2] Such theological refinements pale before the vindication of O'Casey's verdict in the dull fate of Irish labour after its alliance with conservative Sinn Féin.

The Irish Citizen Army none the less followed Connolly into the abyss of insurrection. It is hard to find any distinct socialist reason for their so doing. There appears, from the autumn of 1915, to have been merely an assumption that something had to be done. The ICA itself had been through several transformations since its creation as a workers' militia in 1913, and had ended up as a small force (1,000 members in Dublin city and county) with as high a level of training as limited resources would permit. It made no attempt to develop a new military style and was directly imitative of regular armies. The trivia of military accoutrements had an enchanting effect on everyone from Larkin outwards, and its intensive drill-practice was linked to a conventional idea of future operations.[3] Michael Mallon might write articles on guerrilla warfare, but Connolly was still living in the days of the Blanquist *putsches*.

In a series of articles in the *Workers' Republic* in May–June 1915 under the title 'Street Fighting', the advantages of this type of warfare were analysed on the basis of several

---

[1] S. O'Casey, *The Story of the Irish Citizen Army* (Dublin, 1919), p. 52.

[2] Greaves, op. cit. p. 353.

[3] O'Casey advocated ordinary clothing and irregular fighting methods; Larkin and Markievicz insisted on brassards to give a sense of discipline and *esprit de corps*: O'Casey, *Drums Under the Windows* (London, 1963), p. 610.

nineteenth-century examples. The general point adduced, that

Mountainous country has always been held to be difficult for military operations owing to its passes or glens. A city is a huge maze of passes or glens formed by streets and lanes. Every difficulty that exists for the operation of regular troops in mountains is multiplied a hundredfold in a city,[1]

was sound. But notwithstanding the view that the Citizen Army might expect to participate in a strong defensive action—

Not a mere passive defence of a position valueless in itself, but the active defence of a position whose location threatens the supremacy or existence of the enemy—[2]

Connolly's actual expectations of an insurrection remained an unclear mixture of angry desperation, calculation, and millenarian hope. The 'people' might be ignited by the spark of insurrection, as he assured Bulmer Hobson early in 1916:

He told me that the working class was always revolutionary, that Ireland was a powder magazine and that what was necessary was for someone to apply the match. I replied that if he must talk in metaphors, Ireland was a wet bog and that the match would fall into a puddle.[3]

A similar realism may indeed have been present in Connolly's mind: there was no lack of it in his grim remark to O'Brien on Easter Monday morning, 'We are going out to be slaughtered'. And in reply to O'Brien's question, 'Is there no chance of success', he replied unambiguously, 'None whatever'.[4]

(ii) *Planning insurrection*

I think it was in December 1915 Denis MacCullough told me that the Supreme Council had decided to bring off an insurrection before the end of the European war. This was quite vague, and was never conveyed to me in any

---

[1] 'Street Fighting', *Workers' Republic*, 24 July 1915, repr. J. Connolly, *Revolutionary Warfare* (Dublin and Belfast, 1968). pp. 32–4.
[2] Ibid.
[3] Hobson MSS, quoted in Dudley Edwards, op. cit., p. 250.
[4] Greaves, op. cit., p. 410.

regular manner. It was in direct violation of the constitution of the IRB.

Bulmer Hobson[1]

In my conscientious judgment, an armed revolt at present would be wrong and unpatriotic and criminal.

Eoin MacNeill[2]

The Irish rebellion of 1916 was one of the most singular insurrections to occur in any country. Not the least of its peculiarities was that it was immediately labelled the 'Sinn Féin Rebellion', even though Sinn Féin was a political group (and a small one) committed to moral rather than physical-force resistance. The reason for this was that Sinn Féin was, for its small size and political weight, remarkably well known, thanks to Griffith's incisive writings. The group which actually arranged the rising, on the other hand, was unknown to the general public and the press. Here, indeed, was the culmination of the secret-society insurrection pioneered by Babeuf and Buonarroti, and tirelessly attempted by Blanqui, Mazzini, and others. It suffered from the obvious, though apparently disregarded, handicap that 'the people' who were supposed to rise in response to the insurrectionary call were so taken by surprise as to be incapable of any reaction. Without a mass base, the revolutionary group was doomed to re-enact Emmet's transient street demonstration.

Was the Rising merely a violent rhetorical gesture? Or did its planners envisage real success? The poet James Stephens, a sensitive eyewitness of Easter week, held that the organization of the Rising was minimal, and that the Volunteers' tactics were 'reduced to the very skeleton of "strategy" '. Yet he felt also that 'they expected the country to rise with them, and they must have known what their own numbers were, and what chance they had of making a protracted resistance'.[3] A further strand of reasoning was introduced with the idea that 'their sole aim was to make such a row

---

[1] Bulmer Hobson to Joseph McGarrity, 1934 (Hobson MSS, NLI MS 13171).

[2] Eoin MacNeill, Memorandum I, Feb. 1916. Printed in F. X. Martin (ed.), 'Eoin MacNeill on the 1916 Rising' [n. 7 above], 234–400.

[3] J. Stephens, *The Insurrection in Dublin* (Dublin, 1916), pp. 79–80.

that the Irish question would take the status of an international one', and would be discussed as part of the European
peace negotiations.[1] These common-sense efforts to rationalize the outbreak were typical of those made by commentators then and afterwards.

The key to understanding the function of the insurrection
is to be found in the tussle for control of the Volunteer
organization in the year after the split. The confusion that
caused, and that was caused by, Eoin MacNeill's 'counter-
manding order', reflected a deep division in the leadership's
views of violence and its use. The division, very roughly,
was between those who had repudiated the Volunteer executive's decision, in June 1914, to meet Redmond's demand
to nominate half its membership,[2] and those who had
accepted Redmond's demand in June but who repudiated
his Woodenbridge pledge in September. Pre-eminent in this
second group were Eoin MacNeill and Bulmer Hobson. The
latter, with the egregious achievements of revitalizing the
IRB (and making possible its control of the Volunteers)
behind him, was ruthlessly elbowed out of the brotherhood
after the June compromise. The personal spite vented upon
the alleged renegade was unpleasant, but a real difference
of policy lay behind it. Hobson adhered to the line he had
laid out in *Defensive Warfare*. This meant, in 1915, that he
saw the proper policy of the Volunteer executive as

to go on building an armed Volunteer force, which would defend the
country against any attempt to enforce conscription, developing and
relying on a tactic of guerrilla fighting. . .[3]

In his view an insurrection, under the circumstances (the
match thrown into the puddle, as he graphically put it to
Connolly), 'would be merely a demonstration which would
leave the country defenceless after its suppression', and
would hand on an unfinished struggle to a future generation. He believed that such action, besides being practically

[1] Ibid. p. 81.
[2] The dissident group who signed the 17 June statement were Eamon Ceannt,
M. J. Judge, Con Colbert, Seán Fitzgibbon, Eamon Martin, P. H. Pearse, Seán
MacDermott, and Piaras Béaslai: Martin, *Irish Volunteers*, p. 144.
[3] Hobson to McGarrity, 1934 (Hobson MSS 13171).

ineffective, would be contrary to the IRB constitution. As Dublin Centre he swore in a large proportion of the men who had joined 'the Organization' between 1912 and 1916, and he later declared that 'very frequently men joining had asked for and received an assurance that they would not be ordered out for an insurrection which was merely a demonstration, devoid of popular support'.[1] If so, this was somewhat irregular. But there is no need to dispute Hobson's observation that

Although I was known to be definitely opposed to the policy of insurrection, no effort was ever made or would have succeeded to displace me as Dublin Centre. I undoubtedly represented the views of the great majority of the Organisation at that time.[2]

Cogent objections to an insurrection there may have been. Hobson's alternative policy, however, did not obtain widespread support. As he said, he had 'believed for many years that the only form of active resistance to the English occupation which could be organised with any chance of success was the guerrilla war'. Such foresight was extremely rare in the 1914 generation, whose attitude to rebellion was framed by the 'magic numbers', 98, 48, 67: 'all that delirium of the brave.' For one thing, guerrilla fighting, even as practised by such admired antagonists of England as de la Rey and Smuts, lacked the escapist glamour of traditional warfare. Not for the guerrilla soldier the serried ranks of steel around the green banner. Perhaps more important, its pragmatic nature, and its hit-and-run tactical code, robbed it of the ethical grandeur required by Fenians—not only latecomers like Pearse but founding-fathers like Kickham and O'Leary. For them violence had to have not just a moral basis but a moral mode of expression.

A further difficulty with guerrilla warfare lay in the question of how to train for it. It was not well adapted to the drill-halls in which the local Volunteer companies assembled to learn the art of war. The articles on 'hedge-fighting' in the *Irish Volunteer* indicated the wider possibilities, but

---

[1] Hobson to McGarrity, 1934 (Hobson MSS 13171).
[2] Ibid.

day-to-day training remained locked in a mould borrowed directly from the British army.[1]

The originator of the 'hedge-fighting' idea was himself a soldier of conventional tastes. J. J. ('Ginger') O'Connell, a member of the Volunteer executive, appointed Chief of Inspection in November 1915, was henceforth to loom perennially in the second rank of the Republican leadership. He was the nearest thing to a military expert that the Volunteers possessed, a staunch admirer of German military organization, and a student of Hegel as well as of Clausewitz and Moltke. The Great War shifted his admiration to Foch, but he continued to perceive 'real' armies in the continental way. Battalions were good, big battalions better. All the same, like Hobson, O'Connell was a supreme realist. He was brought in by Hobson, who met him in New York early in 1914, to help organize the Volunteers to meet one of three contingencies:

The first was the landing of a German expeditionary force, the second an attempt to suppress the Volunteer organisation, and the third an attempt to enforce conscription in Ireland. As to the first we proposed to cooperate with the German force if it should come ... An attempt to suppress the Volunteers would have had the effect of driving their organisation underground ... But it was not proposed to remain passive if it came to that. Men in danger of arrest were to form small flying columns in the country, to lie low until they could strike, and to disappear among the rest of the population the moment they had struck. For conscription when it should come the tactics were to be the same: men called up on draft were to go out on flying columns, but only those called up so that the supporting civilian population might be as large as possible.[2]

Hobson and O'Connell decided that it should be a guiding principle that these columns should never bunch together, so that no disaster to a column would involve the loss of more than a few men, and 'no single action could be a decisive or even a severe defeat'. Here in fact emerged the central

[1] See 'Military Instructions for Units, 1914', and 'Scheme of Military Organization for the Volunteers' (Martin, *Irish Volunteers*, pp. 128–9, 170–83). Also O'Rahilly, 'Flags for the Regiments', *Irish Volunteer*, 23 May 1915, and Report by Uniform Sub-Committee, 12 Aug. 1914 (Hobson MSS 13174 (1)). However, J. J. O'Connell noted that Pearse's scheme of organization 'was never approximated to, even in the Dublin-Brigade'.

[2] Holograph notes on origins of Irish Volunteers. Hobson MSS 13169).

principle of modern guerrilla warfare. Equally it had to be accepted that no single military action would be a decisive victory—in other words that the military struggle would be protracted, to use the adjective later made famous by Mao Tse-tung. Such a struggle might not only defeat conscription, but 'make the continued government of Ireland by England impossible'.[1]

A comprehensive and illuminating view of the developing Volunteer organization can be found in an unpublished memoir by O'Connell, amongst Bulmer Hobson's papers. O'Connell noted that as he travelled through the country late in 1914, he realized that the vast majority of Volunteer bodies existed in name only. 'In short the organisation of the Volunteer force began absolutely *de novo* from the split.'[2] A uniform country-wide standard of organization and performance was never achieved. Rather, the discrepancy between Dublin and the rest, noticeable at the outset, became ever greater.[3] The results of local election of officers were generally unsatisfactory: only the Fianna 'selected boys with the touch of iron essential for leadership', (and Fianna officers were later to become the best Volunteer officers). The men of the Volunteers 'commonly selected someone because he was popular or distinguished in some sphere or other'.[4] To overcome these problems O'Connell insisted that rigid military standards should be applied from the start, and opposed those Volunteer leaders who favoured dropping parade-ground drill and 'confining the men's training to shooting and field work as far as country companies were concerned'. The oft-quoted analogy of the Boer commandos did not impress him.

---

[1] Hobson MSS 13169. This was, as Hobson remarked, not a new policy, as it had been outlined by Lalor.

[2] Holograph memoir by J. J. O'Connell, Hobson MSS 13168, ch. I, p. 2.

[3] Ibid., p. 2. The Volunteer General Council, though better conducted than the staff, reflected a one-sided Dublin view: the country men were asked for assent rather than advice (ch. VIII, p. 8). Dublin's officer quality was better, as was its average attendance at weekly drills—some 66 per cent of men on the rolls (ch. XI, p. 1).

[4] Later in the memoir O'Connell remarks that Volunteer commandants were often GAA captains, something which tended to reduce their activity as Volunteers: ch. II, p. 4.

It was my opinion that our differences from the Boers were much more numerous and far-reaching than our resemblances to them. General de Wet's 'Three Years War' was advocated as a text book, but anyone who has read that book cannot fail to recall how frequently the general laments the almost incredible indiscipline of his troops. It was in spite of—not because of—their lack of drill that the Boers achieved so many tactical victories.[1]

He recognized that Dublin headquarters' attempt to organize all districts 'on a preconceived idea without any accurate regard for local facts' led to local resistance. He contended that 'any decent corps should organize its own neighbourhood' without help or interference from Dublin.

Training, however, was a different matter. The problem was to combine proper military discipline with a grasp of the unusual tactical possibilities presented to small bodies of men operating in close country. The main drawback of the Volunteer chiefs, in O'Connell's opinion, was that while thinking themselves 'above sloping arms'—in other words lacking a proper military grounding—they enjoyed playing with grandiose strategic ideas. O'Connell was shaken by the general inefficiency shown in the Dublin Brigade field-day at Stepaside early in 1916. The opposing sides were commanded by Thomas MacDonagh, Director of Training, and Patrick Pearse, Director of Organization. The latter's orders

ran over four closely-typed pages of foolscap and prescribed the most minute details for the conduct of the attack, including the formations of attacking units at definite geographical points and the precise hour at which the assault was to be delivered—neither of which, I need not say, were even approximated to.[2]

Pearse's command concepts, labelled by O'Connell's precocious assistant Eimar O'Duffy 'thinking in Army Groups', surely offer a partial understanding of the Easter Week plans.

O'Connell held that the Dublin staff, whose 'methods . . . were not such as to inspire confidence or respect', had a misconceived organizational policy based on an unrealistic grand-strategic outlook. In a particularly interesting passage he wrote of the need to concentrate on organizing these districts which were ready to be organized.

---

[1] Ibid., ch. I, p. 4.   [2] Ibid., ch. VI, p. 2.

I quite realised that the most easily organisable districts might be remote from anywhere—'of no strategic importance' in fact. But by the mere fact of having their men trained and armed they would at once become 'of strategic importance'. It so happened that the pre-conceived idea of an Insurrection had committed some of my colleagues to the express task of organising districts, of greater importance indeed judged by the map, but where the response was so feeble as not to justify the money expended. For example, there is no doubt that but for the money spent in Kildare we would have contrived in Clare to train men amounting to a formidable numerical strength.[1]

O'Connell admitted that his idea would have given only slow returns—'but it would have given big ones'.

He was of course thinking in purely pragmatic military terms. He shared with others, as he said, 'a fear that the Irish Volunteers might become a revolutionary and not a military body'. By this rather odd verbal distinction he seems to have meant that the Volunteers should not be drawn into insurrection. (The policy he was proposing was thoroughly revolutionary in a military sense, while his ideas about social revolution were hardly more conservative than those of Clarke or MacDermott.) To this end he supported the efforts of Eoin MacNeill to maintain the Volunteers as a 'national safeguard'. Like Hobson he believed that there was widespread agreement with his 'alternative (i.e. non-Revolutionary) policy', and that it would have worked.

It seemed to me that if we had only played our cards fairly we had the Government in a cleft stick. Either they would have to make the first move and suppress us by force, thus raising the country about their ears . . . or they would be compelled to look on our rapidly increasing strength until we would be in a very fair position to demand practically what we wished—and be absolutely certain of making a Hell of a fight of it if denied.[2]

Whether or not this policy retained some ambiguities, it was not seriously discussed by most of O'Connell's superiors.

The secrecy with which the insurrectionist group went about their planning, with the creation of an unofficial 'military council' within the IRB concealed even from members of the Supreme Council, is part of the 1916 legend.

---

[1] Ibid., ch. X, p. 1.
[2] Ibid., ch. XIV, p. 2.

To a large extent the problems and ambiguities of the insurrection plan arose from this double secrecy. Preparatory discussion was at a minimum. The greatest concealment was that within the Volunteer executive, where Pearse's systematic deception of MacNeill was the cause of permanent bitterness.[1] MacNeill was, of course, aware of the insurrectionist tendency, though he was less aware than Hobson of the degree to which the IRB group was capable—or thought itself capable—of directing the Volunteer organization into sudden action. By the beginning of 1916 he and his supporters knew that a sort of internal power-struggle was in process, and that its outcome might prove a decisive juncture in Irish history. They attempted to tighten, or at least to hold, their grip on the organization by increasing their public appearances at parades and so on.[2]   As early as September 1915, when MacNeill attended a Volunteer review in Limerick, he found that some local commanders had received instructions from Pearse to make certain 'definite military dispositions in the event of war in Ireland'.[3] However, though he was alarmed by this discovery, he took no direct action. One eminent historian has suggested that the reason for this may simply be that MacNeill 'was not a military man'; but nor of course were Pearse, MacDermott, or Plunkett.[4]

MacNeill's most substantial effort to halt the slide into rebellion began in January 1916 in response to Connolly's warlike articles in the *Workers' Republic*. The Volunteer executive asked Connolly to a meeting, at which Connolly candidly declared his intention to mount a rising in Dublin. As a result of this, and unknown to MacNeill, Connolly was persuaded to combine his plans with those of the IRB 'military council'. The plans, as will be seen, remained vague. But MacNeill's suspicions were not altogether stilled by Pearse's assurance that he had persuaded Connolly to abandon his

---

[1] Tierney, *MacNeill*, ch. XIV *passim*.

[2] O'Connell memoir, ch. XIV, p. 2.

[3] MacNeill, Memorandum No. 2, in Martin, 'Eoin MacNeill on the 1916 Rising', p. 247.

[4] Indeed the only leader with actual military experience, as a private in the King's Liverpool Regiment, stationed at Beggars' Bush Barracks in the 1880s, was Connolly: Greaves, op. cit. pp. 20, 27. He, however, deferred to Plunkett's self-taught mastery of strategic theory.

insurrectionary ideas. In February he produced a weighty letter to Pearse, which the latter saw fit to read out at an executive meeting, in MacNeill's absence, at the same time smothering discussion of it on the grounds that other members of the executive had not had time to consider the issues in detail.[1]

Hobson, Sean Fitzgibbon, and others attempted to push MacNeill into a direct confrontation, arranging a special meeting of the headquarters staff outside Dublin at MacNeill's house.[2] MacNeill drew up for this meeting a formidable and closely reasoned memorandum which distilled the 'realist' arguments against rebellion.[3] As he wrote later, he had consistently opposed 'all sorts of formulas and ready-made arguments', which in the circumstances were 'practically counsels of despair, like refuges for people who did not find themselves able to think out anything better'.[4] Here he discussed such 'formulas' or 'a priori maxims' as 'it is essential that Ireland should take action during the present war', 'Ireland has always struck her blow too late', or 'the military advantage lies with the side that takes the initiative'. The first he regarded as unprovable, the second as historically untrue (Irish failures had mainly been due to inadequate preparation, as Thomas Davis had said: 'Uprose they ere they ought'), and irrelevant even if it had been true. The third he castigated as 'a sort of magic spell'—as indeed it had been for many French military thinkers before the war—which disguised the fact that real military initiative would always lie with the overwhelmingly powerful British forces.[5]

His deepest thrust was against the psychological weakness which in his view underlay the insurrectionist policy.

To my mind, those who feel impelled towards military action on any of the grounds that I have stated (the a priori maxims) are really impelled by a sense of feebleness or despondency or fatalism, or by

[1] O'Connell memoir, quoted in Dudley Edwards, *Pearse*, p. 248.
[2] Hobson, in *Ireland Yesterday and Tomorrow*, calls it a meeting of the executive.
[3] Copy in Hobson MSS, printed in Martin, 'Eoin MacNeill on the 1916 Rising', pp. 234–40.
[4] MacNeill memoir, quoted in Tierney, *MacNeill*, p. 164.
[5] MacNeill, Memorandum No. 1, Feb. 1916.

an instinct of satisfying their own emotions or escaping from a difficult and complex and trying situation.[1]

Then, moving from condemnation to the positive side of his 'alternative policy', MacNeill asserted that whilst the Volunteers were a military force they should try to achieve their aims without fighting. This was a hard thing to say to a military body, and potentially damaging to its morale—but

it must be remembered that the Irish Volunteers, if they are a military force, are not a militarist force, and that their object is to secure Ireland's rights and liberties and nothing else but that. The reproach of the former Irish Volunteers is not that they did not fight but that they did not maintain their organisation till their objects had been secured.[2]

MacNeill pointed to the very concrete gains which had in fact already been made: England could no longer dominate Ireland by its 'peace establishment' or rule it 'normally by what are called peaceful means'. The government clearly wanted to suppress the Volunteers but dared not: it was 'convinced that it would lose more than it could gain by moving its military forces against us, unless we create a special opportunity for it'. MacNeill of course saw a hopeless insurrection as just such a gift to the government. That it would be hopeless he had no doubt: he thought that those who contemplated a rising were suffering from, amongst other things, the 'childish' illusion that the efficiency of the Dublin Volunteers was duplicated in the provinces.

The crux of the divergence, which was to prove permanent, between MacNeill's pragmatic (or as he called it 'opportunist') approach and that of the extreme group, was reached when he came to deal with the vital question of what constituted Ireland. His words here pre-echoed Arthur Griffith's arguments during the Treaty debate, and encapsulate what may with hindsight be called the 'Fine Gael' outlook.

We have to remember that what we call our country is not a poetical abstraction, as some of us, perhaps all of us, in the exercise of our highly developed capacity for figurative thought, are sometimes apt to imagine—with the help of our patriotic literature. There is no such person as Caitlin Ni Ullachain or Roisin Dubh or the Sean-bhean

---

[1] Ibid., quoted in Martin, op. cit. p. 236.
[2] Ibid., quoted in Martin, op. cit. p. 238.

Bhocht, who is calling upon us to serve her. What we call our country
is the Irish nation, which is a concrete and visible reality.[1]

He added, still more acutely, that it was the duty of the
Volunteers 'to get our country on our side, and not to be
content with the vanity of thinking ourselves to be right and
other Irish people to be wrong'—fundamental democratic
principles allied with purely practical ones. Simply from a
military point of view it was a 'factor of the highest importance to be able to fight in a friendly country'.

MacNeill's reiteration that 'the only possible basis for
successful revolutionary action is deep and widespread
popular discontent' was prophetic. But his assurance that he
personally would not 'give way or resign or shirk any trouble
in opposing' any proposal for insurrection was not altogether
fulfilled. As soon as the discussion in the headquarters staff
began, Hobson recorded, Pearse and MacDermott 'denied in
the most explicit terms having any intention to land the
Volunteers in an insurrection, and reproached the rest of us
for our suspicious natures'. MacNeill quietly slipped his great
memorandum into a drawer, and the issue was never pressed
to a crisis.[2] Hobson was left dissatisfied, later observing
grumpily that MacNeill 'had many great qualities, but he
would not face up to a row'. This was clearly true, yet it
has to be said that Hobson himself, apart from putting
pressure on MacNeill, remained oddly supine throughout
this critical period. He allowed the IRB to be cut from
beneath his feet, and left a leadership vacuum which ensured
the ascendancy of MacDermott and Clarke.

The weighty pragmatism of MacNeill, Hobson, and O'Connell never had the slightest effect on the latter, other than
to force them into minor subterfuges to conceal their
intentions. These intentions were immutably fixed from the
start of the war. The actual military plan for the insurrection
has never been clear, but its core was a stand-up fight in Dublin
framed in the childhood imaginings of Joseph Plunkett.[3]

[1] MacNeill, quoted in Martin, op. cit. p. 239.

[2] Hobson, *Ireland Yesterday and Tomorrow*, p. 73. MacDermott was not in
fact present at the meeting.

[3] On IRB military planning see F. O'Donoghue, 'Ceannt, Devoy, O'Rahilly
and the Military Plan', in F. X. Martin (ed.), *Leaders and Men of the Easter
Rising: Dublin 1916*, pp. 189-201.

The paucity of planning, regarded by the MacNeill group as almost criminal negligence, was of little importance to the insurrectionists. It has been rightly said that 'dominating the whole project there was an objective of greater gravity and significance than the military planning'. This was the declaration of national independence in a manner which 'would take an authentic place in historic succession to earlier efforts to achieve freedom'.[1] Military success was required only so that this effort might be 'on a scale and of a duration which would ensure that it could not be dismissed either as unrepresentative or as a mere riot'. 'Physical force' had changed its meaning significantly. In one sense, the MacNeill group were the true modern heirs to the physical-force tradition. They searched for ways in which the potential strength of the Volunteers could be used to force the British out of Ireland. The insurrectionists, by contrast, proposed to use naked violence only as a preliminary means, to reawaken the supposedly slumbering national spirit. Even such chances as they had of the effective deployment of force they cast aside with a carelessness amounting to contempt.

The biggest such chance was, of course, the gun-running, on a scale even greater than the UVF's, arranged between Sir Roger Casement and the government of Germany. If the Volunteers had landed the cargo of the *Aud*, distributed it, and systematically trained themselves to use it, the transformation of their situation would have been astonishing. Even MacNeill accepted that such an infusion of weapons would make armed struggle a possibility. More importantly, it might have provoked the government into action, which would have given the moral advantage to the Volunteers. It has usually been assumed that the failure to rendezvous with the *Aud*, after she had successfully run the British naval defences and arrived with remarkably punctuality at Fenit, was due to a mixture of misunderstanding, inexperience, and incompetence. The assumption is that the wider plan for the 1916 rising hinged on the use of the huge arms cargo. Such a common-sense view (the view, naturally, held by MacNeill) suggests that Pearse and Connolly, if they hoped

[1] Ibid. p. 193.

for an immediate national upsurge in response to the rising, did not entirely neglect to provide some sort of means for this.

Yet the common-sense assumption that the failure to land the arms shipment rendered the insurrection outside Dublin stillborn neglects the extraordinary context in which the 'misunderstanding' occurred. This was that no detailed arrangements for distributing the arms cargo had been made.[1] It is surely carrying inexperience too far to suppose that such a shipment could have been distributed by *ad hoc* local arrangements.[2] The conclusion which suggests itself is that the planners of the rising in Dublin took very little interest in the fate of the German rifles. This circumstance, coupled with the jejune instructions sent to provincial leaders (the order that the Clare, Limerick and Galway Volunteers should 'hold the line of the Shannon to Athlone' is nearly as notorious as the Citizen Army's digging of trenches on St. Stephen's Green), almost suggests that the Dublin leaders were reluctant to see the brilliance of their own outburst rivalled elsewhere.[3]

(iii) *Rising*

> If they do not win this fight, they will at least have deserved
> to win it. But win it they will, although they may win

---

[1] R. Monteith, *Casement's Last Adventure* (Dublin, 1953), was a strong indictment; for a revealing recent account of local planning see J. A. Gaughan, *Austin Stack: Portrait of a Separatist* (Dublin, 1977), pp. 43–54.

[2] The idea that the cargo could be 'transferred rapidly by rail to three main centres—Cork, Limerick and Galway—for immediate use by the as yet ill-equipped Volunteers' (F. X. Martin. 'The 1916 Rising—A Coup d'État or a "Bloody Protest"?', *Studia Hibernica*, viii (1968), 114) is scarcely realistic. Stack's plans, more complete than any others, look quite unconvincing.

[3] On Pearse's secret provincial instructions, D. Lynch, *The IRB and the 1916 Insurrection*, p. 30. The obsessive Blanquism of the insurrectionists is well displayed by the gun-running episode, which they saw as contingent on the rising and not vice versa. Thus it is still asserted, e.g. by F. O'Donoghue, that the German insistence on timing the *Aud*'s arrival to a bracket of four days—a reflection of the inescapable problems of blockade-running—was 'disastrous from the Irish point of view' because it was 'vitally necessary to synchronize the landing with the start of the rising'. Yet it would have made much better sense both militarily and politically (especially as regards the attitude of MacNeill) if the landing had preceded the rising and the arms been properly distributed and prepared.

> it in death. Already they have won a great thing. They have
> redeemed Dublin from many shames, and made her name
> splendid among the names of Cities.
>
> Patrick Pearse[1]

The events of Easter week 1916, and the shadowy tussle within the Volunteer leadership on the previous Friday and Saturday, have been frequently described—perhaps with greater frequency than depth. The centrepiece of the 'bloody protest for a glorious thing', the realization of Plunkett's vision of a siege of Dublin, has generated a vast literature.[2] It was, as has been remarked, a rhetorical gesture, a genre new to the IRB in spite of its long tradition of verbal extravagance, and one for which the provincial physical-force men were unprepared. Provincial ideas seem to have fallen, in the main, somewhere between the new sacrificalism and the new realism. They remained wedded in effect to the old insurrectionist idea—something more than a mere gesture, but still a sudden great blow, not a protracted struggle. As a result, very little happened outside Dublin. With the Volunteers in general, 'just emerging from the mob stage', as O'Connell put it,[3] and chronically short of arms and ammunition, local leaders could not see how they could strike an effective blow. Thus the ill-fated Tomas MacCurtain in Cork believed that since (*a*) only eighty Volunteers out of an enrolled membership of nearly 2,000 were prepared to stand by their leaders in any event, and (*b*) the quantity of arms and ammunition in the whole of Co. Cork would, if concentrated in the city, only last twenty minutes, he could do nothing.[4] He and Terence McSwiney sat through Easter

---

[1] HQ General Order 28 Apr. 1916.

[2] There is a remarkable survey of the literature, and a mass of details of the rising, in F. X. Martin, '1916—Myth, Fact and Mystery', *Studia Hibernica*, vii (1967), 7–126. One point that Martin makes remains a curiosity—that no professional historian has attempted the task of producing a full-scale account of 1916 since Alison Phillips in 1923.

[3] 'To strike an average of country corps was practically impossible, the range of efficiency was so wide. But taking a wide swathe in the middle of the range it is correct to say that the men could shoot a little, could do a little squad drill, and had a little theoretical knowledge—this last of the vaguest and most rudimentary. They were just emerging from the mob stage' (O'Connell memoir, ch. XI, p. 3).

[4] K. K. McDonnell, *There is a Bridge at Bandon* (Cork, 1972), p. 103.

week glumly, developing a guilt complex which MacSwiney was later to expiate in the grimmest way.

The Limerick City Regiment had planned to move out from Limerick on Sunday morning, camp at Killonan, and commence operations at 7 p.m. by cutting the telegraph and telephone wires and the Dublin and Cork rail lines, below Patrick's Well—leaving the lines to Clare and Kerry open. But 'not knowing anything of what was to happen on Easter Sunday, the Council did not think it fair to lead (the men) to their death as their [sic] was no chance when arms did not land England was prepared'. The commandant agreed to the British commander's demand that their arms be surrendered; and then

When he got home on Monday he found two orders from Pearse there one was to carry on the other all is off their was no time marked on either so he did not know which had arrived first or last and all the city and the county men had been disbanded he could do nothing.[1]

Events in Kerry, where the arms were to have landed, and where in fact Casement landed and fell into the hands of the police, have been justifiably labelled a 'debacle' by the biographer of the Kerry commandant.[2] Austin Stack's future record as an administrator can create no confidence that his arrangements for distributing the German arms would have worked; and his mania for secrecy ensured that confusion would prevail if he himself were incapacitated. Nothing could have been further from the confident staff-work of the UVF. Finally, after Casement's capture, Stack sent his gun to Dublin in the care of Paddy Cahill (future commander of the Kerry Brigade), and delivered himself to the Tralee RIC barrack, where he was promptly arrested.[3] Thus ended the rising in Kerry.

Other local leaders made greater, but still essentially conventional efforts. The well-organized Wexford Brigade under

---

[1] Account of Limerick operations in Easter week by S. J. Dineen, 23 July 1916 (McGarrity MSS, NLI MS17511).

[2] J. A. Gaughan, *Austin Stack*, pp. 25–73 *passim*.

[3] Ibid. p. 61. Stack's ineffectual efforts to forestall the arrest of Casement had, as he felt, been hampered by the strict instructions from Dublin that 'there should be not as much as a single shot fired until general hostilities had begun on Easter Sunday' (Ryan, *The Rising*, p. 238).

Sean Sinnott staged an advance and captured Enniscorthy railway station. It was the best-armed group in Leinster outside Dublin, having started with only eight .303 carbines and 800 rounds of ammunition bought from Hobson for £19, and ended with 300 rifles. Yet one of its leaders remarked on the dramatic contrast between the intense revolutionary activity in Dublin before the rising ('every person one met seemed to be a rebel of some sort') and the atmosphere at home, where 'the first enthusiasm had disappeared and trying to make any headway seemed like rolling a stone up an endless hill'.[1] Its offer of a contingent to assist the Dublin fight was turned down by Connolly, who instructed the brigade to use its strength against British communications. It dominated the south-eastern corner of Ireland for several days, pressing the police hard and leading to reports that 900 rebels were advancing on Arklow, but was unable to take advantage of the opportunity presented by the sensitive reinforcement line Kingstown–Dublin.[2]

The other area in which substantial Volunteer movements took place was Galway, where on 27 April the military reported —by an agreeable slip—no fewer than 1,500 'revels' at Athenry. The naval authorities immediately perceived the danger to the Western Approaches: 'Admiral at Queenstown (Cobh) considers state of affairs at Galway serious'.[3] By next day, however, HMS *Gloucester*, which had dropped several shells near the Volunteer force, reported that the rebels were in retreat from Athenry—a decision reached by a majority of the Galway officers in spite of their commander's wish to stand and 'make the west memorable for a great battle even if they were all to lose their lives'.[4]

Desmond Ryan's exculpatory argument, that 'the isolation of the Volunteer areas from each other prevented the fighters

---

[1] R. Brennan, *Allegiance*, pp. 16, 20. Brennan, though an IRB man (encouraged in this by his local priest), saw the Volunteers from an early stage as 'Sinn Féin Volunteers', and was an admirer of Griffith.

[2] Military telegrams, 27, 28 Apr. 1916 (PRO W.O.32 9510).

[3] Ibid.

[4] C. D. Greaves, *Liam Mellows and the Irish Revolution* (London, 1971), pp. 89–93. An attack was made on the RIC barrack at Oranmore, in which two constables were wounded, and another constable was injured by a shotgun in a small affray at Carnmore.

in the various areas from knowing the real position until after the Rising', is in fact the main condemnation of the insurrection plan.[1] It aimed at a mass uprising without providing the machinery to mobilize and co-ordinate so amorphous a phenomenon. A single exception to the tale of ineffectual action demonstrated what might have been done if a more realistic conception of rebellion had prevailed. In northern Co. Dublin, the Volunteers under the prominent Gaelic Leaguer Thomas Ashe mounted an assault on the RIC barrack at Ashbourne on 28 April. The operation was well prepared, though the attackers were short of explosives and were reduced to a long fire-fight. While this was in progress, RIC reinforcements under County Inspector Gray engaged the outposts of the besieging force. Ashe seems not to have anticipated this elementary riposte, and was momentarily disconcerted. Fortunately for him the very effective fire of his outpost group at Rath Cross led Gray to overestimate the strength of the Volunteers; and, while a precarious stand-off lasted, Ashe's Lieutenant, Richard Mulcahy, devised a flanking movement which pinned down the relief force inextricably. In the end both it and the barrack garrison surrendered, with the loss of 8 RIC killed, including Gray himself, and 15 wounded. This was a truly dramatic triumph for an inexperienced army which had (in spite of Gray's impression) no numerical advantage. Mulcahy's instinctive grasp of small-scale manœuvre laid down, albeit accidentally, the pattern for a new type of warfare. Within a few years Mulcahy was to play a central part in spreading this pattern across the whole country.

For the time being, however, old-fashioned fighting was the order of the day. The Dublin insurgents could do no more than hold the buildings they had seized on Monday morning, and were unable to produce any tactical response to the inexorable isolation and bombardment of each strongpoint. Even fierce fighting like that at Mount Street Bridge, where British conscripts as inexperienced as the Volunteers themselves suffered dreadful casualties—in New Army-style shoulder-to-shoulder attacks that prefigured the Somme in miniature—had little delaying effect. The British response

[1] Ryan, *The Rising*, App. V, p. 266.

was surprisingly swift and uncompromising: all the political hesitations and complexities of the previous five years seemed to be swept away by the direct challenge of physical force. Nevertheless, Pearse was satisfied. In one of the less apparently rhetorical parts of his last public announcement, he held that:

If we accomplish no more than we have accomplished, I am satisfied we have saved Ireland's honour. I am satisfied that we should have accomplished more, that we should have accomplished the task of enthroning, as well as proclaiming, the Irish Republic as a Sovereign State, had our arrangements for a simultaneous rising of the whole country, with a combined plan as sound as the Dublin plan has been proved to be, been allowed to go through on Easter Sunday.[1]

(iv) *Martial law*

Nobody can govern Ireland from England save in a state of siege.

Birrell[2]

Politically, the rising was a godsend to Unionists. It confirmed the treachery and unreliability of the Irish, swept away the tainted administration of Augustine Birrell, and made possible the firm government whose absence, in the Unionist view, had always been a primary cause of the Irish problem.[3] The shift in the British posture in Ireland was sudden, revolutionary. Up to Easter weekend the easy-going regime persisted, notwithstanding the clear warnings of an impending outbreak. The Commander-in-Chief, General Friend, actually went away on leave (or rather without leave) on Friday, while on Monday the British officer-corps was to be found at Fairytown races. As the Viceroy tetchily observed to the Royal Commission, 'Upon the system in Ireland everybody

---

[1] General Order, 28 Apr. 1916; Dudley Edwards, *Pearse*, pp. 298–300. The most careful military analysis of the Rising in Dublin is Col. P. J. Hally, 'The Easter 1916 Rising in Dublin: the Military Aspects', which points to the impressive speed with which the British regained their balance and concentrated forces on the capital: *Irish Sword*, viii. 30 (1967), 51.

[2] Birrell to Asquith, 30 April 1916.

[3] Birrell told Asquith on 30 April, 'A good many "loyalists" here are glad things have happened the way they have ...' (Asquith MSS 36).

seems to be away. There is no coordination'.[1] Friend himself
had made several attempts to improve preparedness, but
effective preparations had been vetoed by Birrell and Nathan
at Dublin Castle.[2]

The suddenness of the fall of this duumvirate may account
for the sharp reversion to violent policy. The discredited
and 'smashed' (in his own word) Birrell had to learn the
news of the rising in London from the military whose warnings he had so often discounted, and could do nothing
but hope that Lord French, C-in-C. Home Forces, would be
able to send enough troops to quell the outbreak.[3] Similarly
Nathan, at first trapped in the Castle but afterwards staying
there through choice, merely assisted the military as best he
could. On Easter Monday, executive power fell unexpectedly
into the hands of Lord Wimborne, secure in the Viceregal
lodge. Lord Basil Blackwood painted a garish picture of the
delighted Viceroy: 'his Ex had simply *swilled* brandy the
whole time . . . had been superlatively theatrical and insisted
on his poor secretaries using the most melodramatically
grandiloquent language down the telephone—standing over
them to enforce his dictation: 'It is His Ex's *command . . .*'[4]
It appears to have been his own decision to proclaim martial
law in Dublin city and district, though the proclamation
was soon to be confirmed and extended by the Cabinet.

Martial law, an object of abhorrence in Britain for over
two centuries, represented a declaration of political and
administrative bankruptcy. In Ireland alone had it been
employed: imposed by statute after the 1798 rebellion and
kept in force for the first years of the Union. Such a prolongation had subsequently been explicitly condemned as an
abuse by the outstanding commentators Hallam and Dicey,

---

[1] Evidence of Lord Wimborne, *Report of the Royal Commission on the
Rebellion in Ireland*, 1916 Cd. 8279. xi. 171.

[2] Notes on measures taken to meet rising, C.-in-C. Home Forces to Secretary
War Office (Asquith MSS 42). Friend had, however, refused the offer of a further
brigade on 7 April, saying that the security situation had improved: Holmes,
French, p. 323.

[3] L. ÓBroin, *The Chief Secretary*, pp. 173-4. This, with its companion volume
Dublin Castle and the 1916 Rising, provides a richly documented view of the
pre-Rising period.

[4] Lady C. Asquith, *Diaries 1915-1918* (London 1968), p. 163.

in whose view martial law was only admissible as an immediate response to desperate emergency.[1] Now, however, amidst the general disorientation caused by total war, this detested recourse was not only invoked—quite properly—in the heat of the moment by the Lord-Lieutenant, but then imposed for an indefinite period after deliberation by the Cabinet. Birrell crossed to Dublin on 27 April and quickly penned a warning against extending martial law to the whole of Ireland.[2] But the decision was already taken, together with the decision— apparently unexpected by Wimborne—that a military governor should be appointed with full powers.

The officer selected for this post, General Sir John Maxwell, was widely, and inevitably, held responsible for the methods employed in suppressing the Rising. But he made a surprisingly leisurely journey to Ireland in the middle of Easter week, and on his arrival found that all military arrangements had already been made by General Friend. Indeed, the first military responses predated even Friend's hasty return to Dublin on 25 April. The army seems to have reacted instinctively in formulating its three-point plan— to recapture the Magazine Fort, to secure the Viceregal lodge, and to relieve and strengthen the Castle garrison.[3] Command of troops in Dublin was assumed at 3.45 a.m. on Tuesday by Brigadier Lowe, bringing in the 25th Reserve Infantry Brigade from the Curragh. As Lowe and Friend elaborated the main thrusts which split up the insurgent groups, they appear to have been following an unquestioned assumption that the rebels must be forced into unconditional surrender as rapidly as possible. No evidence of any other plan survives, or of any political caution at this stage about the speed and weight of the counterstroke.[4] The British riposte was unexpectedly energetic and successful, but this meant, in the circumstances of urban fighting, that it was very destructive.[5]

[1] See above, pp. 94-6.

[2] Birrell to Asquith, 28 Apr. 1916 (Asquith MSS 36).

[3] Hally, op. cit., Part II, p. 48.

[4] Although Basil Blackwood alleged that Wimborne considered a negotiated truce rather than unconditional surrender, a 'floater' designed to sew things up before Maxwell arrived: Lady C. Asquith, loc. cit.

[5] It is a double misconception to suggest, as does M. Caulfield, *The Easter Rebellion* (London, 1964), pp. 187-8, that the British had 'the kind of superior

Hence the well-known employment of field artillery (a form of violence which Connolly had believed was not available to a capitalist government in a commercial centre)[1] and even naval gunfire, and hence the death of ordinary inhabitants of North King Street and elsewhere.

The problem of civilian casualties was to some extent unavoidable, as an order to the first reinforcements disembarking at Kingstown on 25 April shows. In clearing the area between the sea and the Stillorgan, Donnybrook, and Dublin Roads,

> every road and lane in that area must be traversed by patrols, and the head of columns will in no case advance beyond any house from which fire has been opened, until the inhabitants of such house have been destroyed or captured. Every man found in such house whether bearing arms or not, may be considered a rebel.[2]

The chill undertone of that last sentence was not entirely eradicated by the assurance which followed that nearly all Dublin householders were in fact loyal. The psychological reaction of many soldiers (and indeed many civilians) to 'rebels' led to a degree of rough treatment, and in a few cases to something much worse. The 'tiger in our race' was perhaps not uncaged so spectacularly as during the Indian Mutiny, but in the United Kingdom in the twentieth century a few gashes sufficed. The most notorious was the shooting of Francis Sheehy-Skeffington and others by Captain Bowen-Colthurst. Colthurst was found insane (though he ended up as a bank manager); but a wider and, in a sense, more alarmingly unbalanced response was shown by the chief Castle military intelligence officer, Major Price. The account of his torture of Eoin MacNeill, in an attempt to get MacNeill to confess that the real instigators of the Rising were (incredibly) Dillon and Devlin, caused amazement and anger.[3]

---

odds which if they could have been brought to bear on the Western Front, would have ended that war inside a week'.

[1] Connolly's views about the use of artillery in cities were in fact based on the rational premise that artillerymen would be unable to operate at the short ranges required if they were met by concentrated rifle fire.

[2] Orders for OC Troops disembarking, 25 Apr. 1916 (PRO W.O.35 69/1).

[3] *Freeman's Journal*, 6 Sept. 1917; Tierney, *MacNeill*, pp. 223–6.

The historical record of martial law can have held out little hope that in Ireland it would not act as a political irritant, or worse. The first regulations issued by Friend on 26 April, were acceptably straightforward in the midst of crisis. They instituted a curfew, and warned that any civilian carrying arms was liable to be fired on without warning. Their only questionable aspect was the instruction—dear to all military governors—that 'all persons shall give all information in their possession as to stores of arms . . . or of the movement of hostile bodies, to the nearest military authority, or to the nearest police barracks'.[1] Still more unattractive was the proclamation extending martial law throughout Ireland, even to areas where no rebels had been seen, and the suspension in Ireland of the operation of section 1 of the Defence of the Realm Amendment Act of 1915.[2] Henceforth civilians could be tried by courts martial for a range of offences (whose width was not clear). In fact the suspension of Parmoor's amendment would, legally, have sufficed, but as the Irish Attorney-General observed,

undoubtedly the average civilian has an extraordinary belief in the magic term 'Martial Law' and it therefore brings home to loyal and law-abiding people a great sense of security and safety, and upon the other hand the very indefinite knowledge of its powers spreads terror among the disaffected.[3]

This Manichean analysis was, as usual, inadequate. It failed to take account of the third, neutral group within the population. In Ireland this was always by far the largest. Their reaction to martial law rapidly became one of exasperation or hostility.

The two dramatic actions which fixed the nature of martial law or the 'Maxwell regime' in the public mind were the wholesale arrest of Sinn Féiners, and the execution of fourteen leaders of the Dublin rising. Both actions began on 3 May, when Maxwell issued orders to despatch mobile columns 'throughout Ireland with a view to arresting dangerous Sinn Feiners who have actually supported the movement

[1] Regulations to be Observed under Martial Law, 26 Apr. 1916 (Asquith MSS 42, f. 81).
[2] Ibid., f. 80.
[3] Memo., 20 May 1916 (Asquith MSS 42, ff. 148-9).

throughout the country even though they have not taken part in the rising'.[1] On the same day, P. H. Pearse, Tom Clarke, and Thomas MacDonagh were shot in Kilmainham gaol. In the following days 3,340 men and 79 women were arrested by the mobile columns; some 2,000 men and 6 women were tried by courts martial (not military tribunals as might have been employed under martial law, but courts martial legally established by the Defence of the Realm Act). Five of the women and 1,836 men were interned in Britain, mainly at Frongoch in Wales (which became the 'Sinn Fein University'). Sentences of death were passed on 90 prisoners, including Countess Markievicz. Of these fifteen were carried out on 3, 4, 5, 8, and 12 May in Dublin, and on 9 May in Cork.

Contemporary accounts are unanimous in holding that the spinning-out of the secret trials and executions was a primary cause of the shift in public opinion against the authorities. The slowness of the process was, of course, a result of the legalistic punctiliousness with which the trials were carried out. Yet the government got no credit for this: as usual the worst was believed. As Maxwell reported, the unfortunate Bowen Colthurst case gave colour to Dillon's allegations and produced the idea that the military were out of hand. 'This is quoted as a "military execution without trial" and it is spread about that the other military executions were on a par with this.'[2]

Dillon, unlike Redmond, had been an eyewitness of the insurrection in Dublin. His sense of the public mood quickly led him to try to prevent the government from taking repressive action that would be counter-productive. As the initial public bafflement and contempt for the rebels disappeared, Dillon perceived quite clearly that the demonstrative violence of the rising had undermined the policy of collaboration. He was the first Irish MP to brave the patriotic fury of the House of Commons by vehemently denouncing the 'river of blood' let loose in Ireland by the

---

[1] GOC-in-C's Orders, 3 May 1916 (PRO W.O.35 69/1).
[2] Memo. by GOC–in–C. Ireland, in Cabinet Memo. by Prime Minister, 24 June 1916 (HLRO, Bonar Law MSS 63/C/61).

government. This change of front represented a major victory for the policy of violence adopted by the insurrectionists.[1]

Asquith crossed to Ireland immediately after Dillon's speech and halted the executions, though Maxwell was convinced that several more were required. Some earlier political pressure to mitigate death-sentences had been exerted very hesitantly, through French, who had, however, stressed that there was no wish to interfere with Maxwell's freedom of action.[2]

After a fortnight of unfettered freedom, Maxwell was now haled back within the political framework. With soldierly bewilderment he later told the sympathetic Walter Long that, though 'apparently you and other Cabinet Ministers think that I have some definite powers', he was not aware of them. He had been 'sent to Ireland with plenary powers, verbally given, to deal with a state of rebellion', but he had not as Commander-in-Chief been 'given any functions or authority over the machinery of civil government' in Ireland.

Martial law has been proclaimed over the whole of Ireland, but as there is no longer a state of active rebellion or armed resistance to authority, and as the Law Courts and Courts of Summary Jurisdiction are exercising their functions, the Irish law officers are of the opinion that, with the ordinary law and the Defence of the Realm Act and Regulations in force, there is no present justification for the exercise of any special power under Martial law.[3]

Asquith himself told the Cabinet on his return from Dublin that, although 'a number' of the prisoners should never have been sent to Dublin for trial, he was satisfied that 'both before and after Sir John Maxwell's arrival, the officers

[1] House of Commons, 11 May 1916 (HC Deb. 5s, lxxxii, cc. 935-51): F. S. L. Lyons, 'Dillon, Redmond and the Irish Home Rulers', in F. X. Martin, *Leaders and Men*, pp. 34-5. The minor achievement of Dillon's speech, stressed by Lyons, of temporarily staving off the collapse of the parliamentary party, surely pales besides its contribution to the revival of violence as a political medium. Crucially, it was the government, not the rebels, who were accused of 'washing out our whole life-work in a river of blood'.

[2] French's diary, 4 May 1916: Holmes, *French*, p. 325. Maxwell wanted to execute Countess Markievicz, whom he considered 'blood-guilty and dangerous'. He also, according to private information, received Asquith's telegram before ordering the execution of Connolly, and ignored it.

[3] Maxwell to Long, 17, 18 July 1916, in Cabinet Memo. by W. H. Long, 21 July (Bonar Law MSS 63/C/29).

responsible for the general command in Dublin acted, on the whole, with prudence and discretion'. And he added,

It is to be remembered that all the trials and sentences have been conducted, passed and carried out under the statutory powers of the Defence of the Realm Act. There is no single case in which it has been or is likely to be necessary to resort to what is called 'Martial law' and there is no adequate ground for its continuance.[1]

In the circumstances it is remarkable that martial law, far from being abandoned, was confirmed and extended at the end of May.[2] This was contrary to all legal precedent, and Dillon was on sure ground when he demanded to know why martial law had been extended

long after all disturbance has come to an end, for an indefinite period, to the whole extent of Ireland, nine-tenths of which remained perfectly peaceful throughout the recent insurrection.

Asquith in reply did not treat the House to an account of the state of the law since the Boer War and the *Marais* judgment (in which many earlier restrictions on the extent and prolongation of martial law had been overturned),[3] but vaguely announced that martial law was being 'continued' for the time being as a precautionary measure, 'in the hope that its disappearance will be speedy and complete'. In the meantime it would not be resorted to except in cases of urgent necessity—of which there were none.[4]

Martial law had its supporters. Walter Long quoted an Irish judge's opinion that 'If martial law is not maintained for a considerable period we shall have another outbreak'.[5] The redoubtable Hugh de Fellenberg Montgomery spoke for the loyalists when he held that

Nobody approves of Martial law as a permanent mode of governing any country, but as long as the conditions in Ireland remain what they are and the great war with the Central Powers continues, the only safe Rule for Ireland is that of Sir John Maxwell as Military Governor with plenary powers.[6]

---

[1] Memo. by Prime Minister, 19 May 1916 (Bonar Law MSS 63/C/5).
[2] Proclamation, 26 May 1916 (HLRO, Lloyd George MSS D/15/1/5).
[3] Townshend, 'Martial Law', p. 182.
[4] House of Commons, 30 May 1916 (HC Deb. 5s. lxxxii, c. 2542).
[5] Cabinet Memo., 19 May 1916 (Asquith MSS 44).
[6] Note by Montgomery, 25 May 1916 (Lloyd George MSS D/15/1/4; PRONI,

Its opponents were more numerous, however. Many British Liberals, led by the *Manchester Guardian*, condemned the speed and severity of repression.[1] By early June, Lloyd George was writing to Dillon of Maxwell's 'stupid and fatuous' administration and to Asquith that the General's lack of 'tact and restraint' was making agreement impossible.[2] T. P. O'Connor said that unless Maxwell was withdrawn and 'military rule in Ireland brought to an end', settlement would be impossible, and Dillon suggested acutely that

The horrible irony of the situation is that by giving the soldiers and Price a free hand you are making yourselves the instrument of your own worst enemies to defeat your own policy.[3]

The 'madness of your soldiers', and the present 'military dictatorship' had, Dillon declared, roused old historic Irish passions of distrust and hate.

An additional irony, of course, was that, as Maxwell pointed out, martial law *sensu stricto* had not been 'put into operation' anywhere—even in Dublin. Its mere announcement had enabled a grievance to be 'manufactured', all the more easily because people thought that the Defence of the Realm Regulations were 'martial law regulations'. Now all public bodies in Ireland, Maxwell admitted, were spending their time passing resolutions condemning martial law.[4]

Such misunderstandings and reactions were entirely predictable, as were the irritations produced between the civil and military authorities themselves. The whole policy of repression, mild though it may have been in comparison with the treatment which would have been meted out to rebels in, say, France or Germany (as apologists for the government's action have often pointed out), was quite severe enough to

---

Montgomery MSS D.627/429/10). Cf. the murmur about 'governing Ireland' at the Carlton Club on 7 July (Bonar Law MSS 63/C/64).

[1] See J. M. McEwan, 'The Liberal Party and the Irish Question during the First World War', *Journal of British Studies*, xii. 1 (1972), 114.

[2] Lloyd George to Dillon, 9, 10 June; to Asquith, 10 June 1916 (Lloyd George MSS D/14/2/20, 22, 24).

[3] T. P. O'Connor to Lloyd George, 9, 13 June; Dillon to Lloyd George, 11 June 1916 (ibid. D/14/2/23, 25, 27, 35).

[4] Memos. by GOC.-in-C. Ireland, 16, 24 June 1916 (Asquith MSS 42, Bonar Law MSS 63/C/61).

be provocative. In the Irish context it must be judged an over-reaction.

It is true that April 1916 was a hard time for Britain; the surrender of Sir Charles Townshend's little army at Kut, after an agonizingly long-drawn-out siege, was a blow to British prestige comparable with the fall of Singapore twenty-five years later. Yet to say that British public opinion would have turned against the government if the rebels had been treated leniently is only to underline the basic problem of British rule in Ireland—the impossibility of working to purely Irish criteria.

The British response to Easter week reinforced, at several levels, the Irish demand for self-determination. Most importantly, it validated the insurrectionists' attitude to physical force. Dillon was surely right to say that the British, bungling the suppression of the rising by excessive force, made themselves the 'instrument' of the extremists. Yet Dillon's own response also signalled the decrepitude of the constitutionalist politics established by Parnell. The Irish Party, to be sure, was dying from internal paralysis as much as from external shock. The great machine was going the way of all machinery. But what occurred at Easter 1916 was the resuscitation of a very different conception of the political process. The rising was certainly a manifestation of political violence, but it was more than this: it was, to a large extent, a manifestation of violence as politics. It was not the prelude to a democratic national movement which led in turn to the establishment of a 'normal' constitutional national polity. It was, rather, a form of politics which may be called 'demonstration politics', the armed propaganda of a self-selected vanguard which claimed the power to interpret the general will. Cathartic action was substituted for methodical debate; ideal types replaced reality; symbols took on real powers. The Irish Republic, 'virtually established', would not now go away, yet it could never exist—not, at any rate, as the 'noble house' of Pearse's thought.

Demonstration politics proved infectious, perhaps because it simplifies so much. Striking an attitude is morally simpler than hammering out a compromise. The British followed lamely behind: the new Chief Secretary, H. E. Duke, observed in September 1916 that 'Martial law is important to Ireland chiefly as a declaration of policy'—it had no administrative value.[1] Dillon and the blighted constitutionalists, returning to the violent rhetoric of the 1880s, did in their own way likewise.

(v) *Towards insurgency*

> The never failing ingenuity of the Celt has discovered a method of evading martial law, and a series of great demonstrations are now going on at high masses for the souls of the executed men. The relations are received on their leaving church by enormous cheering crowds, and gradually these crowds are developing into processions and demonstrations singing patriotic songs.
>
> John Dillon[2]

> The practice of wearing Irish Volunteer uniforms is increasing, and bodies of men have on several occasions during the past few days been marching about in regular formation both in Dublin and in the county.
>
> Sir B. Mahon[3]

From a loyalist point of view, the worst thing about the martial-law regime was that it was ineffectual. It displayed once again the supreme difficulty of attempting to govern or regulate a modern society by military methods. It set the pattern of administrative policy for the two war years following the lifting of martial law and the departure of Maxwell in November 1916. H. E. Duke, who became the Chief Secretary, was in Alison Phillips's impatient phrase 'a meticulously jealous guardian' of the ordinary law.[4] Yet the extraordinary powers of the DOR Act remained, and continued to be commonly equated with martial law.[5] The government applied its greatest negotiating talent, in the shape of Lloyd George, to the problem of implementing home rule in tandem with conscription. But the failure of the 1916 initiative,

[1] Memo. by Chief Secretary for Ireland, Sept. 1916 (Bonar Law MSS 63/C/37).

[2] Dillon to Lloyd George, 11 June 1916 (Lloyd George MSS D/14/2/25).

[3] Sir B. Mahon to C.-in-C. Home Forces, 25 June 1917 (PRO W.O.32 9513).

[4] Phillips, op. cit. p. 114.

[5] In particular, there was general misunderstanding—wilful or otherwise—of the role of the courts martial.

and the long damp squib of the Convention in 1917 and
1918, destroyed any lingering hope that the Liberal programme of 1912 would be implemented. The face of government slipped back into its traditional expression of mild
coerciveness.[1]

The crisis of 1918 was, of course, precipitated not by
the British government or the Irish executive, but by the
German high command. The April offensive was the final,
and perhaps most crucial, intervention of the Great War in
Irish history. British desperation, 'backs to the wall and
believing in the justice of our cause', made conscription in
Ireland seem inevitable. In the event it remained a threat,
as it had been since 1916, but its political effect in 1918 was
unprecedented. The very persistence of the threat had in
the meantime created the circumstances for a regrouping of
the nationalist movement.

This process may be viewed through the career of Thomas
Ashe. One of the few surviving commandants of Easter week,
and the only one to have won a military victory, Ashe had
enormous prestige amongst nationalists after the Rising.
His earlier work in the Gaelic League gave him a certain
intellectual weight, while his position at the organizational
centre of the republican movement was attested by his
elevation to the presidency of the IRB Supreme Council.
Imprisoned in Lewes gaol, he was not directly involved in the
energetic rebuilding of the 'Sinn Féin' movement at local
level which followed the release of the Frongoch internees.[2]
But he played a catalytic role in the fusion of physical-
force and moral-force nationalists represented by the revived

---

[1] R. M. Henry, _Evolution of Sinn Féin_, p. 231, suggested that 'had the Prime
Minister and his advisers . . . deliberately set themselves to prove that they were
not the wise representatives of an enlightened and friendly democracy . . . but the
jealous and implacable guardians of a subject and hated race . . . it is very doubtful whether they could have bettered their record in a single detail'. Two out-
standingly intelligent historians have used phrases like 'almost inconceivable
foolhardiness' (F. S. L. Lyons) and 'astonishing obtuseness' (D. Fitzpatrick)
to characterize government policy in 1917-18. But Boyce and Hazlehurst, 'The
unknown Chief Secretary', p. 300, contend that Duke's coercive policy, 'far from
amounting to foolish pin-pricks . . . combined flexibility with firmness', and
(perhaps less convincingly) that it was 'fairly successful in containing political
violence'.

[2] H. E. Duke, remarks at War Cabinet, 19 Feb. 1917 (PRO CAB.23/1, W.C.73).

Sinn Féin. It was he who persuaded Joseph MacGuinness, a traditional IRB anti-parliamentarian, to allow himself to be put forward as Sinn Féin candidate at the South Longford by-election on 9 May 1917. According to his biographer, he decided that in returning to a parliamentary strategy the physical-force men 'were not giving recognition to the British parliament but giving the people an opportunity to support Irish freedom'.[1] Such pragmatism clearly marked a new awareness of the need for a mass base, and of the feasibility of channelling the tide of opinion which was rising in favour of the 'advanced' nationalists.

The election of MacGuinness, with the slogan 'put him in to get him out', confirmed the re-establishment of republican control of the national movement. Henceforth physical-force men, whether or not members of the IRB (some, most notably Cathal Brugha, now repudiated the old secret-society tradition), ousted political oddities such as Count Plunkett—and even Arthur Griffith—from leadership of the emerging Sinn Féin coalition.[2] Sinn Féin as a whole began to beat down the Irish parliamentary party and to break up—or take over—its local organization, the UIL. Thomas Ashe, released from Lewes prison, was asked to stand at the next by-election in Clare. His reluctance to enter politics directly (in spite of his advice to MacGuinness) produced the candidature of Eamon de Valera, the other surviving Easter week commandant. The Clare victory was a well-publicized triumph, but the central drama of 1917 was provided by Ashe, following a very different path.

During his first imprisonment, Ashe had conducted prison strikes to demand 'political' treatment—in effect prisoner of war status. Rearrested for an allegedly seditious speech at Ballinalee, Co. Longford, on 25 July, he commenced an uncompromising duel with the government by refusing food.[3] The authorities showed little grasp of the significance of the struggle which developed in Mountjoy gaol. They

---

[1] S. ÓLuing, *I Die in a Good Cause. A Study of Thomas Ashe, Idealist and Revolutionary* (Tralee, 1970), p. 121.

[2] There is a useful account of this process in M. Laffan, 'The unification of Sinn Féin 1917', *IHS* xiv (1971), 353–79.

[3] ÓLuing, op. cit. pp. 165–75.

could not, of course, have foreseen the future role of the hunger-strikes as a republican weapon—a weapon which fused moral appeal with self-directed violence. Yet they might have anticipated that a fatal outcome would have major political impact. Ashe's sudden death after four days of inexpert forcible feeding became in the event a martyrdom at least as potent as the 1916 executions. Only after it, when the damage had been done, did the government make a political response on the matter of prison conditions.[1]

His funeral, exploited with a skill for which a long tradition already existed, cemented the new national movement.[2] It was a great public occasion, and the first Fenian funeral in which a member of the Catholic hierarchy had participated. It also illuminated the new realism of the post-1916 organizers. Comparison between Pearse's speech at the funeral of O'Donovan Rossa in 1915, and the speech delivered by Michael Collins (only just emerging, as Pearse had been, from obscurity) at Ashe's funeral, is instructive. Pearse had delivered a long, traditionally rhetorical—or so most of his hearers must have assumed—oration, culminating in the cry 'the fools! the fools! the fools!—they have left us our Fenian dead, and while Ireland holds these graves, Ireland unfree shall never be at peace'. At Ashe's grave, the Volunteer guard of honour fired a volley, and Collins spoke only two sentences, charged with controlled violence;

Nothing additional remains to be said. The volley which we have just heard is the only speech which it is proper to make above the grave of a dead Fenian.[3]

Collins succeeded to Ashe's inheritance, both as President of the Supreme Council of the IRB and as, in the public mind, the *beau idéal* of the physical-force man.

---

[1] D. G. Boyce and C. Hazlehurst, 'The unknown Chief Secretary: H. E. Duke and Ireland, 1917–1918', *IHS* xx (1977), 298–9.

[2] R. Mulcahy, 'The Irish Volunteer Convention, 27 October 1917', *Capuchin Annual*, xxxiv (1967), 406.

[3] P. Béaslaí, *Michael Collins and the Making of a New Ireland* (London, 1926), i. 166. Interestingly, Macardle's account makes no mention of Collins's address; more unexpectedly, neither does Forester's. O' Broin gives only the second sentence, in a slightly different form.

Unnerved by the public reaction to Ashe's death, the administration retreated into 'cat and mouse' releases. As a result, one judge declared in November 1917 that the government of Ireland had been abandoned.[1] Simultaneously a hitherto unexampled level of organizational efficiency was injected into the movement by Collins, Mulcahy, and others. For the first time an effective command structure was established in Dublin itself, seen by Mulcahy as the strategic centre of Ireland. Within a few years an impressive degree of co-ordination was to be achieved, superficially at least. In reality the dynamism of the new 'Sinn Féin' depended on a mass of local initiatives.[2] Mulcahy himself later recorded, in his oblique manner, that 'small but important moves' had been made even before the release of the Frongoch men, by some of those who had escaped arrest or had been released in the summer and autumn of 1916.[3] The objective of these moves, he suggested, was 'the gathering together of the threads of organization for defence and resistance'—presumably against conscription. But he also admitted that there were other, older motives at work. There was an unmistakable resurgence of agrarian violence, caused primarily by the wartime increase in rural population as emigration was halted. Once more there was pressure on the land, even though the majority of farmers were enjoying a boom caused by war prices and shortages, due to the German submarine blockade.

The reappearance of cattle-driving, tree-felling, forced ploughing, or seizure and parcelling-out of land by rural groups was hardly welcome to the new Sinn Féin

---

[1] Phillips, op. cit. p. 135.

[2] Laffan, 'Unification of Sinn Féin', p. 368, points to—though he does not explain—'spontaneous local initiative' as the cause of Sinn Féin's rapid growth in 1917.

[3] Mulcahy, 'Irish Volunteer Convention', p. 401. A good picture of local activity may be found for Co. Wicklow, a very 'planted' area in which activists could not rely on many farmers' sons. The Volunteers acquired 30 or 40 Martini-Henry rifles from the National Volunteers early in 1916: these were confiscated by the police after the Easter Rising but, amazingly, returned when the Volunteer commandant complained. 'I started off again organising both Sinn Féin and the Volunteers. In every district where I got a Sinn Féin cumann, I saw that I got a Company of Volunteers . . . We soon had sufficient Companies to form two battalions . . .' (manuscript of C. M. Byrne, NLI MS 21142).

movement.[1] The new nationalist leaders were heirs to the social conservatism of their Fenian ancestors, and evinced equal distaste for the small-minded class war of the countryside. Mulcahy recorded that in 1918

> Instructions were issued to all *Sinn Féin cumainn* by the standing committee on 23 February that some of the many cattle drives appeared to be organized unjustly and without due regard to circumstances, emphasising that there was an important distinction between ranches strictly known as such, that is land untenanted or non-residential, and land occupied by relatively small farmers. It was instructed that the *cumann* had authority to organize or conduct a cattle drive without placing the facts before the *Comhairle Ceanntair* and receiving its sanction, and that in special cases references might be made to headquarters.[2]

But, as Mulcahy admitted, 'in many cases individual Volunteers including officers found it difficult not to be involved in agitational movements'.[3] It is clear that much, if not most, of the dynamism of the 'national' movement was agrarian.[4] The central headquarters busied itself in attempting to impose limits, to mould the mass of local Sinn Féin–Volunteer groups (which it hopefully called 'units') into a coherent whole, and to foster public awareness of the political aspect of the movement.[5] But it is unlikely that it would have had such success as it had in this attempt if it had not been for the conscription crisis in 1918.

In resistance to conscription, the Sinn Féin leadership found for the first time a national political issue which could mobilize the mass of the people. The passage of the 'oppressive and inhuman law' brought parliamentarians and Catholic bishops alike to the moral barricades, and many priests were

---

[1] H. D. Duke, however, believed that Sinn Féin was 'being used chiefly in fomenting agrarian trouble in the West and South' (Memo., 19 Feb. 1918, Bodleian, Additional Milner MSS C696/2).

[2] R. Mulcahy, 'Conscription and the General Headquarters' Staff', *Capuchin Annual*, xxxv (1968), 384.

[3] Ibid. Mulcahy made a brave effort to suggest that the 'food position'— i.e. nationalist resistance to British food control measures—brought up the agrarian issue: it 'involved the question of land utilisation; this evoked thoughts of land ownership and division; and from this there arose problems . . .'.

[4] J. A. Gaughan, *Constable Jeremiah Mee, RIC*, pp. 51–2; Hepburn, *Conflict of Nationality*, pp. 106–7.

[5] Ibid.

ready to think in terms of less abstract defences.[1] The pressure continued to intensify. The government, after teetering on the brink of placing the Viceroyalty in commission, appointed Lord French to the post on 11 May. The public impact of this transfer of the Commander-in-Chief, Home Forces, can scarcely be exaggerated: French looked like, and felt like, a military governor, who had been sent to impose conscription, if necessary against resistance.[2] Finally, as if to cement Irish opposition, the unconvincing 'German plot' was brought forth in order to arrest the outstanding Sinn Féin leaders.

A year earlier, Sinn Féin would scarcely have been able to capitalize on this. But in the autumn of 1917 it had managed to create a unified organization, with a leadership acclaimed at the Sinn Féin and Irish Volunteer conventions in October, and a simple political programme. Although deep disagreements persisted, two policies were clarified: the method of abstention (the strict Sinn Féin concept), and the objective of the Republic. The latter was not universally accepted, but it remained, in the Fenian tradition, loosely defined.[3] In voting for Republican candidates at the general election of 1918, nobody could be quite sure what sort of political arrangements were being favoured. Abstentionism was also not unreservedly accepted by all nominal Sinn Féiners, but after April 1918 it was overwhelmingly popular. In short, the Sinn Féin political programme was sufficiently clear to be convincing, and sufficiently loose to be unconstricting. The place of violence in the movement was, like other things, vague. It has rightly been pointed out that the shift of Irish opinion after the 1916 executions towards sympathy with the insurgents 'did not necessarily imply an acceptance of violence as the answer to Irish problems'.[4] But violence

[1] There is an interesting short examination of the church's relationship with Sinn Féin in Henry, op. cit. pp. 271-3.

[2] Holmes, *French*, pp. 383 ff. One modern writer also believes him to have been such: A. J. Ward, 'Lloyd George and the 1918 Irish Conscription Crisis', *Historical Journal*, xvii (1974), 115.

[3] 'The Republic', as Fitzpatrick observes, 'like the Nation once Again, was a vessel into which each man could pour his own dream' (*Politics and Irish Life*, p. 146).

[4] R. Davis, 'The Advocacy of Passive Resistance in Ireland, 1916-1922', *Anglo-Irish Studies*, iii (1977), 37.

undoubtedly remained *an* answer, necessary if not sufficient. The war atmosphere could only emphasize its relevance. An article called 'Ruthless Warfare' in an early edition of the new Volunteer journal *An tOglach* in October 1918 fixed the tone of the new physical-force men. Pungently reversing England's anti-German 'atrocity' propaganda, Ernest Blythe wrote of the still-threatened conscription that

If England decided on this atrocity, then we, on our part, must decide that in our resistance we shall acknowledge no limit and no scruple. We must recognize that anyone, civilian or soldier, who assists directly or by connivance in this crime against us, merits no more consideration than a wild beast, and should be killed without mercy or hesitation as opportunity offers . . . Thus the man who serves on an exemption tribunal, the doctor who treats soldiers or examines conscripts, the man who voluntarily surrenders when called for, the man who in any shape or form applies for an exemption, the man who drives a police-car or assists in the transport of army supplies, all these having assisted the enemy must be shot or otherwise destroyed with the least possible delay.

The hard-bitten realism of this attitude to violence permitted, indeed caused, the development of a new strategy. Its spirit was well conveyed in a letter of Michael Collins to his (then) friend Austin Stack in Belfast gaol: if the present effort fails, 'why we can go into the wilderness again & maybe be better prepared for the next clash'.[1] The strategy of low-level fighting, 'protracted war' in Mao Tse-tung's phrase, a dispersed application of force which can eventually be recognized as guerrilla insurgency, had already begun to appear in 1918. By the spring of that year much of Ireland, and in particular such traditionally 'disturbed' counties as Clare, had once again become virtually ungovernable.[2] But now the traditional agrarian disturbance was to some extent modified and co-ordinated by the sophisticated central command run by Brugha, Collins, Mulcahy, and others. Arms raids developed spontaneously, and the central staff even tried at first to prohibit or limit them. Cathal Brugha reacted furiously when he heard of a shooting incident with the police in Co. Cork. Mulcahy, newly named Chief of Staff, whose relations with the Brugha were from now on less than

[1] Collins to Stack, 7 Oct. 1918 (NLI MS 5848).
[2] Fitzpatrick, op. cit. p. 151.

satisfactory, reflected more philosophically that 'we all had a complete understanding of the limitations and responsibities of the Volunteers'.[1] Such flexible attitudes permitted the avoidance of internal clashes, and fostered the semblance of overall direction which was greatly to increase the political impact of the subsequent campaign of violence.

[1] Mulcahy, 'Conscription', p. 387.

7
Guerrilla Struggle

No nation has ever established its title deeds by a campaign of assassination. The British nation, having come grimly through the slaughter of Armageddon, are certainly not going to be scared by the squalid scenes of sporadic warfare which are being enacted across the Irish channel . . . no course is open to the Government but to take every possible measure to break the murder campaign and to enforce the authority of the law, while at the same time pressing forward the Home Rule Bill.

Winston Churchill[1]

(i) *The end of Constitutionalism*

Honest and intelligent men can always agree on some solution for a question.

H. E. Duke[2]

The intensely British belief that to all political problems a more or less workable 'solution' can be found was to be vindicated, in the short term, between 1911 and 1922. A form of Dominion status was accepted by Sinn Féin leaders for twenty-six Irish counties. The other six lapsed into quiescence under the restricted authority of the only devolved parliament in the United Kingdom. The solution was inelegant but apparently workable, dictated by stubborn realities rather than nationalist or imperialist theories. Lloyd George solved the 'Irish question'—only, as A. J. P. Taylor has pointed out, to be ruined by his success.[3] For Ireland the damage was less sudden and spectacular, but even before the recrudescence of violence fifty years later cracks could be discerned in the façade of settlement. Through them unpleasant débris persistently seeped. The failure of home

---

[1] Article in *Illustrated Sunday Herald*, 13 June 1920.
[2] R. B. McDowell, *The Irish Convention 1917–18* (London, 1970), p. 68; Redmond MSS, T. P. O'Connor to J. Devlin, 15, 16 Feb. 1917.
[3] A. J. P. Taylor, *English History 1914–1945* (Oxford, 1965), p. 161.

rule involved irreparable damage to constitutionalism as a method, and also, perhaps, to the very idea of constitutionalism modelled on the British way in politics. The gun had been brought back into high politics by the Ulster Unionists, but the peculiar form of legitimation which it represented was to flourish on both sides of the new border.

The government contributed materially to the undermining of constitutionalism after 1916 by repeatedly deferring the implementation of home rule. The time-scale originally envisaged when home rule was shelved 'for the duration' was of the order of six months: no one believed that a European war could last longer than that. Nearly two years after the outbreak of war Lloyd George's efforts at a compromise were rendered nugatory by the government's inability to push 'loyal' Ulster into the domain of a nationalist Ireland now tainted with an additional manifestation of disloyalty. Unionist ministers had come as far as accepting home rule in some form, perhaps even before the end of the war: as Balfour noted, if further disorders were to break out during the war he would 'much rather at this moment see a Home Rule government charged with their suppression, than the Imperial government'.[1] But if so they were determined to 'exclude from its operation as much of Unionist Ireland as is possible': Balfour held by the old slogan that 'rather than submit to Nationalist rule Ulster would fight—and Ulster would be right'.[2]

After nearly three years of war, H. E. Duke's administration took hopeful refuge in the device of an Irish Convention. Its faith in the willingness of 'honest and intelligent men' to reach honourable compromise was impressive. The political acumen which led it to conceive that workable arrangements might be made by the Convention was less so. Or is it mere hindsight that sees the old Irish party as doomed to destruction in 1917? Duke believed that an immediate measure of home rule would have salvaged its position. A run of Nationalist election victories in 1918 seemed to support this belief.[3] Yet those by-election successes were not comparable with those

---

[1] Memo. by A. J. Balfour, 24 June 1916 (Whittingehame, Balfour MSS 32).
[2] Ibid.
[3] Cf. O. MacDonagh, *Ireland:the Union and its Aftermath*, p. 90.

of Sinn Féin in the previous year. More important, Duke failed to persuade the Cabinet to guarantee home rule as the price of Irish conscription. On 13 April 1918 he succinctly presented a stark choice:

There are two modes of meeting the imminent crisis. One is an immediate and rigorous course of coercion with wide-spread and preventive arrests. The other is to secure a Home Rule settlement on the terms of Ireland's cooperation in the war. One conclusive reason for the latter course, to my mind, is that the former seems to me impossible as a practical policy.[1]

But the logic which led Duke one way led the Cabinet the other. Three days later Lord French was ordered to Ireland to prepare for the enforcement of conscription. He cut through the restraints which Duke had imposed on the military commander in Ireland, and implemented the policy of mass arrests.[2] The unfortunate results of this policy are substantially attested. It was undertaken in clear opposition to Duke's view that there had not so far, in the 'predatory' Sinn Féin agrarian campaign, been 'any occasion when the interference with the rights of property was attended by conduct amounting to riot which would have warranted repression by armed force.'[3]

Duke had, however, been aware that the basis of the problem in 1918 was 'the avowed determination of the Sinn Féin Leaders to make administration impossible'.[4] Duke had no real idea how to cope with such a subversive opponent. French thought he had; for the next year he applied his energies to prosecuting Sinn Féin on a broad front, aiming at the arrest not only of the leaders but also of the rank and file —which he saw, not absurdly, as a surplus population group, kept in Ireland artificially by the suspension of emigration. To do this he required strong legal measures, in effect martial law. Ironically, most people in Ireland—including some in the administration itself—believed that martial law was still in force.[5] In fact, in 1918, French's most strenuous and persistent

---

[1] War Cabinet, 5 Apr. 1918 (PRO CAB. 23/6); Ward, 'Lloyd George and the Irish Conscription Crisis', pp. 112–13.

[2] Gen. Mahon to Milner, 20 May 1918 (Milner Add. MSS 696/1).

[3] Memo. by Chief Secretary, 19 Feb. 1918 (loc. cit.).

[4] Ibid.

[5] R. M. Henry declared that at the end of the war 'martial law was not relaxed

efforts failed to persuade the government to return to the measure it had applied (in name at least) so liberally in 1916. His attempt to suppress Sinn Féin had to be carried out through the mechanism of Balfour's Crimes Act, coupled with certain provisions of the Defence of the Realm Act. Several counties were 'proclaimed', and Special Military Areas were established to impose controls and punishments upon communities. The overall effect was to give colour to Sinn Féin's portrayal of the government as militarist and repressive, without doing real damage to the developing Sinn Féin-Volunteer organization. The overwhelming Sinn Féin victory in the 1918 general election may not demonstrate a popular mandate for the 'Republic',[1] but it must show general resistance to the administration's policy.

The virtual annihilation of the parliamentary party was thus to a large extent the government's own work. This would have made more sense if the new coalition government had resolved to abandon its attempt to find a *via media* between Nationalists and Ulster Unionists. Appearances notwithstanding, this was not the case. The unconscionable delay in returning to the work of framing a new Home Rule Bill was not deliberate. It was rather the result of the government's perplexity, and its confused reaction to the establishment of Dáil Éireann and the Republican 'government' in the first half of 1919. Even Walter Long, hard-bitten leader of Tory backwoods opinion, who now became the Cabinet's principal intermediary with Ireland, toyed with federalism and the voguish 'home rule all round' idea.[2] Long recognized at the end of 1918, however, that Sinn Féin was 'much the most difficult and dangerous' Irish political organization that the government had faced in the last forty years. He warned grittily that 'it is a fair and square fight between the Irish

or revoked' (*Evolution of Sinn Féin*, p. 277). For the belief of one military intelligence officer, see C. Townshend, *The British Campaign in Ireland 1919-1921* (Oxford, 1975), p. 4.

[1] The best analysis is B. Farrell, *The Founding of Dáil Éireann: Parliament and Nation-Building* (Dublin, 1971), esp. pp. 45-50; see also J. A. Murphy, *Ireland in the Twentieth Century* (Dublin, 1975), pp. 6-7.

[2] On federalism see J. E. Kendle, 'The Round Table Movement and "Home Rule All Round" ', *Historical Journal*, xi, 2 (1968), and 'Federalism and the Irish Problem in 1918', *History*, lvi. 187 (1971).

Government and Sinn Féin as to who is going to govern the country'.[1] In this perception he was following a traditional administrative tendency, albeit with greater justification than had often been the case. The perception of challenge all but dictated the priorities of response. First, the 'restoration of law and order', the enforcement of a return to constitutionalism, and only thereafter the effort to find a political settlement. As before, coercion and conciliation were seen as inseparable. And as usual, few ministers paid much regard to Ireland.[2] None of them, whether Liberal or Conservative, seem to have wondered whether the very necessity of using force to 'restore order' indicated that the ground-base of normality had been fatally eroded.

This erosion, which as will be seen was to cause the stalling of police and military efforts to crush the Republican extremists, resulted in a leisurely schedule for the new home rule measure. As late as September 1919 the Cabinet had to be reminded that as soon as the Treaty of Sèvres was ratified the war would be unarguably over, and the 1914 Home Rule Act would come into operation—unless some new measure replaced it.[3] An Irish Committee was established, into which Lord French was brought, with a seat in the Cabinet. The committee was chaired by Long, who had now come out openly in support of federalism as an arrangement which would side-step the problem of Ulster exclusion and prevent Sinn Féin (which he regarded as irreconcilable) from taking a home rule Ireland towards total separation.[4] Early in November the committee admitted that the Versailles settlements left the Irish issue in rather embarrassing prominence, but rejected the 1914 Act as unworkable. Instead it proposed —since full-blown federalism had failed to gain general acceptance—the creation of two Irish parliaments.[5] As with

[1] Cabinet Memo. by Secretary of State for Colonies, 31 Dec. 1918 (PRO GT 6574, CAB. 24 72/1).
[2] K. O. Morgan, *Consensus and Disunity: the Lloyd George Coalition Government 1918-1922* (Oxford, 1979), pp. 35, 125-32 *passim*. The slight treatment of Ireland in this substantial study underlines the point.
[3] Corr. with Att.-Gen., Sept. 1919 (CAB. 24 89, GT 8210).
[4] Cabinet Memo. by First Lord of Admiralty, 24 Sept. 1919 (CAB. 24 89, GT 8215).
[5] Cabinet Committee on Irish Q., 4 Nov. 1919 (CAB. 24 92, CP 56); Cabinet, 11 Nov. 1919 (C.5 (19), CAB. 23 18).

previous home rule proposals, certain major powers were to be reserved to Westminster. A new vehicle for the increasingly elusive Irish unity was, however, put forward in the Council of Ireland—a body which was to be given further powers if the two parliaments co-operated in it.

The framework for the future was effectively laid down. All that remained was to determine the precise area which was to constitute the separated 'Northern Ireland', and to persuade Nationalists to accept the remainder (an area which had no official name until the creation of the Free State, though the incongruous title 'Southern Ireland' was frequently used). The former problem was settled with a rapidity possible only because Nationalists had been left out of the discussion. The Cabinet itself favoured the separation of the whole 'historic' province of Ulster—nine counties—which looked more viable as a polity and less openly sectarian in its basis than the smaller (four- or six-county) options.[1] The Ulster Unionists themselves simply insisted on six, without argument.[2] By late February 1920 the Cabinet reluctantly brought itself to acquiesce in their demand, reasoning no doubt that if an unsatisfactory solution had to be accepted, it might as well be one that was satisfactory to at least one of the parties.[3]

In this shape the bill went slowly forward, becoming law on 23 December 1920. Elections to the two parliaments were to be held some time before March 1922. However, the problem of finding politically credible Nationalists to work the Southern parliament continued to defy solution. The government remained pinned to its self-imposed task of restoring orderly conditions in which satisfactory elections could take place. By the end of 1920 it was faced with the

[1] Cabinet, 3, 19 Dec. 1919 (C.10, 16 (19), CAB. 23 18). In view of the stress later placed on the 'historic' province of Ulster by Republicans, it is worth recalling that the nine-county province was an English administrative creation, not a Gaelic survival.

[2] On the UUC's demand, and objections from Unionists in Cavan, Donegal, and Monaghan, see P. Buckland (ed.), *Irish Unionism 1885–1923* (NIPRO 1973), pp. 409-20.

[3] The precise process by which the decision was reached is not clear. For attempts at elucidation see D. G. Boyce, *Englishmen and Irish Troubles: British Public Opinion and the Making of Irish Policy 1918–22* (London, 1972), pp. 109-10; C. Townshend, *British Campaign*, pp. 35-6.

fact that the party which would sweep the board in these elections, 'irreconcilable' Sinn Féin, had already gone a long way towards turning itself into an effective rival government. The illegal Irish Republic appeared to exist not only in the minds of fanatical idealists, but on the ground also.

(ii) *The Republic*

> Deputies, you understand from what is asserted in this Declaration that we are now done with England. Let the world know it and those who are concerned bear it in mind. For come what may now, whether it be death itself, the great deed is done.
>
> Cathal Brugha[1]

As has been suggested, objective interpretation of the 1918 election in Ireland indicates that it was not, as Republicans later maintained, a popular mandate for the establishment of a republic *sensu stricto*.[2] The term 'Republican' had been loosely used. For the general public it implied a more aggressively anti-governmental stance than that of the parliamentary party.[3] Arthur Griffith, a monarchist by political nature, was seen as a Republican in this sense, as John O'Leary had been before him. Effective refinement of the concept of the Republic was not to begin until the debate on the Treaty in 1921-2.

However, the men (and still more the woman, Constance Markievicz) elected in December 1918 were undoubtedly separatists committed to methods of action radically different from those of previous Nationalist groups. They might not all have 'done with England' in the way Cathal Brugha would have liked, but they had done with constitutionalism and also with insurrectionism. Their action in assembling on 21 January 1919 as Dáil Éireann, the Parliament of Ireland, was in itself revolutionary. It determined that Irish resistance was henceforth to be expressed through the medium of a

---

[1] Cathal Brugha, Speaker of Dáil Éireann, 21 Jan. 1919: D. Macardle, *The Irish Republic*, p. 253.

[2] Kevin O'Higgins's campaign speeches, for instance, made no mention of the term 'Republic': T. de V. White, *Kevin O'Higgins* (London, 1948), p. 26.

[3] S. Cronin, *Irish Nationalism. A History of its Roots and Ideology* (Dublin, 1980), p. 24.

rival government; a government which unequivocally declared itself to be a state.[1] It created the rudiments of a new political framework: a focus for the claim to national sovereignty, and an executive body claiming public allegiance.[2] Thereafter these bare essentials were fleshed out as the new 'de jure and de facto government' developed a widening range of (often frankly imitative) attributes.

The ideological base of the 'revolution', however, remained very narrow. A rigid insistence on the primacy of nationality characterized the demand for self-determination. This idea of nationality continued to be founded on an almost atavistic sense of identity, notwithstanding Griffith's selective interest in modernity (and, notwithstanding Sinn Féin's non-sectarian attitude, on a deeply Catholic sense of identity).[3] A sense of democratic values existed, but was modified by the belief that Sinn Féin understood what ought to be the will of the people if they were sufficiently nationally aware. Such a Robespierrist vision of the public good contained authoritarian tendencies, which were amplified from other sources. Thus, as Sinn Féin took over the old Irish party apparatus, it also took over its managerial attitudes: one significant result was the conduct of the Sinn Féin convention in May, a display of calculated rigging which reduced democracy to mere game-playing (and recalled the 1909 National Convention, christened the 'baton convention' by William O'Brien, principal victim of the party's strong-arm methods).[4]

The Republic declared by Dáil Éireann was, of course, a one-party state. This was not, as it may appear, inevitable. The Irish Labour party forwent its chance of making a

[1] It has been argued by E. Larkin that an Irish 'state' was effectively in existence by the mid 1880s; however, D. W. Miller's use of the term 'nation' as distinct from 'state' for the dominant Irish political movement up to 1921 is to be preferred, though even this is potentially confusing: *Church, State and Nation*, pp. 559-60 nn. 23, 28.

[2] As de Valera announced in the Dáil on 10 April 1919 (at a public session held in the Dublin Mansion House under the protection of the British police), the Irish people owed 'neither respect nor attachment nor obedience' to 'the other power claiming authority'. 'The sole authority in this country is the authority of the elected representatives of the Irish Nation': R. Mulcahy, 'Chief of Staff 1919', *Capuchin Annual*, xxxvi (1969), 340-1.

[3] Miller, *Church, State and Nation*, p. 495.

[4] J. V. O'Brien, *William O'Brien*, pp. 187-8.

significant impact on the new electorate of 1918, sacrificing itself as had James Connolly on the altar of national unity in the optimistic belief that Sinn Féin's sense of nationality could embrace the idea of social reform.[1] This hope was without much substance. Admittedly, Pearse's sentimental socialism became, after 1916, an ineradicable component of Irish nationalism. However, the harder edge of republican tunnel vision was better displayed by MacDermott, who privately denounced Larkin as 'a danger nationally': 'socialism and the sympathetic strike' were in his view 'dangerous ruinous weapons' which would bring further destruction to Irish manufacture. In addition, he observed, 'all this talk about the friendliness of the English working man and of the Brotherhood of man . . . have a very bad unnational influence'.[2] The 1917 Sinn Féin convention, while affirming the right of workers to a 'fair and reasonable wage', also called on Irish Labour to sever its connection with the British trades union movement. The new official Labour journal *Irish Opinion* commented tartly that the first resolution was one 'to which the assent of even Mr. W. M. Murphy might have been secured'; and referred without enthusiasm to de Valera's vague announcement that 'in a free Ireland, with the social conditions that obtained in Ireland, Labour had a far better chance than it would have in a capitalist England'.[3] De Valera's demand that Labour help to free the country before 'looking for its own share of its patrimony' smacked at best of condescension, at worst of the distaste shown by earlier Fenian purists. *Irish Opinion* observed pertinently 'There are free countries, even Republics, where labour claims "its share in its patrimony" in vain'.

Yet, in spite of this, Irish Labour deferred to Sinn Féin at the crisis of the general election.[4] It never recovered

---

[1] It is of course possible that Labour would have done even worse if it had stood in 1918. Cf. the brief but lucid argument in T. Garvin, *The Evolution of Irish Nationalist Politics* (New York, 1981), pp. 119-20.

[2] MacDermott to McGarrity, 12 Dec. 1913 (NLI, McGarrity MSS 17618).

[3] Quoted in R. M. Henry, *Evolution of Sinn Féin*, pp. 273-4.

[4] B. Farrell, 'Labour and the Irish Political Party system: a suggested approach to analysis', *Economic and Social Review*, i. 4 (July 1970); M. Gallagher, 'Socialism and the Nationalist Tradition in Ireland, 1798-1918', *Eire-Ireland*, xii. 2 (summer 1977).

from its self-abnegation. The Republic remained predictably unenthusiastic towards it. The 'Democratic Programme' adopted at the first meeting of Dáil Éireann was first watered down and then left to evaporate.[1] Even Labour's valiant attempts to obey de Valera's injunction to 'help free the country'—the 'Limerick Soviet' of April 1919, the strike against Motor Permits in the winter of 1919–20, the one-day general strike for the release of hunger-striking Sinn Féin prisoners in April 1920, and above all the long munitions embargo from May to December 1920[2]—were to be relegated to footnotes in future accounts of the national struggle. The Irish revolution was made by labourers and small farmers—at least it was they who supplied the rank and file of the Volunteer forces—but it was socially conservative.[3]

Its intense traditionalism guaranteed that, early Sinn Féin doctrine notwithstanding, the Republic would be surrounded by organized violence. Initial doubts on this matter were more apparent than real. Certainly, the first Volunteer attack in which deaths were inflicted on the police, at Solo-headbeg in Co. Tipperary, was regarded with strong disfavour by many Sinn Féiners. The fact that it occurred on the very day of the first meeting of Dáil Éireann was no more than an odd coincidence, though it was one which was unlikely to appear as such to the government.[4]

Sinn Féin politicians repeatedly tried to put a brake on Volunteer activities, and the Dáil did not bring itself to take public responsibility for the 'military' campaign until April 1921.[5] But the Volunteers themselves never hesitated in their course, and simply assumed that the Declaration of

---

[1] P. Lynch 'The social revolution that never was', in T. D. Williams (ed.), *The Irish Struggle 1916–1926* (London, 1966), pp. 41–54; Fitzpatrick, *Politics and Irish Life*, pp. 254–67.

[2] See C. Townshend, 'The Irish railway strike of 1920: industrial action and civil resistance in the struggle for independence', *IHS* xxi. 83 (March 1979).

[3] Fitzpatrick, op. cit. pp. 203–4, on social profile of Volunteers; 267–80 on 'conservative resurgence'.

[4] Dan Breen, not always the most reliable of witnesses, is undoubtedly correct in stressing the political hostility with which his group was met between Solo-headbeg and the Knocklong Station rescue: *My Fight for Irish Freedom* (Dublin, 1924), chs. 5–7.

[5] K. Nowlan, 'Dáil Éireann and the Army: unity and division (1919–1921)', in Williams (ed.), *Irish Struggle*, pp. 67–77.

Independence had given them absolute legitimacy. The gradual adoption by Volunteer units of the title 'Irish Republican Army' expressed this sense of legitimacy, as did the Volunteer journal *An tÓglach* ('The Volunteer') when it announced (on 31 January 1919) that England and Ireland were at war, and that Volunteers were henceforth justified in 'treating the armed forces of the enemy . . . exactly as a National Army would treat the members of an invading army'.[1]

This declaration was, in Fenian tradition, largely rhetorical. In fact the British forces could not be treated in this way, because they were not like an invading army: they were thoroughly established in every townland of the country. The 'National Army', for its part, was an irregular congeries of local groups which in 1919 were incapable of bringing the smallest military or even police unit to battle. The campaign which these groups developed was quite different from most wars with which soldiers were acquainted. It was shaped by the determination of a few local leaders, primarily in Tipperary, Cork, Clare, Limerick, and Kerry, to strike at the British in any way possible. In these areas Volunteer companies had sprung up in 1917 and 1918 with the spontaneity previously shown by agrarian secret societies, and like their predecessors had begun to arm themselves by seizing weapons and explosives in small quantities.[2] Unlike their predecessors the Volunteers also initiated a relentless and aggressive public boycott of the police, a measure of their political confidence and single-mindedness. By the time that the Volunteer executive in Dublin created a 'General Headquarters' to weld into a military campaign the potentially erratic actions of local groups, the most successful companies were capable of—and preparing for—small attacks on the police.[3] These companies, which had chosen their own officers, never entirely accepted the hierarchical control

---

[1] R. Mulcahy, Notes on the use and origin of the title 'Irish Republican Army' (UCD, Mulcahy MSS P7/D/1/99); P. Béaslai, *Michael Collins and the Making of a New Ireland* (London, 1926), i, 274-5.

[2] L. Deasy, *Towards Ireland Free* (Cork, 1973), pp. 27-56, gives a picture of early organization in West Cork.

[3] F. O'Donoghue, 'Guerilla Warfare in Ireland 1919-1921', *An Cosantoir*, xxiii (May 1963), 294-7.

implicit in the term 'army'. They remained first and foremost groups held together by personal or local loyalties.[1]

The first and most successful organizational effort of the Volunteer GHQ was the regularization of brigade areas in 1918. Some counties accepted Collins's scheme with more or less good grace. In one or two, however, local realities proved too strong for central regulation even in the technical sphere. Co. Clare, for instance, had to be given three brigades so that rival families—Brennans, Barretts, and O'Donnells—could be incorporated. GHQ's attempts to stimulate the organization of Volunteers in quiescent areas enjoyed only modest success.[2] Its final attempt to forge a more centralized hierarchy of command, by creating 'divisions' in the spring of 1921, was likewise equivocal.

Most unexpectedly, GHQ was unable to use the IRB as a nervous system through which central control could be exercised. The IRB remained in existence, indeed. In some areas IRB men took the lead in rebuilding or extending the Volunteer organization in 1917-18.[3] There is, however, little basis for the widespread belief that the IRB shaped and inspired the whole movement.[4] Michael Collins's position as president of the supreme council undoubtedly gave him some additional influence; it enhanced his aura of power, of being a 'big fella', but it did not give him direct control of certain areas where the IRB had been rejected.[5] In addition, several important figures—most notably de Valera and Brugha—had left the Brotherhood, maintaining that the secret society was a harmful survival in an age when the national movement had achieved a mass following. To say

[1] There is evidence of 'independent' Volunteer companies operating in the same areas as 'official' units in narratives in Collins MSS, NLI Pos. 921.

[2] Cf. C. Townshend, 'The Irish Republican Army and the development of guerrilla warfare 1916-21', *English Historical Review*, xciv. 371 (April 1979).

[3] Though Deasy's remark that 'at the back of all these activities hovered the guiding spirit of the Irish Republican Brotherhood' typifies the vagueness with which this connection has been made. Cf. also J. O'Beirne Ranelagh, 'The Irish Republican Brotherhood 1916-24 (Univ. of Kent Ph.D. thesis, 1978), p. 202 (on Sean MacEoin).

[4] e.g. in M. Forester, *Michael Collins* (London, 1971), p. 71.

[5] e.g. in Tipperary: N. J. McGrath, 'A Provincial View of the National Struggle in Ireland 1916-1921—the Case of Tipperary', (Univ. of Keele BA dissertation, 1979), pp. 9, 14.

that Brugha 'was a natural adherent to IRB principles' is very different from saying that he accepted the IRB's position in practice.[1] The old organization was fast losing its pre-eminence and becoming a potential instrument of division.[2] The national movement had outgrown it, in physical scale and also, perhaps, in political sophistication.

The real mechanism through which the Volunteer GHQ was able to exert control was a more abstract one: the process of military professionalization which began to affect, to a greater or lesser extent, the most active units.[3] The primary agent of this process was the guerrilla campaign itself. This campaign, sporadic and almost directionless at the outset, gradually developed a logic and a momentum which drew the Volunteer organization on. Three broad phases in this process can be identified up to the end of 1920. The first was a long period of low-level operations: the boycott of the RIC, occasional violent assaults on isolated policemen, raids for arms, and so on, beginning in 1918 (in some areas, perhaps, earlier still) and continuing until the winter of 1919-20. Soloheadbeg was merely an intensification of these activities, as was Liam Lynch's seizure of military rifles at Fermoy in September 1919. Their result was to drive in the outposts of the RIC. For the first time, the smaller huts containing three or four constables became untenable over wide areas. During the winter the police were withdrawn and concentrated in more defensible 'barracks', with eight or twelve men in each.[4] The RIC, having been with some success morally isolated from the

---

[1] O'Beirne Ranelagh, op. cit. pp. 198-9.

[2] Cf. R. Brennan, *Allegiance*, p. 156. At the same time the loyalty of its own members was necessarily becoming divided. Its revised constitution in Sept. 1919 relinquished its claim to be the government of the republic (to the Dáil), but, inconsistently, retained the claim to Presidency of the republic: O'Beirne Ranelagh, op. cit. pp. 202, 227-8. Cf. J. M. Curran, 'The Decline and Fall of the IRB', *Eire-Ireland*, x. 1 (1975), 16-18; Mulcahy, 'Chief of Staff', pp. 345-6. According to Mulcahy's recollection elsewhere, 'the IRB never interfered in policy in any way and as far as my experience is concerned, the members of the IRB were absorbed in the Intelligence Department that worked under Collins' (Notes, Mulcahy MSS P7/D/36).

[3] See Mulcahy's oddly phrased remarks on 'initiative in a crude state' and 'the malaise in the army command in South Tipperary', in 'Chief of Staff', p. 347.

[4] Townshend, *British Campaign*, pp. 27-8.

community by the boycott, was now clearly pushed towards physical isolation.

The second phase was the inevitable consequence. The Volunteers, having no more easy targets across the countryside, were able—or forced—to develop ways of tackling the larger police posts. Weakly held and amateurishly fortified though they were (with hastily rigged iron shutters and sandbags), these posts were prickly targets. Few Volunteer units were ever able to take them on successfully. Most of the time the only aggression they could manage was sniping at barracks at night, or at patrols by day. The most active units, however, launched a series of full-scale attacks, beginning with that at Carrigtwohill, Co. Cork, in January 1920.[1] In May the barrack at Kilmallock, Co. Limerick, scene of a dramatic assault in 1867, was still more spectacularly burned after an all-night battle. Altogether sixteen occupied barracks were destroyed and twenty-nine damaged during the first six months of 1920. In addition, over four hundred abandoned posts were burned and left as charred signs of the authorities' retreat.[2] Coupled with renewed intimidation of jurors, this pressure brought about the virtual paralysis of the British legal system by the summer. The Dáil assisted in this process by establishing alternative lawcourts, which began, significantly, as arbitration courts to settle land disputes.[3] As will be seen, the British reaction to the humiliation of the summer assizes was to abandon the conciliatory policy initiated in the spring, and to take a definite step towards military rule.[4] The Volunteers thus guaranteed, intentionally or not, the failure of political initiatives and the cohesion of the Republican movement behind the physical-force group.

It was the British intensification of military control under the Restoration of Order in Ireland Act which contributed most directly to the third and most coherent phase of the

---

[1] According to Mulcahy this was the first 'official' attack sanctioned by GHQ. A policy of 'aggression' was, he said, only adopted after the suppression of Dáil Éireann by the government in Sept. 1919: O'Beirne Ranelagh, op. cit. pp. 204, 207; Mulcahy, 'Chief of Staff', pp. 351-2.

[2] Townshend, op. cit. p. 65.

[3] Dáil Éireann, *The Constructive Work of Dáil Éireann* (Dublin, 1921), i. 6, 22.

[4] See below, p. 350.

Volunteer campaign. As the government's hunt for the 'gunmen' and 'murder gang' became more effective, local Volunteers were finally pushed into abandoning their homes and jobs and going 'on the run', in unprecedented numbers. These men formed the basis of the permanent fighting formations—'Active Service Units' in GHQ parlance, 'flying columns' in the vernacular—which appeared in the autumn. Like so many previous creations these were not planned by central headquarters but, in the words of the commandant of the East Clare column, were 'a purely spontaneous development which arose directly from the prevailing conditions'.[1] Several of the most celebrated columns were already formed when GHQ picked up the idea and issued orders for its universal application. The burgeoning of the concept thereafter was probably due not so much to obedience to GHQ as to the inherent appeal, both functional and romantic, of the columns: every brigade, indeed every battalion worth its salt, wanted to have one. By the winter of 1920-1 there were several dozen of them.

The nature of the columns permitted frequent attempts at ambushing of military and police patrols. Ambushes had occasionally been tried before, but they are sophisticated operations which require extensive preparation as well as skilful execution. From September 1920 the number of successful ambushes increased, provoking police reprisals and causing a clear movement of British public opinion away from the government. The culminating event in this phase was the shock annihilation of an élite Auxiliary Division patrol by the West Cork column at Kilmichael on 28 November, which, together with 'Bloody Sunday', transformed British official perceptions of the struggle and paved the way for the reintroduction of martial law.[2]

The columns performed another function, however. Their need for professional training in properly supervised camps gave GHQ its long-sought leverage within the Volunteer

---

[1] Townshend, 'Irish Republican Army', p. 330.

[2] Boyce, *Englishmen and Irish Troubles*, ch. 4; Townshend, *British Campaign*, ch. 12. For a discussion of Tom Barry's account of Kilmichael (*Guerrilla Days in Ireland* (Tralee, 1949), chs. VII-VII) see Deasy, op. cit. pp. 170-2; E. Butler, *Barry's Flying Column* (London, 1971), pp. 62-8; T. Barry, *The Reality of the Anglo-Irish War 1920-21 in West Cork* (Tralee, 1974), pp. 13-18.

officer-corps. At last there was a mechanism by which incompetent or inactive local leaders could be got at: as GHQ noted in April 1921, the Active Service unit was 'not only a standing force of shock troops' [*sic*]; but 'also training units—and it is this that is their most important function'.

The Unit is a testing and a teaching force where those fit for leadership get practice, and those unfit are found out before they have a chance of making blunders on a big scale. It is quite invaluable for 'vetting' officers if properly administered.[1]

Unfortunately this remained, as often as not, a pious hope. It was extremely difficult for GHQ to engineer the removal of higher-ranking commanders it judged unsatisfactory. Indeed, the process of professionalization tended to produce a few units whose rugged independence made them less amenable than ever to central control. None the less, a slow attrition of this independence was achieved by the central command, which insisted with some success, for instance, on receiving regular written reports from all units (a process which presented extraordinary security hazards and which is only explicable as part of a general impulse towards the imitation of 'regular' armies).[2]

To some extent the most substantial function of GHQ was one of political propaganda. Even if it was something of a make-believe 'high command', whose strategic ideas sometimes smacked of *folie de grandeur*—witness its talk of 'shock troops', its grandiose conceptions of 'outflanking' Ulster, and even its less ambitious attempt to create divisional commands[3]—it impressed its opponents as much as it did its notional subordinates. Undoubtedly it increased the credibility of the Republican counter-state as a whole. In one particular sphere, it made a more direct contribution to the conflict. The Directorate of Intelligence under J. J. O'Connell and Michael Collins rapidly developed the capability not only to acquire information but also to penetrate

[1] D/Training, 'Function of A. S. Units', Training Memo. no. 2, 23 Apr. 1921 (Mulcahy MSS P.7/A/II/17).

[2] On the IRA's extraordinary propensity for keeping written records see *inter alia* T. P. Coogan, *The IRA* (2nd edn., London, 1980), pp. 69–70; Townshend, 'Irish Republican Army', p. 336.

[3] Ibid. pp. 337–40.

the British intelligence service (at least that of the Dublin Metropolitan Police) and to carry out, via the 'Squad', destructive operations against it. At the end of July 1919 'the first of the detective spies to forfeit his life was shot' (in the later words of Mulcahy); by January 1920 the DMP 'G' Division had been paralysed. In 1920 efforts were intensified against the special agents brought in from outside Ireland, under the supervision of a new British intelligence chief, Ormonde Winter. 'Bloody Sunday', 21 November 1920, was the most savage manifestation of this hidden struggle: fourteen men were shot in the early morning, a number of them (though not all, as Republican propaganda claimed) British intelligence agents.[1] The shock effect on the British authorities was considerable, but the operation failed to restore the Volunteer intelligence organization to its previous mastery. A noticeable improvement in British intelligence-gathering appeared at the beginning of 1921, and not only in Dublin.[2] The fact was that beneath the brilliant superstructure of Collins's organization in Dublin, the Volunteer intelligence system at large was seriously defective. Local units simply failed to put enough energy into the hard day-by-day grind of collecting and processing information. At times, as a result, they were as much in the dark as their opponents.[3]

The weakness in the intelligence infrastructure of the IRA, together with the fact that the use of terrorism against 'spies and informers' appears to have been on the increase in 1921, threw into relief a central question about the Republic. Did it represent a 'nation in arms'? Republicans have always held that a unified, cohesive popular effort underpinned the demand for separation.[4] Even allowing for the exaggeration necessary (or seemingly unavoidable)

---

[1] J. Gleeson, *Bloody Sunday* (London, 1962); T. Bowden, 'Bloody Sunday— A Reappraisal', *European Studies Review*, i. 1 (1972); C. Townshend, 'Bloody Sunday—Michael Collins Speaks', ibid. ix. 3 (1979).

[2] Townshend, *British Campaign*, pp. 175-7; see also below, p. 357.

[3] GHQ IRA, 'Serious Deficiencies in Country Units', Mar. 1921 (Mulcahy MSS P.7/A/II/17), quoted in Townshend, 'Irish Republican Army', pp. 326-9.

[4] This is well expressed in Mulcahy's idiosyncratic style: 'in 1918 the whole people surfaced in dovetailed organization and co-ordinated will, and . . . they dominated defiantly the political field for the whole time up to the Triumph' ('Conscription and the GHQ Staff', p. 383).

to war propaganda, there is room for doubt on this vital point. The achievement of the Republican counter-state and of the 'army' which bore its name, was at one level remarkable. The organizational resilience and political will displayed by Sinn Féin were greater than those of any earlier nationalist group, and were eventually to prove strong enough to erode those of the government. This resilience stemmed in part from the wide and perhaps deep roots which the movement had put down. In part, however, the penetration of these roots was due to the persistence of older organizations with more traditional aims.

It may indeed be that the real dynamism which underlay the national movement remained the pressure of population on the land. Land hunger, exacerbated by the cessation of emigration, seems to have remained the only force which generated large-scale popular action. Civil resistance of the sort preached by Lalor, Griffith, Hobson, and MacNeill never became a major feature of the political struggle. It appeared, mediated tbrough the forms of local government, in the local councils' break with the local Government Board. It appeared, briefly, in one section of the community in the form of the embargo on munitions of war. But by and large the idea of popular resistance was replaced, rather than reinforced, by that of violent action by smaller groups.[1] It may be true that, as modern guerrilla theory holds, the survival and success of guerrilla groups is dependent on a substantial measure of popular co-operation. Yet this reasoning is finally inconclusive. The title of any government to represent a 'nation in arms' is at best dubious, but that of a subversive movement must necessarily be still more dubious than that of an established state. If the people adopt an attitude of neutrality, the claim of activists to 'represent' them is largely notional, and can only be justified *ex post facto* by official revolutionary historiography.

In the case of Ireland, the claim to be an armed people had observable political impact, on both world opinion

---

[1] Although, as Davis points out in his useful study of 'The Advocacy of Passive Resistance', p. 45, some contemporaries felt that non-violent Sinn Féin was still dominant late in 1920, it is clear that its policy was not being substantially implemented.

(especially in the USA and Dominions, but also in France)
and on opinion in Britain. But it contained, in addition
to its general flaws, a particularly serious flaw in so
far as it was taken to substantiate the claim for Irish
separation: it ignored the refusal of a large and cohesive
minority of the people of Ireland to accept such a claim.

(iii) *Northern Ireland*

> The Government has definitely recognised that there
> are two distinct elements among the population:—
> Those who are loyal to the British Crown and Empire,
> and those who are not. The Government is asking the
> help of all loyalists in Ulster, and proposes to arm with
> Firearms all those called on for duty, to confer certain
> privileges, to recognise them, and to indemnify them
> for injuries incurred by the performance of their
> duties.
>
> Lt.-Col. W. Spender[1]

The year 1920 saw the culmination of the process by
which 'Ulster' separated itself from the rest of Ireland,
a process shot through with violence at many levels. If
it was not made definite until the passage of the Government of Ireland Act in December, separation had been
substantially established for some time. Even before the
upsurge of 1912, the roots of political (or rather, perhaps,
ideological) difference had been bared in events—especially
the 1907 strike— which many people hoped might bury
the evil of sectarianism under the landslide of modernization. Likewise the '44-hour' strike of 1919 produced, at
first, a hopeful display of unity between Protestant and
Catholic workers. However, the political circumstances
of 1920 caused this unity to evaporate with dismaying
rapidity.

In the spring of 1920 the IRA launched a series of attacks
on government offices, including several in the North; where
previously the 'national' struggle had been carried on at a
safe distance, it now impinged directly on Ulster. Some
hostility was soon evident. Symptomatic of this was the offer

---

[1] Memo. to Belfast UVF, 29 Oct. 1920 (PRONI D.1700/5/16).

of Belfast railwaymen to drive northbound trains stranded in Dublin by the munitions strike.[1] The most ominous development was the re-creation in June of the Ulster Volunteer Force. Although the British military commander railed against 'the raising of Carson's army from the grave', the drift of events gathered momentum.[2] When the old citizen militia proved insufficiently adaptable for the new challenge of maintaining order, it was replacd in October by a Special Constabulary.[3] Divided into 'A', 'B', and 'C' categories, the constabulary was in theory to be recruited throughout Ireland. In practice, it was a phenomenon of Ulster, where the part-time paid 'B' Specials were to give a particular stamp to the emerging Northern Ireland state. That polity itself came into virtual existence long before the establishment of the Northern Ireland parliament in June 1921. The effective transfer of administrative functions began in September 1920 with the appointment of a separate Under-Secretary for Belfast.[4]

The decisive stimulus to this process was the outbreak of sectarian riots in the northern capital. On 21 July between two and five thousand 'Protestant and Unionist' workers attended a meeting outside Workman and Clark's south yard, to denounce the IRA guerrilla campaign and Sinn Féin's 'penetration' of Ulster, as well as 'disloyal' trade unionists (pre-eminently the Irish TUC and Labour party) who had allegedly become the industrial wing of the Sinn Féin movement.[5] The dully familiar outcome of this meeting was a swoop by several hundred apprentices and rivet boys from Workman and Clark's into the Harland and Wolff yards,

[1] RIC Reports, June 1920 (POR CO 904 112); H. Patterson, *Class Conflict and Sectarianism*, pp. 129–30.

[2] Gen. Macready to Sir J. Anderson, 18 June 1920 (Anderson MSS, PRO CO 904 188). The revived UVF was commanded by its most talented staff officer, Lt.-Col. Wilfrid Spender; its former Chief of Staff, Hacket Pain, had now become Acting Commissioner of Police for Belfast. Spender's account, very hostile to Macready, is in Buckland, *Irish Unionism*, pp. 445–7.

[3] Extracts from Crawford and Spender diaries, ibid. pp. 442–51.

[4] J. McColgan ' "Ulster's Midwife": Sir Ernest Clark and the Birth of the Northern Ireland Administration', in C. Hazlehurst and C. Woodland, *Irish Government Under Asquith and Lloyd George* (forthcoming).

[5] In fact Sinn Féin appears to have been weak in Belfast: according to the (not infallible) RIC the Volunteers had one battalion of 500 as against 1,300 INV and 6,000 UIL members.

from which Catholic and known socialist workers were driven out. Beaten or pelted with rivets and stones, the first of a long stream of refugees took flight, some of them plunging into the Musgrave Channel to escape.[1] By the end of the week some five thousand Catholic workers had been driven from their jobs, and violence—looting and burning of Catholic shops and houses—had spread to residential areas in east and north Belfast. The intensity of violence in August recalled the riots of 1886, and their lethal effect was greater than all the nineteenth-century riots together. Disturbances erupted sporadically for the next two years; a total of 428 people were killed and 1,766 wounded.[2]

This fearsome explosion has been explained by nationalists as the deliberate work of the Unionist Council, and by socialists as the result of bourgeois manipulation to undermine working-class co-operation. Such explanations are manifestly inadequate, though the first is more informative. The idea that the Protestant workers were directly controlled by any body must be discounted, but their spontaneous action was highly political in content.[3] Its perversity was an expression of the idiosyncratic Ulster-Protestant sense of community—a sense which may convincingly be seen as an arrested development towards modern nationalism. The expulsions were a collective response to the encroaching Republican challenge—or, as the *Boilermakers' Monthly Report* put it, to the 'Sinn Féin murder of D. I. Swanzy'.[4] Ulster Protestants' long-established contractarian attitude to sovereignty obscured their real identity, and has continued to divert them from formulating their status in terms of nationality. Yet by this time it was abundantly clear that the Protestant way of life possessed, for them, an ethnic distinctness equal to that of any national group

[1] RIC Reports, CO 904 112; Patterson, op. cit. pp. 115-6.
[2] A. T. Q. Stewart calls this a 'staggering increase' on the fatalities of the previous century, which had seen a total of 68 deaths between 1813 and 1907 (half of them in 1886).
[3] There is a closely argued analysis of Protestant worker action in Patterson, op. cit. pp. 118-35.
[4] Quoted in Patterson, op. cit. p. 141. Swanzy had been named by a coroner's jury as one of those guilty of the death of Lord Mayor Thomas MacCurtain in Cork on 19 March.

in Europe, and which they would defend if necessary by war. They were neither British nor Irish; their 'Britishness' was a cypher for their resistance to absorption by the Irish. The union flag was a party emblem; the 'British way' of consensus politics was a road on which they would not take a single step. Yet their political dependence on Britain prevented their celebrated self-reliance from extending from the economic into the political sphere.[1]

Ulster separateness had, by 1920, been substantially recognized by the British, though its bases were scarcely comprehended. Irish Nationalists continued to dispute its existence, yet by their own actions made one of the most powerful of all contributions to separation. The Nationalist response to the 'pogrom', articulated by the General Council of County Councils under the aegis of W. T. Cosgrave, Dáil Minister for Local Government, was to organize a boycott of Belfast goods, and to endeavour to cut all commercial and financial links with the city. This policy of sanctions by the exponents of Irish unity appears in retrospect all but incredible, and still more extraordinary was the fact that it was supported by the ILP/TUC and its newspaper *Watchword of Labour*. It was, however, enthusiastically taken up by the Volunteers, for whom the destruction of Belfast goods offered an agreeably 'soft' target and a diversion from the struggle against the Crown forces.[2]

The boycott gave precise shape to Protestant fears of discrimination—or worse—at the hands of a Nationalist government. As such it can only have cemented opposition to republicanism and fostered a determination to use any means to preserve the reality of Ulster separation. The government's forlorn hope, the Council of Ireland, lost

---

[1] The status of Ulster Protestant identity is of course a crucial political issue. The potentially destructive impact of suggestions that it amounts to a form of nationality, or a regional variant of Scottish (rather than Irish) cultural-political identity, on the one-island assumptions of Nationalists may account for the quiet reception of works such as Heslinga's *The Irish Border* and, more recently, Miller's *Queen's Rebels*. Protestants have also been reluctant to face the issue of national independence: see below, p. 393.

[2] The only substantial study is D. S. Johnson, 'The Belfast Boycott, 1920–1922', in J. M. Goldstrom and L. A. Clarkson (edd.), *Irish Population, Economy and Society* (Oxford, 1981), pp. 287–307.

what slender chance it had of producing an Irish solution intelligible to world opinion.

(iv) *'Restoring order': the road to martial law*

> I can see no reason why, with patience and firmness, we may not wear the trouble down in the course of a few years and secure the re-establishment of order together with the acceptance by the Irish people of the responsibility of their own internal government.
>
> Winston Churchill[1]

The essential fact about the government's policy in 1919-21 is that it was not an attempt to reconquer Ireland. A few ministers, no doubt, and perhaps many of the British public, would not have found such a course objectionable. But the home rule solution was generally accepted as inescapable. It was simply a matter of how to implement it in circumstances of veiled rebellion. To begin with, the government was unwilling to identify Irish circumstances in this way. When the Sinn Féin MPs met and declared themselves the parliament of an Irish Republic, the authorities made no move. Indeed, the rebel assembly's meetings in the Dublin Mansion House were, incongruously, guarded by the police.[2] Eight months were to elapse before the Dáil was proscribed. During this time the Liberal Chief Secretary, Ian Macpherson, was in a visibly painful quandary. What should the government do to MPs who would not come to Westminster? As he later explained to Bonar Law, 'we had to allow these members to sit together *in consultation* if they wished'; but when they 'conspired by executive acts . . . to overthrow the duly constituted authority, then we could act'.[3] Macpherson stretched this interpretation a long way. He swallowed the Declaration of Independence as 'consultation'. Only the series of violent acts by the Volunteers culminating in the attack at Fermoy on 7 September, together with

---

[1] Secretary of State for War to CIGS, 18 Sept. 1920 (WO 32 9537).

[2] Phillips, *Revolution in Ireland*, pp. 153-4.

[3] Chief Secretary for Ireland to Ld. Privy Seal, 13 Sept. 1919 (Bonar Law MSS 98/2/12).

the Dáil's move to link the Volunteers to itself by means of the 'oath of allegiance' on 20 August, impelled him to take the step of proclaiming Dáil Éireann an illegal association under the 1887 Crimes Act. Simultaneously, and more sweepingly, the whole Sinn Féin party was proclaimed.

It may be suggested that the peculiar nature of the Lloyd George coalition government played a part in shaping the British response to the Sinn Féin challenge. It is possible that a Liberal government would have been more inclined to negotiate with Sinn Féin straight away on the basis of the *fait accompli* of January 1919.[1] A Conservative government, on the other hand, might have pursued a less hesitant and more effective policy of repression, abandoning home rule for the foreseeable future.[2] As it was, however, the coalition Liberals needed to be particularly firm on the issues of 'constitutionalism' and 'law and order', effectively eradicating the possibility of a negotiated settlement. Much like Forster and Spencer before them, they insisted on a return to proper constitutional practice and a cessation of violence before making an offer of self-government. As violence intensified rather than declined, their responses grew tougher. There remained a tendency to hope month by month that Sinn Féin had 'shot its bolt', but the increasing pressure on the RIC in the early winter of 1919 resolved most doubts on this score. At the end of the year came the most consciously dramatic of the Volunteer operations so far, the attempted assassination of Lord French at Ashtown on the edge of Phoenix Park.

This attack narrowly missed the Viceroy, and though it drew from Lloyd George the cynical comment 'they are bad shots', it precipitated the first major shift of gear in the British campaign. French had long been chafing under the

---

[1] Fisher, Shortt, and Addison were reported in May to be 'disturbed at the suggestion that Sinn Féin be "proclaimed" '. They evidently hoped that Lloyd George, then absent at Versailles, would produce a negotiated settlement on his return: T. Jones, *Whitehall Diary* (ed. K. Middlemas), i (London, 1969), 87.

[2] The alternative Prime Minister, Bonar Law, was to alarm Thomas Jones in January 1921 by saying (privately) that coercion was the only policy; 'the Irish were an inferior race' and the best that could be hoped for was ten years of quiet after the present round of repression: ibid. iii (London, 1971), 49–50.

Cabinet's hesitant policy and the inefficiency of the Dublin Castle administrative system. He and his friend Long gravely misjudged the seriousness of the Sinn Féin policy of abstention, declaring in January 1919 that 'these seventy-three devils' would 'soon go bag and baggage over to Westminster' when they found they could not draw their salaries otherwise.[1] This mistake did not undermine the Field-Marshal's faith in his special understanding of Irish affairs, nor that of Walter Long, who was to inform Lloyd George in 1920 that 'the Irishman is easily dealt with if you stand up to him, but he is the worst man in the world from whom to run away'.[2] French remained convinced of the necessity for the use of force: 'we have taken strong measures and may have to take stronger' he declared in May, adding that he could 'overcome' the militants if only he were given a free hand. He could not convince the Cabinet of the need for such toughness, although it did sanction the application of martial law if the whole Irish executive were agreed upon it. French was forced to admit that 'there is a consensus of opinion here that the declaration of Martial law is not the best way of attaining our object', and that martial law would be no good unless it were 'administered by people who believe strongly in its power and efficacy'. At the same time he despaired of the 'hesitation and indecision' which he felt would 'end in completely demoralising the police forces in this country'.[3]

Long was realistic enough to doubt whether the suppression of Sinn Féin could work, martial law or not, while the authorities lacked the means to carry it out.[4] French had already turned his attention to the weakness of the Castle system, and attempted to establish a new, smaller, and more efficient supervisory body through his 'Viceregal Council'. This administrative innovation failed to take root. French's own influence suffered as a result of his serious illness during

[1] French to Long, and reply, 14, 16 Jan. 1919 (French MSS, quoted in Holmes, *French*, p. 348).

[2] Lloyd George MSS F/33/2/27, quoted in Townshend, *British Campaign*, p. 99.

[3] Ld.-Lt. to PM, 19 May; to Chief Secretary, 4, 11 Nov. 1919 (French MSS, quoted in Holmes, *French*, pp. 350-1; Townshend, op. cit. p. 47).

[4] Long to French, 21 May 1919 (Holmes, *French*, p. 350).

the first three months of Macpherson's period of office, and he was in the end to be altogether eclipsed by Macpherson's successor.

In the intervening period, however, he and Long were able to initiate a revolutionary change in the police force. The RIC's morale appeared very shaky in 1919 (as indeed did that of the London Metropolitan Police), and legislation to improve pay and conditions as recommended by the Desborough Commission was not completed until November. The force remained under strength—though recruitment was in fact rising in the early winter—and poorly equipped. French fumed that the administration was 'continually handicapped in a senseless idiotic manner' by Whitehall's refusal to give war surplus equipment to the RIC. He resolved to rebuild the force, and in December, acting on a suggestion of Long's, he pushed through the decision to recruit extra constables from the pool of English ex-servicemen, removing the protesting Inspector-General in the process.[1] The first of the recruits who were to become known as 'Black and Tans' appeared in Dublin shortly after the Ashtown ambush.

The other aspects of the shift of gear were equally far-reaching. In January 1920 additional legal powers were given to military commanders ('Competent Military Authorities' in DORA terminology) to carry out searches and arrests, and a sweeping programme of arrest and internment was set on foot.[2] Although the new powers were formally revoked in May, the increased military involvement could not be reversed. The policy of internment itself was to prove both provocative and ineffectual.[3] At the same time steps were taken to revitalize the Dublin Castle system. An investigation by the head of the civil service, Sir Warren Fisher, led to the transfer of several capable administrators from Whitehall to Dublin. There, however, they were somewhat inelegantly grafted on to the Castle structure (Sir

---

[1] Townshend, op. cit. pp. 25, 30, 45-6.

[2] GHQ Irish Command, Record of the Rebellion in Ireland in 1920-1, p. 5 (loc. cit. p. 49).

[3] By July 1921, 4,454 Volunteers had been interned (including 19 brigade and 93 battalion commanders) without measureable effect: ibid., App. XII, p. 223.

John Anderson becoming 'Joint Under Secretary') with powers that were not altogether clear. Fisher's idea of supplying consistent, resolute decision-making and control was never realized. Symptomatically, a hesitant attempt to create a 'generalissimo', with command of both police and military forces, came to nothing, partly as a result of traditionalist attitudes.[1] In consequence, uncertainty and disagreement persisted in almost every department of the administration.

The first shift of gear stalled amidst contradictory tendencies. French's own demands were unclear. After Ashtown he put the alternatives thus: 'a large number of men must be arrested and deported; *or else we must have Martial Law*.' But the main function of martial law would surely have been to expedite the arrests. Like almost all coercive policies it was founded on the assumption that resistance could be broken by arrests and exemplary punishment. As Churchill wrote privately,

It is shocking that we have not been able to bring the murderers to justice. If we could get one or two of them we might secure a confession on the steps of the scaffold which would enable us to break up the whole organisation of this murder club. In this, as in so many things, it is the first step that counts.[2]

Martial law was a means of short-circuiting the legal paralysis which was making convictions unobtainable, but it was based on an analysis of Irish resistance accepted by few members of the Cabinet. Apart from Walter Long, Ministers preferred, like Churchill, to believe that hostility was not widespread but was being fomented by a small group of fanatical terrorists. This 'murder gang' might be eliminated by a few successful convictions.

What strikes me is the feebleness of the local machinery. After a person is caught he should pay the penalty within a week. Look at the tribunals which the Russian Government have devised. You should get

---

[1] Record of the Rebellion in Ireland, p. 75. Sir Nevil Macready, who became C.-in-C. in March 1920, rejected the extra function of police chief because it would in his view have made the job too big. Despite his experience as Commissioner of the London Metropolitan Police he had a low opinion of the Irish police and evidently preferred a regular military command: Macready, *Annals*, ii, 425.

[2] Churchill to his wife, 31 March 1920 (M. Gilbert, *Winston S. Churchill* (London, 1975), iv. 449).

three or four judges whose scope should be universal and they should move quickly over the country and do summary justice.[1]

The moderate majority could then be expected to return to legal and constitutional behaviour.

The most enthusiastic exponent of this view was the new Chief Secretary, the Liberal imperialist Hamar Greenwood, who took over from the demoralized Macpherson in April. Greenwood's administration began with the release of the prisoners arrested earlier in the year, many of whom were by then on hunger-strike in Mountjoy gaol. These hunger-strikes were the most successful mounted so far by Republicans, creating an explosive atmosphere in Dublin, where public demonstrations verging on riots were coupled with a one-day general strike. The government's climb-down seemed unavoidable, but Greenwood made a virtue of it by initiating a period of 'conciliation'.

Henceforth a concern for the supposed moderate majority was to dominate policy, curtailing or limiting coercive measures which might, in a technical sense, have 'restored order'. But the political limits of the British campaign remained vaguely demarcated. 'Order' itself was never defined. Lloyd George remarked in June 1921 that the 'Irish job' was 'a policeman's job supported by the military and not vice versa. So long as it becomes a military job only it will fail'.[2] It was on this basis that the police were expanded and rearmed in 1920 under a new Chief, Major-General Tudor. It was a sensible political principle, perhaps the only one feasible in a liberal democratic state. Unfortunately it camouflaged the fact that a militarized police force, such as Tudor set himself to create during the summer, could do even more political damage than the military—perhaps even than martial law. Such was the case in 1920.

Throughout Greenwood's conciliatory period the RIC was energetically expanded and re-equipped. In July 1920 a new formation, the Auxiliary Division, was added, recruited primarily from ex-officers (paid double the rate of ordinary RIC recruits) and stationed in the most 'disaffected' areas

---

[1] Cabinet Committee on Ireland, 31 May 1920 (ibid. 452).
[2] Cabinet, 2 June 1921; Jones, *Whitehall Diary*, iii. 73.

in mobile companies of some 100 men.[1] The government's acceptance of this unorthodox force, and refusal of the military suggestions of special garrison battalions, ensured that the previously sporadic violence of the RIC would intensify. Heavily armed, absurdly lacking in police experience or training, and unrestrained by the discipline normally imposed on armed men under military law, the 'Auxies' pushed violent response to the level of counter-terrorism.[2] Their arrival in Ireland, coinciding with Greenwood's loss of patience with conciliation, marked a second shift of gear in the British campaign. Early in August a remarkable new coercion measure, the Restoration of Order in Ireland Act, was rushed through parliament inside a week by unremitting use of the guillotine. It went beyond DORA in creating what the Judge Advocate-General regarded as 'a form of statutory martial law'. The military authorities henceforth had the power to try a wide range of offences by courts martial, and military courts of inquiry were established in lieu of Coroners' inquests. (Coroners' juries had produced some damagingly hostile verdicts, as in the case of Tomas MacCurtain.)[3]

This was a definite move towards military administration —a clear confession that the ordinary courts, though functioning, were incapable of bringing convictions for IRA violence. A new determination was also evident in the treatment meted out to those arrested—the most outstanding case being that of Terence MacSwiney. (When MacSwiney went on hunger-strike he was neither force-fed nor released. His death on 25 October proved a decisive blow to the

[1] According to GHQ Irish Command the function of Auxiliary Companies 'are those of mobile RIC. They should assist in enforcing the ordinary law, and work in the closest co-operation with the RIC' (6th Div. Orders, 16 Sept. 1920, NLI Pos. 918).

[2] Remarkably, the ADRIC was commanded by an ex-UVF officer, Brig. Crozier, regarded in Dublin Castle circles as a man of uncertain stability. Though he later created a public stir by resigning over ADRIC indiscipline (F. P. Crozier, *Impressions and Recollections* (London, 1930), pp. 265–6), he had almost certainly played a leading part in establishing the pattern of 'economic' reprisals by the Auxiliaries. See Townshend, op. cit. pp. 163–4.

[3] 10 & 11 Geo. V, c. 31, 9 Aug. 1920. The act was followed by 199 principal and 18 supplementary Regulations, including the power to prohibit whistling for cabs: ROI Regs., PRO WO 32 5551.

hunger-strike policy, a fact which might in the long run have outweighed the emotional impact of his martyrdom.) Yet all this was a long way from what soldiers thought of as martial law, which for them was primarily distinguished by the principle of unity of command. The civil structure, though in large part ineffective, remained outside the authority of the military commander, Macready. He himself disapproved of martial law because he thought it could not be employed in an absolute form (the only form that would work) in a liberal democracy. Public opinion would not stand it.[1] Yet the increasingly violent behaviour of the RIC in August led him to advocate it simply in order to obtain control over the police—which, ironically, he had himself refused in March—to prohibit them from actions which he considered politically disastrous.

While he was concerned to restrain the violence of military and police responses, however, the inner Cabinet had decided that violence might be the solvent of the vicious circle of intimidation and criminal immunity which had caused the breakdown of law and order. The central issue was the series of reprisals which occurred with increasing frequency and destructiveness during the summer and autumn.[2] Such reprisals, as Macready conceded, were in one sense inevitable. Any force into which *esprit de corps* had been instilled must respond to attacks on its members. Even with new recruits, 'the fact is that the human endurance of the troops is rapidly reaching a point where restraint will be impossible'.[3] The question was whether the response of angry soldiers and policemen, faced with attackers who vanished into the ordinary population, could be effectively limited by the authorities. Macready proposed a system of 'official reprisals' —public penalties for harbouring rebels or failing to give information of rebel movements—which would release the tension. The main penalty would be the burning of houses

---

[1] C.-in-C. to Chief Secretary, 17 July 1920 (Lloyd George MSS F/19/2/12).

[2] In August the Dublin Castle administrators were 'being urged quietly and persistently that reprisals are the only thing to put down the gun men and hearten the police' (Diary of Mark Sturgis, 24 Aug. 1920, PRO 30/49/1).

[3] C.-in-C. Ireland to WO, 1 Sept. 1920 (POR WO 32 9537 (b)). For strain of continuous duty see also J. C. C. Davidson to E. H. Marsh, 15 Oct. (WO 32 9539).

at the scene of an ambush, or from which shots had been fired (with or without the occupants' consent): such a course of action regularly repeated would put pressure on the public to deny the use of their houses to the IRA or to give information of an IRA presence.

Lloyd George, not surprisingly, disliked this idea. The secretary of State for War, Churchill, agreed with him, responding to Macready with the falsely ingenuous argument that

the greatest help in this respect will be given by the Irish population of towns where troops are quartered if they not only abstain from murdering the soldiers and their officers by treacherous means but also render the assistance which is easily in their power to give for the detection of the actual criminals . . .

I do not believe that the discipline of the army has deteriorated in any fundamental sense . . . Care must be taken not to discourage the loyalty and zeal of the troops in defending themselves from cowardly and treacherous attacks.[1]

Two things were against Macready's proposal. First, that the IRA could win an arson competition easily—it would have a mass of easy targets in the big houses which still sheltered the remnants of the Ascendancy class. Second, and worse, the houses officially burned were likely to be in any case the property of landlords who were the mainstay of the loyal, moderate community.[2] Lloyd George and Churchill preferred the direct personal violence caused by the police in their outbreaks of 'seeing red' after 'intolerable provocation'. (Churchill had already spoken of the need 'to raise the temperature of the conflict to a real issue and shock, and trial of strength' to end the 'prolonged strain that was breaking down the officials in Ireland'.) 'Gunning' rather than 'burning', as evidenced at Balbriggan, let the police get at the gunmen whom they knew but could not legally convict.[3]

---

[1] Secretary of State for War to CIGS, 18 Sept. 1920 (WO 32 9537 (b)). For Lloyd George's reaction ('no government could take the responsibility'), or Sir Henry Wilson's view of it, see Calwell, *Wilson*, ii, 263 (29 Sept. 1920).

[2] In fact the first 'official' reprisal at Midleton, Co. Cork, in Jan. 1921, destroyed houses belonging to the Southern Unionist leader the Earl of Midleton.

[3] Gilbert, *Churchill*, p. 457. Even Wilson was disturbed by the fact that Churchill 'saw very little harm' in the way the RIC had 'marked down certain SFs as in their opinion the actual murderers or instigators and then coolly shot

Nothing else seemed likely to work. The military had been unable to develop successful techniques for dealing with IRA attacks, which reached a massive peak in mid September. The general efficiency of military units in the demanding work of internal security was low. As Macrèady admitted,

The troops are certainly more experienced in the peculiar conditions of this country . . . [but] this is discounted to some extent by the increased activity and boldness of their opponents who are daily becoming better armed, better disciplined, and better established.[1]

There was room for doubt whether the army could deliver results even if it were given the full powers it demanded. However, the Cabinet remained more concerned about the political inadmissibility of military rule than about its chances of success. When the Restoration of Order Act had been framed, it had been felt to be 'a decision of the gravest moment to utilize machinery intended for time of war in time of peace'. Austen Chamberlain had vivid memories of his father's anger at the working of martial law in South Africa in 1900-2. But he admitted that the whole situation was 'most puzzling and most distressing', and even wondered privately, 'Can modern democracy handle such problems successfully?'[2]

Part of the problem, of course, was whether the situation could be seen as one of war rather than peace. Legal understanding of this issue was uncertain.[3] The Cabinet instinctively shied away from identifying the crisis as a war, for fear that such an admission would sustain the Republic's claim to belligerent status. (As Lloyd George told a baffled Lord French, 'you do not declare war on rebels'.) The police strategy was a way of avoiding such an admission, by maintaining the fiction that the 'ordinary' civil authorities were in control. Until late November 1920 there was considerable political optimism that the militarized police, supported by the background presence of the army, were beginning to

them without question or trial' (Wilson MSS, diary, 23 Sept. 1920; Townshend, op. cit. p. 116).

[1] Memo., 6 Aug. 1920 (PRO CAB. 24 110, CP 1750).
[2] Cabinet Conference, 26 July 1920 (CAB. 23 22, C.51 20), App. IV; Austen to Hilda Chamberlain, 24 July (A. Chamberlain MSS 5/1/170). On S. Africa cf. Townshend, 'Martial Law', pp. 176-82.
[3] Ibid. pp. 183-7.

dominate the IRA—had 'murder by the throat' as Lloyd George colourfully expressed it.[1] Such confidence was shattered by two events which pushed the government into a third shift of gear.

The assassinations in Dublin on 'Bloody Sunday', 21 November, followed a week later by the annihilation of an Auxiliary force at Kilmichael, Co. Cork, galvanized the still slack system into a more warlike posture. The order that all service personnel living outside should be brought into barracks was symptomatic of the belated recognition that the IRA challenge must be treated seriously.[2] A wave of arrests followed, over 500 men being seized within a week. Early in December, accepting the argument that Kilmichael resembled a regular operation of war, the Cabinet agreed to the proclamation of martial law in the south-west. The priority of restoring 'law and order' had led the government once again into apparent political bankruptcy.

However, it was impossible for the British political system to plunge headlong into the murky, indefinite region of martial law. It was, rather, feeling its way—very slowly— towards a more modern concept of emergency powers: a mixed system of civil and military administration. Unfortunately, in Ireland in 1921 the mixture was to be very unstable. No sooner was martial law accepted than the Cabinet began to insist on strict geographical limits to its operation. Military demands, backed of course by the Viceroy, for extension of the martial law area, met with steady silence. The army, increasingly obsessed by what it saw as the debilitating anomalies of subdivision, naturally failed to grasp what a politically alert administrator saw as Lloyd George's intention, 'to have martial law in the distant provinces, as a storm on the horizon', but to leave the capital 'free' in the hope of encouraging negotiations.[3]

[1] Even Macready attempted in public to belittle the seriousness of the situation. He told a reporter of the *Petit Parisien* 'Il faudrait fusiller une cinquantaine d'individus et tout rentrait dans l'ordre' (Corr., PRO WO 32 9537 (a)).

[2] Hunting had only been forbidden a month earlier: GHQ Orders 12 Oct., 6th Div. Orders 14 Oct. 1920 (NLI Pos. 918).

[3] Sturgis's diary, 14 Dec. 1920. Even Warren Fisher, however, found this reasoning hard to accept. 'The real fact' in his view was that 'martial law everywhere is an intelligible policy, or martial law nowhere' (Report, 11 Feb. 1921, Lloyd George MSS F/16/1/9).

The Prime Minister was laying the basis for his eventual use of the threat of full-scale war during the treaty negotiations. This political sophistication, however, was unmatched by any corresponding sophistication in the executive machinery. Jolts and clashes increasingly shook the ramshackle structure. Even before the declaration of martial law, when Arthur Griffith was arrested in the burst of raids after Bloody Sunday, the government peremptorily ordered his release. The baffled fury of the military authorities was increased in mid December when they were instructed to desist absolutely from arresting Eamon de Valera on his return from the United States. By February 1921 it became clear that even in the martial law area they were not to be given overall control: the RIC remained substantially independent, and, perhaps worse, legal appeals against the findings of military tribunals were constantly heard in the higher courts. When Macready was forced, humiliatingly, to withdraw an order that the civil courts in the martial law area should close, he became increasingly bitter against political hesitancy. Martial law was rendered all but nugatory. The only major measure adopted under its aegis was the system of 'official reprisals' earlier advocated by Macready; its political unattractiveness finally led the Cabinet to order its prohibition.

Macready's dissatisfaction led him to prepare a set of almost defeatist memoranda for the Cabinet in May, when the elections finally held under the Government of Ireland Act gave Sinn Féin its inevitable sweeping victory. (As Macready glumly noted, the Sinn Féin party was by this time in effect the IRA, with all that that implied for the outcome of 'free elections'.) Echoing Forster's warning of forty years ago, he pointed out amongst other things that the strain of internal security work was telling on the troops, particularly because they were mostly very young and 'fine drawn'.[1] Sir Henry Wilson hoped that the military warning would force the Cabinet out of its indecision, and make it face his crudely expressed ultimatum 'govern or get out'. In this it was successful, if not in the direction Wilson desired. Although reports from the Irish executive as well as from the army

[1] C.-in-C. Ireland, Memo. A, 23 May 1921 (PRO CAB. 24 123, CP 2965).

itself showed that improving military techniques were inflicting severe losses on the IRA, Lloyd George swung decisively
towards a negotiated political solution. The focal event in
this process was the opening of the Northern Ireland parliament on 22 June. In a key speech on the previous day, Lord
Birkenhead made the first public admission that 'a small
war' was going on in Ireland, and that the government was
losing it.[1] The royal plea in Belfast on the 22nd for reconciliation permitted the Cabinet to begin the process of negotiating with men whom they had consistently branded as
terrorists and murderers.

(v) *Peace of exhaustion*

> It is not those who can inflict the most, but those that
> can suffer the most who will conquer.
>
> Facing our enemy, we must declare our attitude simply.
> We see in their regime a thing of evil incarnate. With it
> there can be no parley any more than there can be a truce
> with the powers of hell.
>
> Terence MacSwiney[2]

The government continued to tinker with the possibility
of resorting to full-scale martial law. Under GIA, when the
Southern parliament failed to assemble, Crown Colony
government would follow. The prospect was unpleasant to
Liberal ministers and less than attractive to Conservatives.
Admittedly Bonar Law, now in temporary retirement, had
reached the conclusion that the Irish were an inferior race
whose rebellions must be put down periodically, and who
must otherwise be subjected to resolute government in the
Salisbury style. This sentiment was to have eventual effect
on Lloyd George's political career, but for the time being
the most substantial Conservative leaders remained sympathetic to the Prime Minister.

As a result the Cabinet committee which was to prepare
plans for 'universal' martial law stayed in the background,

[1] 'The history of the last three months is the history of the failure of our
military methods to keep pace with and to overcome the military methods
which have been taken by our opponents' (45 HL Deb. 5s, c. 690).
[2] Speech of inauguration as Lord Mayor of Cork, 1920.

and the government was even ready in July to bow to a questionable legal decision which significantly undermined its martial-law powers.[1] It was evident that the sweeping Sinn Féin victory had shaken its faith in coercive measures, and also in the 'murder gang' theory. Although Frances Stevenson felt that Lloyd George was still hoping as late as the beginning of May 1921 that the Government of Ireland Act could be imposed by force, and he himself declared emphatically in Cabinet that he was not prepared to 'give' Ireland the degree of independence enjoyed by Canada and Australia, he had clearly been shocked when Macready had indicated that the authorities would be powerless to prevent Michael Collins from dictating the outcome of the election.[2]

It was admittedly difficult to assess the military balance in Ireland. A run of British military successes in April struck hard blows at the IRA in Dublin, and more flexible operational methods increased the pressure in the most embattled rural areas.[3] It seems probable that if the activities of the Crown forces had been maintained, or even stepped up (as was planned if Crown Colony government ensued), all but a few of the toughest IRA units would have been reduced to collapse, or forced to suspend operations. It was already beyond the capacity of most of them to carry out demanding operations such as attacks on barracks—the total of successful attacks in the first six months of 1921 was a mere two, as compared with twenty-three in the previous year—and easier undertakings accounted for the still increasing total of outrages.[4] The 'offensive against communications', the persistent felling of trees or digging of trenches to block roads, the breaking of bridges, the shooting of army transport

---

[1] *Egan* v. *Macready* (1921), I IR 265; Townshend, 'Martial Law', p. 187.

[2] She told Sturgis on 11 May that he still hoped 'in his inmost heart that Southern Ireland might still be forced to work his Act without any additions whatsoever' (PRO 30 59/4). Cf. also Cabinet, 27 Apr. 1921 (Jones, *Whitehall Diary*, iii. 62).

[3] F. O'Donoghue, *No Other Law. The Story of Liam Lynch and the Irish Republican Army, 1916-1923* (Dublin, 1954), esp. at pp. 166-7, reveals the pressure on North Cork. Even the Cork No. 3 Brigade complained (to Collins, 9 Feb. 1921) of arms shortages: P. Béaslai, *Michael Collins*, ii. 182.

[4] Townshend, 'Irish Republican Army', p. 342.

mules, and so on, restricted the Crown forces' ability to dominate the countryside, but would only have made real military sense as the prelude of larger-scale operations by the IRA. Large formations never in fact appeared, in spite of the attempt to create 'divisions' in April 1921. The only thing which led the IRA to increase its military weight was the acquisition of the first Thompson sub-machine-guns to be produced—another of the Clan na Gael's pioneering technological initiatives to follow its sponsorship of the Holland submarine fifty years before.[1]

But if the military balance was at last shifting to the British side, it was doing so too late to repair the political damage caused by the government's prolonged failure. Public support in Ireland was never forthcoming, and even British opinion had been sliding irreversibly away from the coercive policy as lurid stories of reprisals became public property. The most symptomatic of the government's failures was its inability to counter Republican publicity. The underground *Irish Bulletin* succeeded in presenting all police or military actions, however trivial (and including some which seem never to have occurred at all), as acts of brutal aggression, usually accompanied by fire and theft. The slant of news-presentation in the ordinary Irish daily press was almost as marked, impaling the government once again upon a dilemma of long standing.[2] Consistently hostile reporting inexorably destroyed whatever chance the government had of recovering public support; yet action to prevent such reporting merely accelerated the process. When the Castle finally moved to prosecute the *Freeman's Journal* for 'spreading false reports' in December 1920, the outcry from the Fleet Street defenders of press freedom was so formidable that the government hastily backed down and ordered the release of the convicted editor and proprietor.[3] The labels

---

[1] J. B. Bell, 'The Thompson Submachine Gun in Ireland, 1921', *Irish Sword*, viii. 31 (1967).

[2] The *Irish Independent*, 30 Oct. 1920, declared bluntly that 'Nobody in Ireland accepts as truthful any statement made by the British government'. This was more than journalistic rhetoric.

[3] In Macready's view this 'abject surrender . . . aroused disgust and contempt in the hearts of those who were risking their lives for the policy of the government' (*Annals*, ii. 476).

applied to events by Republican publicity stuck: thus the
'Croke Park massacre', the 'sack of Balbriggan', the 'looting
of Trim', above all the 'burning of Cork City' are still
remembered today.[1]

In these circumstances it is of limited value to speak of
a purely military balance, or of military 'victory'. The government, advised by Macready, might have appreciated this
much earlier, but it failed to do so. Military success did play
a part in bringing the Sinn Féin leaders into negotiations,
and a bigger part in determining their outcome. However, the
negotiations which began in July 1921 were not the sort
the government had wanted. Instead of obtaining the disarmament or disappearance of the IRA as a precondition,
the Cabinet was forced to approve a 'truce' couched in
formal terms which practically recognized the IRA's status
as an army. Instead of inducing Sinn Féin to act as a political
party within the parliament established by the Government
of Ireland Act, it was compelled to scrap the Act and begin
talks on a completely new basis, with antagonists whom it
had condemned as criminals. The Irish claim to equal status
had perhaps been briefly and semi-officially conceded by the
Kilmainham 'Treaty', but the 1921 treaty negotiations were
at a formal level which had not been admitted since the
Treaty of Limerick. Still, the British held back from recognition of the Republic. The arbitrament of force had brought
them far, but on this issue it was the Republican leaders
who were forced to compromise.

The treaty signed in December 1921 embodied this compromise.[2] It maintained the partition of Ireland, though
with the new element of a Boundary Commission which the
Sinn Féin negotiators hoped would erode the separate status
of the North. It maintained British strategic security in
respect of the vital western sea approaches. Above all,
to guarantee this security it maintained the Crown Link,
expressed   in the form of the Oath of Allegiance to be

[1] For a brilliant quasi-objective 'inquiry' into the Cork affair see *Who Burnt
Cork City? A Tale of Arson, Loot and Murder. The Evidence of over Seventy
Witnesses* (Irish Labour Party and TUC, Dublin, 1921), reprinted as *The Burning
of Cork City* (Cork, 1978).

[2] There is a useful analysis in J. M. Curran, *The Birth of the Irish Free State
1921–1923* (Alabama, 1980), ch. 9.

taken by the legislators of the new Irish Free State. This was the crucial issue for those Republicans who opposed the Treaty, as it was for Lloyd George's Conservative allies.[1] The military foundation of this compromise was tersely exposed by Mulcahy during the Treaty debate, when he reminded the Dáil that the IRA was not capable of driving the British from anything more than a 'fairly good-sized' police barrack. Talk of driving the British out of Ireland by force was, in his view, dangerously self-deluded nonsense. He and Collins certainly believed that if the British carried out their threat to renew and intensify the war, the IRA as it had existed before July 1921 would be crushed.[2] This view was not, however, accepted by all physical-force men— and, indeed, women. Opponents of the Treaty believed that the continued application of violence would result in even greater gains.

(vi) *The function of violence*

> Would the English face a renewal of the Irish war when they might have peace so easily? I doubt it.
>
> Erskine Childers[3]

Physical force, whether or not as a result of its alliance with politically sophisticated Sinn Féin, had demonstrably worked. It had extracted from the British concessions which they had hitherto refused. It had prised open, in the more dramatic metaphor preferred by its adherents, England's grip on

[1] Yet, as Curran points out, in attempting to make it acceptable to the Irish, the British 'so modified the traditional oath of allegiance that it was almost devoid of meaning'. In the acrimony of the Dáil debate on the oath, 'the only point to emerge clearly . . . is that symbols wield more influence over many minds than reality' (ibid. p. 132). Cf. P. S. O'Hegarty's bitter remarks on the 'mystical, hysterical, neurotic worship of "The Republic" ' (*A History of Ireland under the Union* (London, 1952), p. 781) and Erwin Rumpf's suggestion that 'in the absence of an acceptable political system, many had pledged themselves to symbols which they were not prepared to sacrifice even when the real essence of their demands was granted' (*Nationalism and Socialism in Twentieth Century Ireland* (Liverpool 1977), p. 33).

[2] While Macready complained that after the Truce the IRA expanded and rearmed, its leaders felt that having come out into the open they would be much easier targets thereafter.

[3] Childers MSS, NLI MS 15444 (1).

twenty-six out of the thirty-two counties of Ireland. But was this the limit of what it could achieve, as Mulcahy and Collins argued? The answer depended on one's understanding of the function of violence in the political process.

Collins and Mulcahy were the principal representatives of the new realism which had emerged after the rising. Though not pure terrorists, they may be said to have conceived the Volunteer military campaign primarily as armed propaganda. This was an important modification of the old physical-force idea. Collins in particular pursued a campaign in which violence was at bottom symbolic: a guerrilla campaign in the modern sense. Mulcahy seems at times to have hoped, somewhat unrealistically, that the campaign could be carried into a further phase—a phase of open warfare carried on by larger-scale units.[1] This pre-echo of the third phase of Mao Tse-tung's theoretical triad was, however, muted by comparison with Mulcahy's insistence on feasible day-to-day operations.

The cumulative effect of numerous minor operations will give all the desired results. There is nothing gained by hoping against hope for chances of big coups, whereby real small chances pass unheeded.[2]

His evident awareness of the drawbacks of centralization from a technical point of view suggests that his efforts to create a hierarchy of command were primarily aimed at bolstering the political impact of the guerrilla campaign. His acceptance of the Treaty derived from a realization that this impact would have definite limits, beyond which continued violent activity would be profitless or even counterproductive.

Those who opposed the Treaty favoured, *ipso facto*, the continuation of violence. They fell into three main groups. The first, those who perhaps suffered the least mental turmoil in taking up arms against the Provisional Government, may be seen as traditional resisters. They represented an element which had constantly struggled against government and which, after two years of intensified conflict,

[1] Townshend, 'Irish Republican Army', pp. 337-40.
[2] Chief of Staff, IRA, to OC Fingal Brigade, 6 Apr. 1921 (Mulcahy MSS P 7/A/II/17).

would have found it extremely difficult to desist from violence. It is worth recalling that traditional turbulence persisted: a farmer spokesman complained that in Wexford in December 1921

> farmyards are being burned practically daily; fairs and markets are still being held up; roads are being blocked by means of tree-felling; farm produce is being looted; cattle are being driven in thousands by men on bicycles and many of them are being injured.[1]

The republicanism of such 'rebels' was an indefinite quantity; its primary quality was that it had supplied a moral justification for actions which would otherwise have been criminal. The Catholic hierarchy had condemned the IRA's violence, primarily on the ground that it was unlikely to succeed in its object.[2] Hence success was necessary to provide retrospective justification, and only the achievement of the Republic could stand as such success.

A second group, rather Fenian-insurrectionist in outlook, defined the Republic more clearly in terms of sovereign independence, and believed that only the continued application of physical force could bring this about. By 1921 there were undoubtedly many Republicans who believed that the successes of the campaign to date showed that if the pressure were kept up the British could be forced to quit Ireland unconditionally. This attitude was sometimes expressed as 'driving the British out', and some who put it thus may actually have believed that the campaign would end by directly overpowering the Crown forces. Most, however, held, like Cathal Brugha and Erskine Childers, that 'more of the same' would induce the British to withdraw. Mary MacSwiney told the Dáil on 21 December that world opinion would prevent Britain from 'exterminating' the Irish; Harry Boland on 6 January argued that Britain was too deeply enmeshed in overseas problems to carry out its threat of 'war' if the Dáil rejected the Treaty (though he admitted that American opinion regarded the settlement as reasonable).

---

[1] Complaint of M. F. O'Hanlon, Gen. Secretary, Irish Farmers' Union, to Dáil, 15 Dec. 1921: Gaughan, *Stack*, p. 129.

[2] Though, as R. Davis points out, there were other, pragmatic reasons for clerical dislike of guerrilla warfare: surprise attacks were murder of the soul as well as the body, besides which they brought down reprisals on the community: 'Advocacy of Passive resistance', pp. 48–9.

This second outlook merged with a third, which was perhaps less optimistic but which saw it as a matter of honour for Ireland to stand by the Republic. Here all pragmatism was driven out by moral intensity.[1] In particular, the fact of partition dwindled into apparent insignificance alongside the issue of the oath of allegiance. Liam Mellows, preparing to face a firing squad after the capture of the Four Courts, expressed only his comrades' enduring repudiation of the oath.

> Here in this spot (Mountjoy gaol), sacred to the memory of Kevin Barry and other martyrs of the Republic, they deny the authority of any usurping Government, that recognizes the right of the British king in Ireland.[2]

Austin Stack was reduced to near-collapse by the news of the Treaty. He later provided a limpid illumination of the non-rational Republican reaction, in his own harrowed account of the negotiations and their outcome, written while on hunger-strike in Kilmainham in October 1923. In Stack's view, it had seemed evident by late November 1921

> that there could be no agreement in London. The English were not ready to come to the point beyond which we could not touch without dishonour, and, if England wanted more war, well, all we could do was to defend our country's honour with our lives.[3]

This concern with honour, and apparent unconcern for the lives of his less dogmatic countrymen, was the polar opposite of Griffith's cry 'Is there to be no living Irish nation? Is the Irish nation to be the dead past or the prophetic future?' It was based on a sort of anti-pragmatism which had been introduced into the Fenian mental armoury by Pearse. Recalling the plenipotentiaries' account of how they came to sign the Treaty, Stack wrote

> Mr. Griffith, if I remember aright, would not admit duress by the British, Mr. Collins said if there was duress it was only 'the duress of the facts', whatever he meant by that . . .[4]

---

[1] The lone socialist within the leadership, Liam Mellows, declared 'We would rather have this country poor and indigent, we would rather have the people of Ireland eking out a poor existence on the soil as long as they possessed their souls, their minds, and their honour' (Dáil debates, Macardle, op. cit. p. 577).

[2] Holograph note, 30 June 1922 (Childers MSS 15444 2).

[3] Stack memoir, quoted in Gaughan, *Stack*, p. 167.   [4] Ibid. p. 174.

This professed inability to understand or accept facts was to remain a characteristic of republicanism, an 'insulation against failure' in the words of a recent acerbic critic.[1]

The position of Eamon de Valera was, characteristically, slightly apart from all these. De Valera certainly repudiated the Treaty, expressing a belief that

A win meant triumph, definite and final. If we lost, the loss would not be as big as it seemed, for we would be no worse than we had been six months ago. To me the win seemed almost a certainty, but they could not see it.[2]

He blamed the failure on the IRB, which had undermined GHQ—'Tho' the rank and file of the army is right, the head-quarter Staff clean gone wrong—a part of the machine. Curse secret societies!'.[3] But what he saw as 'a win' was not recognition of an absolutely independent unitary republic, but acceptance of his own alternative proposal of 'external association'. This idiosyncratic concept, enshrined in his 'Document No. 2', was in fact accepted by few opponents of the Treaty. Some could not understand it: it lacked the transparent simplicity of absolute independence. Others saw it as essentially similar to the Treaty (accepting in effect Griffith's allegation that it was a 'quibble')—not least in its recognition of separate treatment for Ulster.[4] Yet de Valera's opposition to the Treaty provided a political basis for the renewal of violent resistance.[5] His earlier plea to the Irish not to depart from the 'definite constitutional way of resolving our political differences'[6] was abandoned as soon as that way failed to resolve the difference in his favour.

[1] C. Cruise O'Brien, *Herod: Reflections on Political Violence* (London, 1978), p. 46.

[2] De Valera to McGarrity, 27 Dec. 1921 (McGarrity MSS 17440).

[3] Ibid.

[4] Macardle, op. cit. pp. 953-63; Rumpf and Hepburn, op. cit. pp. 28-31.

[5] The view of P. S. O'Hegarty (*The Victory of Sinn Féin* (Dublin, 1924), p. 72) may be substantially accepted in spite of the fact that, as Rumpf observed, neither de Valera nor anyone else could have persuaded the 'Fenian' group who rejected all compromise to accept the Treaty, even had he wished to do so: op. cit. p. 35.

[6] 'Proclamation to the Irish People', *Irish Independent*, 9 Dec. 1921.

8
Civil Wars

Few as we are have Faith, have Confidence, stand together
as one man, do your real, your whole duty to Ireland, and
a just and all powerful God will guide our forces and crown
their efforts with victory.

Speech at Clan na Gael Convention 1929[1]

(i) *Irregularism*

There are standing in the path today armed men saying to
the massed men of this nation: You must not take a certain
course. That is a position which never has been conceded
in any democratic country. It will not be conceded here.

Kevin O'Higgins[2]

It has often been suggested that during centuries of British
rule the Irish had become indifferent if not hostile to government, so that when political independence came the definition of patriotism had to be changed. Inevitably, it took time
to develop a sense of civic responsibility.[3] The 'great test'
faced by Ireland after 1921 was, in part, whether any government could secure authority that would hold good against
the claims of extremist groups using violent methods. The
Provisional Government which made its bid for such authority
on the basis of the Treaty came increasingly to see its main
task as the creation of a positive sense of political participation. Kevin O'Higgins, its Minister of Justice, produced an
analysis which was probably as close to the truth as could
be reached amidst the dislocation of civil war:

It would perhaps be a generous estimate to say that 20 per cent of the
militant opposition to the Government is idealism . . . . It would be,

---

[1] McGarrity MSS 17534.

[2] Dáil Éireann Reports, i. 959; T. de V. White, *Kevin O'Higgins* (London,
1948), p. 137.

[3] J. M. Curran, *The Birth of the Irish Free State 1921–1923* (Alabama, 1980),
p. 245.

perhaps, a generous estimate also to say that only 20 per cent of it is crime. And between those 20 per cents there flows 60 per cent of sheer futility, that is neither one thing nor the other, but that will go on until some very definite reason is put up to it why it should not go on.[1]

As will be seen, it may be that at root the anti-Treaty resistance, labelled 'irregularism' by the Provisional Government, owed more to traditional local turbulence than to the highly publicized 'split' in the Sinn Féin leadership.

The split was, however, of enduring importance for the political development of Ireland. The outstanding feature of the fracture was its multiple nature. The division in the Dáil in December 1921 was unavoidable in view of the sharp conceptual and personal differences between idealists and realists. The rupture of the Sinn Féin organization, which became evident in January 1922 as preparations went ahead for the 1922 *árdfheis*, was equally certain (though it appears to have surprised and dismayed Austin Stack).[2] Such cleavages might have been confined within de Valera's 'constitutional way' had they not been followed by the disintegration of the IRA. Cracks appeared in the military organization immediately the Treaty terms were announced, but a semblance of unity was assiduously preserved through the next three months while the political rift became absolute.

This fragile cohesion was only maintained through a politically questionable device, the Army Convention. Military support for the idea of a convention showed that the IRA had not accepted a constitutional position within the Republic, and did not feel bound to accept the decision of Dáil Éireann. An ominous gulf in attitudes was emerging. One company officer of the Dublin Brigade later recalled that

Since the days of the Irish party . . . the word 'politician' was never applied to a member of the (advanced national) movement. It was a word of ill-repute. Now nearly all the members of the Dail overnight became in my eyes 'politicians'; a distinction was rapidly being drawn between 'the politicians' and the Army.[3]

[1] White, op. cit. p. 123.
[2] Gaughan, *Stack*, pp. 189–91.
[3] C. S. ('Todd') Andrews, *Dublin Made Me. An Autobiography* (Cork, 1979), p. 208.

The Army Convention was first accepted and then, on 15 March, proscribed as a 'sectional' assembly by the Provisional Government and IRA GHQ. This tardy ban precipitated a move to open opposition by anti-Treaty officers, who proceeded to summon the Convention in spite of the ban—in the knowledge that it would split the Army. 'Army unity' was evidently acceptable only if it followed the ideas of this group, which were curtly expressed by Rory O'Connor (formerly a junior member of the GHQ staff) at a press conference on 22 March. Allegiance to all oath-breaking politicians was repudiated, and in reply to a question whether the group would resort to military dictatorship O'Connor said laconically, 'You can take it that way if you like'.[1]

This lack of interest in constitutional niceties made it easy for the Free State to portray the ensuing civil war as a struggle between democracy and dictatorship. 'The whole question as to whether it is to be a Nation in the future governed by constitutional principles, or whether it is to be a mob dictated to by an armed minority was at stake', as the government's most relentless and gifted spokesman put it.[2] The astounding unconcern with which the anti-Treatyites embarked on a policy of shooting members of the Dáil reinforced this impression. However, whilst such a clash of concepts may illuminate the actions of a few *têtes exaltées*, exhilarated idealists of the sort thrown up in many revolutions, it scarcely provides a basis for understanding the widespread recrudescence of violence in Ireland in 1922. Still less was the key to be found in the machinations of the IRB, as de Valera angrily implied.[3] The old organization faltered in its response to the Treaty, and crumbled into ineffectiveness as a result.[4] Collins's position as president of the supreme council doubtless helped to keep some waverers on his side, but his personal contacts were more important.

[1] Macardle, *Irish Republic*, pp. 616–17; cf. Todd Andrews, 'I did not see anything wrong with an IRA military dictatorship but I resented the breakdown in discipline' (op. cit. p. 218).
[2] White, *O'Higgins*, p. 125.
[3] See above, p. 364.
[4] J. O'Beirne Ranelagh, 'The IRB from the treaty to 1924', *IHS*, xx. 77 (1976), p. 29.

He could not, for instance, repair the loss of Terence Mac-
Swiney in Cork or Dick McKee and Peadar Clancy in Dublin.
McKee's successor as commandant of the Dublin Brigade,
Oscar Traynor, cracked Collins's previously secure grip on
the capital.

The temptation to explain the dynamics of the split and
the civil war as a chain reaction of personal divisions is a
strong one.[1] The most substantial, indeed the only substantial, attempt at social analysis of the conflict, that of
Erhard Rumpf, was hostile to this form of explanation
but was unable to escape from it altogether.[2] Rumpf
accepted that to some extent, impossible to measure precisely, the dispute over the Treaty was a matter of temperament and thus beyond the scope of analysis[3] (except,
presumably, individual psychoanalysis). Further, he acknowledged the importance of local rivalries and the difficulty
of evaluating them, giving as an example the fact that the
split in Co. Kerry followed in part the lines of an ancient
and (politically) irrelevant family feud.[4] He tried, however,
to produce explanations which could be grounded on more
precise evidence, and more comprehensibly modern responses.
In particular he correlated statistics for the intensity of the
'national struggle' of 1919-21 with his general framework of
the 'east–west gradient' on which disturbance and opposition

[1] The oft-remarked personalism of Irish culture provides some justification
for this approach. Cf. D. Schmitt, *The Irony of Irish Democracy*. (Lexington,
Mass., 1973), 45, 55-64.

[2] E. Rumpf, *Nationalismus und Sozialismus in Irland: historisch-soziologischer
Versuch über die irische Revolution seit 1918* (Meisenheim am Glan), 1959.
This pioneering analysis must now be read in conjunction with D. Fitzpatrick,
Politics and Irish Life, and 'The geography of Irish nationalism 1910-1921',
Past and Present lxxviii (1978), which is in part a critique of Rumpf's analysis of
the period up to 1921. After Fitzpatrick's work was written the original thesis
was reissued in translated and slightly revised form as E. Rumpf and A. C. Hepburn, *Nationalism and Socialism in Twentieth Century Ireland.* Further references
are to the work in this form.

[3] Rumpf and Hepburn, op. cit. p. 33. Cf. Todd Andrews, 'I who by temperament could never see but one side to any problem . . . regarded the Provisional
Government as political scoundrels, rascals and murderers supported by oppor-
tunists, gombeen men and West Britons' (op. cit. p. 259).

[4] Rumpf and Hepburn, op. cit. p. 62. It is almost certain that this example
could be multiplied many times; even some 'factions' may well have survived
into the twentieth century.

to British rule increased westwards from the Dublin–Belfast axis.

As an acute critic has recently pointed out, Rumpf's data were unfortunately a treacherous foundation for his elaborate explanatory edifice.[1] He measured regional intensity of conflict by number of incidents, a procedure which could be vitiated by the fact that a low number of incidents in some areas might actually indicate a high level of resistance (as, for instance, the superficial tranquillity of Westmeath in 1871 had demonstrated the power of Ribbonism rather than the strength of the law). Perhaps more seriously, he did not relate these numbers to population, thus distorting his regional comparisons. In addition, the correlation between his maps is far looser than he claimed, and this looseness allowed contradictions to enter his central argument about the dynamics of the civil war. In attacking the personalistic approach to the split, he held that the correlation between his map of the national struggle and that of the split was

too close to be explained simply in terms of the attitude of a few IRA commandants. The fact that anti-British and subsequent anti-Treaty activity went together indicates that the animosities developed during the earlier campaign produced a deep-rooted spirit of intransigence in these areas.[2]

Yet this assertion about the congruence of the two struggles is undermined by his realization that much of the strength of 'irregularism' lay in fact in areas which had *not* been in the forefront of the national struggle, in particular the Gaeltacht/CDB areas of Connacht[3] (though his own map of the split is of limited use, being based on the decisions of divisional commandants rather than subordinate units or rank

---

[1] Fitzpatrick, 'Geography of Irish nationalism', p. 117. Fitzpatrick is particularly critical of Rumpf's reliance on a map of British reprisals as an index of intensity of struggle, and it is unfortunate that this map has been retained in the new edition (p. 39). It is not, however, the case that reprisals were forbidden outside the martial-law area in January 1921, as Fitzpatrick suggests; it is only that 'official' reprisals were then initiated within it (and were carried out quite illegally by the police elsewhere, as by DI Cruise in Galway).

[2] Rumpf and Hepburn, op. cit. p. 57.

[3] Ibid. p. 61. It is obvious that to regard the areas of 1st Western and 1st Midland Divisions as less 'active' in the national struggle than, say, 4th Western or 2nd Northern, is to bend the evidence beyond breaking-point.

and file). Indeed, the remarkable aspect of the civil war is not the continuing military activity of the south-western *exaltados* but the relatively novel activity of the west. This surely indicates, as Rumpf himself declares at a later point, that the social foundation of the civil war differed from that of the 1919–21 struggle.[1]

It is possibly better to view the 'deep-seated spirit of intransigence' in Republican areas after 1921 not as the product so much as a cause of the 'animosities developed during the earlier campaign'. It may be suggested that this intransigence can be identified primarily with traditional rural resistance. Fitzpatrick's research in Co. Clare—the most penetrating local investigation so far—led him to the view that many of the incidents in 1919–21 which were labelled IRA engagements were in reality thinly disguised land seizures, which GHQ had neither the ability nor perhaps the will to prevent.[2] Clare was demographically and economically, as well as geographically, midway between the western (Connacht) and south-western (Munster) regions, and this conclusion may be applicable to some of the 'national struggle' in Munster. The question that arises is why the continuing land war was not 'disguised' in this way in Connacht, where on the contrary the Sinn Féin underground government was early engaged in attempts to control land disturbance through the Dáil courts.[3]

Rumpf's conclusion was that the poorer counties had failed to mobilize effectively in the national struggle because they lacked a substantial middle class. This fact is obviously important, given that Sinn Féin was a middle-class movement. The concomitant conclusion would, presumably, be that nationalism remained an idea confined to the middle class. The areas—the old congested districts above all—where land purchase was least advanced, farm sizes small, and pressure on the land heaviest, were still mobilizing for a different struggle. In this respect it may be argued that the civil war in the west was already in progress before the Truce,

---

[1] Rumpf and Hepburn, p. 68.

[2] Fitzpatrick, 'Geography of Irish nationalism', p. 119.

[3] Rumpf again recognized (p. 55) that 'The social aspirations of landless men were not primarily expressed in terms of hostility to British administration'.

let alone the Treaty. There social groups existed for which the victory of the 'nation' and the achievement of 'freedom' would mean little but the confirmation and reinforcement of a bourgeois regime inheriting and operating the apparatus of the English state.[1] It was that apparatus rather than the dominance of Englishmen as such that had traditionally provoked resistance, though resistance had up to now been applauded and encouraged by nationalist leaders. It was against this resistance, as much as the tyranny of armed fanatics, that O'Higgins—cast in the bronze image of British statesmanship—battled. When he branded his opponents as 'irregulars', an epithet which deeply distressed the devout Liam Lynch, he was condemning a social equation made by the *Manchester Guardian*: 'Irregularism and land grabbing go together'.[2]

This last echo of Whiteboyism lingered in western Ireland well into the 1930s. Before it finally died out it was linked with the cause of a group for whom the convulsion of 1922-3 formed another martyrogenic step in the pursuit of purity, and who were to find a sempiternal holy land in the North. The IRA fought the war, as Pearse had conceived the Rising, as a crusade to save what they judged to be the soul of the nation. They were bereft of feasible proposals, and offered protracted struggle not so much as a mechanism as an ethical assertion; approaching, in effect, an end in itself. Self-validating, autotelic violence became in effect the Republican programme. De Valera's 'Document No. 2' showed that he at least remained concerned with real politics, as he was to demonstrate five years later by taking the Oath of Allegiance. Republicans by contrast defined their position negatively. Their arguments were collected together in September 1922 by the IRA's Publicity Department:

For five years, the nation was united on these fundamental principles, the existence of the Republic, the sanctity of our National Independence and Ireland's territorial integrity.

[1] As Peadar O'Donnell observed, 'in many areas Volunteers were actually used to control the rural masses who would identify the national struggle with their own struggle for land' (*There Will Be Another Day* (Dublin, 1963), pp. 20-2).
[2] (15 March 1923), Rumpf and Hepburn, op. cit. p. 61.

The Treaty violated all three by destroying the Republic, establishing an Irish Colony and partitioning Ireland.

It was impossible for Republicans to sanction this violation because:
1) The Irish people had never recognised British rule as lawful.
2) They had for five years fought a bitter war to maintain the Republic.
3) They had taken lives in its defence.
4) They had sworn to defend the Republic against all enemies, foreign and domestic.
5) The Treaty had been signed behind the backs of the Cabinet of Dáil Éireann and of the Army, and in violation of the signatories' oaths, credentials and terms of reference.
6) The Treaty was signed under a threat of war—an unworthy surrender for a proud and honourable nation.[1]

This moral defensive position found a military counterpart in the strategy adopted both in Dublin, where the seizure of the Four Courts unmistakably followed the hallowed example of 1916, and in the provinces, where Lynch was content to establish a defensive line (not the 'line of the Shannon', though this might have served Republicans better) and wait for the reversal of public opinion which he felt must come.[2] Neither these measures, nor the subsequent reversion to guerrilla strategy, were capable of combating the real power of the state in the hands of the Provisional Government.[3] By threatening the insecure basis of that state, and above all by killing Michael Collins (if indeed they did so), the anti-Treatyites ironically ensured the Anglicization of the Irish political structure.[4] Even Collins had been impelled to borrow British artillery and to consider even more vicious Saxon techniques. His successor, the aggressively realist O'Higgins, was driven by the very ferocity of the Free State

[1] Director of Publicity, N. & E. Command IRA, to all TDs, 8 Sept. 1922 (William O'Brien MSS, NLI MS 13957). 'They' in (2) is ambiguous, referring to 'Republicans' and not 'the Irish people', as might appear.

[2] Todd Andrews records his dismay on realizing that 'the IRA leadership had not merely not envisaged setting up a military dictatorship, but had not considered any alternative policy' (op. cit. p. 218).

[3] McGarrity's impatience with the Republicans' indecision was expressed in a letter to Stack: 'the most essential thing at present is a military victory. If the military fails all fails. If the military wins all fails . . . Propaganda, or resolutions in Congress while your army is driven from the towns is wasted energy and an excuse' (26 Feb. 1923, NLI MS 17640).

[4] J. M. Feehan, *The Shooting of Michael Collins: Murder or Accident?* Cork, 1981), reflects continuing awareness that there are many unanswered questions about Collins's life and death.

Army's response to the Irregulars—with the fearsome emergence of military lynch law—to take refuge in English legal doctrines to assert civil control over the armed forces. Cabinet responsibility was invoked to discipline Mulcahy, the Minister of Defence who acted as Commander-in-Chief; Cabinet government was effectively confirmed.[1] The stable conditions under which a new legal system, as dreamed of by Gaelic revivalists, might have been constructed, were removed. Absent also was constructive criticism (except from Labour) of the new constitution.

The sad irony by which the new state was instantly reduced to the same political bankruptcy as the former British state in countering violent political challenge left an indelible mark on Irish history. Indeed, the special powers resolution of 27 September 1922 went further than the proclamation of martial law in giving discretionary powers to the army, and these powers were dramatically abused on a few occasions, as in the gruesome Kerry affair. These must be seen as evidence of a general demoralization and habituation to violence. Yet the fundamental argument for Irish self-government was rapidly vindicated. O'Higgins's defence of the Free State's actions (including the execution without trial of four Republican leaders) under the maxim *salus populi suprema lex*—'Ultimately all government is based on force, must meet force with greater force if it is to survive' —met with a public acceptance which no British government had obtained. Counter-terrorism worked against resistance which lacked widespread support. The new state's police force, created under the rather outlandish title Civil Guard, was happily Gaelicized into Garda Siochana, and was able to function as an unarmed force on the British model.[2]

No political compromise was offered to the Irregulars, or sought by them. Force succeeded only within its natural limits: it could not abolish political realities. Their very anti-realism made Republicans henceforth an irreducible reality. Symbolically, having considered surrender to the Free

---

[1] White, *O'Higgins*, pp. 119-43.

[2] C. Brady, 'Police and Government in the Irish Free State, 1922-1933' (University College, Dublin, MA thesis, 1977); Garvin, *Evolution of Irish Nationalist Politics*, pp. 152, 192.

State forces, they followed instead Stack's proposal of a 'simple quit'—probably his most enduring contribution to the cause. Republicans quietly hid their weapons and waited for the next opportunity. No instrument of peace ended the civil war.

(ii) *Keeping the faith*

> The reasons and necessity for maintaining a Military Organization are based primarily on the admitted right of the Irish Nation to full and complete control of its affairs . . . and on the principle that any section or proportion of the citizens have the right, and it is their duty, if they feel they can do so, to assert the sovereignty of the Nation. It is the belief of the Army that it is only by military action that the sovereignty of the Republic can be asserted.
>
> IRA Army Council Statement, 1928[1]

After 1922 the IRA was once again an army without a nation, at least in the sense in which the national state had been realized between 1916 and 1921. This was, however, a situation not unfamiliar to the Fenian tradition. The 'new IRA' reverted to guardianship of a national ideal as yet unrealized: more poignantly, in fact, an ideal betrayed by former comrades-in-arms. It disliked, for obvious reasons, the adjective 'new'; but the title 'old IRA' was pre-empted by a group of IRB malcontents in the Free State Army. (This group, which looked much more dangerous to the stability of the state than it proved in the end to be, grew out of an IRB revival organized by Sean OMuirthile in the winter of 1921-2. Its bid to regain influence through the so-called 'army mutiny' of 1924 caused a brief ministerial panic before evaporating.[2]) Republican irreconcilables were commonly labelled the 'new IRA', but a better title might be 'independent IRA'. They saw themselves as standing in a long succession of men and women whose sense of duty and honour 'kept faith' with the cause.[3]

---

[1] Prepared for Clan na Gael Convention 1928 (McGarrity MSS 17533).

[2] The revival of the IRB after the Treaty was observed unenthusiastically by Ernie O'Malley: *The Singing Flame*, pp. 35-7. Strictly the 'old IRA' were called the 'IRA Organization'; Ranelagh, op. cit. p. 37.

[3] Cf. S. Cronin, *They Kept Faith*, (Dublin, 1957); J. A. Murphy, 'The New IRA 1925-62', in T. D. Williams (ed.), *Secret Societies in Ireland*, pp. 150-1.

The independent IRA was marked by intense suspicion of 'political' bodies whose republicanism often proved distressingly flexible. As a result it showed a strong tendency through the next fifty years to stand alone. Throughout this period its commitment to physical force was maintained, but a new uncertainty about how to employ it was noticeable after the failure in the civil war of both open warfare and guerrilla strategy. This uncertainty was to persist. A compensatory willingness to experiment with radical mass movements was to appear and reappear from time to time into the 1960s. On the issue of independence, however, a degree of certainty was evident from the outset of the civil war. The 'Constitution of the Republican Army' drawn up by the proscribed Army Convention in April 1922 redefined the IRA's objects as

(a) To guard the honour and maintain the independence of the Irish Republic,

(b) To protect the rights and liberties common to the people of Ireland,

(c) To place its services at the disposal of an established Republican Government *which faithfully upholds the above objects.*[1]

This political allegiance was so conditional as to move into the region of contract, or even treaty. As such it was extended to the 'Republican Government' established after the split had become a war. Quite clearly it was not the 'government' which validated the existence of the 'army', but the other way about. De Valera's political leadership was accepted in a grudging spirit, because of his public prestige; in the terminology of soldiers he remained a politician. As President of the Republic on the run in rainswept Kerry he exerted less real control than he had two years before, when he was three thousand miles away in the USA.

The decision to stop fighting in 1923 was a military, not a political, one. Had Lynch not been killed it would probably never have been taken. Liam Lynch expressed in pure form the other-worldly Republican rejection of reality. He believed that only diabolical possession could explain the Free State's violent repressive actions; a literal belief, unlike MacSwiney's

---

[1] Macardle, *Irish Republic*, p. 631 (my italics).

rhetorical equation of the British government with 'the powers of hell'.[1]

After the cease-fire, the IRA lapsed temporarily into a state of shocked quiescence. It emerged from this to discover that most of the Sinn Féin 'politicians' were indeed preparing to sell the Republican pass. At the Army Convention in November 1925 Frank Aiken, a northern divisional commandant who was henceforth to adhere to de Valera, admitted that some members of the Republican government were considering entry into the Free State parliament. The reaction was immediate, and a motion to withdraw the IRA from allegiance to Sinn Féin was angrily carried. Its proposer, Peadar O'Donnell, moved into the front rank of the IRA leadership, though he was never able to carry the organization wholly in the direction he wished.[2]

The parting of the ways with de Valera proved to be more final than it was to seem for a decade to come. His new political movement, Fianna Fáil, in spite of its fanciful name, was determined to remain in contact with the real world. Admittedly Fianna Fáil only renounced violence on pragmatic rather than moral grounds, but its argument that the use of force was impossible while 'an elected native government . . . stands in the way with a native army at its command' was revolutionary enough in the circumstances.[3]

Political self-sufficiency meant that the core doctrines of the independent IRA had once again to be defined and refined. The constitution now detailed as

3. *Objects*

(i) To guard the honour and uphold the Sovereignty and Unity of the Republic of Ireland

(ii) To establish and uphold a lawful Government in sole and absolute control of the Republic

(iii) To secure and defend civil and religious liberty and equal rights and equal opportunities for all citizens

[1] Andrews, *Dublin Made Me*, p. 271.

[2] O'Donnell had been selected for the sixteen-man Army Executive by the Convention on 9 April 1922, but he was reckoned a year later to be only in the second rank of leaders: T. P. Coogan, *The IRA* (new edn., Collins, Glasgow, 1980), p. 64.

[3] Fianna Fáil, *A National Policy* (May 1926), p. 6, quoted in D. G. Boyce, *Nationalism in Ireland* (London, 1981), pp. 370-1.

(iv) To promote the revival of the Irish language as the everyday language of the people and to promote the development of the best mental and physical characteristics of our race.

4. *Means*

The means by which Óglaich na h-Éireann shall endeavour to achieve its objects are

(i) Force of arms
(ii) Organising, training and equipping the manhood of Ireland as an efficient military force
(iii) Assisting as directed by the Army Authority all organizations working for the same objects.[1]

The Army Council, delegated as the supreme authority by the General Army Convention, was to have 'power to transfer its services to a Government which is actively endeavouring to function as the de facto Government of the Republic'. But it was itself also invested with governmental powers: it could make peace or declare war on its own authority.[2]

A faint hope that Fianna Fáil might endeavour to function in the desired way remained. After experimenting with a political 'wing', Comhairle na Poblachta, the IRA assisted the Fianna Fáil electoral machinery to its first victories in 1932 and 1933. Immediately after this it opposed—with physical force—the Army Comrades' Association which furnished protection to the defeated Cumann na nGaedheal party. It also tried to hot up the 'economic war' with Britain by acts of sabotage. As the ACA developed into the Blueshirt movement, the IRA was able—with some aplomb—to lambaste the opposition as fascist exponents of political violence.[3] But the presumed alliance between the IRA and Fianna Fáil (presumed by its opponents as well as by some of the IRA—though not its Chief of Staff, Moss

---

[1] Constitution of Óglaich na hÉireann (McGarrity MSS 17529). Cf. the version in Coogan, op. cit. pp. 64-6, which is considerably less full.

[2] Constitution, Arts. 5 (3), 6 (1). The military attitude changed little thereafter. As Sean Russell put it in the mid 1930s, the IRA 'stands ready, as in the past, to cooperate with all groups working towards the ideal of an Irish republic, providing such cooperation in no way imperils or infringes upon the liberty of the army to function in its historic manner' (Confidential declaration, 26 Oct. 1936, McGarrity MSS 17542 (2)).

[3] Attacks in *An Phoblacht*, 20 Aug. *et seq.*: M. Manning, *The Blueshirts* (Dublin, 1970), p. 31.

Twomey)[1] was conclusively demolished when de Valera at last turned his unique political skills to the final suppression of the physical-force party. It was no longer to be tolerated as a state *in potentia* within the established Irish state, now purged by de Valera of its most objectionable features. De Valera's impatience with the near-nihilism of the old organization had already welled up in a letter to McGarrity in 1934.

You talk about coming to an understanding with the IRA. You talk of the influence it would have both here and abroad. You talk as if we were fools and didn't realise all this. My God! Do you know that ever since 1921 the main purpose in everything I have done has been to try to secure a basis for national unity . . . But is all this need and desire for unity to be used as a means of trying to blackmail us into a policy which we know could only lead our people to disaster [?] It has taken us ten years of patient effort to get the Irish nation on the march again after a devastating Civil War. Are we to abandon all this in order to satisfy a group who have not given the slightest evidence of any ability to lead our people anywhere except back into the morass.[2]

This plain speaking (strangely reminiscent of the arguments used by Griffith and Collins against de Valera himself in 1922) was followed in 1936 by the redirection of the apparatus of repression, created to control the Blueshirts, against the IRA. Special tribunals and police harried the organization; it was declared illegal, and Twomey was arrested. The final abandonment of all Republican hope in Fianna Fáil was effectively symbolized when the seven surviving incorruptibles of the 'Second Dáil' transferred their 'authority' to the Army Council. The IRA had re-established its connection with the parliament in the only way possible— by absorbing it.[3]

The Army Council, now the sole Republican authority in theory as well as practice, embarked in 1939 on its first attempt at a systematic campaign of violence since 1923.

---

[1] Twomey told McGarrity on 26 Oct. 1933 that the IRA had come under pressure from Fianna Fáil to disband and merge with the government militia. 'This we could not agree to do.' He believed that Fianna Fáil wanted 'no agreement with the Army'—'in fact, and I should be sorry to do the Fianna Fáil leaders an injustice, I believe that some of them are more bitter towards us than they are to the "Blueshirts" ' (McGarrity MSS 17490).

[2] De Valera to McGarrity, 31 Jan. 1934 (ibid. 17441).

[3] Murphy, 'The New IRA', p. 157.

The bombing raids in Britain were, however, a dramatic reversion to the Clan na Gael methods of the 1880s, a reversion that was the outcome of protracted hesitation and uncertainty over the function of the independent IRA. The organization's drift towards autism was due to its inability to find common ground with other groups rather than to a desire for separation as such. It continually showed an awareness that its commitment to the pure Republic would be vain without some public support. Patriotism was not enough. Hence the hesitant alliance with Comhairle na Poblachta in 1928, and the hopeful clutching of Fianna Fáil's coat-tails afterwards. Moss Twomey felt in 1933 that 'militarily we are in a better position than since 1922', but had to admit (with delicate understatement) that 'politically our situation is not quite satisfactory'.

> Everybody is agreed that force must be the ultimate weapon, but some believe that we cannot get into a position in which force can be effectively used, unless the mind of the country understands the Army, and what it is seeking to achieve.[1]

Some indeed went further than this, and said that the army should try to understand the country. This truly revolutionary argument was tirelessly expounded from the mid 1920s onwards by Peadar O'Donnell, one of the IRA's most gifted publicists.

O'Donnell followed the logic of the most significant support for the Republicans in the civil war, and held that the IRA must identify itself with the land agitation if it was to obtain real strength.[2] It must aim at an agrarian revolution, a true social revolution rather than the abstract political revolution to which Fenians had traditionally been committed. In the general rural depression of the late 1920s this new-New Departure had some appeal to even the most hard-bitten Fenian traditionalists. The creation of *Saor Éire* in September 1931, described as an 'Organization of Workers and Working Farmers', brought the Republican movement to endorse at least the rhetoric of radicalism. The objectives of *Saor Éire*,

---

[1] Twomey to McGarrity, 26 Oct. 1933 (McGarrity MSS 17490).
[2] O'Donnell, *There Will Be Another Day*, pp. 23–30.

1. To achieve an independent revolutionary leadership for the working class and working farmers towards the overthrow in Ireland of British Imperialism and its ally, Irish Capitalism.
2. To organize and consolidate the Republic of Ireland on the basis of the possession and administration by the workers and working farmers, of the land, instruments of production, distribution and exchange.
3. To restore and foster the Irish language, culture, and games,[1]

were not, however, in spite of later claims, unambiguously socialist. 'Working farmers' have little in common with workers, and would only have accepted the second objective if it meant (as it possibly did) not socialization but redistribution of the land. Social ownership of land was not a popular aim amongst agrarian agitators—as had been shown by the fate of Davitt when he adopted the cause of land nationalization—and land-hunger remained the dominant force. Only through ambiguity did O'Donnell's movement to the left make much progress.

From the start it was looked at askance, if not actually opposed, by traditionalists. Even the early 'no tribute campaign' against the payment of land annuities had produced sharp controversy, though it was a tame enough idea compared, say, with the 'no rent' call in 1881.[2] As agrarian disturbances came again to dominate the western countryside in the 1930s, most of the movement's leaders retreated from their radical adventure. The sordid reality of class warfare was, as before, not their idea of physical force. Austin Stack was characteristically recorded as saying,

If we rush into an agitation, the self-seeking will rush after us, and we have no place for that class. We must remember always that we have the custody of a great cause . . . and if we can do no better, we must at least pass it on unsullied to a better generation.[3]

Yet at this time, in the late 1920s, the only direct achievement of physical force was a series of futile political murders,

[1] S. Cronin, *Irish Nationalism*, p. 156. On the agrarian crisis see B. O'Neill, *The War for the Land in Ireland* (London, 1933), pp. 117-58.
[2] Mary MacSwiney in *An Phoblacht*, 7, 28 Apr. 1928; Gaughan, *Stack*, pp. 261-2.
[3] 'Sceilg' in *Saoirse na hÉireann*, June 1928. Gaughan suggests that 'Stack was haunted by the spectre of the Republican, physical-force separatist tradition destroying itself in a welter of greed and self-seeking' (*Stack*, pp. 259-60).

of which the assassination of Kevin O'Higgins was the most spectacular. Even so, traditionalism prevailed.[1] O'Donnell was driven to found a separate movement, Republican Congress, which had only limited success.[2] Under the influence of Sean Russell, purest of physical-force men, the IRA moved almost in desperation towards 'the campaign in England' as the only significant form of action.[3] Self-deceptions were piled one upon another. Russell maintained in September 1938 that the 'organisation in Britain is now as perfect as we can make it', though only four months earlier an Adjutant-General's report had said that 'the state of organisation in the units which exist is poor and loose, and militarily should be described as almost elementary'.[4] The bungled Coventry explosion on 25 August 1939 and the subsequent crack-down by both British and Irish governments confirmed the IRA's weakness and the counter-productive effect of terrorist violence. However, one group within the organization believed its view to have been vindicated by Russell's failure: the advocates of violent action across the border with the 'six counties'.

(iii) *Border wars*

> The numerous explosions carried out under Army orders in Belfast at the time of the King's arrival there, as well as the destruction of practically every excise post along the supposed six county border, gave the world to understand that neither British kings nor British borders will be tolerated in Ireland.
>
> Clan na Gael, 1937[5]

---

[1] As a later disillusioned Republican radical put it, the attempt to reconcile social radicalism and traditional physical-force methods proved 'beyond the IRA's capacity' (Cronin, op. cit. p. 159).

[2] On 3 Jan. 1936 O'Donnell formed an 'Active Service Unit', with objectives that would have raised eyebrows among the ASUs of 1921: Coogan, *IRA*, pp. 111–12.

[3] Russell to McGarrity, 29 Jan. 1937 (McGarrity MSS 17485). Russell was suspended from the IRA and dismissed from his post as Quartermaster-General by his opponents, but reinstated and named as Chief of Staff early in 1938.

[4] Russell to McGarrity, 21 Sept. 1938 (loc. cit); General Report and Comments on Organisation in Great Britain, 6 May 1938 (McGarrity MSS 17544(5)).

[5] McGarrity MSS 17543 (4).

It has frequently been pointed out that the struggle against the Treaty centred not on the concrete question of partition but on the abstract issue of the oath of allegiance (that is, sovereign status). Only a very small proportion of the long Treaty debate—less than three per cent of speaking-time in the Dáil—concerned the Ulster question. The Republican-idealist assumption was, and has remained, that the partition issue was a false one, and would dissolve as soon as the real issue, British control, was resolved. This perspective was a natural extension of traditional Fenian concern with national 'freedom' rather than with the nature of the society that would exist in an independent Ireland.

For the realists who accepted the Treaty, however, the separation of the North was a real fact which posed immediate problems. The signatories believed that they had within the Treaty a mechanism for resolving them. The Boundary Commission, originally proposed by the Ulster Unionists, had been accepted with reluctance. Collins preferred 'local option' to ensure that substantial nationalist population groups were not left in Northern Ireland; but he was under no illusions about the basic difficulty. He told the British negotiators

This is a case which can be settled by Irishmen. By force we could beat them perhaps, but perhaps not. I do not think we could beat them morally. If you kill all of us, every man and every male child, the difficulty will still be there. So in Ulster. That is why we do not want to coerce them, but we cannot allow solid blocks who are against partition in the north of Antrim, through a part of Derry and part of Armagh to Strangford Lough. If we are not going to coerce the North-East corner, the North-east corner must not be allowed to coerce.[1]

Routine optimism was transformed by Collins's ever-maturing realism into a plea—fruitless as it transpired—for a fair partition. He and Griffith had no excessive faith in the Boundary Commission, but, as Griffith said, 'We are not going to use violence because we do not want to have the legacy left by violence among our own people'.[2] The hope that the Commission might so modify Northern Ireland's territory that it would be induced to join the Free State was less extravagant in its first than in its second aspect.

[1] Jones, *Whitehall Diary*, iii. 131.   [2] Ibid.

Unfortunately, the sketchy debate on Articles XI–XIV of the Treaty, which governed the status of the North, failed to reveal the imprecise wording of the crucial Article XII. When the Commission was finally established, it was found to have no power to hold plebiscites (which most people— including Lord Balfour—had assumed would determine the partition on 'Versailles principles'), and its chairman made no attempt to obtain such power.[1] Its tinkering with the border was in the end repudiated by the Free State, and the six-county Northern Ireland as established by the Government of Ireland Act in 1920 became permanent. Even though the large 'Hibernia irredenta', which Balfour had feared would be left in a nine-county Ulster, was reduced to apparently manageable proportions, it remained a major problem—which the Northern Ireland state was almost by definition ill-equipped to handle.

In the meantime a more direct form of nationalist–Unionist conflict was already under way before Collins's death. His effort to preserve the precarious unity of the IRA involved his connivance at—or initiation of—action against 'Carsonia' through the Belfast boycott, and more open violence of which the most public act was the assassination of Sir Henry Wilson in June 1922.[2] Collins, as his attitude in the negotiations showed, regarded the idea of 'coercing' Ulster as futile, and saw such action merely as an intensification of political pressure (by now a familiar Irish approach). The 'statesmanlike' tendency of Free State politics was displayed in the Collins–Craig pact, and was to reach a high point later with O'Higgins's idea that a coronation of the King as King of Ireland might be tolerated as a way of reconciling loyalists to the Free State. (Later still, after the setbacks of the de Valera period, this tendency was to reappear in Garret FitzGerald's campaign to modify the 1937 constitution.[3])

[1] *Report of the Irish Boundary Commission*, intr. G. J. Hand (Shannon, 1969).
[2] Wilson had become security adviser to the Northern Ireland government.
[3] G. FitzGerald, *Towards a New Ireland* (London, 1972); R. Foster, 'Garret's Crusade', *London Review of Books*, iv. 21 (Jan. 1982). The best contemporary analysis of the pact is K. Boyle (ed.), 'The Tallents report on the Craig-Collins pact of 30 March 1922', *Irish Jurist*, xii (1977).

The inescapable difficulty was that violence remained endemic on the northern community boundaries. The Collins–Craig pact was an attempt to deal with the resurgence of collective violence in the summer of 1921, whose immediate occasion had been an IRA attack on three RIC in the Falls Road area on 9 July. The demonstrative flurry of IRA activity in the few days before the Truce had passed off quietly elsewhere, but here it coincided with preparations for the Twelfth. It unleashed a five-hour street battle in which 14 people were killed and 86 wounded.[1] Further rioting broke out on 10 August, and again on 23 September. Protestant Ultras were able to rely on a seasonal preparedness and predisposition for battle to ram home the point that there would be no surrender; 'not an inch' was to become an ever more specific battle-cry now that an actual border existed.

The posture of confrontation at street level was inevitably transferred to the posture of the government whose *raison d'être* was to keep Ulster a 'protestant province'.[2] From 1922 Northern Ireland more than most states may be said to have institutionalized violence. Part of the cause was that it was not quite a state: as the only experiment in devolution so far tried in the United Kingdom, it was a sub-state (rather than a statelet, as it has been pejoratively labelled). The sectarian predisposition of the ruling Unionist politicians was too strong to be neutralized by the demands of statesmanship. A few made the effort, but most were prepared to act as if the Northern Ireland Cabinet was a grand Orange Lodge.[3] Unionist public life was retarded by the dogma of loyalism; political maturity has been slow to emerge. The

[1] RIC Reports, 10–17 July 1921 (PRONI, FIN 18/1/107).

[2] This process is analysed extensively in P. Buckland, *The Factory of Grievances: Devolved Government in Northern Ireland 1921–39* (Dublin, 1979). A critical account making use of the S. G. Tallents MSS (PRO CO 906/30 etc.) is P. Bew *et al.*, *The State in Northern Ireland 1921–72* (Manchester, 1979), pp. 50–62.

[3] Cf. J. Harbinson, *The Ulster Unionist Party, 1882–1973* (Belfast, 1973), ch. 8. Uncompromising partisanship was displayed in the removal of proportional representation (for local elections in 1922, parliamentary elections in 1929), an action condemned by British civil servants as *ultra vires* the Northern Ireland government, 'an abrogation of the rights of the minority . . . and . . . a fatal obstacle to conciliatory efforts' (Cabinet Conclusions, 31 July 1922, App. C, PRO CAB.43/2). British politicians decided to let it pass, however.

situation was conditioned from the outset by the disorders of 1920-2, which stretched the new government in an alarming way. Its restricted powers left it dependent in the sensitive sphere of law and order on Crown forces outside its control. The most substantial recent research has suggested that the confusion in the structure of these forces weakened their response to the 1921 rioting, the result of which was certainly to heighten Protestant anxiety and distrust of Nationalists.[1] Ironically, the government inherited from its parent the legalistic caution which prevented effective repressive action from being taken. This caution would have made sense if the government had intended to bid for the support—or at least the goodwill—of the Nationalist minority. Such may have been Craig's intention, but it did not produce results.[2]

Even the notorious Civil Authorities (Special Powers) Act of 1922, later to be condemned as creating 'a permanent machine of dictatorship', was not immoderate by comparison with the Restoration of Order Act and other earlier coercion laws, in so far as it did not establish special tribunals to try scheduled crimes. Undoubtedly, however, it led to the suspension of Habeas Corpus, and gave wide-ranging discretionary powers to the executive in a manner repugnant to English legal tradition. When it was made permanent in 1933 it cast a grim shadow over the remaining forty years of the sub-state's life.[3] Under it the police, their title less happily translated than in the Free State, from Royal Irish to Royal Ulster Constabulary (the use of the name Ulster to describe the six counties, though it accurately reflects the focus of Protestant identity, has always been regarded as offensive by Nationalists),[4] became a force viewed by the

[1] Buckland, op. cit. pp. 179-81, 187, 194-5.

[2] Ibid. pp. 201-2.

[3] *Report of a Commission of Inquiry appointed to examine the Purpose and Effect of the Civil Authorities (Special Powers) Acts (Northern Ireland) 1922 and 1933* NCCL, London, 1936, pp. 38-40. For a somewhat impressionist argument that 'Northern Ireland has always been and remains a potential police state' see T. Hadden and P. Hillyard, *Justice in Northern Ireland. A Study in Social Confidence* (London, 1973).

[4] Although, as has often been pointed out, the 'historic' province of Ulster was an English administrative creation. See p. 327 above.

Catholic population as violent and repressive. Pre-eminently, however, the tone of the Northern Ireland state was set by the Ulster Special Constabulary. The Class 'B' (part-time) special constables, carrying service weapons which they kept at home when off duty, were direct descendants of the UVF.[1] Seen by their opponents as a 'terrorist militia', the USC gave institutional expression to a Protestant vigilantism which was both traditional and—in its own terms—effective.[2] Ordinary Protestants 'wanted law and order', in the words of a sympathetic historian, and were 'determined that the country should not sink into anarchy as the three southern provinces had done'.[3] A number of northern Catholics concurred to the extent of joining the new force, but the inhibitions were formidable and from the start of recruiting on 1 November 1920 the USC was overwhelmingly Protestant in composition.[4]

The 'B' Specials were in effect an index of loyalism in the North, and a symptom of the IRA's inability to take root across the whole province. It was never in real contention there, and its GHQ took refuge in grandiose fantasies of 'surrounding', 'outflanking' or 'driving wedges into' Carsonia.[5] When the Republicans recovered from the civil war and turned some attention to the North, their hostility expressed

[1] The arming of '30,000 men in Ulster by whom the authority of the Crown could be vindicated' was pressed by Churchill (Cabinet, 23 July 1920); though even Henry Wilson thought him 'a perfect idiot as a statesman' for this (Diary, 26 July 1920: M. Gilbert, *Churchill*, companion vol. iv, p. 1150), and expressed qualms about arming the USC without putting them under military discipline (Cabinet Conference, 2 Sept. 1920).

[2] The process was in fact initiated in 1920 when the centrally directed RIC concentrated in response to the IRA's activities, although these activities were not very substantial in Ulster. Vigilante groups 'using their own arms' moved into the vacuum 'to mount guards at night and patrol their areas against intruders (Sir A. Hezlet, *The 'B' Specials. A History of the Ulster Special Constabulary* (London, 1972), pp. 10–11). However, by 1922 Tallents reported 'the feeling against the Specials and the "B" in particular is more bitter than against the Black and Tans'; even prominent Unionists were telling him 'that this purely partisan and insufferably disciplined force was sowing feuds in the countryside which would not be eradicated for generations' (Tallents to Masterton Smith, Colonial Office, 4 July 1922, PRO CO 906/30).

[3] Hezlet, op. cit. p. 21. Cf. W. Clark's atmospheric memoir, *Guns in Ulster* (Belfast, 1967), pp. 27–73.

[4] Hezlet, op. cit. p. 28; see also below, p. 397, n. 2.

[5] Townshend, 'IRA and development of guerrilla warfare', p. 340.

itself in attacks on the border. The first 'border campaign' was the main IRA strategy in the mid 1930s, preferred by most of its leaders to Russell's plan of terrorism in England. (Tom Barry left the IRA in protest when Russell's plan was implemented.) The project was taken up again, after a twenty-year shelving, in the mid 1950s. 'Operation Harvest', based on plans drawn up in 1956 by Sean Cronin, was intended (as he later put it) 'to reopen the Irish question by confronting Britain directly [*sic*] in the North'.

The question could not be reopened constitutionally because of the Ireland Act of 1949; since no movement existed to organize a campaign of civil disobedience and passive resistance in the North, the only other means was force.[1]

This characteristically obtuse reasoning amounted to saying that since the IRA either could not be bothered or was not competent to create a mass movement, or since there was no prospect of mass support, Republicans could justifiably turn to violence.

Such a rationalization of demonstration politics was instinctively acceptable (and reasonable) to the IRA, but made less obvious sense to outsiders. It manifested the tendency towards autotelic violence which had been a more or less subdued part of Republican thinking since Pearse, and which was evident in the IRA's indecision about the forms which force should take. One authority suggests that the Harvest plan 'aimed at destroying communications, military installations and public property on such a scale as to paralyse the six-county area'—though with what likely result nobody seems to have been sure.[2] Cronin has asserted that a plan to defend the nationalist population by sabotage and civil resistance was 'not an alternative to Operation Harvest' because it was unrealizable.[3]

The border campaign, whose uncertain basis was echoed by untidiness of execution, appears to have been conceived primarily in terrorist terms. As in the 1880s, however, no systematic thought was given to the function of terrorist

---

[1] S. Cronin, *Irish Nationalism*, p. 170. It is of course meaningless to say that the existence of a statute prevented the issue from being raised constitutionally.

[2] Coogan, *IRA*, p. 370.

[3] Cronin, p. 283 n. 180.

acts. There is no trace of any debate such as was conducted by serious pioneers like *Narodnaya Volya* in Russia. Little concern was shown to secure public understanding of the IRA's reasoning. As a result only those who already shared the Republican view of Northern Ireland could see the IRA's use of violence as functional rather than criminal. The real obstacle to any 'constitutional' reopening of the Irish question was not a British statute—however often if might be reaffirmed—but the fixed hostility of the mass of Northern Protestants to the nationalist presumption of Irish unity. In the absence of any prospect of overcoming that hostility, terrorism offered the comforting image of 'confronting' the power which, according to Republican ideology, underpinned it. The operations of the 'Harvest' campaign resembled those of O'Donovan Rossa, not only in their technical competence but also in their negative justification.[1] Even the sympathetic nationalist population failed, in the late 1950s, to accept that violence was an appropriate, much less the sole possible, method of articulating their dissatisfactions.

(iv) *Civil Rights and Provisionalism*

> Violence is the enemy of justice.
>
> Pope John Paul II[2]

The main feature of Irish society as the border campaign limped to a halt in 1962 was the belated modernization of outlooks both north and south of the six-county border. Fianna Fáil under Seán Lemass proved one unlikely agent of this process, as did the Ulster Unionists under Terence O'Neill. Both populations were perhaps more inclined than ever before to reject violence. The movement of the Ulster Catholic community towards integration was especially remarkable: irredentist irreconcilability gave way to serious political activity.[3] An apparently parallel maturing of Unionist

---

[1] Their main achievement was martyrogenic: the death of Fergal O'Hanlon is commemorated in Dominic Behan's extraordinary ballad 'The Patriot Game', the last and probably most successful (and ambivalent) of the 'Come all ye's.'

[2] Sermon at Drogheda, 29 Sept. 1979.

[3] A striking development was the growth of the Catholic professional class.

attitudes suggested that traditional postures of confrontation were being outgrown. When Richard Rose carried out his remarkable survey in 1968, it suggested that fully a third of Northern Catholics approved the constitution of Northern Ireland, in spite of gerrymandering and the absence of proportional representation.[1] Only 60 per cent of Catholics (compared with 83 per cent of Protestants) endorsed the violence used by their co-religionists fifty years before; 83 per cent disapproved of the use of 'any measures' to end partition in the future—primarily because of opposition in principle to the use of force. Rose observed that force was 'disliked in principle, and also rejected as impractical'.[2]

The civil rights movement marked a definite effort to march into the twentieth century. It borrowed its techniques and rhetoric as much from Martin Luther King as from Daniel O'Connell.[3] In so far as it was a front organization for the IRA, it represented an IRA that was itself changed and modernized. The radical impulse first given by Mellows and O'Donnell to the IRA in the 1920s, and subsequently thwarted, seemed finally to triumph in the forging of the link with People's Democracy under the leadership of Cathal Goulding and Eamonn McCann. PD represented itself as a non-sectarian movement based on the ideology of class struggle. The IRA became committed to radical agitation, in alliance with fashionably youthful figures like Bernadette Devlin and Michael O'Farrell. The Civil Rights Association rapidly acquired a mass base, sustaining popular demonstrations which put, for the first time, effective pressures on the Stormont system.

An indicator of this was that Catholic students at Queen's University, Belfast, only 13 per cent in 1941, reached 32 per cent in 1971: J. Darby, *Conflict in Northern Ireland: the Development of a Polarised Community* (Dublin, 1976), p. 149.

[1] R. Rose, *Governing Without Consensus: An Irish Perspective* (London, 1971), pp. 189. Only one-third disapproved, of whom half (14 per cent of total) favoured a united Ireland.
[2] Ibid., pp. 192-3: 81 per cent of Catholics disliked the use of force; by contrast 52 per cent of Protestants approved 'any measures' to keep Northern Ireland protestant. It must be noted that Rose did not ask Catholics if they approved 'any measures' to preserve Catholicism (rather than end partition): self-preservation might have produced a different response.
[3] Cf. R. Rose, 'On the Priorities of Citizenship in the Deep South and Northern Ireland', *Journal of Politics*, xxxviii, (1976).

The events of 1968 were critical. At the beginning of the year, there appeared to be an unprecedented possibility of *rapprochement* between the Protestant regime and the 'disloyal' Catholic community. The Prime Minister, O'Neill, initiated a series of reforms (including franchise reform and the establishment of an ombudsman) intended to meet the genuine grievances of the minority. This was a long way from any promise of real power to that minority, but in the circumstances—after fifty years of unremitting Unionist domination—it was a dramatic *démarche*. The hope of reconstruction was, however, undermined by traditional forces. Instead of integration, a succession of splits on both sides charted a return to violent confrontation.

On the Unionist side, O'Neill's position collapsed with disconcerting speed. Fifty years of 'governing without consensus' had generated a party machine geared to exploiting and bolstering community divisions, which was unable or unwilling to change its approach. A Unionist appeal for Catholic support would lose more Protestant votes than it could hope to gain from the 'enemy'.[1] O'Neill's dismissal of William Craig in December 1968 foreshadowed the Unionist split, which became more certain as the state of public order deteriorated. Here PD played its part: the decisive event, the civil rights march of January 1969, resulted from the first split on the progressive side. O'Neill depended for his survival on some sign that his concessions were having an effect in reconciling the minority. Some minority leaders indeed argued for acceptance of the government's limited reforms in order to strengthen the Prime Minister's position against the Unionist militants, but PD pressed on to intensify the pressure. In so doing it showed a traditionalist contempt for likely practical consequences.[2]

Hardline Unionists, predictably, viewed the CRA with mounting suspicion. Its methods might look modern to outsiders, but they were sufficiently traditional to be instantly recognizable to neighbours. Austin Currie's seizure of an

---

[1] Rose, *Governing Without Consensus*, pp. 180–1.

[2] The Cameron Commission was, surely rightly, 'driven to think that the leaders must have intended that their venture would weaken the moderate reforming forces in Northern Ireland'. See below, p. 391, n. 2.

'unfairly allocated' council house in Caledon, Co. Tyrone, on 20 June 1968 was easily identified as a territorial challenge, as were the CRA marches which began on 24 August. The green–white–orange flag used by marchers as a symbol of non-sectarianism and of peace between Nationalists and Unionists was perceived as a party emblem.[1] Even the universal anthem of the 1960s, 'We Shall Overcome', had a peculiar resonance, not intended by its authors, to Loyalists habituated to siege symbolism. The PD-led march from Belfast to Londonderry was a challenge of major proportions which called forth a reaction of primordial ferocity. Burntollet Bridge on 4 January was a traditional street-fight carried back into the countryside; a violent marker to the limits of modernization. It was followed by the fall of O'Neill in April and, in August, by an extraordinary recreation of the siege of Derry. The opening of the 'Battle of Bogside' illustrates, in the words of an amiably undoctrinaire political scientist, 'how time past and time present can fuse together in an explosive way'.[2] Less metaphorically, it demonstrates the capacity of institutionalized fear to revivify apparently defunct threats.[3] (The Protestant reaction may perhaps be understood as an extreme, but recognizable, social extension of the cognitive tendency labelled by psychologists 'perpetual set'.)

The attack on the Apprentice Boys' march was, in the circumstances, hardly surprising; less surprising, surely, than the fact that the government allowed the march to proceed as 'normal'. But no Northern Ireland government had the political authority—even if it had the will—to prohibit the intentionally provocative assertion of Protestant dominance.[4] The

[1] C. C. O'Brien points out the significance of the fact that Protestants usually describe the tricolour as 'green, white, and yellow'—white and yellow being the Papal colours—a colour-blindness which dramatically reverses the flag's intended message.

[2] Rose, *Governing Without Consensus*, p. 354. On the earlier events see *Disturbances in Northern Ireland. Report of the Commission appointed by the Governor of Northern Ireland*, Sept. 1969, Cmd. 532 (Cameron Commission), esp. pp. 44-8.

[3] See the argument from cognitive dissonance ('Value systems and their effect on perception') in R. S. P. Elliot and J. Hickie, *Ulster. A Case Study in Conflict Theory* (London, 1971), pp. 71-3.

[4] B. Faulkner, *Memoirs of a Statesman* (London, 1978), pp. 60-2, did not consider the 'traditional' marches as an issue for government concern.

government was itself a product and a part of that assertion. The Protestant assault on Bogside, in which the RUC participated, resulted from the composite Loyalist perception of threat in which Catholics refused allegiance to the state and hence were legitimate targets for all law-abiding citizens.[1] (As Rose's survey made clear, and as indeed was obvious, Protestants are not 'rebels in the conventional social sense': their 'willingness to take up arms reflects a rigid political outlook that cannot accept any compromise of the principle of Protestant rule'.[2]) It has been plausibly suggested by other analysts that in a 'polarized' community it is actually easier for divisions and false perceptions to go on worsening than it is for them to diminish. Highly polarized communities show an extraordinary capacity for the rapid transmission of hostile rumour—a tendency evident, for instance, in the inflammatory fabrications of the *Belfast Newsletter*, the major provincial daily paper.[3]

In the wake of O'Neill's fall and the temporary stability provided by the British army, however, Protestant political groups splintered in a way unseen since 1886. Rival Unionist parties, Official, 'Vanguard Progressive', and 'Democratic', battled for the once monolithic Unionist vote. The paradoxical core of Loyalist doctrine itself remained, expressed by Vanguard MP Robert Bradford in 1975:

> It may well become necessary, in the light of further British ineptitude, for the politicians to ask the RUC, the Reservists and the UDR to form a disciplined army to meet the avalanche of IRA horror. We may well have to become 'Queen's Rebels' in order to remain subjects of any kind.[4]

But Vanguard gave expression to a significant but consistently repressed capacity to view 'Ulster' as the essential focus

[1] There is an acute extended analysis of Protestant attitudes in F. Wright, 'Protestant Ideology and Politics in Ulster', *European Journal of Sociology*, xiv (1973), 213-80, and a thoughtful investigation in S. Nelson, 'Discrimination in Northern Ireland: the Protestant Response', in A. Veenhoven (ed.), *Case Studies on Human Rights* (The Hague, 1976), iv. 405-30.

[2] Rose, *Government Without Consensus*, p. 438.

[3] R. Jenkins and J. MacRae, *Religion, Conflict and Polarisation in Northern Ireland*, quoted in Elliot and Hickie, op. cit. pp. 82-7; Darby, *Conflict in Northern Ireland*, pp. 141-2.

[4] *Irish Times*, 29 Aug. 1975; R. Rose, *Northern Ireland: A Time of Choice* (London, 1976), p. 127.

of political loyalty and identity. There has, still, been manifest reluctance to accept the possibility of 'UDI'—a term whose Rhodesian echoes have been used rather to shock the British government than as the basis for a real debate on state-building. Loyalism has remained in effect the avoidance of overall political responsibility.[1]

And in spite of Bradford's threat, and Ian Paisley's efforts to create a 'Third Force', Protestants have not come together into paramilitary organization with anything like the unanimity shown in 1912. The only political threat which effectively mobilized Loyalist energies was the freakish device of 'power sharing' worked out between the British government, Brian Faulkner's Unionists, and the SDLP in 1973, which was massively repudiated by the strike organized by the *ad hoc* Ulster Workers' Council in May 1974. Characteristically, although one UWC leader remarked on television 'it now seems we're running the country', no positive development followed. When Paisley failed to restage the 1974 strike in May 1977, it began increasingly to appear that he could not become the second Carson whom some awaited and others feared. The structural reason is obvious enough: even the 'avalanche of IRA horror' has not been identified as a threat so menacing as home rule.

That avalanche has itself taken split courses. The first and most enduringly important split began early in 1970, as the atavism of the street-fighting in Derry and Belfast overwhelmed the lately acquired Marxoid ideology of the IRA. Once again traditionalists reverted to the primal function of physical force—not to create political waves but to defend territory. The Catholic community recalled the IRA to Defenderism by the unanswerable device of mockery: wall graffiti simply accused the organization of cowardice. The response was a breakaway from the 'Official' IRA of an inappropriately named Provisional body, which returned to the punitive role of older secret societies.[2]

---

[1] For interesting if speculative comments on political immaturity see K. Heskin, *Northern Ireland: A Psychological Analysis* (Dublin, 1980), 102–3. For a selection of views that 'Ulster identity' is growing, see J. R. Archer, 'Northern Ireland: Constitutional Proposals and the Problem of Identity', *Review of Politics*, xl (1978), 268–9.

[2] *Sunday Times* Insight Team, *Ulster* (Harmondsworth, 1972), 176–97;

The campaign subsequently fought by this body has been episodic and Protean, marked rather by resilience than by clarity of intention or effect. In this it has been intensely traditional. If its roots have remained firmly planted in the minority community, its political superstructure has shared with the earlier independent IRA a shadowy air. The Provisional IRA's inheritance of political anti-realism has rendered it vulnerable to sharp attack in the political sphere, and its responses have been unconvincing. Irish people, not least in the Republic, have found little in the way of acceptable policy in such plans as *Éire Nua*, and have indeed sometimes observed that the only political mechanism through which the PIRA could hope to realize its post-Pearsean ideals would be a dictatorship. None the less, outright repudiation has been rare amongst Catholics. Some PIRA methods, particularly prison protests and hunger-strikes (which tap a deep strain of ambivalence towards authority) and regular forays into electoral politics, have generated considerable sympathy. Even at the worst times an ambivalent attitude to IRA violence has produced a general neutrality in Irish public opinion. A characteristic example of this equivocal voice may be found in the collection of talks, articles, and sermons published by the Bishop of Ardagh and Clonmacnois in 1973. The bishop intended to show that the Catholic Church was opposed to IRA violence (except, of course, that used between 1916 and 1921), but he held that 'Denunciation of violence has been, is and will continue to be utterly ineffectual, so long as the policies which provoke violence are persisted in'.[1] This pragmatic disclaimer is in fact—if not intention—a complete and elegant justification of political violence. It may be contrasted with the morally uncompromising, unfashionable challenge delivered by the Pope in 1979. The Pope, however, does not have to live in Ireland.

The exact form to be taken by physical force has never been clearly fixed during the 'long decade' of PIRA operations.

J. Bowyer Bell, 'The Escalation of Insurgency: the Provisional Irish Republican Army's Experience, 1969–1971', *Review of Politics*, xxxv (1973); M. Dillon and D. Lehane, *Political Murder in Northern Ireland* (Harmondsworth, 1973).

[1] Cahal B. Daly, *Violence in Ireland and Christian Conscience* (Dublin, 1973), p. 35.

Any attempt to wage rural or urban guerrilla warfare on the pattern established in 1919-21 (and followed in other wars of national liberation) was limited by the geography of the supporting community. No IRA spark could start a prairie fire throughout Northern Ireland. Away from the 'no-go' areas of Belfast and 'Free Derry', and the borders of Fermanagh and Armagh, PIRA operations were restricted to terrorism. Even so they oscillated between discriminate and indiscriminate attacks. The theoretical underpinning of terrorist action has remained as loose as in the 1880s or 1950s. All that has been clearly fixed is what O'Brien has called the 'desolating durability' of the Republican campaign, and the deep ingraining of violence as a method of defence, control, protest and dialogue.[1] This tendency has been reinforced by further splits within the Republican movement which have produced a new physical-force group, the Irish National Liberation Army. Despite its conservative (albeit rhetorical) title, this group declared itself to be socialist, and may thus be seen as more 'Republican' than the PIRA, which is really a nationalist organization. In size and technique it resembles more closely the international model of urban terrorist forces which became established in the early 1970s. However, its objectives are scarcely more attainable than those of the PIRA under present circumstances, so its appeal to force already has the same air of permanence. The proliferation of violence, more than matched on the Loyalist side by the growth and fission of paramilitary forces, meant that by the mid 1970s it was common for journalists and politicians, as well as analysts, to speak of violence as 'endemic' in Northern Ireland. If in the end this adjective may signify resigned toleration, it produced for a time a kind of despair—a fear that if 'normalization' were deferred the inner structure of Ulster society might be irreversibly dissolved.[2]

[1] C. Cruise O'Brien, *Herod: Reflections on Political Violence* (London, 1978), p. 47. There is a penetrating analysis in E. Moxon-Browne, 'The Water and the Fish: Public Opinion and the Provisional IRA in Northern Ireland', *Terrorism*, v (1981), 41-72.

[2] J. B. Bell, *A Time of Terror. How Democratic Societies Respond to Revolutionary Violence* (New York, 1978), p. 49. See also the modified alarmism of P. Wilkinson, *Terrorism and the Liberal State* (London, 1977), pp. 102-6.

(v) *The crisis of public security*

> We've been fighting the Brits now for eight hundred years.
> And if they're still around in another eight hundred we'll
> still be fighting them.
>
> Anonymous Republican[1]

In his equivocal critique of Republican violence, Bishop Daly showed no hesitation in apportioning responsibility for the Northern Ireland problem. 'Many of us had hoped', he declared, 'that Britain might at last attempt to atone for centuries of harm and hurt in her relations with Ireland'; instead, 'the British government has failed in the most elementary responsibility of a government . . . . It has not led; but it has let itself be misled . . .'[2] This characteristic nationalist view accords little, as in the past, with the facts. It is doubtful whether any party to the Northern Ireland conflict has shown such a desire as the British government to reach a settlement consonant with generally accepted principles of political equity, or pursued so rocky a penitential path, strewn with the debris of successive 'political initiatives', towards it. However, the government has taken a different view of its 'elementary responsibilities'—not so much to lead (in other words to impose) as to elicit from the contending parties an agreed compromise. At the same time, in common with most governments, it has taken as its overriding duty the protection of life and property.

Unfortunately, as so often before, the attempt to maintain law and order has at critical junctures undermined the search for political settlement. In particular, the permanent employment of troops on internal security duty has, far from restoring normality, made normalization increasingly remote and difficult to envisage. Military intervention was the most dramatic and far-reaching administrative action since 1921. It resulted from a sudden toughening of British attitudes to the Stormont government after the events of 1968, and an insistence that the skewed structure of the Northern Ireland state be corrected. This belated volte-face, which would no doubt have come better in 1912 or 1920, altered

---

[1] D. Murphy, *A Place Apart* (London, 1978), p. 226).
[2] Daly, op. cit. pp. 16-17.

the nature of the crisis in progress. No Unionist government would accept British dictation on security matters. The exhaustion and breakdown of the RUC between January and August 1969 thus determined the collapse of the whole system. The critical manifestation of ataxia was the use of Browning machine-guns by Belfast police in the Catholic Divis Street area on the night of 14–15 August. RUC commanders accepted that their men were at the end of their tether, and that military assistance was needed. Some 3,000 troops were immediately committed: welcomed by civilians, especially the battered Catholics, they quickly restored a semblance of order.

If they had been withdrawn soon afterwards, the intervention would have been as successful as any military aid to the civil power. As the army had traditionally argued, the effect of troops in such circumstances is only temporary, and the GOC Northern Ireland, General Freeland, recognized that the period of acceptance by both Catholic and Protestant communities would be finite. They were not withdrawn, however, because the British government now saw the Northern Ireland civil power itself as provocative of disorder. Both the Cameron commission and the Scarman tribunal condemned the structure and actions of the RUC, and the Hunt report decided that the force should be disarmed and the Special Constabulary abolished. The objections of General Macready in 1920 were at last sustained, and the USC was replaced by a force under military discipline, the Ulster Defence Regiment.[1] In effect, 'Carson's army' was regularized, much as the first UVF had been transformed into the 36th (Ulster) Division. Instead of being sent to the Somme, however, the UDR remained on the Lagan and the Foyle.[2] It inherited, inevitably, some of the aura of the Specials along with some of the personnel.

[1] The USC was disbanded on 30 Apr. 1970, by which time the UDR was in theory operational.

[2] Although an initial effort was made to recruit Catholics, large-scale cross-recruitment from the USC to the UDR inevitably occurred. The proportion of Catholics fell from 20 per cent in April 1970 to 16 per cent in November, and to 8 per cent a year later. By 1975 it had dropped to 2 per cent: SDLP Submission to Secretary of State's Conference, 1980; L. O'Dowd, B. Rolston, and M. Tomlinson, *Northern Ireland: Between Civil Rights and Civil War* (London, 1980), p. 185.

Communal violence continued, and took on a new edge as the PIRA began its sporadic early activities.[1]

Paradoxically, it was the PIRA, the organization dedicated to forcing the 'Brits out', that was—and remains—primarily responsible for increasing and perpetuating the British military 'presence'. But the Provisionals' first objective, the destruction of the Stormont system and its replacement by direct rule, was achieved with unexpected swiftness. This was perhaps due in part to British sensitivity to world opinion on human rights issues (though the further IRA hope, that world pressure would induce Britain to hand Northern Ireland over to the United Nations, was not fulfilled in the same way). British involvement produced growing complications, as the army became enmeshed in the Special Powers Act—in the absence of any other delineation of military powers *vis-à-vis* civilians. (The bogey of martial law still hampered political thinking in this area.[2]) The new Conservative administration accepted the Northern Ireland government's demand for the reintroduction of internment without trial, the object being in Edward Heath's oft-reiterated phrase to 'get on top of the gunmen' (an approach reminiscent of the 'murder gang' rhetoric of Lloyd George and Forster). Internment, however, raised political and moral issues which had apparently not been foreseen. It brought the Special Powers Act into the glare of public opinion, and the suspension of Habeas Corpus proved scarcely more acceptable in 1971 than it had been a hundred years before.

The counter-productive effects of internment were far from unpredictable. The government's unfamiliarity with —and distaste for—the situation into which it was being drawn was only too obvious. Even the army, frustrated though it was by the paralysis of the judicial system, was pessimistic about the prospects. In the circumstances the introduction of internment was a mistimed reaction. It has been plausibly argued that early over-reactions may be the

---

[1] For a good if unsympathetic account see R. Moss, *Urban Guerrillas* (London, 1972), pp. 97–106.

[2] R. Evelegh, *Peace-Keeping in a Democratic Society. The Lessons of Northern Ireland* (London, 1978).

best response on the part of democratic polities, since they create the possibility that the problem will have been forcibly resolved by the time that the draconian measures come under public criticism.[1] If such early action is not taken, then sustained under-reaction at least presents a possibility of political negotiation. A belated over-reaction, however, offers a combination of disadvantages, barely disguised by the prospect of negotiating 'from a position of strength'.

Internment brought into focus certain crucial questions bearing on the matter of public security. What exactly was being threatened or destroyed by political violence, and just what was the government upholding? Was it something substantial enough to justify the abrogation of legal rights? Interpreting the challenge of the IRA was not a straightforward business. By the time of internment the PIRA had become, as it has remained, an organization aiming not merely at the defence of its community but at large-scale political reconstruction, however vaguely defined—reconstruction unattainable by constitutional methods. After a phase of instinctive gunfighting in the streets it turned to an indirect strategy in which even such defensive measures as prison protests were designed not to achieve reform of the political–judicial system but as steps in its breakdown. Urban terrorism—whether discriminate or indiscriminate—was unquestionably agitational. It was not, however, the same thing as open insurrection, even when the number of shootings leapt from 213 in 1970 to 1,756 in 1971, and to 10,628 in 1972. Only in south Armagh, where conditions were so favourable that IRA fighters could wear their own uniform with little risk of capture, did recognizable guerrilla warfare emerge. There it might still be said that the government was faced by impenetrable communal resistance drawing directly on rural traditions.

The government hesitated to conclude that the IRA's objects were too extreme to be within the reach of negotiated settlement. Indeed the regime established under direct Westminster rule, with William Whitelaw as Secretary of State for Northern Ireland (a post exceeding the old Chief Secretaryship in power and independence) went to the extraordinary

[1] Moss, op. cit. pp. 110–11.

lengths of negotiatiating a truce with the Provisionals and according 'special category' status to political prisoners. But the renewal and intensification of the PIRA bombing campaign in July 1972, which effectively recognized the inappropriateness of political dialogue, forced it to backtrack demonstratively in order to placate angry Loyalists. The British troop level peaked at 21,000, and operation 'Motorman' was launched to destroy the barricades in west Belfast and Derry. The strange experiment of 'no-go areas' was ended.

This was a reassertion of the 'rule of law', not in the Diceyan but in the vernacular sense: Crown forces patrolling the streets (albeit, unfortunately, in armoured vehicles). It was clear that the existence over a protracted period of well-publicized liberated zones offended against fundamental ideas of government. But it was by no means clear whether the real security of any person or group was being ensured by their elimination. 'Security forces' were moving through the streets to uphold the law, though as before it was apparent that in certain areas 'law' and 'order' remained distinct if not antipathetic concepts. Order had been maintained within the no-go areas by communal methods; law as enforced by government agencies produced disorder. Was this preserving public security? Public security is a generally understood (if seldom defined) and functional concept in societies with a working consensus on public values. *Salus rei publicae* can there be invoked as the supreme law. But in a divided society the inflexible maintenance of law may not be in the public interest.[1]

---

[1] No division has officially been recognized. The Detention of Terrorists Order, 1972, held that detention was justified by the necessity for 'the protection of the public' (cl. 12). The Northern Ireland (Emergency Provisions) Act 1973, whilst detailing 'offences against public security' (Part III), made no attempt to define the concept or to offer an index by which security could be measured. It must be said that even specialist studies like T. Bowden, *The Breakdown of Public Security* (London, 1977), are disconcertingly vague on the central question of the point at which breakdown may be said to have occurred. A similarly impressionistic approach was taken by the European Court of Human Rights (*Ireland* v. *UK*, 1978) when it accepted UK derogation from Art. 5 of the European Convention on Human Rights on grounds of 'public emergency threatening the life of the nation'. The adjective 'public' is clearly ambiguous, and it is obvious that there is a difference—and possibly an antagonism—between state security and what C. H. Enloe calls 'citizen security', Unfortunately, her rather slapdash

Characteristically, by 1971 in west Belfast and elsewhere the legal system had become paralysed. Witnesses and jurors were intimidated, and convictions could not be obtained in 'terrorist' cases. The argument for internment in these circumstances was that unless terrorists could be removed from the streets the state would be failing in its duty to protect its citizens. However, as has been amply proved—and admitted subsequently—neither internment nor any other legal or administrative measure could provide real protection to the public: the bomb-making terrorist simply cannot be stopped by punishments. Internment seems rather to have been designed to protect the state itself from the challenge of rival armies, and against the fear—circulated by several alarmist commentators—that the fabric of modern society was so complex that terrorism might produce general breakdown. Yet the outcome, as Richard Rose pointed out after the abandonment of internment, was a situation in which the essence of the state had fragmented or 'de-institutionalized': there was no longer any body that could claim a monopoly of the use of force, legitimate or otherwise.[1] The government was compelled to abandon the idea of eliminating the IRA, and instead came to talk of an 'acceptable level' of violence.[2] This is certainly a modification of the British image of law and order.

The government's difficulty in defining its objectives echoed the problem repeatedly faced by British governors of Ireland. It ensured that the actions of security forces would always be restricted by the imprecise standards regarded as appropriate to a 'normal' liberal–democratic polity. As Humphrey Atkins declaimed with Roman calm amidst the

work ('Police and Military in Ulster: Peacekeeping or Peace-subverting Forces?', *Journal of Peace Research*, xv (1978); *Ethnic Soldiers. State Security in Divided Societies* (Harmondsworth, 1980), pp. 101-8) does little to resolve the problem, though it furnishes some light relief by speaking of the 'maternal security role' of the British army, and its 'Special Art Service'. In a different class is R. Fisk, 'The Effect of Social and Political Crime on the Police and British Army in Northern Ireland', in M. H. Livingston (ed.), *International Terrorism in the Contemporary World* (London, 1978), 84-93.

[1] Rose, 'Priorities of Citizenship', p. 288.
[2] Reginald Maudling, 15 Dec. 1971; *Sunday Times* Insight Team, *Ulster*, p. 309.

popular outcry that followed the assassination of Lord
Mountbatten and the Warrenpoint ambush in August 1979,
'If we abandon the normally accepted standards of law
then we are playing into the terrorists' hands'. Whilst no
doubt intended as a warning against reprisals, this was also
a declaration that his predecessors' suspension of Habeas
Corpus from 1971 to 1975 had been unjustifiable. And yet
the legal system operating by 1979 was far from normal.
'Diplock courts' trying certain offences without jury, built
into the 1973 Northern Ireland (Emergency Provisions) Act
which replaced the Special Powers law, are indubitably outside the tradition of English law.[1] Their acceptance depends
on the accepted probity of the judiciary, a reputation established over a long period in different historical circumstances.
There is a certain long-term danger in this. The Emergency
Provisions Act, consolidated in 1978, remains a remarkable
coercive measure in the nineteenth-century tradition. The
power of detention without trial was in fact maintained,
though not used, until 1980.[2]

Under these conditions the security forces have been to
some extent successful in coping with political violence.[3] After
1972 British troop levels were progressively reduced, to
14,000-15,000 in 1975-7, and to below 12,000 in 1980. The
challenge of open mass violence diminished, though not
because of military action. As the army itself has been
aware, modern riot control equipment has the effect of placing a further—and maybe critical—gulf between soldiers
and civilians, especially children.[4] Against terrorism a structure

---

[1] For a critical evaluation, K. Boyle *et al., Law and State. The Case of Northern
Ireland* (London, 1975), 78-151. For a defence, Merlyn Rees, 'Terrorism in Ireland and Britain's Response', *Terrorism*, v (1981), 83-8.

[2] The annual renewal of the Act in July 1980 omitted the power of detention
(Clause 12 and Schedule 1). At renewal in 1982 the Secretary of State stated that a
major review of the functioning of security policy—the first since 'the Gardiner
report—would be initiated later in the year'. *Hansard*, 30 June 1982, cols. 943-4.

[3] A quasi-official military account of operations in Northern Ireland may be
found in D. Barzilay's remarkable *The British Army in Ulster*, 4 vols. (Belfast,
1973, 1975, 1978, 1981).

[4] Barzilay, op. cit. iii. 12: 'the thicker the Army's protection gets . . . the more
stoning goes on. When the Army had none of today's sophisticated protection
soldiers . . . either ran away because they were hurt or went in, grabbed the child
who had thrown the missile, took him back to his parents . . . Now troops simply
stand in line like statues . . .'

of techniques has gradually emerged. The most consistently useful of these has probably been the simplest, the Vehicle Check-Point, analogous in principle to the old blockhouse idea, but serving the function of monitoring movement rather than delimiting zones for search and control. When backed up by an increasingly sophisticated intelligence network using automated data processing, VCPs have been able to provide huge quantities of information, as well as occasionally hampering the movement of terrorist groups.[1]

The active pursuit of such groups is a more formidable problem, depending for real success on the development of an integrated civil–military machine as advocated by General Kitson in his book *Low Intensity Operations*, written shortly before he took up the post of GOC Belfast. Such a machine has manifestly not been allowed to develop, though gestures in this direction have occasionally been made, such as the appointment of Sir Maurice Oldfield as intelligence chief after the Warrenpoint ambush in 1979. The introduction of the SAS certainly made counter-terrorist operations noticeably more effective, but at the same time the PIRA reorganized into smaller, tighter cells which were much more secure than its earlier grass-roots formations.[2] New types of weapon have been continually acquired, and while searches for arms have often been surprisingly successful, the 'Winthrop method' is never likely to be a match for the flow of war material from the USA and elsewhere. Only the sustained provision of information from within the community can offer a real mechanism for paralysing terrorist activity. Against rural guerrillas in Fermanagh and south Armagh the army has been frankly unable, helicopters notwithstanding, to do more than maintain a presence— a fact which it has tended, with partial justification, to blame on the existence of a sanctuary across the border of the Republic. The Warrenpoint disaster showed what the technically expert rural IRA can accomplish; conversely, the extraordinary operation 'Petal' mounted by the army

[1] On the limitations of ADP systems, R. B. Pengelly, 'Ulster: the Name of the Internal Security Game', *International Defense Review*, viii (1978), 1301.

[2] Barzilay, op. cit. iii. 16; iv. 12, 18. Cf. the sketchy account in T. Bowden, 'The IRA and the changing tactics of terrorism', *Political Quarterly*, xlvii (1976), 425-37.

in 1980, in which twelve miles of road were saturated with troops to protect the shipment of building materials for strengthening the battered Crossmaglen base, displayed—with its echo of French operations in Indo-China—the marginal nature of the military presence. Thus, although 1980 produced the lowest level of violence for a decade, few confident conclusions could be drawn. Early in 1977 the basis of security policy was redefined as 'primacy of the police', and it has always been evident that only such an approach offered any chance of 'normalizing' Northern Ireland. ('Ulsterization', the semi-official alternative label—also afflicted by Vietnamese echoes—expresses more strikingly the ambiguity of the standards involved.) The army expressed faith in this argument, seeing its task as to convert 'black' areas—in which terrorist operations were frequent—into 'grey' areas in which they were infrequent. The new-look RUC, stripped of its quasi-military Special Patrol Group, could then proceed to turn the grey areas white.[1] This task had been completed to a limited extent by 1981, with military forces removed from many districts, and, probably more importantly, visual evidence of the military presence—the unnerving ubiquity of corrugated iron and barbed wire—progressively dismantled. But the beguiling simplicity of such a colour-code conceals the gigantic problems behind the idea of turning west Belfast into a 'grey' area in which police could function 'normally'.

Military studies must return to the inescapable point that terrorism can never be altogether stopped by external restraints: the initiative will always lie with the bomb-setter.[2] If 1980 came closer to an 'acceptable level' of political violence, this merely showed that as always political evaluations rather than military facts delimit the boundaries of policy. The widely shared belief of the 1970s that it was impossible to talk of political settlement until the IRA had been defeated[3] may perhaps be seen to be an irrelevance stemming from idealized conceptions of public order. In

---

[1] Barzilay, op. cit. iv. 11.

[2] Ibid. iii. 14, 16; iv. 17, 28.

[3] Cf. Moss, *Urban Guerrillas*, p. 111; Lord Chalfont in B. Crozier and R. Moss (Chairman and Rapporteur), *The Ulster Debate* (London, 1972), 90-8.

fact there is no sound reason why political solutions cannot be reached in the midst of war: indeed some of the most realistic and durable arrangements may be arrived at under just such testing pressure.

Epilogue

Contemplation of Anglo-Irish Relations since the mid nineteenth century leaves an impression of English government and Irish resistance locked in a seemingly endless embrace. For protracted periods this embrace has been a violent one. According to English perceptions, violence has repeatedly perverted the normal course of constitutional evolution, calling forth abnormal ('extraordinary') legislation which has in its turn blighted prospects of a solution to the 'Irish question'. From the perspective of Irish nationalists, even the ordinary English law has always been tainted by the violence of conquest. Violence in many forms has been justified as the self-defence of a community under permanent repression. The 'English question' has seemed soluble only by force.

Contemplating the matter of violence itself, it is hard to dispute Hannah Arendt's assertion that 'no one engaged in thought about history and politics can remain unaware of the enormous role violence has always played in human affairs'; or even—ten years on—her observation that it is 'rather surprising that violence has been singled out so seldom for special consideration'.[1] Part of her suggested explanation was that 'no one questions or examines what is obvious to all'. Developments in the academic fields of conflict studies and the analysis of collective violence may to some extent have overtaken this view, but without successfully answering the fundamental point.[2]

Arendt's own contribution was less than conclusive in defining the nature and function of violence in politics. Mere definition of the term has posed real problems. Even the most influential writers have used concepts like 'force', 'power', and 'might' indiscriminately or

---

[1] 'On Violence', in H. Arendt, *Crises of the Republic* (Harmondsworth, 1973), p. 87.

[2] The same may perhaps be said of philosophical excursions such as Ted Honderich, *Three Essays on Political Violence* (Oxford, 1977), and *Violence for Equality* (Harmondsworth, 1980).

ambiguously.[1] 'Violence' may be thought to have remained unambiguous, but a definition that attempts to fix it as 'unambiguously . . . the most direct and severe form of physical power . . . force in action' still depends on two related concepts whose meaning is unclear.[2] Arendt tried to confine 'force' to natural forces, and 'power' to the collective capacity for action, preferring 'strength' as the term for human physical force. Her definition of violence stressed its instrumentality, yet verged on ambiguity by adding

Phenomenologically, it is close to *strength* since the implements of violence . . . are designed and used for the purpose of multiplying natural strength until . . . they can substitute for it.[3]

Even if one can restore 'force' to its normal use to describe human action, it remains doubtful whether 'violence' can be regarded simply as physical force in extreme form. Its well-established usage for vehement or passionate language reminds us that violence may subsist as much in attitude as in action.

'Political violence' presents formidable, perhaps insuperable, problems of definition. Is this composite term to be restricted to acts with an explicit political aim, or should it extend to acts with political impact—or indeed to any violence which occurs because a political system is arranged in a certain way, and which would not occur if certain political changes were made? Any arbitrary definition, the Humpty-Dumpty solution, risks losing important components of the real circumstances in which people are conscious of violence. In so far as a definition underlies this survey, it is no more than classification. Three major categories have emerged: the spontaneous collective violence (or social violence) which may have no explicit political intention but has political

---

[1] See the highly discriminating analysis in d'Entrèves, *The Notion of the State*, pp. 10-11 and *passim*.

[2] H. L. Nieburg, *Political Violence. The Behavioral Process* (New York, 1969), p. 11. It may be noted that *The Oxford English Dictionary* incorporates notions of injury or damage into the primary definition.

[3] Arendt, op. cit. p. 115.

implications;[1] systematic covert intimidation or terrorism; and organized open insurrection. Such forms, in varied permutations, have been a frequent subject for anlaysis. Less frequently studied but more important than their form is their function. It has to be recognized that in some circumstances 'violence pays'.[2] Such circumstances have often been present in Ireland, and it is necessary to ask what they were. The tendency to pass over the question *how* and *why* political violence works, and thus why it is used,[3] seems to result from the feeling that it is, in Arendt's words, 'obvious to all'. Yet it is not altogether obvious why terrorism, say, should be dominant in some circumstances and ineffectual or even counterproductive in others.

The functionality of violence should certainly be a prime concern of governments confronted by it, if they hope to do anything more than deal with external symptoms. Unfortunately for rational policy-making, the term 'violence' is politically loaded. From the viewpoint of the state, political violence is by definition the *illicit* use of force for political ends (the state itself uses 'force' to impose the law or to wage war).[4] Its illegitimacy justifies, and in fact requires, the use of counter-force by the state—the English legal doctrine of 'repelling force with force'. The development of England in the nineteenth century was widely seen as a progress from violence to order (or, from Sorel's opposite viewpoint, a decadence from violence to cunning). The duty to maintain law and order in Ireland has always been a non-partisan issue. No party, indeed hardly a single individual, has publicly questioned the possibility or necessity of maintaining or 'restoring' order under all circumstances.

---

[1] This corresponds roughly to Tilly's 'reactionary' or 'reactive' category, and perhaps to Rummel's category of 'turmoil'. Cf. T. R. Gurr, *Why Men Rebel* (Princeton, 1970), p. 10.

[2] C., L., and R. Tilly, *The Rebellious Century* (London, 1975),. pp. 280-5 (though they add the important caveat that if properly organized 'repression works' as well).

[3] As in the extended classification of forms in P. Wilkinson, *Terrorism and the Liberal State* (London, 1977).

[4] The term 'state' is used here in spite of traditional English lukewarmness towards it, and contemporary American assaults on its descriptive value (as in D. Easton, *The Political System* (New York, 1953) especially). It is taken to include not merely the political system, but more importantly the accretion of notions analysed by d'Entrèves.

Yet it is surely clear that the feasibility of repression of disorder is directly related to the legitimacy of the state.[1] On the face of it the existence of disorder implies some breach in legitimacy. If the breach is small, the authority— and hence power—of the state remains ample. If it is large, authority must be eroded and power may become insufficient. Such, it may be suggested, has tended to be the case with the English state in Ireland. In circumstances of breakdown or paralysis of the civil government, it has been driven back on the exercise of force. In effect this has meant open or disguised military rule.

The police in Ireland under the union, and in Northern Ireland since 1921, have always been a semi-military 'gendarmerie' of the continental rather than the English type.[2] Their capacity to influence disorder has varied, but has usually been inadequate. The recourse of 'tinkering with the police' has been as evident in the disarming and rearming of the RUC in the 1970s as in the creation of the Black and Tans in 1920 or the frequent adjustment of the old RIC organization.[3] Most of their problems derive from the artificial position of a state (that is, centralized) constabulary which has never entirely removed the label of an 'army of occupation' fastened upon it by nationalists.

Regular military forces have scarcely proved more effective in curbing lawlessness and disorder, while they act of course as a political irritant. Only in crushing open insurrection have they enjoyed unqualified success. The experience of garrisoning Ireland under the union was not a happy one for the British army. Amongst other effects it revealed on several occasions the inherent weakness of military rule in a liberal

---

[1] Legitimacy is rooted in collective beliefs; indeed, in the sense of forming a community. Cicero's 'I cannot conceive of a people unless held together by consent to law' is approximately re-expressed in Nieburg's formula: 'It is the consensus that supports the informal polity that constitutes the nation. Those who occupy the offices of state power face each day the continuing task of validating the legitimacy of the state . . .' (*Political Violence*, p. 55).

[2] Cf. T. Bowden, *Beyond the Limits of the Law. A Comparative Study of the Police in Crisis Politics* (Harmondsworth, 1978), 168-70.

[3] For a renewed argument for 'normalization' see G. H. Boehringer, 'Beyond Hunt: A Police Policy for Northern Ireland of the Future', *Social Studies*, ii (1973), 399-414.

polity.[1] The 'martial law problem' was, in part, that armies are not technically equipped to regulate modern societies, even when they are physically strong enough. Such capacities as they possess have been consistently undermined by legal ambiguities. Despite a recurrent state of emergency, military powers necessarily remained curtailed. A true *état de siège* in the continental sense remains unknown to the British constitution, in spite of an accretion of emergency powers Acts. The more vaguely conceived 'martial law' was always abhorred precisely for its vagueness. Yet the military often found themselves in an uncomfortably high profile in Ireland, their role readily exaggerated by public opinion. Nothing is more symptomatic of this problem than the fact that martial law could be believed to be in force even when it was not, as in 1916-17.

British government in Ireland has shown the uncanny knack of getting the worst of both worlds; of appearing to rest on force while seldom exerting enough force to secure real control. By contrast, armed resisters have repeatedly used 'physical force' as an adjunct to 'moral insurrection', and secured the benefit of both combined. What the authorities have condemned as violence, lawlessness, or terrorism has broadly been accepted under the neutral title 'physical force' as a legitimate instrument of political struggle or as enforcement of an 'unwritten law'. Of the three categories of political violence, the last, open insurrection, has always failed—not merely to defeat the government, but also to mobilize widespread popular support. The persistence of the second form, however, indicates that this reflects the lack of credibility rather than the lack of legitimacy of the physical force policy. Certainly, failure has not undermined it: rather the reverse. The 'triumph of failure' has become a moral force in its own right. Its most fecund source is, of course, the Easter rising. Pearse was unique as a moralist of political violence in Ireland: his assertion of the 'cleansing and sanctifying' power of blood-sacrifice bears comparison with Sartre's chilling claim that 'violence, like Achilles' lance,

---

[1] Cf. the classic analysis of S. E. Finer, *The Man on Horseback. The Role of the Military in Politics* (London 1962), ch. 3. For a more pessimistic recent view, J. Woddis, *Armies and Politics* (London, 1977), esp. pp. 275-300.

can heal the wounds it has inflicted'.[1] It is impossible to exaggerate the power of such a conception to mobilize the intellectual leadership of armed resistance.

No such exalted ideas, however, have been necessary to legitimize social violence or systematic terrorism. Frequent use has been made of the terms 'endemic violence' or 'the habit of violence' to delineate the circumstances of the Irish countryside and certain Irish cities. Excessive weight should not perhaps be placed on subjective perceptions which have sprung to some extent from alarmist local authorities. However, these terms suggest a basis for the analysis of social violence and of certain forms of intimidation. It is evident that, unlike open insurrection, enforcement terror was directly functional. As a number of historians, following Hobsbawm, have observed of pre-modern popular disturbances, such collective actions successfully regulated the powers of landlords and even employers. Their success depended on the existence of fundamental ideas—for instance the 'moral economy'—amounting to an unwritten law; popular action was triggered and legitimized by breaches of this law. Such rules were well attested in nineteenth-century Ireland. Collective action is, however, made effective not by stimulus but by organization, albeit primitive.[2] In Ireland the crucial organizational framework was provided by a mass of rural secret societies, loosely connected by common outlook (as embodied in initiation oaths) rather than by formal links. Recruitment into these groups—'associations' in their own terminology, 'gangs' in the government's—became a process so regular as to form part of rural socialization.[3] In this sense, the deployment of violence became habitual. Most importantly, the expectation of violence became habitual. Threats of violence were widely

---

[1] In his preface to Fanon's *The Wretched of the Earth*; subjected to partial criticism in R. Aron, *History and the Dialectic of Violence* (Oxford, 1975), 188-92. It must be said that even the cult of Pearse has never moved into the exaltation of violence which has characterized romantic notions of superman morality.

[2] This is the whole drift of the work of Tilly and his associates, as against the analysts of deprivation and frustration-agression.

[3] Transported with added resilience into Belfast; cf. Rose's account of 'socialization into conflict', ch. ix of *Governing Without Consensus*.

believed. The ubiquity (as much imagined as real) of the associations ensured the credibility of their terror, and credibility is the key to functionality.

Indeed, it should be stressed that, in contrast to T. P. Thornton's idea that agitational terror functions to the extent that it is indiscriminate and unpredictable,[1] enforcement terror depends on its discrimination and predictability. Like the law which it opposes, its long arm must reach unerringly to strike down offenders. No group has been more conscious of the need for this predictability than the Fenians and their successors, who have carefully cultivated the myth of infallible vengeance against 'spies and informers'.[2] In so doing so they have merely extended the pre-existing methods of focusing or orchestrating action against land-grabbers and other objects of popular hostility.

The result of all this, it must be concluded, was to restrict the legitimacy of the British government of Ireland. The state was widely perceived there as a mere relation of forces rather than a higher juridical or ethical entity. The extent to which it visibly rested on force undermined its claim to the monopoly of force, and its claim that violent resistance was illicit. In the state's own logic, 'there is no state where other associations arrogate to themselves the exercise of compulsion'.[3] In contradistinction to the ethos of the liberal state there developed something like a 'subculture of violence', which in the view of one analyst becomes 'legitimate and normative in backward societies where frontier conditions and the absence of higher normative systems . . . forces the use of the only values available, a large proportion of which are necessarily negative'.[4] It would of course be absurd to suggest that higher normative systems were absent in Catholic Ireland; but the negativity of attitudes to the state and of nationalist political orientation ('break the connection'; 'Brits out')

---

[1] Thornton, 'Terror as a Weapon of Political Agitation', p. 81. His assumption is that the function of terror is the 'disorientation' of an increasingly 'atomized' population.

[2] The most resonant example of this was 'remember Carey', the 1882 informer shot (by chance) in South Africa.

[3] R. M. MacIver, *The Modern State* (Oxford, 1926), p. 230.

[4] Nieburg, *Political Violence*, p. 85.

clearly legitimized the use of force.[1] This subculture of violence persists, even if within a narrowed base. In Northern Ireland it is amplified by a competing tradition which preserves to an extraordinary extent the atmosphere of frontier conditions. The longevity of these traditions can offer scant comfort to those who hope that the state, with its insistence on refusal to 'give way to men of violence', can find an integrative mechanism capable of functioning in the absence of shared assumptions about the nature of politics.

[1] P. Alter, 'Traditions of Violence in the Irish National Movement', in W. J. Mommsen and G. Hirschfeld (eds.), *Social Protest, Violence and Terror in Nineteenth and Twentieth Century Europe* (London, 1982), p. 139.

Bibliography

I. *Unpublished Papers*

Asquith MSS	Bodleian Library, Oxford
A. J. Balfour MSS	(*a*) British Library
	(*b*) Whittingehame
Bonar Law MSS	House of Lords Record Office
Bryce MSS	Bodleian
Buller MSS	Public Record Office
Cardwell MSS	PRO
Carnarvon MSS	PRO
Chamberlain MSS	Birmingham University Library
Childers MSS	National Library of Ireland
Collins MSS	NLI
French MSS	Imperial War Museum
W. E. Gladstone MSS	BL
Viscount Gladstone MSS	BL
Hart MSS	Public Record Office of Northern Ireland
W. V. Harcourt MSS	Bodleian
L. Harcourt MSS	Bodleian
Hobson MSS	NLI
Kilmainham (Irish Command) MSS	NLI
Larcom MSS	(*a*) NLI
	(*b*) Trinity College, Dublin
Lloyd George MSS	HLRO
Luby MSS	NLI
McGarrity MSS	NLI
Milner MSS	Bodleian
Montgomery MSS	PRONI
Mulcahy MSS	University College, Dublin, Archive
Sir G. Murray MSS	PRO
Nathan MSS	Bodleian
O'Beirne-Ranelagh MSS	UCD Archive
W. O'Brien MSS	NLI
O'Donoghue MSS	NLI
O'Hagan MSS	PRONI
O'Malley MSS	UCD Archive
Anna Parnell MSS	NLI
Royal Irish Constabulary (Crime Special) MSS	State Paper Office, Dublin
Saunderson MSS	PRONI

Strathnairn (Rose) MSS	BL
Tallents MSS	PRO
Wilson MSS	IWM

II. *Official Papers*

Report of the Commissioners of Inquiry into the origin and character of the riots in Belfast in July and September 1857; with minutes of Evidence and Appendix. HC 1857–8, XXVI. 1.

H. J. Brownrigg, Examination of Some Recent Allegations concerning the Constabulary Force of Ireland, in a Report to His Excellency the Lord Lieutenant, 9 April 1864.

Report of the Commissioners of Inquiry, 1864, respecting the magisterial and police jurisdiction, arrangements, and establishment of the Borough of Belfast. HC 1865, XXVIII. 1.

Report of the Commissioners appointed by the Home Department to inquire into the treatment of certain treason-felony convicts in the English convict prisons. HC 1867, XXXV. 673.

General Orders for the Guidance of the Troops in Affording Aid to the Civil Power in Ireland. Stationery Office, Dublin, 1870 and 1882.

Return showing, for each month of 1879 and 1880, the number of Land League meetings held and agrarian crimes reported to the Inspector General of the Irish Constabulary. HC 1881, LXXVII. 793.

Return of the Outrages reported to the Royal Irish Constabulary Office from 1st January 1844 to 31st December 1880. HC 1881, LXXVII (C. 2756).

Numerical Returns of Outrages reported to the Constabulary Office in Ireland during 1881. HC 1882, LV (C. 3119).

Report of a Committee of Inquiry appointed by the Lord Lieutenant of Ireland, 17 August 1882. HC 1883, XXXII (C. 3577).

Report of the Belfast Riots Commission, with Evidence and Appendices. HC 1887, XVIII (C. 4925).

Report by One of the Commissioners of Inquiry, 1886. HC 1887, XVIII (C. 5029).

Return of Lists of the districts proclaimed under the Criminal Law and Procedure (Ireland) Act, 1887, showing the portions of the Act so put in force in each proclaimed district, and the date of the proclamations. HC 1887, LXVII. 525.

Memorandum as to the principle upon which outrages are recorded as agrarian, and included as such in the returns laid before Parliament. HC 1887, LXVIII. 25.

Return showing, by provinces and counties, the number of cases of Boycotting, and the number of persons wholly and partially Boycotted throughout Ireland, on 31st July 1887 and on 31st January 1888. HC 1888, LXXXIII. 287.

Returns of agrarian offences, exclusive of threatening letters and notices, for the first six months of 1882 and of 1887; and analysis of returns during the first and second six months of 1882 and 1887. HC 1888, LXXXIII. 411.

A Return by Counties of all cases of shooting and bomb outrages, including firing at the person, into houses, &c, reported to the Police in Ireland since the Government dropped the Peace Preservation Act. HC 1912-13, LXIX. 725.

Disturbances in Northern Ireland. Report of the Commission appointed by the Governor of Northern Ireland, 1969. Cmd. 532.

Report of the Advisory Committee on Police in Northern Ireland (Hunt Report), 1969. Cmd. 535.

Violence and Civil Disturbances in Northern Ireland in 1969 (Scarman Report), 1972. Cmd. 566.

Review of the Operation of the Prevention of Terrorism (Temporary Provisions) Act 1976 by The Rt. Hon. Earl Jellicoe, 1983. Cmd. 8803.

III. *Books, Pamphlets, Articles, and Theses*

Akenson, D. H., *Education and Enmity: the Control of Schooling in Northern Ireland 1920-50*, David and Charles, Newton Abbot, 1973.

Amery, L. S., *The Plot Against Ulster*, Union Defence League, 1914.

Anderson, R., *Sidelights on the Home Rule Movement*, Murray, London, 1906.

Andrews, C. S., *Dublin Made Me. An Autobiography*, Mercier, Dublin and Cork, 1979.

Arendt, H., *Crises of the Republic*, Penguin, Harmondsworth, 1973.

Arensberg, C. M., *The Irish Countryman. An Anthropological Study*, London, 1937.

Bahlman, D. W. R. (ed.), *The Diary of Sir Edward Walter Hamilton 1880-1885*, 2 vols., Clarendon Press, Oxford, 1972.

Baker, S. E., 'Orange and Green. Belfast 1832-1912', in H. J. Dyos and M. Wolff (edd.), *The Victorian City: images and realities*, vol. ii, RKP, London, 1973.

Balfour, A. J. (ed. Mrs. E. Dugdale), *Chapters of Autobiography*, Cassell, London, 1930.

Barry, T., *The Reality of the Anglo-Irish War 1920-21 in West Cork. Refutations, Corrections and Comments on Liam Deasy's 'Towards Ireland Free'*, Anvil, Tralee, 1974.

Barzilay, D., *The British Army in Ulster*, 4 vols., Century Services, Belfast, 1973, 1975, 1978, 1981.

Beames, M. R., 'Rural conflict in pre-famine Ireland: peasant assassinations in Tipperary 1837-1847', *Past and Present*, lxxxi (1978).

Becker, B. H., *Disturbed Ireland: Being the Letters Written during the Winter of 1880-81*, Macmillan, London, 1881.

Beckett, J. C., *The Anglo-Irish Tradition*, Faber, London, 1976.

Bell, G., *The Protestants of Ulster*, Pluto, London, 1976.
Bell, J. B., 'The Escalation of Insurgency: the Provisional Irish Republican Army's Experience 1969-1971', *Review of Politics*, xxxv (1973).
—— *A Time of Terror. How Democratic Societies Respond to Revolutionary Violence*, Basic Books, New York, 1978.
Bew, P., 'The Problem of Irish Unionism', *Economy and Society*, vi (1977).
—— *Land and the National Question in Ireland 1858-82*, Gill and Macmillan, Dublin, 1979.
—— 'Les Fenians et l'indépendance de l'Irlande', *L'Histoire*, xxxiii (1981).
—— *C. S. Parnell*. Gill and Macmillan, Dublin 1980.
——, Gibbon, P., and Patterson, H. *The State in Northern Ireland 1921-72. Political Forces and Social Classes*, Manchester UP, 1979.
Binchy, D. A., 'Irish History and Irish Law', Parts I and II, *Studia Hibernica*, xv (1975); xvi (1976).
Birmingham, G. (J. O. Hannay), *Irishmen All*, Foulis, London, 1913.
Blake, H. A., 'The Irish Police', *The Nineteenth Century*, lvii (1881).
Blunt, W. Scawen, *The Land War in Ireland*, Swift, London, 1912.
Boal, F. W., Murray, R. C., and Poole, M. A., 'Belfast: the Urban Encapsulation of a National Conflict', in S. E. Clarke and J. L. Obler (edd.), *Urban Ethnic Conflict: A Comparative Perspective*, N. Carolina Univ., Chapel Hill, 1976.
Boehringer, G. H., 'Beyond Hunt: A Police Policy for Northern Ireland of the Future', *Social Studies*, ii (1973).
Boulton, D., *The UVF 1966-1973*, Gill and Macmillan, Dublin, 1973.
Bourke, M., *John O'Leary: a study in Irish separatism*, Anvil, Tralee, 1967.
Bowden, T., *The Breakdown of Public Security. The Case of Ireland 1916-1921 and Palestine 1936-1939*, Sage, London, 1977.
—— 'The IRA and the changing tactics of terrorism', *Political Quarterly*, xlvii (1976).
—— *Beyond the Limits of the Law. A comparative study of the police in crisis politics*, Pelican, Harmondsworth, 1978.
Boyce, D. G., *Nationalism in Ireland*, Croom Helm, London, 1982.
Boyle, K., 'The Tallents Report on the Craig-Collins Pact of 30 March 1922', *Irish Jurist*, xii (1977).
——, Hadden, T., and Hillyard, P., *Law and State. The Case of Northern Ireland*, Robertson, London, 1975.
—— —— —— *Ten Years on in Northern Ireland*, Cobden Trust, London, 1980.
—— —— —— 'Northern Ireland: the communal roots of violence', *New Society*, vol. 54, 6 Nov. 1980.
Brady, C., *Guardians of the Peace*, Gill and Macmillan, Dublin, 1974.
Brennan, R., *Allegiance*, Browne and Nolan, Dublin, 1950.
British and Irish Communist Organization, *The Two Irish Nations: Against Ulster Nationalism*, B & ICO, Belfast, 1975.

Broeker, G., *Rural Disorder and Police Reform in Ireland 1812-36*, RKP, London, 1979.

Brown, T. N., 'Nationalism and the Irish Peasant, 1800-1848', *Review of Politics*, xv (1953).

Buckland, P., *Irish Unionism 1885-1922*, Historical Association, London, 1973.

— *Irish Unionism 1885-1923. A Documentary History*, Public Record Office of Northern Ireland, Belfast, 1973.

— *The Factory of Grievances. Devolved Government in Northern Ireland 1921-1939*, Gill and Macmillan, Dublin, 1979.

Budge, I., and O'Leary, C., *Belfast: Approach to Crisis. A Study of Belfast Politics 1613-1970*, Macmillan, London, 1973.

Bull, P. J., 'The Reconstruction of the Irish Parliamentary Movement 1895-1903', Ph.D. thesis, University of Cambridge, 1973.

Burton, F., *The Politics of legitimacy. Struggles in a Belfast community*, RKP, London, 1978.

Cambray, P. G., *Irish Affairs and the Home Rule Question. A Comparison of the Attitudes of Political Parties towards Irish Problems*, Murray, London, 1911.

Carleton, W., *Traits and Stories of the Irish Peasantry*, 4 vols., London, 1846; repr. Mercier, Cork, 1973.

Casey, D. J., and Rhodes, R. E. (edd.), *Views of the Irish Peasantry, 1800-1916*, Archon, Hamden, Connecticut, 1977.

Casey, J., 'Republican courts in Ireland 1919-22', *Irish Jurist*, v (1970).

— 'The genesis of the Dáil courts', *Irish Jurist*, ix (1974).

Chamberlain, J., *A Political Memoir 1880-92*, Batchworth, London, 1953.

Christianson, G. E., 'Secret Societies and Agrarian Violence in Ireland, 1790-1840', *Agricultural History*, xlvi (1972).

Clark, S., 'The social composition of the Land League', *Irish Historical Studies*, xvii (1971).

— 'The Political Mobilisation of Irish Farmers', *Canadian Review of Sociology and Anthropology*, xii (1975).

— 'The importance of agrarian classes: agrarian class structure and collective action in nineteenth-century Ireland', *British Journal of Sociology*, xxix (1978).

— *Social Origins of the Irish Land War*, Princeton UP, 1979.

Clark, W., *Guns in Ulster*, Northern Whig, Belfast, 1967.

Clarkson, J. D., *Labour and Nationalism in Ireland*, Columbia UP, New York, 1925.

Cluseret, G. P., 'My Connection with Fenianism', *Littel's Living Age*, cxiv (1872).

Comerford, R. V., *Charles J. Kickham. A study in Irish nationalism and literature*, Wolfhound, Dublin, 1979.

— 'Anglo-French tension and the origins of fenianism', in F. S. L. Lyons (ed.), *Ireland Under the Union*.

Connolly, J., *Revolutionary Warfare*, New Books, Dublin, 1968.

Coogan, T. P., *The IRA*, new edn., Fontana, London, 1980.

Cooke, A. B., and Vincent, J., 'Herbert Gladstone, Forster, and Ireland, 1881-2', Select Documents XXVIII, *Irish Historical Studies*, xvii (1971).

—— —— *The Governing Passion. Cabinet Government and Party Politics in Britain 1885-6*, Harvester, Brighton, 1974.

Corfe, T., *The Phoenix Park Murders. Conflict, Compromise and Tragedy in Ireland, 1878-1882*, Hodder, London, 1968.

Cronin, S., *Irish Nationalism. A History of its Roots and Ideology*, Academy Press, Dublin, 1980.

Crozier, B., and Moss, R., *The Ulster Debate. Report of a Study Group of the Institute for the Study of Conflict*, Bodley Head, London, 1972.

Cullen, L. M., and Smout, T. C., *Comparative Aspects of Scottish and Irish Economic and Social History*, Edinburgh, 1977.

Curran, J. M., 'The Decline and Fall of the IRB', *Eire-Ireland*, x (1975).

—— *The Birth of the Irish Free State 1921-1923*, Alabama UP, 1980.

Curtis, L. P., *Anglo-Saxons and Celts*, Conference on British Studies, Bridgport, Connecticut, 1968.

—— *Coercion and Conciliation in Ireland 1880-1892. A Study in Conservative Unionism*, Princeton UP, 1963.

—— *Apes and Angels. The Irishman in Victorian Caricature*, David and Charles, Newton Abbot, 1971.

Curtis, R., *The Irish Police Officer*, Ward, Lock, London, 1861.

—— *The History of the Royal Irish Constabulary*, Simpkin, London, 1869.

Daly, C. B., *Violence in Ireland and Christian Conscience*, Veritas, Dublin, 1973.

Dangerfield, G., *The Damnable Question. A Study in Anglo-Irish Relations*, Constable, London, 1976.

Darby, J., *Conflict in Northern Ireland. The Development of a Polarised Community*, Gill and Macmillan, Dublin, 1976.

—— and Williamson, A. (edd.), *Violence and the Social Services in Northern Ireland*, Heinemann, London, 1978.

D'Arcy, W., *The Fenian Movement in the United States*, Catholic University of America Press, Washington, 1947.

Davis, R., *Arthur Griffith and Non-Violent Sinn Féin*, Anvil, Dublin, 1974.

—— 'The Advocacy of Passive Resistance in Ireland, 1916-1922', *Anglo-Irish Studies*, iii (1977).

Davitt, M., *The Fall of Feudalism in Ireland, or the Story of the Land League Revolution*, Harper, London, 1904.

Deasy, L., *Towards Ireland Free. The West Cork Brigade in the War of Independence 1917-1921*, Mercier, Cork, 1973.

D'Entrèves, A. P., *The Notion of the State*, Clarendon Press, Oxford, 1967.

Derby, Earl of, 'Ireland and the Land Act', *The Nineteenth Century*, lvi (1881).

Devlin, B., *The Price of My Soul*, Deutsch, London, 1969.

Devoy, J., *Recollections of an Irish Rebel*, repr. Irish UP, Shannon, 1969.

Dewey, C., 'Celtic agrarian legislation and the Celtic revival: historicist implications of Gladstone's Irish and Scottish Land Acts 1870-1886', *Past and Present*, lxiv (1974).

— 'The rehabilitation of the peasant proprietor in nineteenth century economic thought', *History of Political Economy*, vi (1974).

Dicey, A. V., *England's Case Against Home Rule*, Murray, London, 1886.

Dillon, J., 'The Coming Winter in Ireland', *The Nineteenth Century*, cxvii (1886).

Donnelly, J. S., *Landlord and Tenant in Nineteenth Century Ireland*, Gill and Macmillan, Dublin, 1973.

— *The Land and the People of Nineteenth Century Cork*, RKP, London, 1975.

— 'The Whiteboy movement, 1761-5', *Irish Historical Studies*, xxi (1978).

Drudy, P. J. (ed.), *Ireland: Land, Politics and People*, Cambridge UP, 1982.

Dunbabin, J. P. D., *Rural Discontent in Nineteenth Century Britain*, Faber, London, 1974.

Edwards, O. Dudley, *The Sins of Our Fathers. Roots of Conflict in Northern Ireland*, Gill and Macmillan, Dublin, 1970.

Edwards, R. Dudley, *Patrick Pearse: the Triumph of Failure*, Gollancz, London, 1977.

Enloe, C. H., 'Police and Military in Ulster: Peacekeeping or Peace-Subverting Forces', *Journal of Peace Research*, (1978).

— *Ethnic Soldiers. State Security in a Divided Society*, Pelican, Harmondsworth, 1980.

Evans, E. Estyn, *The Personality of Ireland: Habitat, Heritage and History*, Oxford UP, 1973.

Evelegh, R., *Peace-Keeping in a Democratic Society. The Lessons of Northern Ireland*, Hurst, London, 1978.

Eversley, Baron (Shaw-Lefevre), *Gladstone and Ireland: the Irish Policy of Parliament from 1850-1894*, Methuen, London, 1912.

Farrell, B., *The Founding of Dáil Éireann: Parliament and Nation-Building*, Gill and Macmillan, Dublin, 1971.

Farrell, M., *Northern Ireland: the Orange State*, Pluto, London, 1975.

Feingold, W. L., 'The tenants' movement to capture the Irish Poor Law Boards, 1877-1886', *Albion*, vii (1975).

Fergusson of Kilkerran, J., *The Curragh Incident*, Faber, London, 1964.

Fitzgerald, F. (ed.), *Memoirs of Desmond Fitzgerald 1913-1916*, RKP, London, 1968.

Fitzgerald, G., *Towards a New Ireland*, Knight, London, 1972.

Fitzpatrick, D., *Politics and Irish Life 1913-1921. Provincial Experience of War and Revolution*, Gill and Macmillan, Dublin, 1977.

— 'The geography of Irish nationalism 1910-1921', *Past and Present*, lxxvii (1978).

Flackes, W. D., *Northern Ireland. A Political Directory*, Gill and Macmillan, Dublin, 1980.

Fogarty, L. (ed.), *Collected Writings of James Fintan Lalor*, Talbot, Dublin, 1918.

Foster, R. F., *Charles Stewart Parnell. The Man and his Family*, Harvester, Hassocks, 1976.

— *Lord Randolph Churchill*, Clarendon Press, Oxford, 1981.

— 'Parnell and his people: the Ascendancy and Home Rule'. Unpublished TS.

— 'Garret's Crusade', *London Review of Books*, Jan. 1982).

Gallagher, M., 'Socialism and the nationalist tradition in Ireland 1798–1918', *Éire-Ireland*, xii (1977).

Gardiner, A. G., *The Life of Sir William Harcourt*, 2 vols., Constable, London, 1923.

Garvin, T., 'The destiny of the soldiers: tradition and modernity in the politics of de Valera's Ireland', *Political Studies*, xxvi, 1978.

— *The Evolution of Irish Nationalist Politics*, Holmes and Meier, New York, 1981.

— 'Defenders, Ribbonmen and others: underground political networks in pre-famine Ireland', *Past and Present*, xcvi (1982).

Gatrell, V. A. C., 'The Decline of Theft and Violence in Victorian and Edwardian England', in V. A. C. Gatrell *et al.*, *Crime and the Law. The Social History of Crime in Western Europe since 1500*, Europa, London, 1980.

Gaughan, J. A., *Austin Stack: Portrait of a Separatist*, Kingdom Books, Dublin, 1977.

— (ed.), *Memoirs of Constable Jeremiah Mee, R.I.C.*, Anvil, Dublin, 1975.

Gibbon, P., *The Origins of Ulster Unionism: the Formation of Popular Protestant Politics and Ideology in Nineteenth Century Ireland*, Manchester UP, 1975.

— and Curtin, C., 'The Stem Family in Ireland', *Comparative Studies in Society and History*, xx (1978).

Gilley, S., 'English attitudes to the Irish in England 1780–1900', in C. Holmes (ed.), *Immigrants and Minorities in British Society*, Allen and Unwin, London, 1978.

Gladstone, W. E., 'Notes and Queries on the Irish Demand', *The Nineteenth Century*, cxx (1887).

Gleichen, Gen. Lord Edward, *A Guardsman's Memories*, Blackwood, Edinburgh, 1932.

Gooch, J., 'The War Office and the Curragh Incident', *Bulletin of the Institute of Historical Research*, xlvi (1973).

Gray, T., *The Orange Order*, Bodley Head, London, 1972.

Grey, Earl, *Ireland. The Causes of its Present Condition, and the Measures Proposed for its Improvement*, Murray, London, 1888.

Gurr, T. R., *Why Men Rebel*, Princeton University Press, 1970.

Gwynn, D., *The Irish Free State 1922–1927*, Macmillan, London, 1928.

Gwynn, S., and Tuckwell, G. M., *The Life of the Rt. Hon. Sir Charles W. Dilke*, 2 vols., Murray, London, 1917.

Hadden, T., and Hillyard, P., *Justice in Northern Ireland: a study in social confidence*, Cobden Trust, London, 1973.

Haire, D. N., 'The British Army in Ireland 1868-90', M.Litt. thesis, Trinity College, Dublin, 1973.

Hamer, D. A., *John Morley. Liberal Intellectual in Politics*, Clarendon Press, Oxford, 1968.

Hammond, J. L., *Gladstone and the Irish Nation*, Longman, London, 1938.

Hardinge, A. *The Fourth Earl of Carnarvon*, 3 vols., H. Milford, Oxford, 1925.

Harris, R., *Prejudice and Tolerance in Ulster. A study of neighbours and 'strangers' in a border community*, Manchester UP, 1972.

Harvie, C., 'Ideology and Home Rule: James Bryce, A. V. Dicey and Ireland, 1880-1887', *English Historical Review*, xci (1976).

— 'Ireland and the Intellectuals, 1848-1922', *New Edinburgh Review*, xxxviii/xxxix (1977).

Hawkins, R., 'Gladstone, Forster, and the release of Parnell, 1882-8', *Irish Historical Studies*, xvi (1969).

— 'An Army on Police Work, 1881-2. Ross of Bladensburg's Memorandum', *Irish Sword*, xi (1973).

— 'Government versus Secret Societies: The Parnell Era', in T. D. Williams (ed.), *Secret Societies in Ireland*.

— 'Liberals, land and coercion in the summer of 1880: the influence of the Carraroe ejectments', *Journal of the Galway Archaeological and Historical Society*, xxxiv (1974-5).

Henry, R. M., *The Evolution of Sinn Féin*, Talbot, Dublin, 1920.

Hepburn, A. C., 'The Ancient Order of Hibernians in Irish Politics 1905-14', *Cithara*, x (1971).

— (ed.), *The Conflict of Nationality in Modern Ireland*, Arnold, London, 1980.

Heskin, K., *Northern Ireland: A Psychological Analysis*, Gill and Macmillan, Dublin, 1980.

Heslinga, M. W., *The Irish Border as a Cultural Divide. A Contribution to the Study of Regionalism in the British Isles*, Van Gorcum, Assen, 1971.

Hezlet, A., *The 'B' Specials. A History of the Ulster Special Constabulary*, Tom Stacey, London, 1972.

Hobsbawm, E. J., *Primitive Rebels. Studies in Archaic Forms of Social Movement in the 19th and 20th Centuries*, Manchester UP, 1969.

— and Rudé, G., *Captain Swing*, new edn., Penguin, Harmondsworth, 1973.

Hobson, B., *Defensive Warfare. A Handbook for Irish Nationalists*, West Belfast Branch of Sinn Féin, 1909.

Holmes, R., *The Little Field-Marshal. Sir John French*, Cape, London, 1981.

Hopkinson, M., 'Collins, De Valera, Mulcahy, Liam Lynch: Attitudes to the Irish Civil War', Unpublished paper read to Irish Historical Society, Sept. 1980.

Hoppen, K. T., 'National Politics and Local Realities in Mid-Nineteenth Century Ireland', in A. Cosgrove (ed.), *Studies in Irish History*, UCD, 1979.

Horgan, J. J., *Parnell to Pearse*, Browne and Nolan, Dublin, 1948.

Hunter, J., 'The Gaelic connection: the Highlands, Ireland and nationalism 1873-1922', *Scottish Historical Review*, liv (1975).

— *The Making of the Crofting Community*, Donald, Edinburgh, 1976.

Hurlbert, W. H., *Ireland Under Coercion. The Diary of an American*, Douglas, Edinburgh, 1888.

Hurst, J. W., 'Disturbed Tipperary 1831-1860', *Éire-Ireland*, ix (1974).

Hussey, S. M. (comp. H. Gordon), *Reminiscences of an Irish Land Agent*, Duckworth, London, 1904.

Inglis, H. D., *A Journey throughout Ireland during the Spring, Summer, and Autumn of 1834*, 5th edn., Whittaker, London, 1838.

Irish Boundary Commission, *Report and Documents* (intr. G. J. Hand), Irish UP, Shannon, 1969.

Irish Labour Party and TUC, *Who Burnt Cork City*, Dublin, 1921.

Irish Loyal and Patriotic Union, *Publications Issued during the Year 1890*, Dublin and London, 1890.

Irish Magistrate, *The Irish Magistracy*, Gill, Dublin, 1885.

Jalland, P., *The Liberals and Ireland. The Ulster Question in British Politics to 1914*, Harvester, Brighton, 1980.

Janke, P., 'Ulster: a Decade of Violence', *Conflict Studies*, cviii, Institute for the Study of Conflict, London, 1979.

Kee, R., *The Green Flag. A History of Irish Nationalism*, Weidenfeld, London, 1972.

Kohn, L., *The Constitution of the Irish Free State*, Allen and Unwin, London, 1932.

Laffan, M., 'The unification of Sinn Féin in 1917', *Irish Historical Studies*, xvii (1971).

Laqueur, W., *Terrorism*. Weidenfeld, London, 1977.

— 'Interpretations of Terrorism: Fact, Fiction, and Political Science', *Journal of Contemporary History*, vii (1977).

Larkin, E., 'The Devotional Revolution in Ireland 1850-75', *American Historical Review*, lxxvii (1972).

— 'Church, State and Nation in Modern Ireland', *American Historical Review*, lxxx (1975).

— *The Roman Catholic Church and the Creation of the Modern Irish State, 1878-1886*, Gill and Macmillan, Dublin, 1975.

Leadam, I. S., *Coercive Measures in Ireland, 1830-1880*, National Press Agency, London, 1881.

Lebow, R. N., 'British Historians and Irish History', *Éire-Ireland*, viii (1973).

— *White Britain and Black Ireland. The Influence of Stereotypes on Colonial Policy*, Institute for the Study of Human Issues, Philadelphia, 1976.

Le Caron, H., *Twenty-five Years in the Secret Service. The Recollections of a Spy*, Heinemann, London, 1892.

Lee, J. J., *The Modernisation of Irish Society 1848-1918*, Gill and Macmillan, Dublin, 1973.

—— 'The Ribbonmen', in T. D. Williams (ed.), *Secret Societies in Ireland*.

LeFanu, W. R., *Seventy Years of Irish Life, being Anecdotes and Reminiscences*, E. Arnold, London, 1893.

Lewis, G. Cornewall, *Local Disturbances in Ireland*, B. Fellowes, London, 1836.

Lloyd, C. D. C., *Ireland Under the Land League. A Narrative of Personal Experiences*, Blackwood, Edinburgh, 1892.

Locker-Lampson, G. L. T., *A Consideration of the State of Ireland in the Nineteenth Century*, Constable, London, 1907.

Lynch, D. (ed. F. O'Donoghue), *The IRB and the 1916 Rising*, Mercier, Cork, 1957.

Lyons, F. S. L., 'Vicissitudes of a middleman in county Leitrim 1810-27', *Irish Historical Studies*, ix (1955).

—— *John Dillon. A Biography*, RKP, London, 1968.

—— 'The Political Ideas of Parnell', *Historical Journal*, xvi (1973).

—— *Charles Stewart Parnell*, Collins, London, 1977.

—— *Culture and Anarchy in Ireland 1890-1939*, Clarendon Press, Oxford, 1979.

—— *Ireland Since the Famine*, Weidenfeld, London, 1971.

—— and Hawkins, R. A. J. (edd.), *Ireland Under the Union. Varieties of Tension*, Clarendon Press, Oxford, 1980.

Macardle, D., *Tragedies of Kerry 1922-1923*, [? Dublin], 1924.

—— *The Irish Republic. A Documented Chronicle*, Gollancz, London, 1937; new edn., Corgi, London, 1968.

McCartan, P. (ed.), 'Extract from the papers of Dr Patrick McCartan', *Clogher Record* (1964, 1965).

McCarthy, M. J. F., *Five Years in Ireland 1895-1900*, 10th edn., Hodges and Figgis, Dublin, 1903.

McCord, N., 'The Fenians and Public Opinion in Great Britain', *University Review*, iv (1967).

MacDonagh, O., 'The Politicization of the Irish Catholic Bishops, 1800-1850', *Historical Journal*, xviii (1975).

—— *Ireland. The Union and its Aftermath*, Allen and Unwin, London, 1977.

McDowell, R. B., *The Irish Administration 1801-1914*, RKP, London, 1964.

MacGiollaChoille, B., 'Fenians, Rice and Ribbonmen in County Monaghan, 1864-67', *Clogher Record* (1967).

—— 'Fenian documents in the State Paper Office', *Irish Historical Studies*, xvi (1969).

McHugh, J., 'The Belfast Labour Dispute and Riots of 1907', *International Review of Social History*, xxii (1977).

MacLochlainn, A., 'Gael and Peasant—A Case of Mistaken Identity', in D. J. Casey and R. E. Rhodes (edd.), *Views of the Irish Peasantry*.

MacLochlainn, A., 'Thomas Davis and Irish Racialism', *Irish Times*, 20 Nov. 1973.

McManus, F. (ed.), *The Years of the Great Test. 1926-39*, Mercier, Cork, 1967.

Macready, C. F. N., *Annals of an Active Life*, 2 vols., Hutchinson, London, 1924.

MacStiofáin, S., *Memoirs of a Revolutionary*, Cremonesi, [Edinburgh], 1975.

Mandle, W. F., 'The IRB and the beginnings of the Gaelic Athletic Association', *Irish Historical Studies*, xx (1977).

Manning, M., *The Blueshirts*, Gill and Macmillan, Dublin, 1970.

Martin, F. X., '1916—Myth, Fact and Mystery', *Studia Hibernica*, vii (1967).

— 'The 1916 Rising—a *Coup d'État* or a "Bloody Protest"?', *Studia Hibernica*, viii (1968).

— (ed.), 'Eoin MacNeill on the 1916 Rising', *Irish Historical Studies*, xii (1961).

— (ed.), *The Irish Volunteers 1913-1915. Recollections and Documents*, Duffy, Dublin, 1963.

— (ed.), 'The McCartan Documents, 1916', *Clogher Record* (1966).

— (ed.), *Leaders and Men of the Easter Rising: Dublin 1916*, Methuen, London, 1967.

— and Byrne, F. J. (edd.), *The Scholar Revolutionary, Eoin Macneill 1867-1945 and the Making of a New Ireland*, Irish UP, Shannon, 1973.

Melville, C. H., *The Life of Gen. the Rt. Hon. Sir Redvers Buller*, 2 vols., E. Arnold, London, 1923.

Miller, D. V., *Church, State and Nation in Ireland 1898-1921*, Gill and Macmillan, Dublin, 1973.

— 'Irish Catholicism and the great famine', *Journal of Social History* (fall 1975).

— 'Presbyterianism and "modernization" in Ulster', *Past and Present*, lxxx (1978).

— *Queen's Rebels. Ulster Loyalism in Historical Perspective*, Gill and Macmillan, Dublin, 1978.

Mitchell, A., *Labour in Irish Politics 1890-1930: the Irish labour movement in an age of revolution*, Irish UP, Dublin, 1974.

Mommsen, W. J., and Hirschfeld, G. (edd.), *Social Protest, Violence and Terror in Nineteenth and Twentieth Century Europe*, Macmillan, London, 1982.

Monteagle, Baron, 'The Crimes Act', *The Nineteenth Century*, c (1885).

Moody, T. W., 'The New Departure in Irish Politics 1878-9', in H. A. Cronne *et al.*, *Essays in British and Irish History*, Muller, London, 1949.

— 'Thomas Davis and the Irish Nation', *Hermathena*, cii (1966).

— 'Anna Parnell and the Land League', *Hermathena*, cxvii (1974).

— *The Ulster Question 1603-1973*, Mercier, Cork, 1974.

— *Davitt and Irish Revolution 1846-82*, Clarendon Press, Oxford, 1981.

— (ed.), *Nationality and the Pursuit of National Independence*, Appletree, Belfast (Historical Studies, 11), 1978.

— and Ó Broin, L. (edd), 'The IRB Supreme Council 1868-78', Select Documents, *Irish Historical Studies*, xix (1975).

Morley, J., 'Irish Revolution and English Liberalism', *The Nineteenth Century*, lxi (1882).

— *The Life of William Ewart Gladstone*, 3 vols., Macmillan, London, 1903.

Moss, R., *Urban Guerrillas. The new face of political violence*, Temple Smith, London, 1972.

Moynihan, M. (ed.), *Speeches and Statements by Eamon de Valera 1917-1973*, Gill and Macmillan, Dublin, 1980.

Mulcahy, Gen. R., 'The Irish Volunteer Convention, 27 October 1917', *Capuchin Annual*, xxxiv (1967).

— 'Conscription and the General Headquarters Staff', *Capuchin Annual*, xxxv (1968).

— 'Chief of Staff, 1919', *Capuchin Annual*, xxxvi (1969).

Murphy, D., *A Place Apart*, Murray, London, 1978.

Murphy, J. A., 'The New IRA 1925-62', in T. D. Williams (ed.), *Secret Societies in Ireland*.

— *Ireland in the Twentieth Century*, Gill and Macmillan, Dublin, 1975.

Nelson, S., 'Discrimination in Northern Ireland: the Protestant Response', in A. Veenhoven (ed.), *Case Studies on Human Rights*, iv, The Hague, 1976.

Newsinger, J., 'Revolution and Catholicism in Ireland, 1848-1923', *European Studies Review*, ix (1979).

Nieburg, H. L. *Political Violence. The Behavioral Process*, St. Martin's Press, New York, 1969.

Nowland, K. B., 'The Fenian Rising of 1867', in T. W. Moody (ed.), *The Fenian Movement*.

O'Brien, C. Cruise, *Parnell and his Party, 1880-1890*, Clarendon Press, Oxford, 1957.

— *States of Ireland*, Hutchinson, London, 1972.

— *Herod: Reflections on Political Violence*, Hutchinson, London, 1978.

O'Brien, J. V., *William O'Brien and the Course of Irish Politics 1881-1918*, California UP, Berkeley, 1976.

O'Brien, R. Barry, *Dublin Castle and the Irish People*, Kegan Paul, London, 1909.

Ó Broin, L., *Fenian Fever. An Anglo-American Dilemma*, London, 1971.

— *The Chief Secretary: Augustine Birrell in Ireland*, London, 1969.

— *Dublin Castle and the 1916 Rising*, rev. edn., Sidgwick and Jackson, London, 1970.

— 'Revolutionary nationalism in Ireland: the IRB, 1858-1924', in T. W. Moody (ed.), *Nationality and the Pursuit of National Independence*.

— *Revolutionary Underground. The Story of the Irish Republican Brotherhood, 1858-1924*, Gill and Macmillan, Dublin, 1976.

O'Casey, S., *The Story of the Irish Citizen Army*, Dublin, 1919.
— *Drums Under the Windows*, Macmillan, London, 1945.
O'Connor, T. P., *The Parnell Movement, with a Sketch of Irish Parties from 1843*, Kegan Paul, London, 1886.
O'Donnell, Patrick, *The Irish Faction Fighters of the Nineteenth Century*, Anvil, Dublin, 1975.
O'Donnell, Peadar, *There Will Be Another Day*, Dolmen, Dublin, 1963.
O'Donoghue, F., 'Plans for the 1916 Rising', *University Review*, iii (1962).
— 'Guerilla warfare in Ireland', *An Cosantóir*, xxiii (1963).
— 'The Failure of the German Arms Landing at Easter 1916', *Cork Historical and Archaeological Society Journal*, lxxi (1966).
O'Dowd, L., Rolston, B., and Tomlinson, M., *Northern Ireland: Between Civil Rights and Civil War*, CSE Books, London, 1980.
O'Farrell, P., *Ireland's English Question. Anglo-Irish Relations 1534-1970*, Schocken. New York, 1971.
— *England and Ireland since 1800*, Oxford UP, 1975.
O'Hegarty, P. S., *A History of Ireland Under the Union*, Methuen, London, 1952.
O'Higgins, K., *Civil War and the Events which Led to it*, Talbot, Dublin, 1922.
O'Luing, S., *Fremantle Mission*, Anvil, Tralee, 1965.
— *I Die in a Good Cause. A Study of Thomas Ashe, Idealist and Revolutionary*, Anvil, Dublin, 1970.
O'Malley, E., *The Singing Flame*, Anvil, Dublin, 1978.
O'Neill, B., *The War for the Land in Ireland*, M. Lawrence, London, 1933.
Orridge, A., 'Explanations of Irish nationalism: a review and some suggestions', *Journal of the Conflict Research Society*, i (1977).
— 'Who Supported the Land War? An Aggregate-Data Analysis of Irish Agrarian Discontent, 1879-1882', *Economic and Social Review*, xii (1981).
Ó Tuathaigh, G., 'The Irish in Nineteenth Century Britain: Problems of Integration', *Transactions of the Royal Historical Society*, 5th ser., xxxi (1981).
Palmer, N. D., *The Irish Land League Crisis*, Yale UP, New Haven, 1940.
Palmer, S. H., 'The Irish Police Experiment: the Beginning of Modern Police in the British Isles, 1784-1795', *Social Science Quarterly*, lvi (1975).
Patterson, H., *Class Conflict and Sectarianism. The Protestant Working Class and the Belfast Labour Movement 1868-1920*, Blackstaff, Belfast, 1980.
Phillips, W. A., *The Revolution in Ireland, 1906-1923*, Longman, London, 1923.
Pollard, H. B. C., *The Secret Societies of Ireland: their Rise and Progress*. Edinburgh, 1922.
Power, J. O'Connor, 'The Irish Land Agitation', *The Nineteenth Century*, xxxiv (1879).

Power, P. F., 'Violence, Consent and the Northern Ireland Problem', *Journal of Commonwealth and Comparative Politics*, xiv (1976).

Provisional Sinn Féin, *Where Sinn Féin Stands*, Dublin, 1970.

— *Social and Economic Programme*, Dublin, 1970.

Quinault, R., 'Lord Randolph Churchill and Home Rule', *Irish Historical Studies*, xxi (1979).

Quinlivan, P., and Rose, P., *The Fenians and England 1865-1872*, Calder, London, 1982.

Reid, T. Wemyss, *The Life of the Rt. Hon. W. E. Forster*, 2 vols., Chapman and Hall, London, 1888.

Rose, P., *The Manchester Martyrs. The story of a Fenian tragedy*, Lawrence and Wishart, London, 1970.

Rose, R., *Governing Without Consensus. An Irish Perspective*, Faber, London, 1971.

— 'On the Priorities of Citizenship in the Deep South and Northern Ireland', *Journal of Politics*, xxxviii (1976).

Rumpf, E., and Hepburn, A. C., *Nationalism and socialism in twentieth-century Ireland*, Liverpool UP, 1977. (Rev. trans. of *Nationalismus und Sozialismus in Irland: historisch-soziologischer Versuch über die irische Revolution seit 1918*, Hain, Meisenheim am Glan, 1959.)

Ryan, D., *The Phoenix Flame: a study of Fenianism and John Devoy*, A. Barker, London, 1937.

— *The Rising. The Complete Story of Easter Week*, Golden Eagle, Dublin, 1949.

— *The Fenian Chief: a biography of James Stephens*, Gill, Dublin, 1967.

Schmitt, D., *The Irony of Irish Democracy. The impact of political culture on administrative and democratic political development in Ireland*, Heath, Lexington, 1973.

Semple, J. A., 'The Fenian Infiltration of the British Army', *Journal of the Society for Army Historical Research*, lii (1974).

Senior, H., *Orangeism in Ireland and Britain 1795-1836*, RKP, London, 1966.

Shaw, F., SJ, 'The Canon of Irish History—A Challenge', *Studies* (1972).

Short, K. R. M., *The Dynamite War. Irish-American Bombers in Victorian Britain*, Gill and Macmillan, Dublin, 1979.

Snoddy, O., 'The Midland Volunteer Force, 1913', *Journal of the Old Athlone Society* (1968).

Solow, B., *The Land Question and the Irish Economy, 1870-1903*, Harvard UP, Cambridge, Mass., 1971.

Steele, E. D., 'Gladstone and Ireland', *Irish Historical Studies*, xvii (1970).

— 'J. S. Mill and the Irish Question', *Historical Journal*, xiii (1970).

— *Irish Land and British Politics. Tenant Right and Nationality 1865-1870*, Cambridge UP, 1974.

— 'Cardinal Cullen and Irish Nationality', *Irish Historical Studies*, xix (1975).

Steele, E. D., 'Gladstone, Irish Violence, and Conciliation', in A. Cosgrove (ed.), *Studies in Irish History*, UCD, Dublin, 1979.

Stephen J. Fitzjames, 'On the Suppression of Boycotting', *The Nineteenth Century*, cxviii (1886).

Stephens, J., *The Insurrection in Dublin*, Maunsel, Dublin, 1916.

Stevenson, J., *Popular Disturbances in England 1700-1870*, Longman, London, 1979.

Stewart, A. T. Q., *The Ulster Crisis*, Faber, London, 1967.

— *The Narrow Ground. Aspects of Ulster 1609-1969*, Faber, London, 1977.

Strauss, E., *Irish Nationalism and British Democracy*, Methuen, London, 1951.

Sullivan, A. M., *New Ireland*, 6th edn., Sampson Low, London, 1878.

Thornton, T. P., 'Terror as a Weapon of Political Agitation', in H. Eckstein (ed.), *Internal War. Problems and Approaches*, Free Press, Glencoe, 1964.

Tierney, M., *Eoin MacNeill, Scholar and Man of Action, 1867-1945*, Clarendon Press, Oxford, 1980.

Tilly, C., 'Collective violence in European perspective', in H. D. Graham and T. R. Gurr (edd.), *Violence in America: Historical and Comparative Perspectives*, Bantam, New York, 1969.

— 'The Changing Place of Collective Violence', in M. Richter (ed.), *Essays in Theory and History: An Approach to the Social Sciences*, Harvard UP, Cambridge, 1970.

— *From Mobilization to Revolution*, Addison-Wesley, Reading, Mass., 1978.

—, Tilly, L., and Tilly, R., *The Rebellious Century. 1830-1930*, Dent, London, 1975.

Townshend, C., *The British Campaign in Ireland 1919-1921*, Oxford UP, 1975.

— 'The Irish railway strike of 1920: industrial action and civil resistance in the struggle for independence', *Irish Historical Studies*, xxi (1979).

— 'The Irish Republican Army and the development of guerrilla warfare, 1916-21', *English Historical Review*, xciv (1979).

— 'Bloody Sunday—Michael Collins Speaks', *European Studies Review*, ix (1979).

— 'Martial Law: Legal and Administrative Problems of Civil Emergency in Britain and the Empire, 1800-1940', *Historical Journal*, xxv (1982).

Treble, J. H., 'The Irish Agitation', in J. T. Ward (ed.), *Popular Movements c.1830-1850*, Macmillan, London, 1970.

Turner, Gen. A. E., *Sixty Years of a Soldier's Life*, Methuen, London, 1912.

Vaughan, W. E., 'Landlord and Tenant Relations in Ireland between the Famine and the Land War 1850-78', in L. M. Cullen (ed.), *Comparative Aspects of Scottish and Irish Economic and Social History*.

Vaughan, W. E., 'An assessment of the economic performance of Irish landlords, 1851-81', in F. S. L. Lyons (ed.), *Ireland Under the Union.*

Vincent, J., 'Gladstone and Ireland', Raleigh Lecture, 1977, British Academy, London, 1978.

Ward, A. J., 'Lloyd George and the 1918 Conscription Crisis', *Historical Journal*, xvii (1974).

Waters, M. J., 'Peasants and Emigrants: Considerations of the Gaelic League as a Social Movement', in D. J. Casey (ed.), *Views of the Irish Peasantry.*

Weekly Irish Times, *Sinn Féin Rebellion Handbook*, Dublin, 1917.

White, T. de V., *Kevin O'Higgins*, Methuen, London, 1948.

Williams, T. D. (ed.), *The Irish Struggle 1916-1926*, RKP, London, 1966.

— *Secret Societies in Ireland*, Gill and Macmillan, Dublin, 1973.

Wright, F., 'Protestant Ideology and Politics in Ulster', *European Journal of Sociology*, xiv (1973).

Wright, T., *The Historical Works of Giraldus Cambrensis*, Bohn, London, 1863.

Index

police (*cont.*):
    patrolling, 79–81, 134, 145–7, 219
        n. 2
    Belfast, 85–6, 189 n. 3
    assaults on, 150, 152
    strike, 176
    'tinkering with', 189, 409
    boycott of, 332, 334
    Garda Siochana, 373
    See also constabulary
Price, Maj. I., 306
Property Defence Association, 154
Protestantism, as basis of social segre-
        gation, 39, 42
    and 'siege mentality', 40
    ritual parades, 42–3, 45–6
    law and constitution as ascendancy,
        88, 188, 191
Provisional Irish Republican Army
        (PIRA), and socialist IRA,
        393
    as Defenders, 393–5
    operations, 398, 399, 400, 402,
        403
'public banding', 40, 249
public security, 400

Queen's County, 21

Redmond, John, INP leader, and Great
        War, 278
    and control of Irish Volunteers,
        287
    and rising, 308
Reed, Sir Andrew, Inspector General
        RIC, 264
reprisals:
    unofficial, 99, 351
    official, 351–2
Republicanism, 13, 25, 27, 28, 224,
        240, 319, 328, 362, 382,
        388
    anti-Treaty 'irregularism', 370–3,
        374
    See also Fenianism; Irish Republi-
        can Brotherhood
Resident Magistrates (RMs), 53, 57,
        137, 146, 170, 173, 175,
        199, 203
    Special ResidentMagistrates(SRMs),
        138, 143, 175
    Divisional Magistrates (DMs), 175,
        203

resistance, popular, 12–13, 16, 20, 24,
        106, 125, 339
    and deprivation, 108
    and rising expectations, 109
    and modern state, 243
    See also collective violence; civil
        resistance
Restoration of Order in Ireland Act,
        1920, 335, 350, 353
Ribbonism, 14–24
    See also Westmeath
Rice, James Blayney, IRB Centre,
        Monaghan, 29
Richardson, Gen. Sir G., UVF Com-
        mander, 250
Ridgeway, Sir Joseph West, Under-Sec.,
        Dublin Castle, 210, 216, 217,
        218, 220
riot control, 76–8, 84–7, 100, 186–7,
        189, 209, 402
Roberts, Field-Marshal Earl, 231, 250
Ros, Gen. Lord de, on police in Ire-
        land, 76, 79–82
    on riots of 1864, 84–5
Roscommon, County, 55, 232
Rose, Sir Hugh, *see* Strathnairn, Lord
Rose, Richard, 389, 391, 392, 401
Ross of Bladensburg, Sir John, 143
        n. 3
    Chief Commissioner, DMP, 276
Rossa, Jeremiah O'Donovan, 24, 28,
        36
    and 'skirmishing', 120, 123, 159–
        61, 163, 388
Rossmore (Roslea) incident, 183–4
Royal Irish Constabulary,*see* constabu-
        lary
Rumpf, Erhard, 368–70
Russell, Seán, IRA Chief of Staff, 381,
        387
Ryan, Desmond, 301

Salisbury, Earl of, Prime Minister, 127,
        181, 192, 197, 204, 206,
        207, 212, 217
Saor Eire, 379–80
Sartre, Jean-Paul, 410–11
Saunderson, Col. E. J., Ulster Union-
        ist leader, 182 n. 2, 191
Scotland, economy, 3
    crofters' land war, 207–8
secret societies:
    agrarian 'associations', 14–17, 20,

Turner, Col. A. E., 170
Commissioner for Kerry and Clare, 209 n. 1, 215, 217-19
Twomey, Maurice, IRA Chief of Staff, arrested 1933, 377-8
on the 'mind of the country', 379
Tyrone, County, 249, 391 (Caledon)

Ulster, 38-46, 181-91, 257, 323, 327, 340, 364, 382-3
'Ulster custom', 38-9
and Protestant identity, 182, 342-3, 384, 385
crisis of 1912-14, 237, 245
Solemn League and Covenant, 248, 250
'Collins-Craig pact', 383-4
'Ulsterization', 404
See also Loyalism; Northern Ireland
Ulster Defence Regiment (UDR), 397
Ulster Defence Union, 191
Ulster Unionist Clubs, 247-8
Ulster Unionist Convention, 1892, 191
Ulster Unionist Council, 246, 247, 250, 327 n. 2, 342
Ulster Unionist Party, fission of, 382, 392
Ulster Volunteer Force (UVF), *see* Volunteers
United Ireland, 199
United Irish League (UIL), 226-34
as INP organization, 236, 237-8
United Irishmen, 27
United Nations, 398
United States of America, 25, 119
Irish civil war veterans, 91, 168 n. 3

vigilantism, 40, 182, 386
violence:
nature of, 5-7
political function of, 7-8, 27, 38, 107, 118, 126, 148-9, 200, 229, 245, 282-5, 294-5, 319, 331, 360-4, 406-8
institutionalization of, 38-9, 47-8, 384
social function of, 45
police and, 68, 211, 217, 350
language, 151, 155-6, 204, 407
See also crime, collective violence

Volunteers:
movement of 1782, 156, 224, 295
in Protestant organizational history, 40, 41
Protestant 'levée en masse', 184
Irish Volunteers (IV) and Irish National Volunteers (INV), 226, 255
Provisional Committee, 258
organization, 259-60, 274-5
gun-running, 260-1, 274-5
1916 rising, 277, 286, 287
split Sept. 1914, 278-9
reconstruction, 319-20
war against Britain, 331-2, 344
See also Irish Republican Army
Ulster Volunteer Force (UVF), 245, 249-55, 264, 266, 269, 270
formation and organization, 250
'Special Service' force, 251, 253
plans for coup, 252
gun-running, 252-3, 255, 260, 276
rebirth 1920, 341, 386
and 'B' Specials 1970, 397
and UDR, 397
See also drilling, illegal

Waterford, County, 92 (1867 election), 98-9 (1868 election)
Watchword of Labour, 343
West Mayo United Irish League, *see* United Irish League
Westmeath, County, 1870 Ribbon disturbances, 7, 15, 16, 17 n. 2, 50, 62, 369
'Westmeath Act' (Protection of Life and Property (Ireland) Act, 34 Vict. c. 25), 63, 134 (graph)
Wexford, County, 56, 57 (Newtonbarry), 300, 362
Whiteboyism, 15, 16, 19, 22, 371
Whitelaw, William, Sec. of State for Northern Ireland, 399
Wicklow, County, 52
Wilson, Maj.-Gen. (later Field-Marshal) Sir Henry, and Curragh crisis, 268-73, 355
assassinated, 383
Wimborne, Ivor Guest, 2nd Baron (later